Cities of Hope

Cities of Hope

People, Protests, and Progress in Urbanizing Latin America, 1870–1930

Edited by

Ronn Pineo and James A. Baer

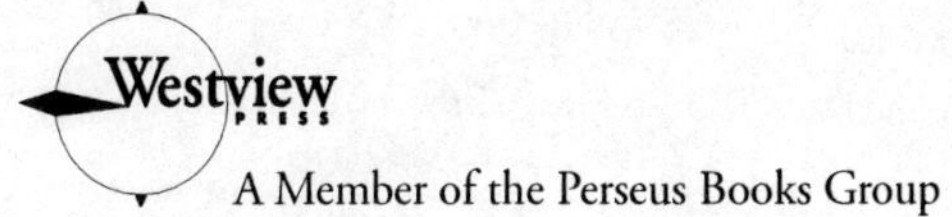

Published in 1998 in the United States of America by Westview Press, 5500 Central Avenue, Boulder, Colorado 80301-2877, and in the United Kingdom by Westview Press, 12 Hid's Copse Road, Cumnor Hill, Oxford OX2 9JJ

Library of Congress Cataloging-in-Publication Data
Cities of hope : people, protests, and progress in urbanizing Latin America, 1870–1930 / edited by Ronn Pineo and James A. Baer.
p. cm.
Includes bibliographical references (p.) and index.
ISBN 0-8133-2443-2 (hc) —ISBN 0-8133-2444-0 (pb)
1. Working class—Latin America—Political activity. 2. Urbanization—Latin America. 3. City and town life—Latin America. 4. Working class—Housing—Latin America. 5. Working class—Medical care—Latin America. I. Pineo, Ronn F., 1954– . II. Baer, James A.
HD8110.5.C56 1998
322.4'4'098—dc21 97-45103
CIP

The paper used in this publication meets the requirements of the American National Standard for Permanence of Paper for Printed Library Materials Z39.48-1984.

10 9 8 7 6 5 4 3 2

To my parents, Martha P. Baer and Charles A. Baer,
whose support and love have been with me always
James A. Baer

To Ardis and Tommy
Ronn Pineo

Contents

Illustrations

Tables

Figures

Photos

Maps

Foreword

Samuel L. Baily

Although cities have always been important to the societies of Central and South America, they have been especially so since the last quarter of the nineteenth century. At that time the rapid growth in the export economies of the region stimulated an unprecedented increase in the pace of urbanization, and this phenomenon has continued with some fluctuation ever since. Because of improved health conditions the existing local populations expanded. In addition, between 1870 and 1930 millions of foreign immigrants (primarily Italians, Spaniards, and Portuguese) flocked to Buenos Aires, Montevideo, São Paulo, and to a lesser extent to other urban areas. Subsequently millions of migrants from the rural sectors of these countries moved to the cities and contributed increasingly to their growing populations. Today Latin America is a predominantly urban area and has some of the largest cities in the world. In the twenty-first century, Latin America will contain even more of the world's largest cities.

The populations of the urban areas of Latin America grew so rapidly during the past century and a quarter primarily because the cities held out the promise of jobs and economic advancement. To many a move to the cities seemed to be the best option to improve one's economic position, but there were no guarantees that those who came would be able to take advantage of the available opportunities. Clearly there was opportunity for some, but not necessarily for all. Much depended on which city they moved to, when they moved, the nature of the labor market at the time, the skills they had, and who else was in the city to compete with them. Despite the wide variation in personal fortunes, a sufficient number of individuals succeeded well enough that others continued to believe in the promise and to move to the cities.

Pineo, Baer, and their colleagues offer valuable insights into the nature of urban life in nine Latin American cities of various sizes and types at the turn of the past century. They are concerned primarily with the living conditions of working people, how working people responded to the problems they encountered, and what collective strategies were most successful in addressing these problems. They skillfully show the constant tension between, on the one hand, the promise and opportunity of the city and, on the other, the reality of city life, which rewarded some but not others. The growing number of urban dwellers confronted structures (labor and housing markets, wages, prices) over which they had little control, but they were not helpless. They protested against bad working and living conditions and fought to improve them. Combined, the chapters in this volume provide a very solid basis for understanding the impact of urbanization on the working classes of Latin American cities and the variety of their responses to their situations.

One of the major contributions of this book is to draw attention to the importance of consumer- as well as job-related issues for the urban working classes. We are presented with detailed information on housing and health conditions and on working-class responses to them in a number of places. For example, we see a pattern of a specific type of protest regarding housing. Between 1907 and 1925 working-class residents were so angered by housing conditions in Buenos Aires, São Paulo, Veracruz, Mexico City, and Panama City that they informally organized rent strikes. In Buenos Aires (1921) and Veracruz (1923) this informal working-class organization was sufficient to encourage the governments to become involved and to pass rent laws. Although only some of the numerous strikes and other forms of protest were successful, the authors conclude that the working classes seemed less threatening to the elites when they organized as consumers and therefore were more likely to achieve their objectives in that context.

This collection contributes much to our knowledge and understanding of the impact of urbanization on the working classes of Latin America and their efforts to improve their living and working conditions. It is essential reading for those concerned with the contemporary cities of the area and their problems, for these problems, clearly rooted in the period around the turn of the century, are ably discussed in this book.

Acknowledgments

Many individuals have helped the authors in preparing this book. Among those who have provided the most assistance are the National Endowment for the Humanities, for introducing the authors through a Summer Seminar and for providing additional funding through Summer Stipends and Study Grants; David Rock at the University of California, Santa Barbara; Barbara Tenenbaum and the staff at the Hispanic Division at the Library of Congress; Barbara Ellington; Sam Baily; and Elizabeth Lambert Johns, chair of the Social Science and Public Service Division of Northern Virginia Community College, Alexandria Campus.

James A. Baer and Ronn Pineo

Latin America. Reproduced and adapted by Elizabeth F. Paskey from Cathryn L. Lombardi and John V. Lombardi, with K. Lynn Stoner, Latin American History: A Teaching Atlas *(Madison, Wisc.: Conference on Latin American History, University of Wisconsin Press, 1983).*

Introduction

James A. Baer
and Ronn Pineo

This collaborative book brings together new research, analysis, and comparison on a critically important but little studied topic: the dawn of modern urbanization in late-nineteenth- and early-twentieth-century Latin America. We have focused our attention on the ordinary people of these cities, the working men and women who faced the task of dealing with the ramifications of the broad social, political, and economic transformations that were taking place all around them. This book offers a sense of what life was like for these urban residents, examining the conditions they confronted and exploring their experiences. We consider the myriad ways that these people responded to the problems of urban life and analyze how these actions affected the politics and the dynamics of urban reform at the time. Our goal is to offer a deeper understanding of the links between urban conditions, the informal politics of urban working men and women, and the process of urban social reform.

Cities are places of excitement. In the cities that we have built one can find nearly everything people have invented that make life most exhilarating. Seemingly all of these creations are offered up, are pressed upon us at the very same time in the city. Cities present opportunities: a better chance for getting work, for meeting people, or for hearing the latest news. But more, cities provide opportunities that cannot exist elsewhere. In cities one can find work in rare, even odd, specializations; meet people who share an unusual, even peculiar, interest or hobby; and find fully and loudly expressed a bewildering cacophony of novel, even bizarre, ideas. The noise, the music, the odors, the food, the criminals, the lovers—the city. Cities are all of us at our best and worst.

Cities may best be distinguished from their rural surroundings by emphasizing several key characteristics, each of which may be thought of as being set on a continuum from urban to rural. Of course, cities are places of more people, of higher population density, and of greater building density. But more than that, cities are places of functional specialization: in "law, government, religion or economic exchange" but not farming or mining.[1] Cities are places where the hands and face of the clock have eclipsed the sun and the seasons in marking the periods of our lives.

Background: The Urban Traditions of Latin America

For Latin America cities have long been of paramount importance. In both the Hispanic and pre-Columbian traditions, the city served as a critical economic, social, and political center. In medieval Spain cities obtained *fueros* (special legal rights) that included taxation and law-making privileges, and the *vecinos* (citizens of the cities) guarded these prerogatives jealously. Indeed, Spanish citizenship was not of the nation but of one's municipality. Wherever the Spanish went, they established new towns and ruled the countryside from their cities.

Even prior to the arrival of Europeans in the Americas, cities already functioned as great centers of civilization and empire. Cuzco, the Inca capital in the Peruvian Andes, served as the center of an empire that spanned nearly all of the western side of South America. In Cuzco the ruling Inca lords brought together and enjoyed the tributes collected from many subject peoples. The Inca mandated that all local chiefs make a yearly pilgrimage to Cuzco and required that the sons of the chiefs receive their schooling in Cuzco.

The Aztec city of Tenochtitlán in the Valley of Mexico was a vast city of more than 200,000 inhabitants, with many great pyramids and temples. The Aztec capital developed as the religious, political, military, and economic center of an empire that stretched to the shores of the Gulf of Mexico on the east and to the Pacific coast on the west. Tenochtitlán was larger than many European cities of the 1500s and, according to Bernal Díaz, a foot soldier who accompanied conquistador Hernán Cortés, grander than many of the cities he had seen in the Mediterranean. Cortés began his campaign of conquest in Mexico by founding the city of Veracruz, which gave him the power to establish a political authority based on the Spanish municipality. His soldiers became the citizens and elected him leader, giving him legitimacy in his relationship with the king of Spain. After he had destroyed the Aztec capital after a long siege, Cortés was determined to build the capital of New Spain on the ruins of Tenochtitlán, despite its location hundreds of miles from the coast and in the middle of a lake. Cortés understood that symbolically this placed the new authority of the Spanish above that of the Aztecs. His action also recognized the importance of the site as the center of power in Mexico.

Throughout the conquest and the creation of empire, the Spanish built cities as anchors for their control of territory. Francisco Pizarro created Lima as a new capital in Peru, Pedro Avila de Arias built Panama City on the South Sea (the Pacific Ocean), and Pedro de Valdivia founded Santiago to control the central valley of Chile. Later, on the periphery of empire, smaller cities like Saint Augustine, San Antonio, Santa Fe, and Los Angeles served as the focal points from which the Spanish projected their power.

The colonial Spanish were quintessentially urban people, living in cities and directing their exploitation of the Americas from cities. Throughout the colonial period, Latin American cities continued to serve as the centers of imperial control of politics, commerce, and society, even if most wealth derived from the mines and land worked by natives and African slaves and even if most people still lived in rural areas.

Spanish colonial life was centered in the city. Symbols of church and state, the great cathedrals and viceregal palaces in Mexico and Lima stood together on the central square of each colonial city. Universities and theaters, shops and workshops, hospitals and monasteries, homes of the wealthy and the poor lined the evenly spaced streets on rectangular blocks. In this way the Spanish imposed their vision of order upon the land and over the people throughout the city.

The independence movements in South America began among the juntas of Creoles and merchants of Buenos Aires and Caracas, and the newly formed governments were established in these and other cities. After independence, one of the most critical issues for many of the new republics was that of the domination of a capital city and central government over the countryside and the provinces. In the early nineteenth century, civil wars and political battles were fought over the importance of the capital city and its relationship to the countryside. This period of turbulence would not be resolved until the middle of the century in most Latin American countries.

With the nineteenth-century creation of the mining and agro-export economies tied to European and U.S. markets, port cities emerged as centers of wealth, and if they were not the capital cities they vied for power with the capital. Exports brought a general increase in economic activity and urban growth. This, in turn, led to immigration from abroad and migrations from the interior that completely altered many cities, ultimately making them overwhelmingly large centers of population.

During the nineteenth century it was Western Europe that first underwent rapid urbanization. Urbanization and industrialization are concomitant developments. Still, even though nearly all of the largest cities in the world at that time were located in the center of the world economy, that is, in Western Europe and the eastern United States, parts of Latin America nevertheless shared in the general trend toward urbanization. In 1890, when London was the largest city in the world (4.2 million), Latin America still boasted two cities, Rio de Janeiro and Buenos Aires, among the world's largest twenty. By 1900 Latin America counted thirteen cities with populations of 100,000 or more and eighty-two more that numbered in excess of 20,000. By the next decade, Buenos Aires had a population of about 1.6 million, and Rio de Janeiro had a population of about 1.2 million. By 1920 more than one-quarter of the population of both Uruguay and Chile lived in cities with populations greater than 20,000, as did one-third of the Argentine population. Of all the less-developed regions of the world, Latin America was the most urbanized. Latin America was more urbanized than East Asia, South Asia, or Africa, and by 1930, 17 percent of the Latin American population lived in cities of 20,000 or more.[2]

Today the cities of Latin America have grown to spectacular size. Mexico City is the world's single largest city; São Paulo has more people than New York City. But many problems have come with this growth. The dilemmas are manifest, from cholera raging through the sprawling "young towns" of Lima to the suffocating air pollution of Mexico City to the unwanted and cruelly abused street children of Rio de Janeiro.

Policymakers and scholars have usually sought to understand these enormous concerns as strictly post–World War II phenomena, the powerful immediacy of the contemporary crises leading them to emphasize short-term causes. But although the extent of the present challenges must not be denied, their roots run deeper, reaching back to the critical period between 1870 and 1930.[3] We believe that the urgent urban problems of today can only be successfully addressed if we first achieve a far better understanding of their historical origins.

The Genesis of Modern Urban Latin America: 1870–1930

Beginnings can count for a great deal in most things, and for Latin America the period from 1870 to 1930 was an especially important beginning. This period marked the start of the modern urban age. Visitors to Latin America in the years before the 1870s often commented that the cities "generally . . . appeared small, poor and broken down," but "during the last decades of the nineteenth century, . . . the urban landscape of Latin America was completely transformed."[4]

The late nineteenth and early twentieth centuries brought exciting changes and new challenges to Latin America. Rising raw material exports generated riches, but the concomitant process of rapid urbanization inexorably created heightened social tensions. During these years, most Latin American cities rebounded from their postindependence slump in population and economic growth, responding to export opportunities in the international economy. Large markets emerged in Western Europe and the United States for Latin American exports. Raw materials from Latin America became much more sought after as industrialization spread. Latin America sent copper, tin, rubber, cotton, nitrates, and wool to Western Europe and the United States. At the same time, the rise in the number of middle-class employees and better-paid workers in Western Europe and the United States meant more consumers of other Latin American exports, such as coffee, sugar, wheat, beef, cacao, and tobacco. With this broad surge in global demand, the value of Latin America's total exports increased remarkably: Brazil's nearly doubled from 1869 to 1905, Mexico's rose seven times over in the years between 1877 and 1911, and Argentina's increased 800 percent from 1873 to 1910. Overall, world trade rose twenty-five times over in the years from the mid-nineteenth century to the start of World War I.[5]

This trade increase also depended upon the development of new technology. Steamships with iron hulls greatly reduced the time and costs of transoceanic shipping. Railways fanned across the Argentine pampa, the Brazilian coffee country, and elsewhere, further reducing transport costs, especially for bulky commodities. Barbed wire kept cattle away from crops, modern windmills brought up groundwater, new plows broke virgin sod, and repeating rifles killed off the remaining native Americans who still thought the land belonged to them. Telegraph cables reached across the Atlantic to South America and enabled foreign investors to get the latest word on the progress of their investments. Technology effectively brought Latin America closer to the centers of world commerce.

As Latin America's exports rose in these years, cities of different functions emerged. Many Latin American cities developed as vital entrepôts. Export-preparation industries—for example, the meat-packing industry in Buenos Aires—developed in cities where the export item required processing prior to shipment. Further industrialization followed in some cities, as in Buenos Aires; São Paulo; and Santiago. Still, this manufacturing usually remained limited to relatively small-scale enterprises, chiefly oriented toward serving domestic needs for consumer nondurables, such as inexpensive textiles or processed foods. Finally, capital cities grew in size and power as government bureaucracies expanded with rising import and export taxes.

Together, economic change and urbanization began to generate new patterns of politics for Latin America in the years from 1870 to 1930. Previously, in the chaotic years following independence, tough, charismatic, rural strongmen had come to dominate national politics in much of Latin America, and their endless personal wrangling had left most of the young republics in a state of near-perpetual disorder. But by the late nineteenth century, political stability, requisite for continued economic growth, had become a more urgent concern. As states employed their increased resources to centralize and expand their power, the achievement of stability at last become possible. The emerging urban elite, more prosperous and more numerous than ever before, successfully ended the disruptive governance of the old rural *caudillos*. Indeed, the landed elite now often moved to the cities, the principal venues for conspicuous consumption by the elite, old and new. As cities now assumed a more central role in the economy, they also assumed a more central role in government. In these years, then, the locus of political power in Latin America shifted away from the countryside and toward the city, in effect, a restoration of their prior colonial position of ascendancy.

Critical changes also came in elite attitudes toward the urban underclass in the years prior to the turn of the century. Traditional paternalistic acceptance of a measured responsibility for the welfare of the urban poor began to erode; the colonial, elite-directed urban social order was collapsing. As Michael Conniff has noted:

> An important attribute of colonial Latin American cities . . . [had been] social solidarity. This meant that everyone, no matter how poor or wretched, had a definite place. To be sure, places were hierarchically arranged. Though inequality was accepted, charity and concern for the downtrodden were important, and this responsibility became vested in both Church leaders and the wealthy.[6]

In the swiftly changing social milieu of the growing cities of Latin America before the turn of the century, a new culture of individualism was arising, replacing colonial notions of shared communal concern. It no longer seemed necessary to care as much about the urban underclass; fewer now took pity upon them; fewer now saw their many hardships as something the community had to address. If some people were poor, their own sloth must have caused it, many now believed.

The dominant philosophic view of government and business leaders regarding the proper role of the state was to favor a laissez-faire government. That is, most opinion shapers and policymakers generally held that the government should not be too large and that it should not interfere in the natural currents of trade. Nevertheless, the capacity for state action was daily increasing as government revenues rose swiftly from taxes on the rising foreign commerce. But if there were more state funds to spend, this did not mean that urban reforms to benefit the poor followed. Instead, city fathers had other agendas: plans for urban renewal that they believed would make their cities look more attractive (that is, more like Paris) or plans for public works that favored elite interests. Still, sometimes the elite pressed for citywide sanitation reform that benefited everyone, especially if epidemics led to quarantines that closed off commerce or killed the loved ones of rich and poor alike.

Most important of all, the sweeping economic changes brought by rising exports led to a basic reconfiguration of the social structure in Latin America. As a consequence, Latin American patterns of politics began to change, reflecting the new distribution of power in society. New-money elites emerged from the export-import trade or from mining and industry. These new wealthy interests now pressed to join Latin America's landed elite and the other members of the traditional oligarchy, the church and military, in ruling their nations.

The middle class, that quintessentially urban grouping, also grew in size and changed in its composition in these years. The middle class was no longer just a small collection of skilled handicraft workers and professionals who lived on the edges of elite lives, dependent upon the patronage and favor of the well-to-do. Advances in commerce and the increasing size of government created a wider demand for clerks, accountants, and bureaucrats to sort and keep track of the rising profits and tax revenues. Middle-class opportunities also opened up in small businesses. As the middle class emerged, its members would demand political inclusion.

In these years a modern urban working class also began to appear with the many new laborers in the railways, on the docks, in factories, and in other advanced economic sectors. Such workers began to forge modern labor unions and to press for better conditions, for urban reform, and in time for political inclusion. Such demands might be repressed, but as the unions grew in size they could no longer simply be ignored. Nevertheless, in this period most workers, even the most advantaged ones, failed to win the right to vote in Latin American nations, with but a couple of noteworthy exceptions. As a result, workers had little choice but to express their politics informally and thus generally less consistently and effectively.

The elite generally viewed these new organizations of workers with great discomfort, seeing their presence as threatening. The elite at the beginning of the twentieth century in Latin America typically turned to repression as the appropriate manner for dealing with increasingly obstreperous workers. For the first time, modern police forces were necessary to control the urban underclass; ordinary people would no longer be usually self-policing as had generally been the case in the colonial cities of the past.

By the 1920s and with gathering speed in the 1930s and after, these mounting changes in the social structure finally ruptured most of the old-style political arrangements of elite hegemony across Latin America. By this time the urbanized population in many nations began to reach a critical threshold: The urban working class had grown and with increasing momentum was pushing for political inclusion. The old political pattern of oligarchic exclusion was breaking down.

The era of populist-style politics that followed in the late 1920s and after was, in the words of historian Michael Conniff, an attempt "to correct abuses of elitist government and accommodate rapid urbanization."[7] Thus began the transition to urban working-class political incorporation, albeit under clientistic, less than fully democratic, populist arrangements. Populism emerged as an answer to the threat of working-class insurrection from below, especially after the violent general strikes during and after World War I in cities across Latin America. The populist governments that appeared were multiclass coalitions, distributive if not redistributive, channeling benefits to loyal supporters. However, populist leaders had no plans to challenge urban elite interests in order to benefit the masses (although rural elite interests were sometimes looted). Therefore, to pay for the programs needed to assure popular support, populist leaders usually had to hope for an export boom that would boost revenues. Failing this, they turned to loans or, ultimately, just printed the money they needed. Charismatic populist leaders wanted everyone to benefit and no one to pay. Some early examples of populism can be found in José Batlle's Uruguay or Hipólito Yrigoyen's Argentina, but as Conniff correctly noted: "The general prosperity of the 1920s fostered the new urban politics that became populism."[8]

This change was fitful, uneven, and often reversed, but in time the transition to the new politics was complete. This book explores the patterns of urban working-class lives and politics in the years that stood between the old and the new: between the old of traditional elite paternalism and exclusionary politics and the new of mass-based, multiclass, inclusionary populist politics and an active state.

Studies of Urban Latin America

Given the central role of the city in the Latin American experience, it is remarkable that they have been so little studied. In the words of leading scholars, works are "few and far between" and there are so many gaps that the entire field must be judged "relatively unexplored."[9]

The critical 1870–1930 period presents further historiographical concerns. Although the economic history of Latin America's export-led growth of the late nineteenth and early twentieth centuries has been the subject of serious study (Roberto Cortes-Conde and Stanley J. Stein provide an extensive discussion and guide to the literature in their 1977 publication *Latin America: A Guide to Economic History 1830–1930*), the social history of Latin America for this era remains extremely underdeveloped.[10]

We need better historical treatment of working-class life and living conditions in the cities. We need to know much more about the employment patterns, the social conditions, and the politics of housing, health care, and general urban social reform for late-nineteenth- and early-twentieth-century cities of Latin America. As it stands, we have only a very rough sense of conditions in turn-of-the-century cities and, more seriously, only a limited understanding of the difficult and complicated process of effectively responding to these conditions with needed social reforms.

The lack of study of Latin American social and urban history stems partly from the lack of source material. Several serious difficulties have complicated the research task. Historians exploring the social history of urban Latin America for this era have discovered to their dismay that the rich sources mined by urban scholars of Western Europe and the United States seldom exist in Latin America.[11] This is especially true for the smaller and economically less successful nations, which could not always afford the costs of ordinary record keeping. There are few synthetic sources of the kind that yield convenient tabulations covering a series of years. To obtain information about health care, births, deaths, population, and other topics, researchers are forced to dig the information out year by year. In some cases, though documents exist they are not organized; they are piled up in storage rooms filled with boxes of various scattered papers.[12]

One especially important contribution of this book is to provide a strong empirical account of basic conditions in the city: housing, transportation, potable water, sewage disposal, sanitation, vaccination, health care, and other aspects of urban life. The chapters will similarly provide long-needed basic information on urban demography: population size, growth rates, ethnicity, gender ratio, age, marriage, and births, among other topics. This book brings together difficult-to-gather data on critical aspects of the Latin American urban experience.

The existing literature is especially weak in making comparisons, discerning patterns, and constructing theories. Because urbanization has been more extensively studied for Europe and North America, theories drawn from that experience have often been employed in an effort to understand Latin America. This is unwise, for these theories are ill-suited to Latin America, where cities were historically less industrialized and far less politically inclusionary than those of the United States and Western Europe.

Within Latin America, generally only the few great primate cities have been studied; historians have given little consideration to the many nonindustrial, nonprimate cities. Unfortunately, too many scholars have made the convenient assumption that the economic, political, and social patterns found in the few large cities must also hold for the many medium-sized ones.

We believe that this book helps take urban social history in an important new direction, and in so doing it directly addresses the major historiographical gaps in urban history and in Latin American social history. Moreover, by exploring urbanization in Latin American cities, in both industrial and nonindustrial cities, in primate and nonprimate cities, this work brings into question many of the assumptions of what existing historiography there is. It is our hope that this study will help to stimulate further inquiry and to suggest a path for future research on urban Latin America.

Methodology

This book seeks to provide a basis for understanding the relationship between the impact of urbanization on the working class in Latin American cities and the variety of responses by that group in the critical years between 1870 and 1930. In the chapters that follow, we also explore the many factors that contributed to or hindered urban social reform in these years.

Each of the authors has produced an original chapter based on his or her own research. Each author in this book has taken one city and highlighted a key urban issue for that city. All the chapters are new, not previously published, and have been written especially for this book.

The case study sites selected for this volume provide a mix of Latin American city types. We have included capital cities of large nations (Rio de Janeiro, Brazil; Mexico City, Mexico; Lima, Peru; and Buenos Aires, Argentina) and capital cities of medium-sized or smaller nations (Bogotá, Colombia; Panama City, Panama; and Montevideo, Uruguay). We have selected for study a secondary city in a large nation (Veracruz, Mexico) and a secondary city in a medium-sized nation (Valparaíso, Chile). We have included a tropical city of non-European immigrants (Panama City). In this way the urban experience in all the largest nations of Latin America is covered, and we still offer a sampling of cities from the medium-sized and smaller countries. Because we could not cover every Latin American city, we have instead directed our attention to a sampling of those that experienced the most urban growth, even if this means that some regions that saw less urbanization, notably the Caribbean, are not covered here.

The case studies address a variety of critical topics, engaging an array of issues in working-class conditions, the patterns of worker politics, and the process of urban social reform. We have clustered several chapters around two key working-class concerns, housing and health care, in order to facilitate comparison between case studies. Unfortunately, we cannot offer complete coverage for all issues that affected workers. Some themes, such as crime and education, will have to await further research and treatment elsewhere.

This volume is cooperative in the richest sense. Although every author developed her or his own emphasis and argument, we found common territory in our shared analytical approach and research agenda. Three core questions inform all of the chapters in this study. First, what were the living circumstances for working women and men in the growing cities at the end of the nineteenth century in Latin America? Second, how did this population respond actively to the problems they faced and act to improve the quality of their lives? And, third, what circumstances and what strategies were most likely to have a lasting impact? It is our contention that although each city contained unique characteristics, a pattern of working-class response emerged during this period that affected the political process of the nation. Each of the chapters in this volume focuses on one aspect of that variegated and intermittent reaction.

In looking for answers to these questions, no single, dominant cause has risen above all others. Causes vary with local circumstances. For instance, an inadequate city transport system might be explained by an impoverished city government, by too-hilly terrain, by disruptive civil wars, or by a combinations of these or other factors. Likewise, high city death rates might be attributable to an uncaring city government, to inadequate revenues, to a lack of local sources of potable water, or again to a combination of these and other factors. To be sure, it is possible that for a particular problem in a particular city one sole factor stands out in explaining why the problem existed or why reform came or did not come. But what works to explain what happened in one city can often be irrelevant in another.

Accordingly, in the case studies that follow each author has sought to examine conditions, politics, and reform and to build an argument that is sensitive to the exigencies of local circumstance. In the concluding chapter we will explore the combinations of cause and the explanatory patterns that have begun to emerge from these case studies.

David Sowell's study of urban growth in Bogotá and its impact on the social structure emphasizes the importance of the city's working class in the shaping of Colombia's political culture. He shows the years between 1870 and 1930 to be a period of dramatic population growth for Bogotá, especially after the War of the 1,000 Days (1899–1902). This growth produced problems for the working class: lack of housing and municipal services in workers' neighborhoods. It also created opportunities for skilled laborers. This combination provided the opening for informal as well as formal political impulses by members of the city's working class. These activities included riots, assassinations, and public intimidation, as well as strikes and demonstrations. Nevertheless, working-class demands for reform, although often uncoordinated and not sustained, did have an impact on the two major political parties, which either sought the votes of urban workers or attempted to repress urban disturbances.

Contention over urban space in Montevideo is highlighted in Anton Rosenthal's chapter on the introduction of the electric streetcar. Rosenthal shows how the need to improve urban transportation not only transformed the physical characteristics of Montevideo but also shaped social interaction and altered labor relations. The electric streetcar produced many changes in Montevideo's society.

City residents traveled more often and farther on the electric streetcar: to beaches and resorts on the edge of the city and to entertainments within the city. They suffered death and injury from accidents with electric streetcars, which were faster and quieter than the old horse-drawn trolleys. The streetcar became a billboard for advertisements and political electioneering and a stage for public spectacle where crimes of passion were committed. The electric streetcar companies, both foreign owned, emerged as the largest landowners in the city as well as employers of a workforce that grew from 2,000 to 5,000 between 1911 and the 1930s. This important labor force, in turn, would provide critical support to the Colorado party, which had ousted the Blancos in 1904. So critical to this regime were both the streetcar workers and the cheap transportation provided by the trolleys that prices for tickets remained unchanged from before World War I until 1936, even as the government gave the workers a 15 to 25 percent raise in 1922 to settle a strike.

The importance of labor issues combined with urban growth and social transformation is underscored by John Lear in his chapter on the working class of Mexico City during the Mexican Revolution. Lear addresses the previously unexplained relationship between the defeat of the general strike by organized labor in Mexico City in 1916 and the pro-labor codes written into the 1917 Constitution. By reviewing the structure of work and community in Mexico City after 1870, Lear finds that working-class mobilization became most effective when it extended beyond the traditional issues of the workplace and included questions of food supply for the capital during the revolution. He shows how this network of support resurfaced in a tenant strike in 1922, revealing the importance of viewing Mexican workers as active participants in political contention even though their official institutions become subject to the influence of the ruling party.

Housing is the focus of the research by Andrew Grant Wood. He finds that the tenant strike in Veracruz in 1922, which began a nationwide movement that included Mexico City, illustrates the significance of consumer issues within the ongoing development of postrevolutionary politics. The events in Veracruz brought together anarchist traditions of direct action by labor, a growing crisis in the availability of affordable housing, and the political opportunity provided by Veracruz State governor Adalberto Tejeda. This intricate combination allowed members of the working class to demand urban reforms of the emerging postrevolutionary party and provided a common focus of complaint that led to collective action.

This relationship between increasing urban problems, especially in housing, and the entry of the working class into the political arena, albeit in a nonformal manner, is taken up by James A. Baer in his study of the 1921 rent law in Argentina. Baer indicates that housing issues had evolved over time, leading to tenant leagues, a rent strike in 1907, and a National Commission on Affordable Housing. However, the postwar crisis of rising rents created an ad hoc and even unintentional coalition of Catholic reformers, conservative politicians, the leaders of the Radical party, the Socialists, and working-class women and men who rented. This coalition of groups, each for its own reasons, came to support legislation for governmental regulation over housing costs and rental agreements that was nothing short of a radical departure from the past laissez-faire approach of Argentine governments. Baer suggests that this event should be seen as one element in the emergence of Argentine populism and that it is necessary to recognize the importance of working-class action for change.

David S. Parker expands the analysis to include both housing and public health in Lima, showing why urban reform in that city was so much less successful than in Veracruz and Buenos Aires. The key, he believes, was the racism of reformers, who held that poor hygiene and tenement life were the fault of inferior peoples, both indigenous native populations and immigrant Asians. He shows that attempts at reform inevitably refused to recognize the structural roots of many urban problems and often were thinly veiled attempts to impose greater control over the urban working class. That this did not lead to a unified response from Lima's working class owed in part to the racial divisions among its disparate members.

The city of Valparaíso, Chile, presents both contrasts and similarities to Lima with respect to the failure of urban reforms. Ronn Pineo uses detailed analyses of hospital records and other sources to show that public health officials in Valparaíso and Chile knew what measures needed to be enacted. However, the dynamics of national politics and the inherent belief in the inferiority of the city's working class produced a multiplicity of responses that failed to improve effectively the lives of the urban poor. Thus Valparaíso, although it was Chile's most important seaport and second largest urban center, continued to lag behind in public health improvements.

Sam Adamo focuses on the campaign to improve both the image and the public health of Rio de Janeiro and its citizens. As a national capital and port city, Rio reflected on Brazil as a whole. The country's leaders wanted to overcome their capital's image as a disease-ridden tropical backwater and set about to transform the city. Public works projects forced poor residents, most of them Afro-Brazilians, out of the city center and added to an already serious housing shortage. Public health measures attempted to improve the health of the city's residents and make the city more attractive to European capital and immigration. Although these reforms did improve the looks and the sanitation of the city, their impact on the population varied, often by race. The city's poor generally suffered from nutritional deficiencies and a lack of sanitation in their marginal neighborhoods that affected their health. The success of urban reform in Rio thus needs to be measured by race.

The final case discussed in this book is Panama City, where the issue of race was a key component in the development of the urban working class. Sharon Phillipps Collazos studies the impact of the immigrant Caribbean workers who were brought to Panama to help dig the Panama Canal. English-speaking, Protestant, and black, these Caribbean immigrants settled in the Canal Zone and in Panama City, becoming a significant yet distinct part of the working class. These divisions within the Panamanian working class and between the Canal Zone controlled by the United States and the city controlled by Panamanians made it more difficult for labor organizations to unite workers. Again, the problem of housing provided one of the few issues that brought together much of the Panamanian working class.

It is our overall goal for this volume to offer a broader understanding of urban history and to make a significant contribution to Latin American social history. By adding to our knowledge of ordinary people in everyday life, we not only achieve a fuller and more complex understanding of our collective past, we also develop a more democratic vision of history. By exploring the genesis of modern Latin America's urban explosion, we gain a valuable perspective and hence greater insight into the severe urban dilemmas that are the challenge of the present.

Notes

1. See the discussion by Philip D. Curtin in his preface to *Atlantic Port Cities: Economy, Culture, and Society in the Atlantic World, 1650–1850,* ed. Franklin W. Knight and Peggy K. Liss (Knoxville: University of Tennessee Press, 1991), xi.

2. During this era, Latin America's population increased markedly: from 30.5 million in 1850 to 61 million by 1900 and nearly doubling again by 1930 to 104 million people. Latin America's population grew at a rate faster than that of Europe or North America in the years from 1900 to 1930; James Scobie, "The Growth of Latin American Cities, 1870–1930," in *Cambridge History of Latin America,* ed. Leslie Bethell, vol. 4, *C. 1870 to 1930* (Cambridge: University of Cambridge Press, 1986). Also see John J. Johnson, *Political Change in Latin America: The Emergence of the Middle Sectors* (Stanford: Stanford University Press, 1958), 32; Eric E. Lampard, "The Urbanizing World," in *The Victorian City: Images and Realities,* ed. H. J. Dyos and Michael Wolff, vol. 1 (London: Routledge and Kegan Paul, 1973), 9, 33; Ruth Berins Collier and David Collier, *Shaping the Political Arena: Critical Junctures, the Labor Movement, and Regime Dynamics in Latin America* (Princeton: Princeton University Press, 1991), 66.

3. This point was suggested by Gerald Michael Greenfield, "The Development of the Underdeveloped City: Public Sanitation in São Paulo, Brazil, 1885–1913," *The Luso-Brazilian Review* 17 (Summer 1980): 107.

4. Scobie, "Growth of Latin American Cities." See also Knight and Liss, *Atlantic Port Cities,* 5, and passim.

5. William P. Glade, *The Latin American Economies: A Study of Their Institutional Evolution* (New York: American Book, 1969), 215–216; Desmond Christopher Martin Platt, *Latin America and British Trade 1806–1914* (London: A. and C. Black, 1972), esp. chap. 4; Celso Furtado, *Economic Development of Latin America,* trans. Suzette Macedo (Cambridge: Cambridge University Press, 1976), esp. chap. 4; Nicolas Sanchez-Albornoz, *The Population of Latin America: A History,* trans. W. A. R. Richardson (Berkeley: University of California Press, 1974), 168, 178–179; Collier and Collier, *Shaping the Political Arena,* 59. W. Arthur Lewis, *The Evolution of the International Economic Order* (Princeton: Princeton

University Press, 1978), notes that the last part of the nineteenth century marked the point when the world divided into primary-product exporters and industrial exporters. With this "second" industrial revolution of the late nineteenth century, the developed world come to depend upon the less developed nations for supplies of many basic raw materials.

6. Michael L. Conniff, "Introduction: Toward a Comparative Definition of Populism," in *Latin American Populism in Comparative Perspective,* ed. Michael L. Conniff (Albuquerque: University of New Mexico Press, 1982), 9.

7. Michael L. Conniff, *Urban Politics in Brazil: The Rise of Populism, 1925–1945* (Pittsburgh: University of Pittsburgh Press, 1981), 3.

8. Conniff, "Introduction," 6.

9. Gerald Michael Greenfield, "New Perspectives on Latin American Cities," *Journal of Urban History* 15, no. 2 (February 1989): 213; Richard J. Walter, "Recent Works on Latin American Urban History," *Journal of Urban History* 16, no. 2 (February 1990): 205. See also John K. Chance, "Recent Trends in Latin American Urban Studies," *Latin American Research Review* 15 (1980): 183–188; Richard M. Morse, "Trends and Patterns in Latin American Urbanization, 1750–1920," *Comparative Studies in Society and History* 16, no. 4 (September 1974).

10. Roberto Cortes-Conde and Stanley J. Stein, *Latin America: A Guide to Economic History 1830–1930* (Berkeley: University of California Press, 1977). Exceptions include Peter DeShazo, *Urban Workers and Labor Unions in Chile 1902–1927* (Madison: University of Wisconsin Press, 1983); June Hahner, *Poverty and Politics: The Urban Poor in Brazil, 1870–1920* (Albuquerque: University of New Mexico Press, 1986). On the evolution of writing on the social history of Latin America from 1870 to 1930, see John J. Johnson, "One Hundred Years of Historical Writing on Modern Latin America by United States Historians," *Hispanic American Historical Review* 65, no. 4 (1985): 745–765; Geoffrey Barraclough, *Main Trends in History* (New York: Holmes and Meier, 1978), 117; Eugene Sofer, "Recent Trends in Latin American Labor Historiography," *LARR* 15 (1980): 167; K. P. Erickson, P. V. Peppe, and Hobart Spalding, "Dependency vs. Working Class History," *LARR* 15 (1980): 177–181.

11. See the comments by Hahner, *Poverty and Politics,* xii, 168.

12. See the discussion in Julia Kirk Blackwelder and Lyman L. Johnson, "Changing Criminal Patterns," *Journal of Latin American Studies* 14 (1982): 70–371. For example, the Ministry of Labor and Social Welfare in Ecuador started to collect such information only after 1925; Alan Middleton, "Division and Cohesion in the Working Class: Artisans and Wage Labourers in Ecuador," *Journal of Latin American Studies* 14 (1982): 185.

1

Political Impulses: Popular Participation in Formal and Informal Politics, Bogotá, Colombia

David Sowell

"Of all the South American capitals, Bogotá has remained the most backward, and it cannot be compared with Caracas, Lima, Santiago, or Buenos Aires." Miguel Samper described 1860s Bogotá as a city in which homeless people filled the streets, the poor existed on public charities (and therefore had no desire to work!), economic conditions were deplorable, Conservatives manipulated a guileless society, and a flawed, violent political culture prevented civic advancement.[1] Thirty years later, Samper commented upon the much-improved state of public welfare, economic conditions, civil order, and civil amenities. Still, he viewed the city as behind other Latin American capitals, especially in its political culture.[2] The elite-dominated Conservative and Liberal parties had proven unable to sustain a political life that avoided periodic bloodshed, such as would soon occur in the disastrous civil war, the War of the 1,000 Days (1899–1902). However, in the first decades of the twentieth century, a political stability unknown to Samper's time dominated the nation.

Studies of Colombian political culture are very rich. In particular, the unusual longevity of the Conservative and Liberal parties (1840s to the present) has focused scholarly attention upon the relationship of the parties to the nature and formation of the Colombian political system. Partisans are keenly interested in their particular organizational, intellectual, and personal histories; others tend to be more concerned with the relationships of the laboring classes to parties and political power.[3] Charles Bergquist, drawing upon dependency theory, suggests that coffee laborers forced partisan political accommodations that shaped contemporary Colombian politics.[4] Bergquist places less importance upon the profound changes wrought by rapid urbanization,[5] although David Bushnell notes that the resurgence of the Liberal party after the 1930s is directly associated with the rapid growth of urban centers, where that party is historically more influential.[6] Ruth and David Collier, in their influential *Shaping the Political Arena*, identify the expanded demographic base that accompanied urban and commercial development, especially that of the capital city, as central to the socioeconomic context of twentieth-century politics.[7] Their top-down analysis, however, fails to fully appreciate the active role of laborers in shaping the political process, a serious misreading of Colombian political culture avoided by Bergquist.

This chapter relates the "condition of the city" to the world of politics. How did Bogotá's demographic and economic growth between 1870 and 1930 affect the city's social structure? How were the interests of the "popular" classes articulated? How did their actions affect the political culture of the city and nation? These sixty years constitute a critical stage in the socioeconomic and political development of the Colombian capital. Small producers, including artisans, engaged in a wide variety of formal and informal political expressions that forced the dominant Conservative and Liberal parties to at least partially accommodate their interests. Just as small producers in the coffee sector forced the parties to respond to their social concerns within the polity, so too did the urban artisans win a voice in shaping Colombia's twentieth-century political culture.

Demographic and Socioeconomic Change

After its foundation in 1538 in one of the most heavily populated regions of the northern Andes, Santa Fe de Bogotá grew slowly, reaching a population of about 20,000 by the start of the nineteenth century. The city served as a center of religious, political, and institutional authority for much of northern South America.[8] Bogotá, like Lima and other cities of the interior, began to expand in the second half of the nineteenth century, primarily because of a quickening pace of economic activity, the increased importance of the city as a political center, and the establishment of nascent manufacture. (See Table 1.1.)[9] Although Bogotá never had a reputation as being particularly unhealthy, it did suffer from periodic epidemics and from diseases common to highland Latin American urban centers. Even in the late nineteenth century, population growth occurred because of migration from the countryside, not because of an excess of births over deaths. (See Table 1.2.) Not until the early twentieth century did public health conditions and other factors improve so that the number of people who were born outnumbered those who died in the city. In addition, economic opportunities in factories and construction began to draw more and more people from the countryside, especially from the rural areas of Cundinamarca and Boyacá. Improved urban health conditions generated internal population growth that, when combined with the increased rates of in-migration, accounted for the rapid rate of urban growth.[10] The city's population reached 235,421 in 1928 (a sixfold increase over its 1870 to-

TABLE 1.1 Comparative Latin American Urban Population Growth: 1791–1914

Bogotá	*Lima*	*Buenos Aires*
21,394 (1801)	52,627 (1791)	40,000 (1801)
40,000 (1843)	54,628 (1836)	55,416 (1822)
40,883 (1870)	89,434 (1862)	177,787 (1869)
95,813 (1895)	100,194 (1895)	663,854 (1895)
121,257 (1912)	143,000 (1908)	1,575,814 (1914)

SOURCES: Peter Walter Amato, *An Analysis of the Changing Patterns of Elite Residential Areas in Bogotá, Colombia* (Ph.D. diss., Cornell University, 1968), 138; Richard E. Boyer and Keith A. Davies, *Urbanization in 19th Century Latin America: Statistics and Sources* (Los Angeles: Latin American Center, 1973), 7, 37–39, 59–61; Anderson, "Race and Social Stratification," 215.

TABLE 1.2 Births and Deaths in Bogotá, 1877–1892

Year	*No. Births*	*No. Deaths*
1877	1,370	2,188
1881	1,769	2,274
1885	2,050	3,088
1886	1,975	2,754
1887	2,295	2,591
1889	2,264	2,570
1890	2,557	2,231
1891	2,305	3,159
1892	2,402	2,344

SOURCES: *Diario de Cundinamarca,* January 25, 1878; *El Heraldo,* January 22, 1890; January 16, 1892; January 11, 1893; *El Orden,* January 1, 1891.

tal), topped 700,000 by 1951, and had more than doubled to 1,697,311 in 1964.[11] The 1985 census counted 4,207,657 residents in the city. These rates of expansion applied to other cities as well, so that whereas only 30 percent of the nation's populace lived in urban areas in 1938, 52 percent did so in 1964, and a full two-thirds were urbanites in 1985.[12]

Bogotá served as a highland economic hub throughout the colonial period, although its most important function was as the seat of government. Mid-nineteenth-century liberal economic policies stimulated momentary growth, although the export economy was subject to alternating booms and busts, a situation compounded by civil wars, such as that of 1859–1862, which helped produce the conditions cited by Samper in *La miseria.* The economy fluctuated through the end of the century as capital from tobacco and then coffee exports ebbed and flowed into the city. After the War of the 1,000 Days, the capital entered a period of expansion that lasted, with a few short recessions, through the 1920s. Capital from increasingly profitable exports and from the growth of internal manufacture and an influx of foreign capital served as the stimuli for this economic growth.

The site of the Colombian capital greatly affected its spatial development. The city lies hundreds of kilometers from the nearest coast and is located at an elevation of 2,600 meters on the vast Sabana de Bogotá. *Hacendados* divided this fertile plain into large estates for the production of cattle, vegetables, and grains early in the colonial period. These estates, in combination with a mountain ridge that rises to the east of the city, dictated the city's growth along a generally north-south axis. The city's initial four *barrios* (wards) contained the population until the period of late-nineteenth-century expansion, when population growth forced the creation of new *barrios*. By 1930 the number of *barrios* had increased sixfold and included the once-autonomous town of Chapinero, about two kilometers north of the central plaza.[13] Most of those who moved northward were more affluent, whereas the working classes and poor settled near the older central and southern sections of the city, where costs tended to be lower. This spatial distribution of socioeconomic groups contrasts with that of the colonial period, when the elite dominated the urban core, which was ringed by commercial, artisanal, and poorer social classes.[14]

Bogotanos faced various socioeconomic pressures caused by the growth of the city. A shortage of housing for workers became a public concern in the 1890s; ten years later a variety of groups clamored for some sort of public action on this need. *Barrios obreros* (workers' neighborhoods), which lacked municipal services, developed in the southern and western areas of the city. These neighborhoods were dominated by single-story brick shops that often doubled as stores.[15] In 1908 the editors of *El Artista* urged that the city council extend basic services to the southwest portion of the city, as many laborers were forced to live in their shops in unhealthy and unsafe conditions.[16] Similar requests were made in the early 1910s, but not until 1913 did the city council authorize such construction. The barrio Antonio Ricaurte was officially dedicated as a *barrio obrero* in 1914, although water lines did not reach the barrio until several years later, a problem shared with many of the newer areas of the city populated by the working classes and the poor.[17] By 1920, at least eighteen *barrios obreros* existed throughout the city.[18]

Significantly, economic processes in both rural and urban settings enhanced the numbers and socioeconomic status of small producers, a change that had profound political consequences. Although Bergquist focuses on the growth and importance of small rural producers,[19] their urban counterparts have received less attention. In the early nineteenth century, most urban males worked in manual trades as skilled or unskilled laborers or in the public sector, and women tended to labor in domestic service or in sewing activities, mainly as unskilled workers. (See Tables 1.3 and 1.4.) Artisans enjoyed a socioeconomic position that both afforded them more economic independence and sustained their sense of social worth.[20] The small consumer industries that developed in the last third of the nineteenth century utilized low technology and unskilled labor and did not com-

TABLE 1.3 Comparative Male Occupational Structure, Bogotá, 1851, 1888

	1851		*1888*	
Category	*N*	%	*N*	%
Unskilled	69	12.7	89	20.1
Semiskilled	13	2.4	11	.9
Skilled	196	36.3	163	36.9
Commercial	57	10.5	52	11.8
Religious	21	3.9	5	1.1
Professional	26	4.8	17	3.8
Other[a]	158	29.3	105	23.7
Total	540		442	

[a] Includes police and military.

SOURCES: Manuscript Returns, 1851 Census, AHN: *República,* Miscelánea, vol. 17, pp. 65–165; *El Telegrama,* data extracted from October 1887 through December 1888; Cupertino Salgado, *Directorio general de Bogotá: Año IV, 1893* (Bogotá: n.p. 1893).

TABLE 1.4 Comparative Female Occupational Structure, Bogotá, 1851, 1888

	1851		*1888*	
Category	*N*	%	*N*	%
Unskilled	574	78.2	316	79.0
Semiskilled	55	7.54	221	5.5
Skilled	7	.9	11	2.7
Commercial	89	12.1	38	9.5
Religious	1	.1	4	1.0
Professional	6	.8	5	1.3
Other	2	.3	4	1.0
Total	734		400	

SOURCES: Manuscript Returns, 1851 Census, AHN: *República,* Miscelánea, vol. 17, pp. 65–165; *El Telegrama,* data extracted from October 1787 through December 1888; Cupertino Salgado, *Directorio general de Bogotá: Año IV, 1893* (Bogotá: n.p., 1893).

pete with skilled labor; nor do they appear to have reduced the percentages of skilled laborers in the workforce.[21] In the early twentieth century, as construction activity increased, mechanical shops developed, and early manufacturers were established, the numbers of skilled laborers both in and out of the factory setting grew.[22] Not until the late 1930s did factory production slowly begin to replace handicraft production in most trades. (See Tables 1.5 and 1.6.)

These changes recast the city's occupational profile. By the beginning of the twentieth century skilled (artisanal) and unskilled workers were joined by increasing numbers of wage laborers and *industriales* (producers on the cusp between skilled and managerial status). Just as they had in the nineteenth century,

TABLE 1.5 Manufacturing and Factory Workforce, Bogotá, 1870–1978

	Manufacturing % of Total Workforce	*Factory % of Total Workforce*	*Factory % of Manufacturing Workforce*
1870	20	1	5
1900	18–18.5	2	
1938	14		
1950	12		
1978	16–18	7–8	50

NOTE: A factory is a plant with five or more workers.

SOURCE: Albert Berry, "A Descriptive History of Colombian Industrial Development in the Twentieth Century," in *Essays on Industrialization in Colombia,* ed. Albert Berry (Tempe: Center for Latin American Studies, Arizona State University, 1983), 9, 22.

TABLE 1.6 Trends in Cottage Shop and Factory Employment in Manufactures, Bogotá, 1944–1945 to 1973 (in thousands)

	Cottage Shops	*Factories*
1944–45	308.4 (66.5%)	155.6 (33.5%)
1953	287.0 (59.2%)	199.0 (40.8%)
1964	327.5 (51.4%)	310.0 (48.6%)
1973	496.2 (50.4%)	488.8 (49.6%)

SOURCE: Cortes, Berry, and Ishaq, *Success in Small and Medium-Scale Enterprises,* 444–445.

artisans sought to obtain effective political representation and tariff protection for their industries. Unskilled workers, joined by wage laborers, expressed concerns about the rate of pay, housing conditions, the price of food, and other quotidian issues. *Industriales,* a new segment of the labor force, shared an interest in tariff protection and political influence with artisans. Each of these groups had different socioeconomic interests and assumed distinct political stances, although small producers continued their socioeconomic and political prominence.

Political Impulses

Informal and formal political impulses were closely associated with partisan politics, Bogotá's social structure, and the socioeconomic tensions caused by the city's rapid population growth. Formal politics refers to the routine, accepted, institutionalized structures of authority through which "legitimate" political claims are made upon a government. Elections, political parties, city councils, and legislatures, for example, fit within this category. Informal politics lie outside the bounds of formal politics and include such behaviors as riots, assassinations, and public intimidation. Some political actions, such as strikes or demonstrations, can be either formal or informal, depending upon the political culture of a particular place or time.[23]

A set of highly diffuse and weakly articulated regional political networks operated within a remarkably light state structure to shape Colombia's colonial political culture. Generally quiescent middle-class and popular sectors supported an "unwritten constitution" in which Spaniards, Creoles, middling, and popular groups maintained a balance between formal and informal politics. Early-nineteenth-century elites and some middle sectors added formalized political organizations that hinged on (1) relations to colonial bureaucracy, (2) independence-era associations, and (3) regional political networks. The Conservative and Liberal parties struggled with issues of political economy, mechanisms of social control, and the nature of the state structure (especially centralism versus federalism). The Constitution of 1886, interpreted by the Conservative-dominated governments of the late nineteenth century, resolved most of these issues. Liberal opposition to the Conservative agenda resulted in the War of the 1,000 Days, whose outcome was to cement Conservative control of the national government, albeit under more moderate leadership. During the twentieth century, the control of the state, the incorporation of new political interests into the polity, and social tranquillity have dominated the agendas of the dominant parties.

Nineteenth-century partisan contention led to a more widespread participation in formal politics. In urban areas, both Conservatives and Liberals attempted to tip the scale in their own favor in the struggle for political control during bitterly contested elections by recruiting eligible voters. Craftsmen played an important role in this process, first as subordinated voters and then in a more independent manner. After the Democratic and Popular Societies (in the 1850s) and the Alliance (in the 1860s) threatened to emerge as autonomous popular movements, elite political parties attempted to channel popular political expressions into formal (and nonthreatening) activities. Select representatives of artisanal and other sectors were offered low-level, uninfluential positions in city or departmental governments. In the twentieth century, both the Conservative and Liberal parties, especially the more leftist Liberals, made strong overtures toward urban dwellers, particularly the artisanal sector.

Not all popular political expressions fit within formal boundaries. Popular groups often used direct action to make their interests known, making informal politics a central component of the city's political culture. After considerable contention in the late colonial period,[24] direct action by crowds diminished in frequency until the 1870s, when a series of public "disturbances" upset social tranquillity, revealing the tensions of a "modernizing" city. Food, public order, and wages were among the concerns that motivated popular sectors to engage in formal and informal politics.

The political economy of food was one realm of contention. In January 1875, the "*pan de a cuarto*" riot developed after a coalition of bakers combined to drive up the price of wheat flour and bread by over 20 percent and to eliminate the production of a small loaf consumed by the popular sector. Thousands of people, mostly workers and other members of the popular classes, flocked to the Plaza de

Bolívar on January 23, where they demanded that President Santiago Pérez drive down prices. He refused, whereupon the crowd stoned more than thirty bakeries and houses of offending monopolists. Injuries in the riot were limited, but heavy damage was inflicted on several properties. Shortly thereafter, the price of wheat and bread began to drift downward.[25]

Explanations for the riot suggest some of the relationships between formal and informal politics. For individuals, such as President Pérez, who were vested with power and had a particular ideological agenda (in his case liberalism), formal political expressions best addressed their interests. As they had done so often in the past, two factions of the Liberal party sought partisan advantage by attempting to draw artisans into the debate over the riot's causes, tactics that suggest the value of that class in the upcoming presidential elections. However, craftsmen who participated in various formal political organizations, from distinct partisan orientations, refused to criticize the violence, instead condemning the monopolistic practices of the bakers.[26] Rather than noting a partisan cause for the riot, these social commentators saw in the event a clash between liberal economic ideology and the "moral economy of bread," divisions that often disrupted the city's marketplace.[27] Members of the crowd, for whom the price and availability of bread had an immediate impact upon their lives, could interpret the presidential refusal to intercede on their behalf as evidence of the futility of formal politics and the usefulness of direct action in obtaining lower prices.

Elite plans to create an "orderly city" also contributed to informal political violence. The effort to "professionalize" Bogotá's police force by the importation of a French agent to supervise and reorganize the police force in 1892 redefined the relationship between the capital's populace and the police, all in the effort to instill an elite vision of proper urban order. Many Colombian elites, as did their counterparts elsewhere in Latin America, envisioned Paris as the epitome of urban development and sought to reproduce its architecture, street layout, cultural centers, and system of policing.[28] At the same time, the growth of the city and drastically increased food prices put pressures upon urban consumers.[29] Further, the presidential campaign of 1891 had splintered the National party of Rafael Núñez, encouraging Liberals to renew their partisan mobilizations.

These changes, especially in policing, sought to redefine a sense of urban order. They did not, however, spark the riot of January 16, 1893. Instead, the riot originated in artisanal anger at an author who had blamed the city's moral decay upon the gambling and alleged abuse of alcohol by the capital's artisans and other laborers. This touched a sensitive nerve among craftsmen, who were under increasing pressures from foreign imports and economic change that together helped to undermine their productive, social, and political status. As had happened in 1875, an attempt was made in the early stages of the unrest to appeal to formal political authorities to redress some of the crowd's grievances. The refusal of acting executive Antonio B. Cuervo to censure the offending author led artisanal delegates back into the streets, where violence ensued. The riot left almost fifty people dead, resulted in countless injuries, led to mass arrests, and caused considerable property damage and the destruction of all police stations save one.[30] The 1893 tumult was fundamentally a reaction to the policing reform and to the slander of the artisanal class and was grounded in the city's unsettled economic and political conditions. As it had in the past, the failure of formal politics to satisfy popular expressions again preceded direct, informal action.

The 1893 riot heralded a fifteen-year crackdown on both informal and formal political dissent. Conservatives, who had joined the Núñez regime in 1886, were now fearful that partisan divisions in the ruling alliance might allow a Liberal resurgence. As a result, police and governmental authorities became increasingly vigilant against "conspiracies." For example, workers were implicated in a Liberal attempt to overthrow the government in January 1895, a movement that was easily suppressed.[31] The deep fears of popular conspiracy against the government resurfaced after the War of the 1,000 Days. The nominally Conservative president, Rafael Reyes, limited partisan violence and restrained potential popular challengers with his heavy-handed rule. In the first years of the Reyes regime, artisans and others placed a great deal of pressure for tariff protection upon the administration.[32] The Reyes regime allowed very little public dissent, so that an alleged conspiracy resulted in the arrest on June 1, 1906, of several newspaper editors and dozens of workers, many of whom were sent to military colonies or prisons in other areas of the country.[33]

The city's increasingly differentiated labor structure resulted in several new labor initiatives. Owners of small handicraft factories (*industriales*), artisans, and workers founded the short-lived Union of Industriales and Workers in 1904 to support higher tariffs on goods that were seen as competitive with domestic production. This organization faded under the repression of the Reyes regime, but many of its leaders appeared again in the National Union of Industriales and Workers (UNIO) in 1910. The UNIO expressed a traditional demand for tariff protection, but it also called for higher wages, workers' compensation, a reduction in the number of working hours, and Sunday off, while pointing out its concerns about inadequate education, housing, and other welfare programs. These new concerns are directly related to the rapidly expanding city and the changing character of the workforce, in which the needs of wage laborers now supplemented the concerns of artisanal workers. Despite serious differences in the objectives of these labor groups, the UNIO promised to work with the established parties, but it also strove to establish itself as an independent political force. Other workers' organizations of the 1910s and 1920s sought similar ends either through cooperation with dominant parties or through their own efforts.[34] By the end of the 1910s, a fledgling Socialist party had emerged in the city, an organization that wielded considerable political clout in the next decade. However, divisions among laborers often weakened the overall political influence of Socialist and other labor organizations.

Bogotá's dismal socioeconomic conditions in the wake of the War of the 1,000 Days led various groups to organize to assist those in need. Mutual aid societies, which had first been organized by artisans and white-collar workers in the 1870s, attempted to organize food kitchens and to arrange health and welfare benefits for their members. The Catholic church led this effort, helping to establish several important societies, including the Sociedad de la Protectora (1902) and the Sociedad de Santa Orosía (1907).[35] Catholic mutual aid societies tended to distance themselves from overt political action, whereas those organized by artisans cooperated with other organizations.

Strike activity increased as the numbers of wage laborers grew, an example of an informal political action that would in time be formalized. Workers on the savannah railway struck in 1916 for higher wages, while workers at the national capital project walked off the job in 1913 in an effort to force the government to allow them to take part in a local festival.[36] Six years later workers won a conditional right to strike, but the full right to organize and strike would not be granted until 1931.[37] Workers on the savannah railroad were among the most active strikers in the 1920s, engaging in at least six major walkouts, some of which stimulated sympathy strikes among the capital's workers.[38] Strike activity increased dramatically in the 1930s, especially after the election of Alfonso López Pumarejo in 1934.

All major political alliances appealed to workers in an attempt to win their allegiance and votes. Conservatives, especially those closely related to the Catholic church, in keeping with the Social Action movement, used mutual aid organizations as their initial overture. In addition, the Jesuit-sponsored Workers' Circle (1911) created a savings bank, a restaurant, a school, and various other social services for its members.[39] The Workers' Circle remained active in Bogotá through the end of World War II, and although it had an uncertain impact, it certainly provided important material support to a needful populace. In combination with the strong loyalty to the church among the city's craftsmen, these initiatives provided a firm base of support among wage laborers for the Conservative party.

In the aftermath of their defeat in the War of the 1,000 Days, Liberals seemed less concerned with the material and religious concerns of workers and more concerned with acquiring workers' votes to sustain their political restoration. In 1904 the Liberal leader Rafael Uribe Uribe declared in favor of "socialism from above" that would expand the role of the state in economic development, in the protection of workers, in the establishment of savings banks, and in the protection of national industries.[40] In 1911 before the UNIO, Uribe Uribe articulated his concern for electoral reform, better public education, improved public hygiene, and "rational protection" of the nation's industries.[41] Uribe Uribe appears to have made serious progress in gaining political support among Bogotá's workers, but his 1914 assassination blunted reform sentiments within the Liberal party. His death opened the political space in which more autonomous popular mobilization could take place, especially among the nascent socialist groups. By the mid-1920s, however, a new generation of Liberals, "Los Nuevos," led by Jorge Eliécer Gaitán and Gabriel Turbay, again made direct overtures toward the popular sectors and achieved important electoral successes.[42]

Local and departmental elections revealed the increasing value of workers' votes to traditional parties. Although efforts to forge an independent workers' political party failed because of the varied concerns of different types of laborers, Liberals and leaders of the short-lived Republican party actively courted groups such as the UNIO, the Colombian Workers' Union, and the Workers party. Successful alliances among these groups, such as during the 1915 congressional and municipal council elections, resulted in the defeat of the dominant Conservatives and the election of several workers to public office. When workers' organizations urged their supporters to withhold their votes, as they did during the 1917 departmental elections, their political importance was equally evident in the easy Conservative victory.[43] This same pattern continued into the 1920s, when the fledgling Socialist party emerged as an electoral force that was short-lived but that won several seats in Congress in the 1921 elections, a victory that shaped the "new liberalism" of Gaitán and Turbay.

Informal political behavior did not stop after the turn of the century, but it increasingly paralleled formal political concerns. For example, the UNIO helped to organize the 1910 *20 de julio* centennial parade, which, according to most accounts, proceeded smoothly. The evening bullfight, by contrast, was the scene of a violent confrontation between spectators and the police as spectators left the bullring upset with a disappointing fight. Police overreacted to these public emotions and opened fire on the crowd, leaving at least nine people dead and scores injured. Once again, the workers' organization bore the burden of blame for the violence, although objective commentators noted the overreaction by untrained police as the primary cause of the violence.[44]

The events of March 16, 1919, clearly united workers' formal and informal political activities. Spiraling inflation resulting from the economic dislocations of World War I had generated a tremendous wave of strikes on the northern coast of the nation the previous year.[45] The nation's first socialist Workers' Assembly opened in late January, an unsettling turn of events for President Marco Fidel Suárez. The March protest originated in workers' opposition to the importation of military uniforms and other supplies that could be produced domestically. A Workers' Assembly demonstration on March 16[46] turned violent as prepositioned army troops fired on the protesters, killing at least seven and wounding many others. Numerous workers' leaders were arrested, and the government imposed martial law.[47]

The March violence accelerated the pattern of confrontation between organized workers and the state. The Conservative party, in control of the nation's executive branch until 1930, demonstrated increasing willingness to use lethal force against labor and other emerging sectors. Considerable violence surrounded labor disputes in the 1920s, notably in the Barrancabermeja oil fields and in the banana groves of Santa Marta. The Socialist party grew after its 1919 congress but could not make electoral inroads into the constituencies of either major party. Younger elements of the Liberal party, led by Jorge Eliécer Gaitán and Los Nuevos, renewed Uribe Uribe's overture toward laborers but could accomplish little given their political weakness. The Liberal presidential victory of 1930 signaled a new era in Colombian politics, one in which labor would figure prominently.

Conclusion

The "modernization" of Bogotá and Colombia necessitated the reformation of the country's political culture. Social classes grew or were created by socioeconomic changes in both urban and rural settings. Members of the expanded artisanal sector and newly created *industriales* reacted to the conditions of the "new" city by way of petitions, mutual aid societies, informal violence, demonstrations, and political organizations. Artisans and *industriales* often joined in formal politics, and informal expressions came from a broader segment of the laboring classes. Workers' political organizations were commonplace but tended to be most influential when they allied with the dominant parties, although they were very effective in placing items of concern to workers on the parties' agendas. Partisan electoral mobilizations both continued nineteenth-century traditions and shaped the framework of twentieth-century Colombian political culture. Socioeconomic problems, such as the need for housing, were addressed only after a lengthy process that tended to demonstrate partisan disinterest. The violence of March 16 signaled the readiness of the government to quell "subversive" challenges, especially when sponsored by a socialist organization that called for fundamental changes in the country's political economy, an unfortunate feature of twentieth-century political culture shared by both parties.

Political impulses "from below" forced the Conservative and Liberal parties into a critical juncture; they had to develop repressive mechanisms more fully or reach an accommodation with these growing urban sectors. Ruth and David Collier, in their authoritative *Shaping the Political Arena*, suggest that the Colombian "incorporation period" occurred in the 1930s and 1940s, as the state legitimated and shaped an institutionalized labor movement.[48] The institutionalization of the labor movement took place as the Liberal party helped to organize the Confederation of Colombian Workers (CTC) in 1935, after which the Conservative party facilitated the organization of the Union of Colombian Workers (UTC) in 1946. These unions served as channels through which organized workers could express their interests vis-à-vis the state, albeit in a manner that subordinated their interests to the needs of the parties. Smaller, more radical unions coexisted with these large confederations, but with less effective political voice.

Artisans and small producers most frequently participated in socialist, Communist, or left Liberal political initiatives, tendencies that came to fruition in the 1930s as Gaitán tapped the energy of this long-ignored social sector.[49] Gaitán emphasized the importance of independence and self-worth in his political messages, themes that paralleled the ideology of many artisans.[50] The increased capitalization of production that occurred after the 1920s seriously undermined the socioeconomic independence of this crucial social sector, especially as immigrant and national entrepreneurs developed a domestic putting out system and imported finished goods.[51] By the mid-1940s Gaitán had come to dominate the Liberal party and thus was able to represent the interests of urban small producers, which were often quite distinct from those of the wage laborers of the CTC and UTC. With his April 9, 1948, assassination, however, labor's influence was blunted, leaving the traditional Conservative and Liberal parties in a position of dominance over organized labor.

The tragic failure of Colombian political culture lies not in the willingness of its citizens to formally assert their interests vis-à-vis the polity but in the insistence by institutionalized leaders that nonelite interests be subordinated to their own. In this, the urban crucible of the Colombian capital revealed patterns of political accommodation that would be reshaped and extended throughout the nation.

Notes

An earlier version of this paper was presented at the 1995 Latin American Studies Association. The author would like to thank James Baer, Ronn Pineo, and Sharon Phillipps Collazos for their helpful comments.

1. Miguel Samper, *La miseria en Bogotá y otros escritos* (Bogotá: Universidad Nacional, 1969), 7–13, passim.

2. Ibid., 135–193.

3. See, for example, Martín Alonso Pinzón, *Historia del Conservatismo*, 2nd ed. (Bogotá: Ediciones Tercer Mundo, 1983); Gerardo Molina, *Las ideas liberales en Colombia*, 3 vols. (Bogotá: Tercer Mundo, 1970–1977); Edgar Caicedo, *Historia de las luchas sindicales en Colombia* (Bogotá: Ediciones CEIS, 1982); or Jonathan Hartyln, *The Politics of Coalition Rule in Colombia* (New York: Cambridge University Press, 1988).

4. Charles Bergquist, *Labor in Latin America: Comparative Essays on Chile, Argentina, Venezuela, and Colombia* (Stanford: Stanford University Press, 1986).

5. Ibid., 291–293.

6. David Bushnell, *The Making of Modern Colombia: A Nation in Spite of Itself* (Berkeley and Los Angeles: University of California Press, 1993), 199–200.

7. Ruth Berins Collier and David Collier, *Shaping the Political Arena: Critical Junctures, the Labor Movement, and Regime Dynamics in Latin America* (Princeton: Princeton University Press, 1991), 63–64.

8. Juan Friedel and Michael Jiménez, "Colombia," in *The Urban Development of Latin America, 1750–1920*, ed. Richard M. Morse (Stanford: Center for Latin American Studies, Stanford University, 1971), 61–76; William Duane, *A Visit to Colombia, in the Years 1822 & 1823* (Philadelphia: Thomas H. Palmer, 1826), 464–465.

9. Richard E. Boyer and Keith A. Davies, *Urbanization in 19th Century Latin America: Statistics and Sources* (Los Angeles: Latin American Center, 1973), 7, 9–10, 37–39, 59–61.

10. Alfredo Iriarte, *Breve historia de Bogotá* (Bogotá: Fundación Misión Colombia, Editorial Oveja Negra, 1988), 145.

11. Alan Udall, "Urbanization and Rural Labor Supply: A Historical Study of Bogotá, Colombia, Since 1920," *Studies in Comparative International Development* 15, no. 3 (Fall 1980): 71.

12. Bushnell, *The Making of Modern Colombia*, 277, 287.

13. Iriarte, *Breve historia de Bogotá*, 137.

14. Peter Walter Amato, "An Analysis of the Changing Patterns of Elite Residential Areas in Bogotá, Colombia" (Ph.D. diss., Cornell University, 1968).

15. Mauricio Archila Neira, *Cultura e identidad obrera: Colombia, 1910–1945* (Bogotá: CINEP, 1991), 58.

16. *El Artista*, July 11, 1908. All newspaper citations are from Bogotá.

17. David Sowell, *The Early Colombian Labor Movement: Artisans and Politics in Bogotá, 1830–1919* (Philadelphia: Temple University Press, 1992), 145; *Unión Industrial*, August 21, 1909; *El Resumen*, March 1, 1913.

18. Archila, *Cultura e identidad obrera*, 58.

19. Bergquist, *Labor in Latin America*, 275–276.

20. For a discussion of nineteenth-century artisanal ideology, see Sowell, *Early Colombian Labor Movement*, chap. 4.

21. Luis Ospina Vásquez, *Industria y protección en Colombia, 1810–1930* (Medellín: FAES, 1987), 264–269, 303–314.

22. Gary Long, "The Dragon Finally Came: Industrial Capitalism, Radical Artisans and the Formation of the Colombian Working Class, 1910–1948" (Ph.D. diss., University of Pittsburgh, 1994), 11, passim.

23. This conceptualization borrows from the work of Charles Tilly. See Charles Tilly, Louise Tilly, and Richard Tilly, *The Rebellious Century* (Cambridge, Mass.: Harvard University Press, 1975).

24. See, for examples, Anthony McFarlane, "Civil Disorders and Popular Protests in Late Colonial New Granada," *Hispanic American Historical Review* 64, no. 1 (February 1984): 17–54.

25. *La América*, January 26, 27, 29, 30, 1875; *La Ilustración*, January 25, 26, 1875; *El Tradicionista*, January 26, 29, 1875.

26. David Sowell, "The 1893 *bogotazo*: Artisans and Public Violence in Late-Nineteenth Century Bogotá," *Journal of Latin American Studies* 21 (May 1989): 267–282; *La América*, January 30, 1875.

27. *La Ilustración*, January 26, 1875.

28. Oscar de J. Saldarriaga Vélez, "Bogotá, la Regeneración y la policía, 1880–1900," *Revista Universidad de Antioquia* 37, no. 211 (January–March): 37–55; Alvaro Castaño Castillo, *La policía, su origen y su destino* (Bogotá: Lit y Edit "Cahur," 1947), vol. 8, 12–18.

29. On prices see Miguel Urrutia, "Estadísticas de precios, 1846–1933," in *Compendio de estadísticas históricas de Colombia*, ed. Miguel Urrutia and Mario Arrubla (Bogotá: Universidad Nacional de Colombia, 1970), 85.

30. Sowell, "The 1893 *bogotazo*," passim.

31. Charles Bergquist, *Coffee and Conflict in Colombia, 1886–1910* (Durham, N.C.: Duke University Press, 1978), 44–45, 49; *El Telegrama*, January 12, 1895; *Los Hechos*, January 23, 1895.

32. Eduardo Lemaitre, *Rafael Reyes: Biografía de un gran colombiano* (Bogotá: Banco de la República, 1981), 246–255, 316–324; Bergquist, *Coffee and Conflict in Colombia*, 219–223.

33. *El Correo Nacional,* June 4, 5, 6, 8, 13, 1906.

34. Sowell, *Early Colombian Labor Movement,* 137–147; *La Capital,* February 7, 1911.

35. Sowell, *Early Colombian Labor Movement,* 134–135.

36. *Gaceta Republicana,* January 27, 1913.

37. Miguel Urrutia, *The Development of the Colombian Labor Movement* (New Haven, Conn.: Yale University Press, 1969), 158–159.

38. Archila, *Cultura e identidad obrera,* 221–231; Daniel Pécaut, "Colombia," in *The State, Industrial Relations and the Labour Movement in Latin America,* ed. Jean Carrière, Nigel Haworth, and Jacqueline Roddick (New York: St. Martin's Press, 1989), vol. 1, 264–266; Urrutia, *Development of the Colombian Labor Movement,* 64–68.

39. Guillermo and Jorge González Quintana, *El Círculo de Obreros: La obra y su espíritu, 1911–1940* (Bogotá: Editorial de la Litografía Colombiana, 1940), 9–21; *Primer congreso eucarístico nacional de Colombia* (Bogotá: Escuela Tipografía Salesiana, 1914).

40. Jorge Orlando Melo, "De Carlos E. Restrepo a Marco Fidel Suárez. Republicanismo y gobiernos conservadores," in *Historia política,* part 2, vol. 1 of *Nueva historia de Colombia,* directed by Gloria Zea, 8 vols. (Bogotá: Planeta, 1989), 223.

41. *El Liberal,* October 27, 1911; Vincent Baillie Dunlap, "Tragedy of a Colombian Martyr: Rafael Uribe Uribe and the Liberal Party, 1896–1914" (Ph.D. diss., University of North Carolina, 1979), 221.

42. Urrutia, *Development of the Colombian Labor Movement,* 76–80.

43. Sowell, *Early Colombian Labor Movement,* 144–145, 148.

44. *La Gaceta Republicana,* July 5, 21, 24, 27, 29, 1911; *El Tiempo,* July 22, 25, 1911; *El Día Noticioso,* July 22, 25, 27, 1911; *Colombia,* July 8, 1911; *La Unidad,* July 27, 1911; *El Liberal,* July 25, 1911; *Comentarios,* July 21, 1911.

45. Urrutia, *Development of the Colombian Labor Movement,* 56–59; René de la Pedraja Toman, "Colombia," in *Latin American Labor Organizations,* ed. Gerald Michael Greenfield and Sheldon L. Maram (Westport, Conn.: Greenwood Press, 1987), 181.

46. *El Correo Liberal,* March 14, 1919; *La Gaceta Republicana,* March 14, 1919.

47. *La Gaceta Republicana,* March 22, 1919; *El Correo Liberal,* March 17, 18, 1919; Urrutia, *Development of the Colombian Labor Movement,* 63–64.

48. Collier and Collier, *Shaping the Political Arena,* 7, 289, passim.

49. Herbert Braun, *The Assassination of Gaitán: Public Life and Urban Violence in Colombia* (Madison: University of Wisconsin Press, 1985), 9, 49; Long, "The Dragon Finally Came," 235.

50. Long, "The Dragon Finally Came," passim; Sowell, *Early Colombian Labor Movement,* chap. 4 and passim.

51. Long, "The Dragon Finally Came," 255–259.

2

Dangerous Streets: Trolleys, Labor Conflict, and the Reorganization of Public Space in Montevideo, Uruguay

Anton Rosenthal

The city of Montevideo experienced a phenomenal rate of growth in the late nineteenth and early twentieth centuries, a growth driven by immigration from Europe, particularly from Italy and Spain, as well as by migration from Uruguay's rural interior. Montevideo expanded from a backwater capital of about 70,000–105,000 inhabitants in the 1870s to a small port city of 267,000 in 1900 to a thriving metropolis of 655,000 by 1930.[1] The strains of this six- to ninefold increase in population were felt in a variety of sectors: A scarcity of housing for these immigrants led to the proliferation of *conventillos* (slum tenements) both in the center and on the periphery of the city; epidemics, some a direct consequence of this poor housing, became a constant fixture of urban life; construction of both private and public buildings proceeded at a fever pitch between the turn of the century and the Great Depression as the city stretched northward and eastward; a new mass transit system was created, featuring the electric trolley as its centerpiece; and finally, public space became more delineated, more contained, and more contested by masses and elites.

This chapter examines the intersection of space and class by showing how the electric streetcar became a lightning rod for social conflict in the opening decades of the twentieth century. The trolley redefined order in the streets of Montevideo and reconfigured the social nature of public spaces in the city. The streetcar's speed shrank distances and brought outlying areas within the grasp of center-city residents. This led to the emergence of new suburbs and recreational beaches along the eastern shoreline, the incorporation of previously independent towns to the north, and increased accessibility to large parks, the zoo, soccer stadia, and other public areas for the city's working class. In short, leisure areas became democratized by the electric streetcar.[2] Furthermore, the streetcar helped foster a vibrant urban culture that drew on the tango and jazz, cafés and cabarets, theaters and the cinema. By 1921, the city's two trolley companies were offering all-night service on several routes to feed the growing demand for transportation to these entertainments.[3] The annual number of riders on the network in that year surpassed 126 million, more than six times the number carried on the old horse trams in 1904.[4]

But the increased speed offered by the electric trolleys also had a downside. As the trolley competed with other forms of transport and as vehicular traffic increased, the street became an increasingly dangerous locale for pedestrians, children, cart drivers, and even streetcar passengers. The high incidence of accidents resulting from this traffic alarmed the public and the press well into the post–World War I era. By 1930, traffic fatalities had risen to over 60 per year.[5] The street, and by extension the streetcar, also became objects of fear during epidemics and crime waves throughout the early twentieth century. But the most terrifying aspect of life in the street came with the advent of severe labor strife in 1918. As Montevideo was hit by the global wave of postwar inflation and a severe increase in unemployment, streetcar workers, port workers, and their supporters took to the streets in the city's second general strike. In plazas, intersections, and on streetcar platforms, workers and police fought to preserve differing notions of social order, with tragic consequences.

This chapter focuses on a central paradox—a privately managed, foreign-owned public utility that served the needs of urban masses and stockholders—and demonstrates its differing impacts on a reformist government, a rapidly changing working class, and an evolving middle class that sprang from the expanding state bureaucracy. The chapter also examines the development of the streetcar as a public space in its own right, the scene of mixing between different social groups as well as the locus of political and commercial interactions. Lastly, the chapter details the 1918 general strike and the consequent emergence of the streetcar as a contested terrain between its workers, the two foreign companies that owned the network, the city government, the police, and the public.

Economic and Political Change

At the turn of the twentieth century, Uruguay was just emerging from a long period of destructive civil wars and political instability. The chief consolidator of peace and security was President José Batlle y Ordoñez (1903–1907 and 1911–1915), who dominated the nation's politics for the first three decades of the century and was the architect of the first welfare state in the Americas. He promoted centralized state authority, secularization, and the modernization of the capital, at the expense of the rural sector, which had been a hotbed of revolt during the late nineteenth century.

Batlle made a name for himself by experimenting with the forms of government (proposing, for example, the replacement of the presidency by an executive committee), by instituting reforms that redressed imbalances in wealth and power, and by showing sympathy for the working class's struggles with utility companies and factory owners. Between his two terms of office, he traveled extensively in Europe and drew ideas on political management and democracy from the Swiss. When he returned home, he embarked on a campaign to restructure Uruguayan society along European lines, delving into the family as well as the economy. University education was opened to women, capital punishment and bullfights were abolished, and divorce was liberalized so that it could be initiated by wives. The state bank was reorganized, and state monopolies in insurance and some utilities were created. Workers were protected by an eight-hour-day law, a compulsory day of rest after five days of work, state regulation of workplace conditions, prohibition of night work for women, and the establishment of pensions, workmen's compensation, severance pay, and universal public education.[6]

But the pace of change in the economic sphere often outdistanced the scope of these reforms and of the government bureaucracy that monitored them. Workers organized unions and pressed hard for changes in the conditions of work, taking advantage of the reduced levels of police repression of the labor movement during Batlle's presidencies. Montevideo underwent a highly compressed industrialization in the late nineteenth and early twentieth centuries as new technology for freezing meat, a modern railroad network, and a modernized port drove the expansion of an export economy based on livestock. By 1930 there were nearly 80,000 industrial workers in 4,859 establishments in Montevideo, 90 percent of which had been founded since 1900.[7] Militant workers emerged among meat packers and transport workers. These industrial workers joined artisans in construction, bakeries, furniture and shoe factories, and print shops to form a very active labor movement imbued with radical ideologies such as anarchism and socialism. Large strikes became common, and by the late 1920s they had crept into the public sector, with police and firemen staging walkouts. Into this boiling cauldron of social discontent, the electric streetcar was introduced, with immediate consequences for urban disorder.

Creating Public Space

Prior to the introduction of electric trolleys in 1906, Montevideo had a distinctly rural character. While thousands of European immigrants entered its port in search of factory work or commercial opportunities in the last decades of the nineteenth century, waves of new residents also poured into the city from Uruguay's interior, contributing to the persistence of rural culture in the capital.[8] The city's streets were filled with horse carts of all types, horse-drawn carriages, and horse trams. The pace of life was still leisurely, and the daily press carried few complaints about traffic congestion. The horse trams, operated by seven different companies, ran at irregular schedules at slow speeds, stopping for passengers who hailed them from their houses.[9]

The arrival of the faster and larger electric streetcars in December 1906 was warmly greeted by the press and was seen by the city's elite as an opportunity to bury Montevideo's rural component, to zone the municipality into controllable sectors, and to socialize the masses into more predictable urban behavior.[10] The trolley also lessened the elite's fear of disease and crime by permitting the construction of new quarters on the outskirts of the rapidly expanding city for the emerging working class and thus promising to help eliminate the *conventillos.* But the *eléctrico* could fulfill only part of this promise of a more "civilized" future. As speculators drove up land prices and inflation cut the real wages of the working class, the *conventillos* persisted and grew even more densely populated.[11] Indeed, it was mostly the elite who followed the trolley lines out to the new seaside suburb of Pocitos. Furthermore, the growth of the city occurred in an uncontrolled fashion, following the dictates of land auctioneers and developers rather than a central plan. By 1919 the magazine *Mundo Uruguayo* complained that public spaces and plazas, hygiene, and beauty had received little attention from developers, who had opened up streets and avenues "without order or harmony" in their search for wealth.[12]

But this complaint ignored a key fact about the streetcar companies themselves: They were the largest landowners in the city and from the first had sought to convert some of their land into public attractions that would boost ridership. The consolidation of the 157-mile streetcar system in the hands of two companies, one British and one German, permitted the creation of new public spaces across the city. La Sociedad Comercial, the British company, rebuilt the Hotel Pocitos at the terminus of its line on what became the city's premier swimming beach; they equipped the hotel with 600 rooms, a French restaurant, and a terrace that extended over the water.[13] This perfectly placed hotel became a meeting place for young middle-class and upper-class couples, who flocked to the locale on Sundays. The company also built a soccer field next to its station in Pocitos in 1921; it drew thousands of Sunday riders. In addition, the company developed the lands of the Parque Central, a major city recreational area that eventually became the home of an 80,000-seat stadium, the largest in South America at the time, and the scene of the first World Cup of soccer in 1930.[14]

La Transatlántica, the German company, converted its land at Capurro Beach into a park with a terrace and bandstand and built two soccer fields of its own. In addition, each company developed routes to tourist areas such as Playa Ramirez, Parque Rodó, the Prado Hotel, and the zoo at Villa Dolores, as well as routes that linked the city's twelve plazas. Special services were also run to the cemeteries, and the companies reportedly carried 600,000 people on the weekend commemorating the Day of the Dead in 1909.[15] Within a short time, Montevideo's residents became completely dependent upon the trolley, and annual ridership grew from just over 30 million in 1906 to a peak of 154 million in 1926.[16] In this latter year, the traffic represented nearly thirty monthly trips for each man, woman, and child in the city.[17] Such usage led at least one foreign observer to remark that Montevideo was "over-trammed."[18]

The immense increase in the movement of people along the city's streets set off a chain of developments. The city embarked on an extensive program of street paving, it extended sewer services to suburbs, and a building boom commenced that changed the city's architectural image along its main avenues and plazas. Among the notable events: In 1908 the Standard Life Insurance building, soon to house a major department store, was finished; the next year the renovation of the port was completed and the 200-room Parque Hotel was opened across from Playa Ramirez; in 1911 the penitentiary at Punta Carretas and the new university were erected and the Prado Hotel was opened; and in 1913 the British Hospital was inaugurated and the Mercado Agrícola in La Aguada was finished.[19] In the 1920s the architectural face of the city underwent a complete renovation with the construction of landmarks such as the Palacio Salvo on the Plaza de Independencia, the new customs house overlooking the port, the stunning Palacio Legislativo and the Hotel Carrasco, and a beach resort and casino on the eastern edge of the city. In addition, work was undertaken on the downtown headquarters of the Banco de la República and the Jockey Club. This building boom was financed by both public and private capital. (See Map 2.1.)

The Street as Public Spectacle

The Uruguayan chronicler Luis Enrique Azarola Gil remarked in his memoirs that men and women in twentieth-century Spanish America were street-oriented. Men left home to seek entertainment in cafés, clubs, bars, restaurants, theaters, or the racetrack, and women went to the movies, shopping, dancing, or visiting at teatime.[20] Other chroniclers and newspaper reporters suggest that Uruguayans in particular sought out simple pleasures in public spaces—from the bustle of the Sunday market at Tristan Narvaja to the afternoon promenade of women along Calle Sarandí, from card-playing at neighborhood cafés to outdoor concerts in the Parque Capurro. Streetcars were at the center of the city's daily rituals and special events, bringing the populace from their homes and workplaces into these public spaces.

The street and its connected spaces were a source of constant entertainment in the preradio and pretelevision era. Markets offered an array of diversions along with their produce, including snake charmers and fortune-tellers. Lottery tickets were sold throughout the city in cafés, illegally until the 1930s.[21] Beggars, hawkers, and prostitutes roamed the streets of the Old City, occasionally, as reported in the newspapers, disturbing the middle class's sense of urban order, which resulted in police sweeps. One department store offered a lunchroom on the fourth floor,

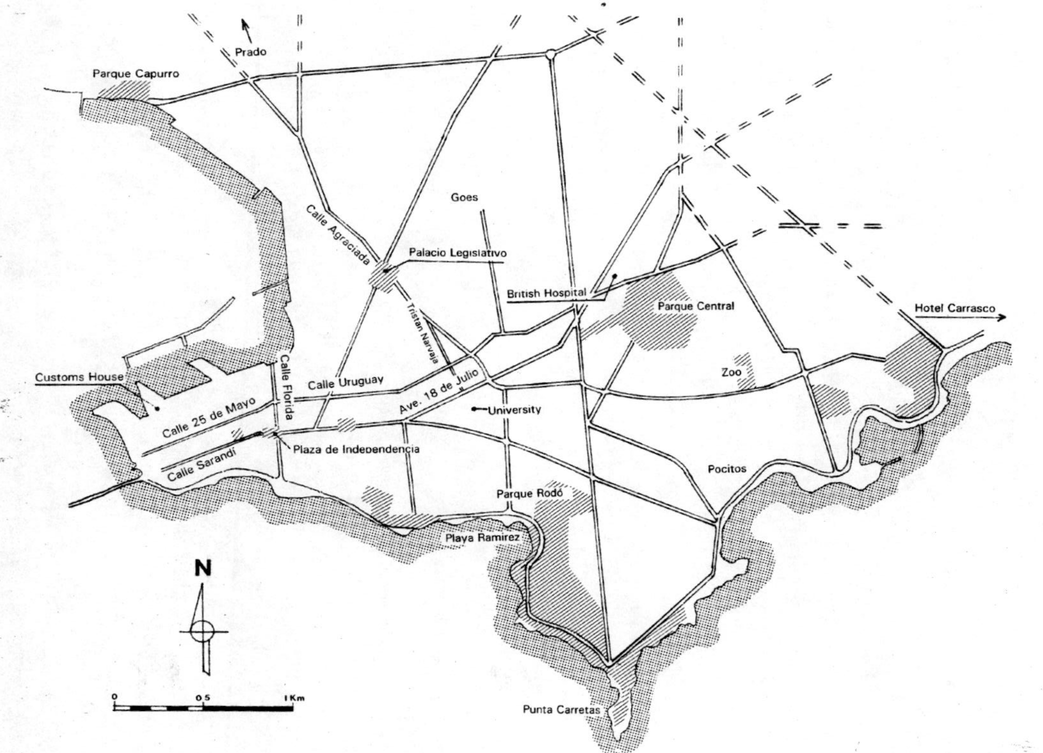

MAP 2.1 *Montevideo, Uruguay, about 1930. Drawn by Werner Rosenthal.*

so that hungry shoppers did not have to wander back out onto the street, where they might be accosted by the small armies of child beggars who periodically worked that district.[22] The city's streets were also plagued by rabid dogs into the 1920s.[23]

Almost anything could happen in public spaces, without warning, which was no doubt part of their attraction. In the prewar period, newspapers carried many accounts of Montevideans committing suicide in parks and plazas, sometimes taking trolleys to these sites. In one case, a man rode a trolley to the penitentiary, sat on a bench in the plaza across from it, and put a bullet in his head, leaving a note in his clothing.[24] In another example, a twenty-year-old man riding a streetcar along Calle Uruguay waited until the trolley came to a stop, pulled out a revolver, and shot himself, dying instantly.[25] Even foreigners engaged in public suicides, as evidenced by the case of a violinist with the visiting Vienna Philharmonic Orchestra who slit his wrists and then flung himself out of a third-floor window of the Hotel Globo, falling across the trolley line on busy Calle 25 de Mayo and killing himself instantly.[26] Waves of such incidents occasionally led to calls for legislation to restrict newspaper coverage of these deaths, since such coverage was thought to be encouraging an epidemic of suicides.[27] Some public demises, however, were less intentional. In the middle of an autumn afternoon in 1916, a young Italian peanut vendor died when he made the mistake of closing an escape valve in his portable stove, in order to sound the whistle, and blew himself up in Plaza Matriz.[28] In general, however, small plazas were places of exchange and socialization for the city's immigrants:

> The small plaza is the scene where human anguish develops: The discussions are her fruit, as are the fights, a typical manifestation of passion.
>
> In the lonely nights, when the soul is invaded by an inexplicable desire to go there, to see the fights, to listen to the picturesque commentaries spoken in different dialects, forming an appealing spectacle, it is a pleasurable pastime which makes one forget everything.[29]

The nights were also filled with entertainments as the streetcar extended its hours of service; the new, nighttime activity propelled the city to improve its lighting. Montevideo's first twenty-four-hour pharmacy opened to a large crowd of onlookers in 1918. It was located across from the Teatro Solís and was named La Gran Farmácia Norte-Americana.[30] But the zone that radiated out from the Plaza de Independencia already featured late-night bakeries, gambling dens, cabarets, and houses of prostitution disguised as soda fountains. In the period from 1913 to 1917, the tango moved out of the vice-ridden Bajo district and into respectable establishments in the Centro district and competed with jazz in café concerts. The rise of this café culture was fed by the streetcar, almost as if one were an extension of the other. One chronicler tells of trolleys disgorging passengers in the Plaza de Independencia who headed for the nearby Bar Victoria, which announced its musicians on signs placed on the sidewalk. He also describes the debut of a tango group brought from Buenos Aires to the Café au Bon Marché on Calle Florida in 1915 as a major event: "As the place quickly filled, people thronged on the sidewalk and often crowded into the street, impeding the passage of the trolleys."[31] Juan Carlos Patrón claimed that the Viejo Café Vaccaro in the Goes neighborhood attained such fame in the 1920s that whoever boarded a No. 12, 13, or 17 trolley in the Centro district and put two coins in the hand of the guard, only needed to say "¡Al Vaccaro!" to be understood.[32]

Trolley workers themselves were key links between this café culture and the new transport network. They often had their own favorite cafés in the vicinity of the various tram stations, where they no doubt discussed their lot.[33] In 1916, meeting in the Café Sportman, trolley workers laid the plans for an aborted strike.[34] Two years later, when their well-organized strike shut down the entire city, cafés, *confiterías* (tea shops), and bars were among the establishments that sent them money.[35] It is no accident that the rise and demise of café life in Montevideo coincided almost exactly with the birth and death of the trolley.

The streetcar was also a key force in bringing masses of people together for parades and other special events, and it was always heavily used. The various inaugurations of electric streetcar service in 1906–1907 brought tens of thousands of spectators into streets along the routes, eager to see the new technology in operation.[36] The single event that brought all the city's social classes together in an atmosphere of ritualized disorder was the annual Carnival celebration. This festival was so well staged in Montevideo that it attracted tourists from as far away as Buenos Aires. The necessity of moving an immense number of people across the city at all hours greatly taxed the streetcar system during Carnival. With trolleys packed like sardine cans, churches and other groups canceled or postponed meetings, recognizing the difficulty faced by members trying to get across the city during the revelry. The *eléctrico* also occupied a prominent place in the city's irregularly staged transport parades. In 1917 La Sociedad Comercial won a gold medal for its entry in one such parade, a three-hour event that was viewed by a large Sunday crowd.[37] Streetcars also became important parts of the public space in official civic events. When the city celebrated the bicentennial anniversary of its founding in 1926, it decked out the streetcars in special lights and national flags, as if they were extensions of the main plazas, which were specially lit for such events.[38] On national holidays, the trolley poles were customarily wrapped in the national colors.[39] This type of symbolic connection between streetcars and public space was deepened and democratized in various spontaneous "assaults" on trolleys following important national events. In 1924, for example, youths mobbed streetcars, hoisted national flags on their platforms, and draped them with homemade banners in celebration of Uruguay's Olympic soccer championship.[40] During the 1933 coup, many city residents poured out into the streets and rode streetcars in a collective response to the first interruption of democratic government in three decades.

The streetcar provided more than a grid for the rapidly expanding city, a spur to its physical restructuring, and an efficient system for the daily movement of tens of thousands of new immigrants and workers. It also served as a social space that moved between the public and private spheres of the city and cut across class lines, thus promoting a degree of social leveling and impeding the strict segregation of urban districts by class. The lines between public and private were not firmly drawn, and their negotiation became part of the conflict brewing between elites and masses in Montevideo.

Disorder in the Street

Streets plazas, and parks were central to the life of Montevideo, but they also had their dangers. The most obvious dangers were related to the rapid increase of street traffic, aided by the streetcar. The number of trolleys grew from 272 at the initiation of electric service to around 650 by the mid-1920s as the two streetcar companies sought to accommodate the demand for service that they had helped create through the development of recreational areas. In addition, Montevideo had to cope with the practice of a "double commute," that is, the practice among some workers and most middle-class employees of returning home for a hot lunch.[41] The *eléctricos* had to share the public way with thousands of autos and dozens of buses, in addition to the declining number of slow horse carts used to deliver bread and other goods.[42] Automobiles appeared slowly in Montevideo, with only 109 registered at the time of the debut of the *eléctricos*. The Ford Model T arrived in 1910, and by 1920 there were 2,000 cars on the city's streets. Significant growth in automobile use came during the 1920s, when the number of registered cars reached 20,000, a far larger proportion than in Buenos Aires.[43] All of this traffic transformed the street from a place of casual encounters into a danger zone. Newspapers were replete with accounts of accidents as trolleys demolished carts, crashed into each other, ran over careless pedestrians who crossed the rails without looking, and jumped their tracks on curves or during collisions, flying into sidewalks, stores, and houses.[44] Perhaps most at risk were working-class children, who escaped the confining world of the *conventillos* by playing soccer in the residential streets or worked as messengers and newsboys criss-crossing the thoroughfares of the commercial district. The increased speed of the electric trolleys, which had fostered the spread of the city, made them more difficult to stop than horse trams. La Sociedad Comercial employed handbrakes instead of airbrakes on its cars in the early years, which resulted in longer stopping times. Often the only option a motorman had when confronted with a child playing in the street was to sound the bell, lower the *salvavidas* (cowcatcher), and hope for the best.[45] This was not always a successful maneuver. Juan Carlos Patrón recounted an incident in which a childhood friend was killed by a streetcar as he crossed the street to buy an ice cream, and Patrón noted that for Montevideo's children the trolley was sometimes their first direct contact with death.[46]

The streetcar and its occupants also faced dangers from the increasing numbers of automobiles in the city. Impatient motorists often whizzed around streetcars at

The collision of public spaces. Reprinted Courtesy of the Intendencia Municipal de Montevideo, Uruguay.

The dangerous streets. Reprinted courtesy of the Intendencia Municipal de Montevideo, Uruguay.

stops and ran over descending passengers. An indicator of the drivers' obliviousness was a newspaper editorial that castigated them for repeatedly running over a dog in the middle of a central intersection, seemingly without noticing the dead animal.[47] On occasion, motorists also hit line maintenance workers for the trolley companies, with tragic results.[48]

Public outcry over the dangerous state of the streets resulted in the creation of special traffic police in 1914 to regulate the disparate speeds of carts, streetcars, and autos. This led to a temporary decline in accidents, but by the 1920s the city's boulevards and streets were again overwhelmed, and officials had to create a motorcycle traffic brigade to force motorists to comply with traffic laws.[49] The state of decline in public safety can be gauged by the following anecdote from the popular press, describing a man with two children attempting to cross the city's primary artery, 18 de Julio, at 7 P.M., just after the race track closed:

> A man with two children tried to cross the avenue from North to South and had to stop three or four times due to the speed with which the automobiles were passing there. Finally, and perhaps remembering the tragic death of Mr. Vega who was run over a block away, he pulled out a revolver, put his children behind him and pointing the gun, crossed the street followed by his kids with complete happiness.
>
> How long will these things go on?[50]

Newspapers ran photo after photo of damaged trolley cars, and they were always surrounded by dozens of curious onlookers. The trolley accident had become a public event, commented on in the street as well as in the press. The movable public space had been converted into a spectacle.

The Trolley as Public Space

In a variety of ways, the trolley functioned as an extension of Montevideo's streets and public halls. There were written and unwritten codes of behavior to follow, criminals plied their trades, passengers exchanged germs, and the crew of the streetcar worked under public supervision and criticism. In this way, the streetcar connected many different sectors of Montevideo's society.

From the beginning of service, rules were established for the proper behavior of passengers. These were set out by the city, which relied on policemen for enforcement, and by the two streetcar companies, which issued directives to trolley conductors, who were responsible for the passengers' compliance. These rules ranged from restrictions on general behavior, such as prohibitions on entering a trolley when intoxicated, using offensive language, spitting or smoking cigarettes in any part except the rear platform, and bringing animals on board, to provisions to ensure the smooth functioning of the trolley, such as regulations for boarding and leaving, regulations requiring that large parcels be stowed on the front platform, and the prohibition on talking with the motorman. The city regulation Article 36 even ordered conductors not to allow anyone with a "visibly repugnant illness" to board.[51] The regulations were posted inside the streetcars and were also published in daily papers.[52] Through a system of fines assessed by roving inspectors and the vigilance of well-behaved passengers who complained to newspapers and the companies about infractions, the conductors were converted into policemen. They were to enforce these rules, using the authority represented by their company uniforms, and they were to respond tranquilly to all passengers who came into their domain, no matter what conflicts arose. The municipal code demanded order, and the companies required that the conductors be the public face of their businesses. The trolley also served as a public space by promoting consumerism, becoming one of the first vehicles of mass advertising in the city. The roofs, platforms, and insides of hundreds of trolleys were plastered with advertisements for products including mineral water, soft drinks, beer, champagne, syrup, oatmeal, tea, and even funeral services. Some advertising was especially designed to take advantage of the swaying motion of the trolley, such as a soap ad that showed a woman scrubbing clothes or a man drinking wine with his arm in motion.[53] This usage of public space to sell commodities was satirized by Felisberto Hernández in a short story in which a man riding a trolley receives an unwanted hypodermic injection from a passing vendor, only to find hours later that a jingle for a furniture store is playing incessantly in his head and he can neither sleep nor think.[54]

The streetcar also functioned as a public place through the exchange of political ideas and social commentary. The primary activity of trolley riders, judging from cartoons and photographs, was the reading of newspapers. Even on crowded trolleys, men leaned out over the platform perusing the latest sports and political news. News vendors made the trolleys one of their major marketplaces, jumping on at a signal from a passenger or coming aboard yelling the latest headlines. The ambience of a moving reading salon no doubt contributed to the conversion of the rear platform into a popular forum where strangers of different social classes and cultural backgrounds debated each other and argued with the guard. In a 1934 essay on the "culture of the platform," Antonio Soto catalogued the variety of themes daily discussed there: sports, real estate taxes, politics, law, the economy, urban development, and the lottery.[55] In addition, streetcars became a focus of political activity during election campaigns, with party placards adorning their sides.[56] Not all exchanges of ideas on the streetcar were peaceful, nor did they always conform to middle-class notions of propriety. In 1910 words exchanged between two trolley passengers led to a duel, when this was still a fashionable method of settling "questions of honor."[57] During a strike by news vendors in 1920, the workers boarded streetcars and took copies of boycotted newspapers from the hands of passengers, leading the outraged *Uruguay Weekly News* to demand: "It is time some serious effort was made to make them behave in a reasonable and orderly manner."[58]

The streetcar also served as a democratizing agent by extending the public space accessible to the lower class. The trolley was a relatively inexpensive form of transport that allowed workers to get out of their own neighborhoods, visit public parks, and even take part in demonstrations. The basic fare for short trips was set by the city of Montevideo and the national legislature at four *centésimos* in 1906 for both lines, and it did not increase for some thirty years, much to the chagrin of the companies and their stockholders. By contrast, the general cost of living in Uruguay rose 39 percent from 1914 to 1921 alone.[59] Furthermore, there were special worker trolleys that ran during rush hours and charged only half fare. In 1913 the Oficina del Trabajo estimated that the average expense of traveling by streetcar constituted just over 3 percent of a worker's budget and just under that percentage for a family of six with two incomes.[60]

The connection between democratization and the trolley also extends to the stations and the surrounding plazas, which were frequently disorderly areas in the post-1914 period. The plaza in front of the Pocitos streetcar station was the scene of numerous demonstrations in 1916: speeches against the military draft organized by the Socialist party in March and October and a night meeting organized by the trolley workers' union in April in support of a fourteen-point list of demands.[61] The area surrounding the La Transatlántica station on Calle Agraciada became the scene of a violent incident at the May Day march in 1920, an incident in which seven people were wounded, one a trolley conductor.[62]

As it became a popular form of transportation, the trolley was perceived by its passengers as an increasingly dangerous conveyance. Drawing millions of monthly riders, often in crowded conditions, the trolleys became a favorite hunting ground of pickpockets. Preying on middle-class passengers, thieves used razor blades to cut pants pockets or, working in pairs, used distractions to lift wallets, jewels, and, on one occasion, an insurance policy.[63] Nor were trolley passengers spared the sight of more violent crimes. In the midst of Carnival in 1922, passengers were shocked as a motorman bending over the platform to switch the points on Avenida General Flores was stabbed in the back by someone in costume. The assailant turned out to be a young woman who was avenging herself for the "dishonest intentions" shown her by the motorman.[64] Trolley workers were also occasionally the aggressors. Conductors were known to throw punches at irritating passengers, but they reserved their greatest hatred for their superiors.[65] In 1909 a disgruntled former conductor shot a ticket inspector on a tram, and two years later a former motorman attacked an inspector as he was leaving a trolley; the inspector turned around and shot the motorman five times.[66]

These, however, were sensational and somewhat rare events. The major daily fear of trolley passengers was of contracting contagious diseases, especially tuberculosis, which was responsible for nearly one out of every five deaths in Montevideo in the late 1920s.[67] The Anti-Tuberculosis League constantly lobbied for the enforcement of the regulation against spitting on the cars, but apparently without much early success.[68] Fear of tuberculosis was also behind plans to ban smoking on trolleys altogether.[69] Trolley crews were submitted to screening for tuberculosis, and conductors were fired if it was discovered that they had the disease. Special ticket-dispensing machines were placed in service as a means of reducing the possibility of contagion from conductors. During the influenza epidemics of 1918 and 1919, trolleys were one of the few public spaces to remain open (schools, cinemas, and theaters were closed); special provisions were made to wash down the aisle walkways when the cars finished their runs.[70] But the public was occasionally admonished to be careful when traveling on trolleys and to open the windows even in inclement weather.[71] *La Tribuna Popular*, in a column complaining about unannounced changes in trolley routes, declared in 1921: "There are moments in which, apart from the jams, the impertinence and the discomforts, one runs the risk of carrying home some parasite caught from contact with people at odds with hygiene."[72] To some degree, this association of trolleys with disease and contagion reflected an unease at the social mixing that the streetcars had so effectively promoted since their inception.

The Politics of Public Utilities

Underneath this evolving experience of the streetcar as public space lay a broader political history of the streetcar as the perceived agent of imperialism. Montevideo had been the beneficiary of early British interest in telephone, electricity, gas, and water services. It was the first South American city with an electric power plant for street lighting (1886), and by the turn of the century it had the largest per capita telephone usage on the continent.[73] This modernization was financed largely by British investors, who operated monopolies in gas, water, and railroad transport, though the electric company was taken over by the state in 1897. The streetcar system remained a semi-competitive venture between British, German, and then Spanish interests until the mid-1920s, when it too became a British monopoly.

The various utilities in Montevideo followed different business fortunes, and for the most part they earned an excellent rate of return for their foreign investors and also negotiated a working relationship with Batlle's Colorado party at both the municipal and national levels of government. The exception was the British streetcar network, which posted solid earnings in the prewar era but failed to pay any dividends from 1916 to 1924, a period of significant labor conflict, and again from 1929 to 1935.[74] One of the reasons for the poor profits of the streetcar companies in the later years of operation was the failure of the national and municipal governments to grant them permission to raise the basic fare. The companies were hamstrung by the terms of the original concession, worked out before Batlle had built up his constituency in the labor movement, which gave enormous regulatory powers to the government. Uruguayan legislators were always deeply suspicious of the streetcar and feared being tied to a system that might become obsolete very quickly, so they drove a hard bargain with the streetcar companies, which resulted in the delayed entry of the trolley to Montevideo and a situation in which the only hope for sustained company profits lay in a high volume of traffic. Like the other utilities, the streetcar came under public criticism for poor service, criticism that Batlle effectively used as leverage in the pages of *El Día* to bring public sympathy to the side of the company's workers. The company was portrayed as an agent of British imperialism, much abuse was leveled at Juan Cat, the general manager and a prominent member of the Blanco party, and the nationalist card was played to secure labor's loyalty to the Colorado party. During the 1911 shutdown and again in later strikes, the city government levied fines on both streetcar companies for failing to provide the service outlined in their operating contracts, as a means of bringing the companies to the bargaining table with their workers.

Commenting on this first general strike, Batlle clearly marked out the national interest as antithetical to that of the companies:

> The strike has, therefore, obliged the companies to pay out 13,725 pesos monthly, which will be transformed into a little more bread and a little less fatigue. Besides, 150 new families have their poor existence assured.
>
> Without the strike . . . this money, which represents the appetizing sum of 167 pesos per year, would have continued to go to London and Berlin along with other fat profits, with the pleasant prospect of making the pockets of the British and German stockholders a little heavier. Now these 167,000 pesos will stay in the country and be spread—along with a little bit of happiness—among the poor people.[75]

The *batllista* state further showed its antipathy to the streetcar by openly supporting the creation of bus service that became a serious rival to the streetcar by the 1920s. All in all, the relations between the trolley companies and the government were icy.

The battle over rates reveals the political importance of the streetcar as a public space, as well as the electoral clout of Montevideo's working class in the early twentieth century. The Colorado party was keenly aware that the streetcar companies were among the largest employers in the capital city, maintaining a workforce of nearly 2,000 in 1911 and almost 5,000 by the 1930s. They badly needed the allegiance of these workers to preserve the social order that they had created with the military victory over the Blanco party in 1904. In 1918 they tried to nationalize the streetcar by buying out the two private companies, but the 20-million-peso price asked by the latter was seen as out of the question. In that same year, as a consequence of a strike that we will shortly examine, the streetcar companies pressed to have the basic fare increased from four to five *centésimos*. This required legislation at the national level that was effectively stalled by Colorado senators. Later attempts to revive the measure were successfully counteracted by pressure from workers.[76]

It was only in 1936, as part of yet another trolley strike, that the streetcar company, now a functioning monopoly in serious financial trouble, was granted this increase in the basic fare, a rate already charged by the more popular bus companies. Surveying this history in the late 1930s, Simon Hanson wrote: "It is probable that by taking full advantage of an unusually fortunate concession urban transportation was obtained at a lower cost than that at which even a well-managed non-profit State enterprise might have been able to provide it."[77]

The streetcar, then, stands out from other foreign-owned utilities in its relations with the state and with the working class. It touched far more lives on a daily basis than did gas or telephones, thus becoming an object of mass consumption. It was a workplace in the public purview, but one guided by a private industrial regimen. It was extensively regulated by both the city and the national governments, yet its intransigent managers were backed by European stockholders hungry for a proper return on their investments. Depending on which voice of the daily press one consulted, the streetcar was either sucking wealth out of the country or the victim of socialistic bureaucrats and demagogues intent on abusing the companies for their own narrow political ends.

The Streetcar as a Contested Public Space (1918–1922)

The role in which the trolley functioned as a public space in its own right, as an extension of the rapidly changing street life, gave it a special emotional charge. It was difficult for any resident of Montevideo to feel neutral toward something that had so profoundly altered the physical and mental landscape of the city in so short a time. With the trolley at the center of public life, it was only natural that it became a focus for labor strife and violence during the immediate postwar period.

The key element in making the streetcar into a contested urban space was the disjunction between its role as the primary form of mass transit until the mid-1920s and the fact that it was controlled by private capital. Dating from its inauguration, questions of fares, wages, frequency of service, extension of lines to new zones, and worker discipline all became entangled in the web of power relations between the national government, the municipal government, the local management of the two trolley companies, their shareholders, the passengers, and the thousands of workers who labored as motormen, conductors, linesmen, inspectors, and mechanics.[78] La Transatlántica and La Sociedad Comercial effectively formed a transportation monopoly in the city, operating together to resist workers' demands for wage increases, union recognition, and changes in the work regulations until their formal merger in 1933. The relationship between these companies and the trolley crews was often tense, and occasionally the resentments flared into violence.

A strict industrial regimen, combined with the intransigence of the companies, led to strikes in which the riding public and the city government became active participants. In May 1911, trolley workers staged their first systemwide strike; it developed into Montevideo's first general strike and involved an estimated 60,000 workers. At issue was the arbitrary authority exercised by each of the companies over the workforce, evident in forced overtime, low wages, mandatory deposits on uniforms, lack of rest periods and accident insurance, and the usage of dangerous handbrakes.[79] Their complaints resonated with the press and the general populace. Merchants and workers supported the strikers with donations of food, services, and money, and when the companies appeared to be victimizing strike leaders, nearly forty unions came together to shut down the city for two days in a collective protest. There were incidents in the streets as newsboys and other workers attempted to impede the running of trolleys; meanwhile, the national government sent troops to protect the private property of the companies from sabotage and to control the public space of streets and plazas. In the words of an Italian diplomat summing up the actions for his government: "Many windows and some heads were broken."[80] One motorman was killed in the clashes, and there were several accidents, one with fatal consequences. The streetcar workers achieved only a partial victory from the three-week-long walkout, but the strike changed the way in which the public viewed the streetcar. From this point onward, it became a symbol of both capital and foreign authority dominating the citizens of Montevideo, who saw the system as part of their patrimony.

In the period after World War I, civil unrest became more common in Montevideo, and increasingly it focused on the trolley as a vulnerable part of the urban geography. During a strike of *frigorífico* workers (meat packers) in 1917, a bomb was placed on one trolley that was bringing workers to the Cerro, the meat-packing district, and another streetcar was attacked and shots were fired.[81] As already noted, the 1920 May Day parade of workers was marred by violence outside the Calle Agraciada trolley station as demonstrators hurled stones at a motorman operating a streetcar. In October 1921 streetcars of both companies were stoned in connection with protests surrounding the death sentences handed down on Nicola Sacco and Bartolomeo Vanzetti in the United States.[82] Following another tumultuous May Day in 1923, a group of workers stopped a tram from the Cerro and then trashed it and two other trolleys before police chased them off.[83]

The streetcar lines themselves were the scene of intense labor conflict from 1918 to 1922. Trolley workers reconstituted their union in 1916, demanding recognition, increased wages, interest paid on uniform deposits, airbrakes, summer uniforms, windows on platforms, worker waiting rooms in all stations, standardized shifts, and the provision of lawyers and wages for motormen jailed as a result of accidents.[84] But the union was not yet strong enough to force these issues, and no strike was mounted. Meanwhile, World War I continued to erode the wages of trolleymen, diminishing their buying power by 13 percent from 1914 to 1920.[85] In August 1918 streetcar workers were sufficiently organized to stage a walkout, and as in 1911 their conflict evolved into a citywide strike. Again they asked for wage improvements and union recognition, in addition to changes in the practices of fines and compliance with the eight-hour-day law.[86] The strike marked a conjunction of three important elements: First, it drew on a tradition of resistance among the trolley workers dating back to 1906, including at least some union leaders who had participated in the 1911 strike and so brought a significant institutional memory to bear on questions of strategy.[87] Second, the dispute followed fast on the heels of a successful port strike, which served as inspiration for the trolley workers.[88] Finally, the trolley workers were able to gain the sympathy and support of the city's working class and turn their walkout into a general strike within ten days. Supported by the anarchist labor confederation, known as the Federación Obrera Regional Uruguaya (Uruguayan Regional Workers Federation), the strike was joined by port workers, meat packers, garbage collectors, linotypists, news vendors, and restaurant workers.[89] But this time the dispute took on aspects of an urban insurrection, with pitched battles in the streets. No less than 494 policemen were sent to guard the stations and ride on the streetcar platforms at the first rumor of a strike, an action that only served to infuriate the crewmen and their allies.[90] Workers and others attacked trolleys with stones, lime, and tar, shattered their windows, cut cables, pulled up switching points in the street, and placed small bombs on the rails. On some occasions, shots were fired, and scores of workers and police were injured in street fighting. A mechanic from the streetcar shops was fatally shot in a street battle, and many others died over the course of the strike.[91] The funerals of workers became mass protests that involved thousands of marchers and often turned into further bloody incidents when they crossed paths with a functioning trolley.[92] Eventually, soldiers were brought in to patrol the city and its suburbs and to collect the garbage.[93] Despite this violence, neither side gave in. By the end of the month, with the strike committee in jail and the resources of the striking streetcar workers exhausted, the workers either returned to work or found new jobs in the port.[94] In spite of the loss and the government repression, they continued to hold meetings, plan strikes, and press the companies for improvements in the workplace over the next four years.

The conflict between the notion of the streetcar as a public service and the reality of the system as a private enterprise came to a head in 1922. Once again, workers initiated action by closing down the streetcar system for three weeks in the hopes of securing some relief from the continuing inflation. This time they employed a new tactic: They organized boycotts of bars, stores, and barber shops frequented by nonstriking workers. This proved to be an effective strategy in leveraging public support.[95] The companies sought to divert the strike toward their own goal of raising revenues through increased fares by openly stating that they supported the workers' wage demands and would accede to them as soon as the government allowed higher fares. But the city councillors, led by Batlle's son, took a different tactic, portraying the companies as greedy and themselves as guardians of the public interest. They voted to intervene in the two companies and briefly took over their daily administration, paying the workers a 15–25 percent wage increase without raising the fares. This action gained the support, in principle, of the nation's oldest conservative daily newspaper, *El Siglo*, which ran an editorial campaign for the nationalization of the trolley service. This situation lasted for six months, until the companies successfully overturned their "occupation" in the courts.[96] Yet the fares, and in large measure the wages, remained at these same levels until 1936, without any further strikes on the lines, thus marking a temporary victory for the city's workers. By 1930, the trolleys were suffering from the competition afforded by the buses, and they went into a period of decline that lasted until their phased disappearance in the 1940s and 1950s.

The understanding of space is important to the understanding of urban class conflict within the broader history of modern Latin America. The electric streetcar was a powerful shaper of both public space and collective behavior in early-twentieth-century Montevideo. It transformed the street in a myriad of ways, some dangerous and others wondrous. For the city's working class, it both opened up new physical spaces and helped to bring it into the political life of the evolving metropolis. At the same time, the streetcar also came to symbolize the limits of municipal patrimony and of a collectively shared notion of public space that conflicted with the demands of stockholders sitting across the ocean in European capitals. By focusing on the trolley as a contested political space, this chapter has revealed the somewhat atypical role of the national and city governments in labor relations during this period and the centrality of the transport sector to the evolution of the urban labor movement in Uruguay.

The trolley was both an agent of social change and a socially constructed space in itself. In its technology, its size, and its regimen, it was an industrial workplace. Yet it was also a vital service that was consumed by the city's working and middle classes and promoted by commercial interests, and as such it was subject to political pressures over fares and quality of service within Uruguay's evolving democracy. The streetcar's thousands of workers did not toil invisibly behind factory walls but were contained in the changing life of the street and open to public eyes. Just as the streetcar formed a new type of transport network, its workers used its space to create new social networks that helped them rise to a position of leadership within the national labor movement and to effectively combat two foreign companies on issues of safety, wages, and dignity. The short history of the electric streetcar thus reveals the importance of urban space as a factor in determining the contours of local labor history.

Notes

1. Luis B. Vicario, *El crecimiento urbano de Montevideo* (Montevideo: Ediciones de la Banda Oriental, 1968), 16; J. A. Zahm, *Through South America's Southland* (New York and London: Appleton, 1916), 141; Juan Rial, *Estadisticas historicas del Uruguay, 1850–1930* (Montevideo: CIESU, 1980, mimeograph), 3 (estimates are for the Departmento [province] of Montevideo); Reginald Lloyd, *Impresiones de la República del Uruguay en el Siglo Viente* (London: Lloyd's Greater British Publishing, 1912) estimates that Uruguay's population grew by nearly 50 percent from 1883 to 1908.

2. Anton Rosenthal, "Streetcar Workers and the Transformation of Montevideo: The General Strike of May 1911," *The Americas: A Quarterly Review of Inter-American Cultural History* 51, no. 4 (April 1995): 474–475.

3. *Uruguay Weekly News*, January 30, 1921.

4. *El Libro del Centenario* (Montevideo: Capurro, 1925), 746.

5. Raúl Lerena-Acevedo, *Tráfico y transportes* (Montevideo: Impresara Uruguaya, 1932), 20.

6. Simon G. Hanson, *Utopia in Uruguay: Chapters in the Economic History of Uruguay* (New York: Oxford University Press, 1938), 20–21.

7. Banco de la República Oriental del Uruguay, *Sinopsis económica y financiera del Uruguay* (Montevideo: Impresara Uruguaya, 1933), 170.

8. José Pedro Barrán and Benjamín Nahum estimate that 30 percent of Montevideo's population in 1908 were immigrants and that 12 percent had rural origins; *Batlle, los estancieros y el imperio britanico,* vol. 1: *El Uruguay del novecientos* (Montevideo: Ediciones de la Banda Oriental, 1979, 1990), 40, 105.

9. R. Lerena-Acevedo, in *Tráfico y transportes,* notes that in 1907 some 97 percent of Montevideo's vehicular traffic was animal-driven, whereas by 1927 this figure had dropped to only 6 percent. A. Zahm, a visitor to Uruguay in 1916, commented: "Montevideo is the youngest of South American capitals and has an air of modernity about it that is totally absent from La Paz, Quito and Bogotá. [I]t everywhere manifests enterprise and prosperity. But, although everyone is busy, no one seems to be in a hurry." Zahm, *Through South America's Southland,* 138. See also Juan Carlos Pedemonte, "56 años, 7 meses y 6 días," *Almanaque del Banco de Seguros del Estado, 1988* (Montevideo, 1987): 59; Diego Fischer and Rosario Cecilio, *Noventa y tantos . . .* (Montevideo: Fundación Banco de Boston, 1991), 97.

10. For details on the inauguration of streetcar service and the debate about urban development that it engendered, see Anton Rosenthal, "The Arrival of the Electric Streetcar and the Conflict over Progress in Early Twentieth-Century Montevideo," *Journal of Latin American Studies* 27, no. 2 (May 1995): 319–341.

11. *El País* reported that although the number of *conventillos* declined by nearly 30 percent between 1905 and 1919, and the number of rooms in them declined by 26.4 percent, the number of inhabitants only dropped by 16 percent; January 1, 1920. In one of its first issues, *Mundo Uruguayo* demanded that city authorities demolish the *conventillos* because they constituted "a shame for a modern and hygienic city"; no. 7, February 19, 1919, unpaginated.

12. *Mundo Uruguayo,* no. 6, February 12, 1919, unpaginated.

13. Edward Albes, "Montevideo: The City of Roses," *Bulletin of the Pan American Union* 45 (July–December 1917): 453.

14. Tony Mason, *Passion of the People? Football in South America* (London and New York: Verso, 1995), 30, 39.

15. *Uruguay Weekly News,* November 7, 1909.

16. Eduardo Acevedo, *Anales Historicos del Uruguay,* vol. 5 (Montevideo: Casa A. Barreiro y Ramos, 1934), 458, and vol. 6 (Montevideo: Casa A. Barreiro y Ramos, 1936), 318.

17. Banco de la Republica, *Sinopsis económica y financiera del Uruguay,* 11.

18. J. A. Hamerton, *The Real Argentine: Notes and Impressions of a Year in the Argentine and Uruguay* (New York: Dodd, Mead, 1915), 384.

19. Fernando O. Assunçao and Iris Bombet Franco, *La Aguada* (Montevideo: Fundación Banco de Boston, 1991), 79; Alfredo R. Castellanos, "Guión Cronológico," *Cuadernos de Marcha,* no. 22 (February 1969): 96; C. Altezor and H. Baracchini, *Historia urbanística y edilicia de la ciudad de Montevideo* (Montevideo: Junta Departmental de Montevideo, 1971), 305; and Leopoldo C. Artucio, *Montevideo y la arquitectura moderna* (Montevideo: Editorial Nuestra Tierra, 1971).

20. Luis Enrique Azarola Gil, *Ayer, 1882–1952* (Lausanne: Imprimeries Réunies, 1953), 26.

21. *Memoria de la Policia de Montevideo, 1919–1922* (Montevideo: A. Barreiro y Ramos, 1923), 14.

22. Roberto J. G. Ellis, *Del Montevideo de ayer y de hoy* (Montevideo: Editorial VYP, 1971), 37–38; *Uruguay Weekly News*, March 11, 1917, sección castellana 2.

23. The *Boletín Mensual de Estadística Municipal* (Montevideo) for January through December 1927 lists a total of 151 rabid dogs remitted to the city's chemistry laboratory.

24. *El Día*, August 20, 1918.

25. *El País*, December 9, 1920.

26. *Uruguay Weekly News*, August 12, 1923.

27. *Uruguay Weekly News*, April 28, 1907, June 23, 1907.

28. *La Tribuna Popular*, March 23, 1916.

29. *Renovación*, I:1, July 1918.

30. *La Razón*, August 22, 1918.

31. Emilio Sisa López, *Tiempo de Ayer Que Fue* (La Paz: Ediciones Vanguardia, 1978), 30 (quote), 102–103 (Bar Victoria).

32. Juan Carlos Patrón, *Goes y el viejo Café Vaccaro* (Montevideo: Editorial Alfa, 1968), 140.

33. Ibid., 107.

34. *La Tribuna Popular*, March 3, 1916.

35. *El Día*, August 23, 1918.

36. A. Rosenthal, "The Arrival of the Electric Streetcar," 326–329.

37. *La Tribuna Popular*, April 19, 1921, April 20; *Uruguay Weekly News*, April 29, 1921.

38. *Mundo Uruguayo*, no. 417, January 6, 1927, inside cover.

39. Omar M. Gil Soja, *18 y Yi* (Montevideo: Arca, 1993), 61.

40. *Mundo Uruguayo*, no. 439, June 9, 1927, p. 12.

41. R. Lerena-Acevedo, *Tráfico y transportes*, 25.

42. *El Libro del Centenario*, 746; R. Lerena-Acevedo, *Tráfico y transportes*, 14.

43. R. Lerena-Acevedo, *Tráfico y transportes*, 14; Alvaro Casal Tatlock, *El automóvil en el Uruguay: Los años heróicos, 1900–1930* (Montevideo: Ediciones de la Banda Oriental, 1981), 22, 24, 62. There are statistical discrepancies between these two sources.

44. *Uruguay Weekly News*, July 31, 1921, October 23, 1921; *Mundo Uruguayo*, no. 34, August 28, 1919, unpaginated.

45. The *salvavidas* was a mechanical device dependent upon the reflexes of the motorman and on maintenance by the company. The *Uruguay Weekly News* reported that one car's *salvavidas* failed to function, and the car ran over and killed an eight-year-old girl who stood in the street "paralyzed with fright"; March 12, 1922. See also *La Tribuna Popular*, April 9, 1916. On the other hand, a ten-year-old telegraph messenger nicknamed "Marconi" was picked up suddenly on the fender of a car and was found to be still smoking his cigar; *La Tribuna Popular*, June 7, 1907.

46. Patrón, *Goes y el viejo Café Vaccaro*, 46.

47. *La Tribuna Popular*, January 4, 1920.

48. *La Tribuna Popular*, January 2, 1920.

49. *Mundo Uruguayo*, no. 75, June 17, 1920, unpaginated.

50. *La Tribuna Popular*, January 5, 1920.

51. Junta E. Administrativa, Dirección de Rodados, *Reglamento de Tranvías Eléctricos* (Montevideo: Talleres Graficos Juan Fernandez, 1910).

52. *La Tribuna Popular*, December 8, 1906.

53. Gil Soja, *18 y Yi*, 28.

54. Felisberto Hernández, "Muebles el canario" in *Nadie encendía las lámparas* (Madrid: Ediciones Catedra, 1993), 179–182. The ultimate commoditization of public space was il-

lustrated in a nightmarish 1936 cartoon featuring the character Don Tranquilo as an advertising agent who has found a way to have plants in Parque Rodó, the Prado, and along Avenida 18 de Julio grow in such a way that they spell out advertising slogans; *Mundo Uruguayo*, no. 877, February 13, 1936, p. 83.

55. Antonio Soto, "La plata forma del tranvía, foro ambulante y crisol de tipos," *Mundo Uruguayo*, no. 800, May 10, 1934, p. 5.

56. *Uruguay Weekly News*, November 30, 1919.

57. *Uruguay Weekly News*, July 3, 1910.

58. *Uruguay Weekly News*, March 14, 1920.

59. República Oriental del Uruguay, Ministerio de Industrias, *El salario real (1914–1926)* (Montevideo: Imprenta Nacional, 1927), 52.

60. *Boletín de la Oficina del Trabajo*, no. 2, April 15, 1913, 290, 294. Félix Etchevest made even lower estimates of absolute expenditures on trolley fares in 1914 and 1918 in his *Salario Vital* (Montevideo: Imprenta de Juan L. Domaleche, 1918), 35.

61. Archivo General de la Nación, Uruguay: Archivo Virgilio Sampognaro, box 219, file 1, Letters to Jefe Político Virgilio Sampognaro, April 30, 1916, October 14, 1916; *La Tribuna Popular*, March 3, 1916.

62. *El País*, May 3, 1920.

63. *Mundo Uruguayo*, no. 456, October 6, 1927, pp. 2–3; *La Razón*, May 30, 1911, for insurance policy.

64. *Uruguay Weekly News*, March 12, 1922.

65. *El País*, December 7, 1920, for guard hitting passenger.

66. *Uruguay Weekly News*, January 10, 1909; *La Razón*, August 4, 1911. Occasionally these animosities developed away from streetcars. In 1921, a recently fired conductor entered the offices of La Transatlántica and fatally shot the chief of traffic and a porter who came to his aid, before jumping through a window and landing on a bread seller on the sidewalk, severely injuring both of them; *Uruguay Weekly News*, June 5, 1921, and *La Tribuna Popular*, June 13, 1921.

67. Great Britain, Public Record Office, FO 371/15143/A1489/1489/46, Annual Report 1929, March 13, 1930, Mr. E. Scott to Mr. A. Henderson, p. 13.

68. *Uruguay Weekly News*, December 8, 1912.

69. *El Día*, May 12, 1911; smoking was allowed on worker cars, Gil Soja, *18 y Yi*, 62.

70. *La Siembra*, III:27, October, 1918.

71. *La Razón*, October 31, 1918.

72. *La Tribuna Popular*, November 9, 1921.

73. Charles S. Sargent, "Uruguay" in *Latin American Urbanization*, ed. Gerald M. Greenfield (Westport, Conn.: Greenwood Press, 1994), 482.

74. Hanson, *Utopia in Uruguay*, 190; M. H. J. Finch, "British Imperialism in Uruguay: The Public Utility Companies and the *Batllista* State, 1900–1930" in *Latin America, Economic Capitalism, and the State*, ed. Christopher Abel and Colin M. Lewis (London and Dover, N.H.: Athlone Press, 1985), 263; *The Sun*, April 28, 1936.

75. Quoted in Milton Vanger, *The Model Country* (Hanover, N.H.: University Press of New England, 1980), 132.

76. Great Britain, Public Record Office, FO 371/10632 A1004/1004/46, Annual Report on Uruguay for 1924, January 23, 1925, p. 25.

77. Hanson, *Utopia in Uruguay*, 194.

78. Rosenthal, "Streetcar Workers," 475–491.

79. *El Socialista,* I:9, May 14, 1911..

80. Carlo Umilta, quoted in Juan Antonio Oddone, *Una perspectiva europea del Uruguay* (Montevideo: Universidad de la República del Uruguay, 1965), 91.

81. *Uruguay Weekly News,* June 10, 1917.

82. *La Tribuna Popular,* October 29, 1921.

83. *Uruguay Weekly News,* May 6, 1923.

84. *La Tribuna Popular,* March 3, 1916.

85. Ministerio de Industrias, *El salario real,* 31, 41.

86. *Montevideo Times,* August 6, 1918; A. G. N., Archivo Virgilio Sampognaro, box 219, file 4, Memorandum of August 1.

87. *El Día,* August 31, 1918.

88. Fernando López D'Alesandro, *La fundación del Partido Comunista y la división del anarquismo (1919–1923)* (Montevideo: Vintén Editor, 1922), 23–25.

89. *La Prensa* (Buenos Aires), August 13.

90. Archivo General de la Nación, Uruguay: Archivo Virgilio Sampognaro, box 219, file 4, "Personal Que Se Necesitara para Custodia de Las Estaciones de los Trenvias", August 2, 1918.

91. *La Razón,* August 5, 1918; August 9, 1918; *Uruguay Weekly News,* August 11, 1918, sección castellana; August 18, 1918; *La Prensa,* August 10, 1918; Archivo General de la Nación (Uruguay), Archivos Judiciales, Juzgado del Crimen, Primer Turno, 1918, No. 102, letter to Virgilio Sampognaro from Third Section of Police, August 14.

92. *Montevideo Times,* August 11, 1918.

93. *La Prensa,* August 14, 1918.

94. *Montevideo Times,* August 31, 1918.

95. Alfredo Errandonea and Daniel Costabile, *Sindicato y sociedad en el Uruguay* (Montevideo: Fundación de Cultura Universitaña, 1969), 114.

96. *Uruguay Weekly News,* January 15, 1922; January 29, 1922; *El Siglo,* January 24, 1922; February 1, 1922.

3
Mexico City: Popular Classes and Revolutionary Politics

John Lear

Many of the patterns of massive urban growth and marginal living conditions commonly associated with Latin American cities after 1945 were evident in the urban transformations of primary cities at the turn of the century. From changes in the size, conditions, and social differentiation of major cities emerged a broader pattern of challenges to the traditional oligarchs who dominated authoritarian political systems and benefited from unequal economic growth during Latin America's "golden age." Along with members of the commercial, administrative, and professional middle classes, workers organized in new "modern" associations and attempted to assert themselves in the workplace and in municipal and national politics.[1]

The late 1910s in particular was a period of widespread labor mobilization in Latin America as well as the United States. This cycle was exacerbated at the global level by the economic exigencies of World War I and by the inspiration of the Russian Revolution and at the national level by crises of political legitimacy that swept the region. For example, in the five years from 1916 to 1921, general strikes occurred in Buenos Aires, Santiago, Rio de Janeiro, Lima, and Mexico City, among other cities in the region.[2] This cycle of labor mobilization can be seen as a precedent for later and more lasting organization and political incorporation of workers throughout Latin America after World War II.

Mexico City experienced a pattern of organization and mobilization that resembled and differed from that of the rest of Latin America. As did those of other major cities that underwent dramatic growth at the turn of the century, Mexico City's workers and popular classes experienced unprecedented mobilization and organization, culminating in a general strike in Mexico City in July 1916. A major difference between mobilizations in Mexico City and those of other cities in Latin

America was the context of the Mexican Revolution, a far deeper social and political crisis than was experienced elsewhere in Latin America. Because of that context, urban workers emerged from the revolution with a considerable level of organization and significance in the power structure.

The Mexican Revolution began in 1910 as an electoral revolt against a dictator of more than thirty years, President Porfirio Díaz. But it soon evolved into a profound and bloody social conflict that divided the nation for the next decade, a conflict in which a variety of factions and social actors contested national power before a cohesive military and social coalition emerged by 1920. While scholars of the Mexican Revolution debate its popular peasant roots and transformative character,[3] all agree that it was not primarily a revolution of urban workers.

Studies of Mexican labor and the revolution often use events in Mexico City to generalize about the working class, but none have looked closely enough at local structures and ongoing organizational processes within Mexico City during this period. When urban workers are discussed at all in the literature of the revolution, with few exceptions the focus has usually been on the six-month period in 1915 when a group of workers from Mexico City, affiliated with the anarchist group the Casa del Obrero Mundial (House of the World Worker), took up arms to support the military faction that eventually triumphed. Thus the workers of the so-called Red Battalions are celebrated in the orthodox view for their support of the revolution and condemned in the revisionist view for their early dependence on the state that emerged from that faction.[4]

Much of the historical literature on Mexican workers in the twentieth century has focused on particular unions or strikes to the exclusion of other aspects of the lives of working people[5] or on the relations of union leaders to the postrevolutionary state, relying largely on corporatist paradigms borrowed from political science.[6] Just as peasants were lost from the revisionist narrative of the revolution, workers were credited with only limited agency in these histories—at best, unions and the working class they represented are seen as dependent instruments of the state.

In this chapter I explore three related processes: In the first part of the chapter I explore the patterns of industrialization and urbanization that transformed work and community in Mexico City at the turn of the century and helped to undermine the Porfirian consensus that had made growth possible; in the second, I identify the organizational forms and specific demands of workers and popular classes that emerged during the "parenthesis of freedom" that was the revolution; finally, I describe two cycles of mobilization, the first leading up to the general strike of 1916 and the second leading to the rent strike of 1922. Both cycles challenged and shaped the emerging political order in Mexico City and demonstrate some of the possibilities and limitations of urban mobilization in this period.

I argue that although the actions of urban workers and masses rarely paralleled the armed insurrection of much of the peasantry during the revolution, urban workers and masses were nevertheless transformed by changes of the Porfiriato, the last decades of the reign of Porfirio Díaz, and by the events of the revolution and that through their mobilizations they were able to enhance greatly their role in local and national politics in the postrevolutionary period. The prominence of labor after the revolution was the result of a continuous cycle of largely autonomous urban organization that had begun years earlier. Finally, these mobilizations took on greatest significance when they extended beyond the workplace—linking skilled and unskilled workers, men and women—and echoed the demands of the popular classes.

The Roots of Mobilization

The urban mobilization in Mexico City had its roots in changes in the structure of work and community itself. The urban geographer David Harvey has described the changing social identity that can emerge from this dual transformation as the formation of "a community of class, and a class of community."[7] In other words, class can be defined by identification within or across places of work, that is, by one's identification as a worker, but also by identification around space, by one's position in a community of working people. Both types of identification, in relation to work and in relation to community, were well advanced by 1910.

The lives of two working people who rose to varying degrees of prominence in the labor movement during the revolution serve to illustrate broader patterns of work and class formation in turn-of-the-century Mexico City. Esther Torres arrived in Mexico City at the age of thirteen from her native city of Guanajuato in 1910 to join her younger sister and her recently widowed mother. Why move to Mexico City? According to Esther's mother, the only men to marry in Guanajuato were miners and mule drivers; now that her miner husband was dead, she needed to support her family, but the only work in Guanajuato for her or her daughters was as domestic servants, earning one and a half pesos a month. Esther explained years later that "as far away as there [Guanajuato] the news arrived that in Mexico City, there was a factory where women worked." Indeed, right off the train in Buenavista Station, Esther's mother approached a woman in a tortilla shop to ask where she could find work. The next day, the *tortillera*'s niece brought Esther's mother to meet the *maestra* of La Cigarrera Mexicana, who immediately hired her. When Esther joined her mother months later, she and her sister were hired at La Cigarrera as well, their first of many similar jobs in the city.[8]

Jacinto Huitrón was born in a tenement house near the center of Mexico City in 1885 of parents who had migrated from towns in the central states of Hidalgo and Mexico. His father, a cobbler, died when Jacinto was seven, and to get by his mother opened a tiny variety shop in the north of the city. After finishing primary school, Jacinto was apprenticed to a blacksmith at a peso a week and continued to take classes for four years at the trade school on San Lorenzo Street. After 1900 he got work constructing carriages, as a mechanic, as a blacksmith, and as an electrician. In 1910 he was laid off from his job in the railroad shops, and after a brief stint of work and opposition politics in Puebla, he returned to the capital to work as a mechanic and plumber in several of the city's big shops.[9] During the revolution, working people as different as Esther Torres and Jacinto Huitrón came together in organizations and mobilizations.

Porfirian progress brought to the capital city a particular type of development.[10] After 1876 Porfirio Díaz succeeded in creating an authoritarian government from Mexico City that could impose peace and order and subordinate regional interests to those of an increasingly centralized authority. The Díaz government finally managed to implement the liberal economic project, which opened Mexico up to foreign capital, reduced long-standing restrictions on subsoil use and commerce, and initiated a period of unprecedented export-oriented growth in mining and agricultural products. A secondary aspect of Porfirian development was the creation of large-scale industries serving relatively weak domestic markets; these industries were owned largely by foreign-born merchant-financiers or foreign investment companies and were protected by direct and indirect tariffs and by close ties to the Porfirian political elite.[11]

Aided by a national system of railways, Mexico City consolidated its traditional role as the nation's political, financial, and commercial center and experienced a rapid growth in population, a growth fueled primarily by migration. From 1895 to 1910 the city grew by 50 percent, to just under 500,000 people. Although still far from recovering its colonial status as the largest city in the hemisphere, Mexico City at the turn of the century was the third-largest city in Latin America, after Buenos Aires and Rio de Janeiro.[12] The revolution would only accelerate a pattern of primacy that would become extreme after 1940: During the decade of fighting, refugees swelled the city by a third, and during the decade of the 1920s, the city grew again by 58 percent, to almost 1 million people.[13]

In 1910 almost half of the population had been born outside of the Federal District, and a significant portion of migrants, like Esther Torres, came to the capital from the more urbanized states of central Mexico, such as Mexico State and Guanajuato, where the decline of mining and traditional artisanal industries forced many urban workers to look elsewhere for work. Although they were probably a minority of those who migrated to the city, the presence of these already-urbanized migrants, many of whom found work in factories and skilled trades, facilitated subsequent worker organization.[14]

Even more important to social change than migration was the transformation of the nature of production and work in the city. In spite of the presence of new and traditional elites and a significant increase in the number of middle-class professionals, bureaucrats, and merchants, the capital was a city of workers.[15] But the orientation of much of the urban economy toward this privileged group of consumers very much shaped the working class. Work remained oriented toward commerce, services, and the production of consumer goods instead of toward the heavy or dominant industries that characterized other Mexican cities, such as the northern city of Monterrey, with its metallurgical industries, or the southern town of Orizaba, where a quarter of the city's 40,000 residents were employed in textile mills.[16]

Spurred by the introduction of electricity by Anglo-Canadian companies in the 1890s, French and Spanish immigrant merchants installed large modern factories in Mexico City and the surrounding Federal District and helped give rise to a small but significant factory proletariat. Factory production, involving heavy machinery and a large number of workers, was limited primarily to two industries, textiles and tobacco. Of the twenty-two factories in the city proper, only two employed more than a thousand workers: La Carolina, a modern textile mill, employed more than 1,000 workers, and the model cigarette factory El Buen Tono had close to 2,000 workers, mostly female, around 1907.[17] The number of Mexico City factory workers rose 400 percent from 1895 to some 10,000 in 1910. In the latter year, a third of factory workers were women, and in the largest factories, about 10 percent of workers were children. Women and children were generally relegated to lower-paid jobs involving the preparation and finishing of textiles and, as was true for Esther Torres and her sister, the packing of machine-made cigarettes.[18]

These new, modern factories drastically undercut the livelihood of artisanal weavers and tobacco workers, whose actual numbers in the city dropped by over half from 1895 to 1910 and by similar numbers nationally. At least in Mexico City, the number of new factory positions created exceeded the number of artisanal cigarette and textile workers lost, so the displacement of artisanal workers was probably less dramatic there than in other areas of the country, or, rather, the more severe difficulties faced by artisanal workers in other parts of the country was manifest in the stream of migrants from old artisanal zones to the capital.[19] At the same time, the process of proletarianization was further mitigated in the city itself by the creation of some highly skilled jobs within factory settings and by opportunities elsewhere in the urban economy, opportunities made possible by the production of textiles, such as the burgeoning growth of seamstress work.[20]

But for all the importance of the rise of modern factories in a relatively short period, factory workers still made up only 4 percent of the Mexico City workforce.[21] Overall, although the emergence of a factory proletariat in Mexico City was important, factory workers were neither numerically nor organizationally the most important sector of the working class.

Of greater significance in shaping the working class of Mexico City was the reorganization of the traditional manufacturing crafts. Artisanal production had deep roots in the colonial capital and had survived intact through much of the nineteenth century in spite of the tentative openings of free trade and the elimination of colonial guilds.[22] But starting in the 1880s, new machinery, increasing shop size, and new shop organization began to transform the nature of work, making many journeymen and master craftsmen redundant in the face of medium-sized, semimechanized shops, often owned by foreign corporations or immigrants. In some cases, these shops grew to be virtual factories, such as the Excelsior shoe factory, which began as a small shop manufacturing large needles and grew by 1911 to employ 800 workers and produce 1,200 pairs of shoes daily. Two other shoe companies employed around 200 workers each.[23] As a result, the number of cobblers, men like Jacinto Huitrón's father, dropped by a third from 1895 to 1910 as a few large plants went far toward eliminating the once-ubiquitous shoe shop and itinerant shoemaker of old.[24] The numbers of other craft workers, such as bakers, weavers, and tannery workers, experienced similarly dramatic drops. Of course this pattern was not uniform, and many craft workers held their own in numbers, such as printers and metal workers, or grew modestly, such as construction workers. And some trades grew dramatically, such as plumbers and mechanics.[25]

But even where small craft shops remained numerous, in most manufacturing sectors they were no longer the predominant form of production in terms of share of production or even in number of workers. As a result, the existence of many craft workers in small shops became more precarious as their relative share of the market became smaller. Even where the introduction of new technologies in manufacturing increased the demand for skilled workers or where workers retained a high degree of control over the work process, as in metallurgy shops, the circumstances of their employment—wage labor, larger shops, the separation of shop from home, and ownership based on property rather than skill—were significantly different from those of nineteenth-century artisanal settings.[26]

The growth of the urban economy degraded many crafts, but it also created new opportunities. People like Jacinto Huitrón, who thirty years earlier might have pursued his father's profession, instead moved from one trade to another as boundaries between many traditional trades faded and new jobs were created. For example, the business card that he used in 1913 as treasurer of the Casa del Obrero Mundial had printed on the back: "I do all types of work, plumbing, welding, forging, mechanical, inventing, fine machinery, installation and all kinds of repair."[27] These were all tasks much in demand in Mexico City, though they required a man of some education and craftsman-like abilities. Machines and migrants reduced the boundaries, both of skill and of culture, between trades that had existed before, at least among skilled workers. As suggested by patterns of organization after 1910, this weakening of boundaries among traditional handicrafts probably also facilitated involvement in working-class politics and broad-based, working-class organizations.

The introduction of elements of a modern urban infrastructure, such as electricity and electric streetcars, also entailed the creation of new skilled and semi-skilled occupations. Railroads, electrical plants, and tramways all demanded mechanics, drivers, and electricians, people able to operate and maintain expensive machinery. The cost of their equipment and the importance of their work to the smooth functioning of the urban economy gave these workers an importance far beyond their considerable numbers in the workforce. The Anglo-Canadian electrical and streetcar companies in Mexico City employed 1,000 and 4,000 employees respectively. Similarly, the Nonoalco railroad repair shop employed 1,200 people. Of course many of these workers were unskilled "peons," but skilled positions abounded, and labor organization after 1910 increasingly occurred at the plant level.[28] By gathering together large numbers of workers, these new industries facilitated a high degree of consciousness among workers. Furthermore, the control of these industries by foreign capital and foreign managers, almost always American or English, injected workers' consciousness with a fierce nationalism.[29] Workers in these industries acquired great strategic importance after 1911 and through the 1920s as their strikes repeatedly brought the city to a standstill.

This type of metropolitan industrialization meant displacement as well as opportunities for factory, skilled, and strategic workers. In large-scale enterprises, it set the stage for direct confrontation between labor and capital, and among workers in small shops, it created significant resentments over both the monopolistic control of large producers and merchants and their often-foreign origins. Not surprisingly, much of the organizational initiative of labor in Mexico City after 1910 came from these three groups: skilled workers in changing craft industries, strategic workers in new infrastructure and transport industries, and textile factory workers. After 1911 alliances between these groups occurred relatively easily. But together they made up barely 12 percent of the labor force.[30]

The process of industrial change in Mexico City resembles that of many European and U.S. cities in the nineteenth century, but there were a few significant differences: First, industrialization in the form of investment and technology came to Mexico City late and rapidly, in a period of barely two decades after 1885. Second, changes led to a very high concentration of production and commerce in a few hands. Third, those hands often belonged to a few foreign companies and foreign-born entrepreneurs. Fourth, this "modernization" was very incomplete and left the majority of the labor force engaged in casual and unskilled labor.

Far and away the majority of the city's population worked in unskilled manufacturing and service occupations. The type of economic growth that occurred in Mexico City perpetuated and even expanded the need for unskilled and casual labor. Domestic service workers grew in number by 52 percent in the fifteen years before 1910 and in that year remained the largest single occupational category in the city, at 28 percent of the workforce. For recent migrants from the countryside, many of them indigenous, domestic service provided a transition to Spanish, to city life, and to alternative jobs.[31]

This is particularly true for women. Women made up more than one-third of the paid labor force, but over 40 percent worked as domestic servants.[32] With the exception of a few growing middle-class occupations in teaching and private and government offices, for women the alternatives to working in domestic service were to work as shopkeepers and attendants or in the garment industry and factories. Esther Torres and her sister, for example, left their jobs in the cigarette factory to work as seamstresses in a variety of sweatshops. When Esther could no longer get work in sweatshops because of her organizing work, she sewed out of her home.[33] The great bulk of the urban workforce, men, women, and children, worked as servants or in commerce, sweatshops, hotels, restaurants, street sweeping, or the generic categories of peon and day laborer.[34]

Mechanization increased wages for some groups and reduced or maintained low wages for others. A basic mechanic or metallurgical worker earned two to five pesos a day, and adult factory workers in textiles and tobacco generally earned around one peso a day. The basic wage for unskilled workers in Mexico City in 1910 was between seventy-five centavos and a peso a day for men and was as low as twenty-five centavos a day for women. Children, often with the euphemistic title of "apprentice," worked for as little as ten centavos a day or else worked unpaid in factories and sweatshops helping their parents do piecework.[35]

With the cost of living in Mexico City rising after 1900, it became impossible for an individual to support a family on the wages from unskilled work.[36] One U.S. observer carefully estimated the annual income and minimum cost of living for an unskilled worker in 1910 and remarked on the resulting gap: "It seems, in contemplating the cold figures of the city peon's budget, as if it were impossible for him to exist, and yet exist he does, even though his children die like flies and his wife grows old at thirty."[37] Of course the explanation of this mystery, besides the reality that many did not survive, was clear from his calculations: In most working-class families, women and children entered the workforce regularly. In the many cases where the nuclear family could not be sustained in such circumstances, extended households of relatives sent multiple workers out into the labor market in order to survive.[38]

Organization among these workers was made more difficult by the extreme instability and the informality of much of their employment. Work could vary dramatically from one season to the next or from one recession to another. Except for a core of skilled workers, industries such as construction and garments alternately absorbed and laid off large numbers of workers from one job and season to another. During the 1907 recession, and again during the worst years of fighting during the revolution, unskilled and even skilled work became scarce. For many, work remained precarious, and they pursued numerous types of occupations. The reserve army of the underemployed made for a constant downward pull on wages and considerable structural obstacles to organization.[39]

In short, industrialization transformed the Mexico City workforce in a way that divided workers into the skilled and the unskilled. This dichotomy went beyond the workplace to include both social and cultural aspects of their lives. Unskilled workers were more likely to have rural origins, whereas skilled workers were more commonly from urban backgrounds. Skilled workers were far more likely to be literate[40] and were often versed in liberal and even radical European thought. For example, Jacinto Huitrón finished primary school and entered the Escuela Obrera, where he read classics of Mexican history and culture and thrilled to Mexican poet Salvador Díaz Mirón's ode to Victor Hugo. Inspired by liberal and anarchist thought, he would even name his children Anarcos, Acracia, Autónomo, Libertad, and Emancipación.[41] By contrast, Esther Torres had barely been able to finish the third grade in her native city of Guanajuato before entering the labor market, and even this minimal education distinguished her from many unskilled workers.[42] Unskilled workers, men in particular, were more prone to drink and honor Saint Monday, and in spite of the much more secular environment of the city, religious belief and veneration for the Virgin of Guadalupe remained important, especially for women.[43]

Skilled workers, more than unskilled workers, maintained a deep-rooted tradition of corporate organization (mainly mutual aid societies) and of political participation dating back to the nineteenth century.[44] Huitrón, for example, joined the Union of Mexican Mechanics in 1909 while working for the railroad, and during a brief stay in Puebla he became involved with Aquiles Serdán and the Maderista opposition to Porfirio Díaz. In the case of Esther Torres, as with many unskilled workers, unionization and political participation would come with the revolution and with help from skilled and educated workers like Huitrón. Although Huitrón was exceptional in many ways, the pattern of organization among skilled workers can be generalized. As William Sewell argues for nineteenth-century French artisans: "Serious involvement in working-class politics required a level of information, organizational experience and commitment, and a freedom from the most pressing material wants," a pattern that describes a small minority of skilled Mexican workers.[45]

The dichotomy in the workforce between skilled and unskilled meant that for effective citywide mobilization to occur, alliances between the minority of skilled and the majority of unskilled workers were necessary. The organizational link between these two groups could be made around universal demands for improving basic work conditions, even though those work conditions might differ dramatically among skilled and unskilled. But skilled and unskilled workers often lived in close proximity, and they shared a resentment of the presence of foreigners, whether as employers, managers, or shopkeepers, as well as the increasing physical inequalities apparent in the city itself. Thus broader issues of consumption and community could help bridge the dichotomy between skilled and unskilled, particularly in times of economic crisis and organizational freedom. Although organizational leadership frequently came from skilled workers, the participation and demands of unskilled workers often shaped the course of the mobilization.

Another basis for mobilization came from the redefinition of space and community in Mexico City. During the last half of the Porfirian regime, the city underwent profound changes in its physical layout, a sort of redefinition of geographical class relations. In the late nineteenth century, electric tramways and broad central avenues deliberately patterned on those of Paris were laid out, increasing the circulation of people and goods from one part of the city to another. The result was that different areas of the city became more specialized in function, and different social groups were pushed physically further apart.

Three trends were already very clear by 1910: First, much of the new elite and middle classes abandoned the traditional multiclass downtown for the more exclusive residential divisions on the western periphery of the city, primarily along the Paseo de la Reforma (today the tourist district known as the Zona Rosa). Second, the core colonial downtown area—once characterized by its mixture of wealthy and poor, commerce and crafts—became increasingly devoted to commerce and finance rather than residences. The most exclusive streets were dominated by banks, insurance offices, railroad and transportation offices, social clubs, or five-story department stores. Third, high rents and deliberate policies of demolition pushed many workers and urban poor from the core downtown area. But in spite of Porfirian attempts to make the central axis of the old colonial downtown an exclusive showcase of commerce, finance, and statehood and in spite of the resulting rise in rents, many of the lower classes remained nearby in crowded tenements in order to be close to sources of work servicing the shops, markets, and restaurants of the center. A fringe of crowded tenement houses grew up east of the central plaza. Other working-class neighborhoods formed around the railroad stations in the north and around the factories in the south of the city. Marginal colonies of the poor, areas with few or no basic services, the predecessors of post-1945 squatter settlements, sprang up around the workshops, prisons, and railroad stations, particularly on the eastern edges of the city.[46]

Structural changes that relegated the poor to peripheral areas were supplemented by attempts by Porfirian reformers to eliminate what the Mexican positivist Miguel Macedo identified as "the deleterious environment of the lost classes: cheap eating houses, taverns, public dances, gaming houses and brothels."[47] In particular, measures were taken to keep prostitutes, peasants, and the homeless off the streets in the central district and in the wealthy new residential neighborhoods and parks.[48] But these measures proved largely ineffective, doing little more than filling up the new Porfirian jails and creating increasing resentment toward police and government authorities among both workers and popular classes.[49]

These trends led to the creation of a mosaic of neighborhoods in which workers and popular classes increasingly lived and worked far from the wealthiest classes, and they set the stage for a growing assertiveness of workers and urban poor that overcame previous patterns of respect for wealth and a consensus over political authority. Many poor and working-class Mexicans came to see themselves more and more as apart from wealthy classes, and they came to identify not with the multiclass community of the past but, rather, with the "other" Mexico that grew up in the shadows of Porfirian glitter. For example, on Independence Day in 1909, the inaugural edition of a new workers' newspaper complained that "nobody has shown concern except for the public boulevards," presented to visiting foreigners, and that foreign factory owners felt "the disgust and fear that the tenements workers live in inspire." The editorial ended by warning the "*señores burócratas*," the positivist-inspired technocrats known as *científicos*, that now "the people have awakened."[50] In the opposition presidential campaign of Francisco Madero a few months later, sentiments of worker resentment and emerging popular identities were manifest in the outpouring of support from what one newspaper called "the great unwashed."[51]

During and after the revolution, these nascent communities of class and space attempted to reassert themselves in the workplace and in public areas. Many workers, especially streetcar and electrical workers, became conscious of their power within the new spatial arrangement of the city. Many of the public demonstrations of workers after 1909, such as their support for Madero's presidential campaign in 1910, the first May Day celebration in 1913, or the general strike of 1916, can be interpreted as conscious attempts to reassert their presence in the exclusive downtown areas, where they had historically been central social actors.[52] These attempts are also evident in community-based demands for services and affordable food and housing, such as the food riots that occurred throughout the revolution and the massive rent strike of 1922. Their collective demands, whether to local authorities, to employers, or to landlords, made them difficult to ignore and often a threat to the larger order.

Organization and Demands

If solidarity among working people was shaped by the changes in the structure of space and work, the emergence of new forms of organization was also the product of the revolution itself: of its ideological currents; of the greater political freedom that was due largely to weakened and constantly changing local and national authorities; and finally, of the material changes in the urban environment brought on by military and economic turmoil.

For much of his thirty-four-year reign, the government of Porfirio Díaz sustained its control over the working class in Mexico City.[53] The regime's control over labor weakened as the nature of production, work, and community changed and as workers began to elaborate a critique of the Porfirian system using elements of liberal ideology and references to their rights as inscribed in the 1857 Constitution. During the presidential elections of 1910, a significant portion of workers in Mexico City rejected Porfirian paternalism and backed the candidacy of Madero, a wealthy northern landowner and industrialist who promised "a real vote, and no boss rule." In supporting Madero, workers in Mexico City, led in particular by textile workers and printers, emphasized the historical role of workers in building the nation, both through their own labor and through their participation in nineteenth-century battles against foreigners and conservatives. The struggle against the tyranny of Díaz's political system was equated with workers' struggles against abuse and exploitation in the workplace, both of which were linked to the role of foreigners in Mexico.[54] But when Madero's repressed presidential campaign turned to armed rebellion, his support came from the countryside. Mexico City remained largely quiet, except for a massive protest against Díaz by some 15,000 mostly poor citizens on May 24, 1911, in the central plaza, which probably hastened Díaz's resignation the next day.[55] But after the fall of Díaz, the political participation that workers exercised in the 1910 presidential campaign proved to be limited and frustrating during Madero's brief presidency (November 1912 to February 1913) and during the ensuing conservative dictatorship of Victoriano Huerta (February 1913 to August 1914), pushing urban workers to strengthen their own organizations in the workplace and their own communities.[56]

Although strikes occurred and workers formed organizations with increasing frequency at the turn of the century, these initiatives clearly accelerated after the fall of Díaz. Since the demise of the colonial guilds, mutual aid societies had been the only form of worker organization sanctioned by employers and the government, and during the first year of Madero's presidency they flourished and expanded their membership and activities, providing an important stepping-stone to the formation of unions that were combative as well as more pragmatic.

But after 1912 many of these new societies broke with the recent past and attempted to consolidate workers from a single sector into a single organization, a pattern different from previous patterns, in which the mutual aid societies either included workers from a variety of occupations or were based in a particular shop or factory. Unified mutual aid societies with between 500 and 1,000 members were soon organized in Mexico City among a variety of craft workers, for example, printers and stonecutters, as well as office workers, restaurant workers, federal employees, and shop employees, in addition to a number of small new mutual aid societies.[57]

These new organizations briefly teetered between the goals and ideology of mutualism, those of small producer organizations concerned with issues of security and cultural and moral improvement, and those of workers who sought to assert themselves within the structure of modern industry. This was particularly true among societies representing traditional crafts. An important example is the Confederation of Printers, which was established in May 1911 on the same day that crowds pushed Porfirio Díaz to resign. Printers like Rafael Quintero were steeped in liberal traditions and had participated actively in the Madero presidential campaign the year before. Such traditions were further influenced by the anarchism and utopian socialist traditions brought by southern European immigrants such as the Spaniard Amadeo Ferrés, founder of the Confederation of Printers. The confederation sought, primarily through their newspaper and cultural events, to enlighten fellow workers, especially in other sectors, and attempted to create a cooperative press for unemployed printers. The confederation and other groups of workers first incorporated a mild language of class, which identified a common interest among all workers that was distinct from that of owners, and eventually moved to more direct confrontation with employers. This shift reflected the struggle within the confederation between printers like Ferrés, rooted in nineteenth-century small-craft traditions, and printers like Rafael Quintero, who worked in big modern print shops and newspapers such as the *Diario Oficial*. Quintero would eventually lead this group out of the confederation.[58] A similar tension existed within other groups, such as the Union of Tailor Workers, whose founder was the radical tailor Luis Méndez, who owned a modest tailor shop himself.[59]

The initial consciousness of these craft workers was rooted in an increasing articulation of the idea that modern industries had created unfair monopolies in traditional crafts, factories, and sweatshops. Even the conservative mutualist newspaper *El Obrero Mexicano* in November 1911 commented positively on a strike by 200 women garment workers and acknowledged that not alcohol but "monopolies are the greatest enemies of our class, the means of exploitation to bleed the worker and take away his energies."[60] Similarly, monopoly was often associated with foreign entrepreneurs and foreign firms, an identification unmistakable in the call by stonecutters to form a union in September 1911, which began: "It is sad and shameful that Mexican workers serve as a stepping-stone [*escalón*] so that foreigners can climb up and treat us worse than caciques or foremen."[61]

These workers made continuing attempts to participate in management decisions and to retain a degree of control over production and employment, often through the formation of cooperatives or attempts to bypass perceived monopolies and middlemen.[62] But by 1913 many of the new workers' organizations had taken on the name of *sindicato* (union). In the process, they moved from artisanal concerns about security and control over production to more direct confrontation with large employers and demands for government regulation. As with the printers, this shift probably reflected the rise to prominence within these organizations of workers from large rather than small shops and the reorientation that came from increasing association among workers from different trades and skill levels.

The leadership and cultural orientation for much of worker organization and the definitive move away from mutualism was led by the Casa del Obrero Mundial. The Casa was formed in 1912 by various organizations of craft workers, individual workers like Jacinto Huitrón, and intellectuals, such as Antonio Díaz Soto y Gama, who had previously helped found the Partido Liberal Mexicano and would soon go on to join the Zapatistas. The Casa functioned first as a cultural organization, holding night classes and poetry readings and instructing workers in both self-improvement and the writings of radical European thinkers, with a preference for Spanish anarchists. Within a year of its founding, the Casa del Obrero Mundial moved away from emphasizing education and moral regeneration to more directly criticizing the terms of labor and the political sources of inequality, a trend that began under the presidency of Madero and intensified under the counterrevolutionary regime led by General Victoriano Huerta, who had toppled Madero in 1913. By then, the Casa's role was as a catalyst for the formation of unions and the implementation of "direct action," generally through strikes.[63]

Under President Madero, the Casa and its affiliated unions had remained staunchly independent, rejecting most overtures from the newly established Department of Labor, as well as from powerful and occasionally sympathetic ministers such as Jesus Flores Magón. Under the dictatorship of General Huerta, the Casa continued its stance of political neutrality, though it occasionally engaged in public demonstrations, such as the city's first May Day in 1913, which could only be construed by Huerta officials as a blatant political challenge.[64] In May 1914, after closing down Congress and benefiting from sham presidential elections, an increasingly desperate Huerta sent troops to close down the Casa and curtailed most independent organizational activity by workers.[65]

Three months later, after General Huerta's military defeat in August 1914 at the hands of the northern-based Constitutionalist armies led by Venustiano Carranza, Álvaro Obregón, and Francisco Villa, the Casa and the union movement in Mexico City reemerged with a heightened vibrancy. Within two years of the Casa's founding, many of the principal workers' groups in the city had formed unions and joined the Casa, and mutualist groups were increasingly marginalized. Besides the dominant craft workers, component unions from an early date included many "respectable" groups, such as waiters, shop clerks, and government employees. But this latest phase of organization also saw the creation and incorporation of new and powerful industrial unions, such as those of the streetcar workers and the electrical workers, powerful unions that would play an ever-greater role in leading strikes and challenging the craft-based leadership within the Casa.[66]

A similar transformation occurred, if hesitantly, among factory workers. To some extent, their organization and political participation was shaped by a series of strikes by textile workers in late 1911 and 1912 in which Madero's newly formed Department of Labor intervened. The result was a Textile Convention in which industrialists hammered out a voluntary agreement with the government, with minimum input from a national Permanent Central Committee of textile workers. The committee of textile workers had no formal union rights at the factory, local, or national levels, and its existence and relation to the government shaped labor relations in that sector for the next decade, limiting the participation of Mexico City's textile workers in citywide movements. Even so, local textile workers' organizations underwent similar transitions and formed tentative ties across sectors in ways that challenged the structures imposed by the 1912 convention. For example, the Union of Textile and Related Arts reorganized in September 1914 to affiliate with the Casa del Obrero Mundial. Their statutes allowed half of their dues to go for "the class struggle" and the other half to go to a mutual aid fund that would provide the traditional security against unemployment or death ("taking into account that some *compañeros* cannot give up old patterns of 'mutualism'"). By January 1915 this union claimed to represent the majority of textile workers in the Federal District and insisted that the Department of Labor allow elections to reconstitute a new Permanent Central Committee of textile workers.[67]

Perhaps most unusual of all, given the gap between skilled and unskilled workers, is that many of the more marginal and unskilled workers in Mexico City began to organize in this period. Their unions often were organized as a result of efforts by the Casa del Obrero Mundial to bring into its ranks less-skilled workers and those in occupations where women predominated. For example, just weeks after their victory over the fashion shops of downtown Mexico, the Union of Tailors backed the efforts of lower-paid seamstresses at the Palacio de Hierro department store to form a union of their own.[68] Given the precarious position of these workers in the labor market, such efforts were not always successful, but in the space of months, and often with the sympathy of occupying revolutionary generals, bricklayers, seamstresses, female cigarette workers, and even the marginalized workers of the corn tortilla mills formed unions.[69]

When at the end of 1914 the triumphant Constitutionalist forces split along regional and social lines between the Convention forces led by Emiliano Zapata and Francisco Villa and the Constitutionalist forces led by Venustiano Carranza and Alvaro Obregón, the Casa reported a membership of 52,000.[70]

During the revolution, even the most radical workers and the organizations they led never advocated the immediate seizure of the means of production, except on a few occasions involving a foreign company, and even then only when the instrument of intervention was the state or revolutionary generals.[71] More often their increasing militancy was aimed at lessening the worst abuses of the capitalist system, asserting greater control over aspects of the work process, and claiming citizenship rights to which they felt entitled by their role in Mexican development.

The new mass constituency of the Casa after May 1913 also required a shift in strategy by the craft workers who led the Casa to accommodate the needs of the unskilled. The skilled craft workers who made up the initial organizations and the leadership of the Casa aspired to participate in management decisions and retain a degree of control over production and hiring decisions. These aspirations were commonly shared by skilled workers in factories, the streetcars, and the electrical company. But the most common demands among the unskilled workers, who soon became the majority of the Casa, were over long-standing issues of stable wages, an eight-hour day, and an end to arbitrary abuse by managers. The demand for respect from owners or managers, who were often of foreign origin, provided a catalyst for many strikes, particularly among the most poorly paid and among women workers.[72] Given the nature of work, the desire for improved working conditions, particularly the eight-hour day, was more widespread among Mexico City workers than the specific concerns of craft workers to control production and employment, and thus helped unify a citywide union movement.[73] Pressing for such universal demands allowed the Casa to incorporate much of the city's working class in strikes, demonstrations, and appeals to authorities for protective legislation or military decrees, even as it increasingly compromised their professed anarchist rejection of the state.

Although anarchist principles suggested otherwise, most unions and even the remaining mutual aid societies pushed authorities to establish "*personalidad jurídica*" (legal status), which would give stability to their organizations and allow them to press demands within the workplace and in the judicial system.[74] And at least at the outset of the revolution and again after 1917, electoral representation and access to elected political officials remained important issues for workers.[75]

Other unifying demands were those that extended beyond work to consumer issues of food, rent, and provision of basic services. This was a relatively natural link, given mutualist and anarchist traditions, but it was also a response to the increasing concentration of production and commerce in the capital that had occurred during the reign of Porfirio Díaz.[76] Moreover, the military conflicts throughout Mexico brought drastic changes in the material conditions of the city and in turn helped radicalize worker demands and methods. During the worst years of fighting, the increasing importance of consumer issues helped to straddle the division between skilled and unskilled workers and between unions and popular classes. This pattern is suggested by the petition presented by the Casa del Obrero Mundial to Constitutionalist military authorities on October 3, 1914. Besides presenting a series of ambitious labor proposals that included the eight-hour day, a minimum wage, and the elimination of piecework and work at home, the Casa went much further and called for a mix of regulations and participation by workers to force prices of basic goods down to their 1912 levels, to reduce rents by a third, to triple the tax on empty rooms, and to enforce housing sanitation regulations, with Casa del Obrero Mundial workers acting as inspectors and construction teams to implement improvements.[77]

This link to consumer issues had important consequences for the mobilization of women.[78] In Mexico City, women provided the initiative and primary participation for a series of mobilizations in this period that ranged from taking over food shops in order to administer a just exchange to occupying government buildings in order to press demands for food and services. Throughout much of July 1915, women led widespread food riots and confiscations and even took over the convention parliament to demand that the Villista and Zapatista delegates resolve the problem of hunger in the city.[79] The link between food riots, demonstrations, and union activities is suggestive but somewhat ambiguous. In general Mexico City unions endorsed riots and confiscations as morally justified "direct action," though insisting that sacking shops alone could not solve the problems of the poor.[80] Still, these actions, almost invariably led by women, pushed the unions to orient their concerns toward consumption issues and to further incorporate women in unions and public demonstrations.

As workers and consumers, women mobilized in their own organizations and on their own initiative, but they also extended crucial or definitive support to initiatives that came from male-dominated organizations, particularly when the link to consumer issues was clear.[81] This would prove to be the case in both the general strike of 1916 and the rent strike of 1922.

Alliance and Defiance: The 1916 General Strike and the Rent Strike of 1922

As previously mentioned, the Casa is probably best known for its alliance of February 1915 with the Constitutionalist forces. In that month, a portion of the Casa leadership and component unions abandoned their stance of political neutrality and chose to take up arms in the Constitutionalist forces of Venustiano Carranza in his battle against the Convention forces of Villa and Zapata. In March some 5,000 to 7,000 soldiers in five Red Battalions abandoned Mexico City and followed General Alvaro Obregón to Veracruz.[82] As noted, this alliance had and continues to have great significance. Various factors and explanations for the alliance bear mentioning: the dire shortages and unemployment in the city that made the guaranteed pay and corporate structure of the Red Battalions attractive; the personal intervention of Constitutionalist general Alvaro Obregón and his middle-class intellectual allies; the failure of the Convention forces to appeal to or court urban workers or to resolve urban shortages; internal conflicts within the Casa; and according to Gilly, the "petty bourgeois" mentality of the Casa "artisans."[83]

Through much of the nineteenth century, two traditions coexisted within the ranks of Mexican workers: a determination to confront employers directly, without interference by political authorities, and the use of political alliances, particularly at the municipal level, to guarantee basic workers' rights.[84] Within the constituent Casa unions and the Casa leadership, these strategies competed uneasily, and in February 1915 resulted in the Pact with the Constitutionalists. Anarchism provided a powerful catalyst to organization and direct action, but although skilled workers and their unions were generally the least likely to turn to political authorities in their conflicts with employers, they also had a deep-rooted tradition of political participation dating back to the early republic.[85] For example, many of the craft workers most versed in anarchist precepts had, like Jacinto Huitrón and Rafael Quintero, actively supported Madero in his 1910 electoral challenge to Díaz. Their deeply held belief that Mexican workers were key figures in the history of the nation may have made it difficult for them to remain neutral in the war that divided the country; indeed, the alliance was seen by many Casa members as a type of social charter that acknowledged the historical role of workers as citizens. Casa leaders may also have seen the alliance as affirming their role as leaders of less-skilled workers and workers elsewhere in the nation and as the quickest way to deliver on key demands of these rapidly organizing groups.[86]

Less attention has been paid to other aspects of popular mobilization that challenged and shaped the consolidation of the victorious middle-class factions at a key moment during the revolution. For the purpose of this chapter, it is worth noting, first, that the majority of the Casa members and key component unions remained in Mexico City rather than joining the Red Battalions, whether because of political disagreement, personal rivalries, or simply the need to remain close to employment and family.[87] Second, worker and popular mobilization continued in Mexico City under the Convention government of Villa and Zapata during the six-month absence of the Red Battalions, particularly among workers in large and strategic industries that could best survive the dire conditions imposed by war. For example, the Electricians Union undertook two largely successful strikes for wage increases and union recognition and gave support to a variety of other groups of workers in the city.[88] And finally, the Red Battalions quickly ran into problems with First Chief Venustiano Carranza because of their determination not only to fight his military battles but also to organize workers and call for strikes in the regions they occupied.[89] Carranza quickly dissolved the majority of the Red Battalions in August 1915, and the fairly quick reconciliation of these returning soldiers and union leaders with the workers that had stayed in Mexico City initiated a renewed cycle of autonomous mobilization at an unprecedented level that culminated in the general strike of July 1916.[90]

It was in this period of consolidation that union organization reached people like Esther Torres, who had struggled through the toughest years of the revolution working as a seamstress at a variety of sweatshops between prolonged periods of unemployment. Hunger and unemployment first brought her to the Casa, where she received work distributing food in outlets organized by the Casa and municipal authorities.[91] Having watched other working people organize and join the Red Battalions over the years, she finally got permission from her mother to attend one of the Casa meetings. There, she recalled years later, she listened to Rafael Quintero explain "what kind of thing a union was." The next week, in November 1915, she brought a group of seamstresses to the Casa, where with the help of Jacinto Huitrón, they organized a seamstress union.[92]

An innovation that solidified the organizational ties among different sectors was the revitalization of the Federation of Workers' Unions of the Federal District in January 1916. The federation, while closely tied to the Casa and sharing its headquarters, went beyond the loose encompassing structure and cultural focus of the Casa and ceded more influence to independent-minded unions such as the powerful Electricians Union, which had rejected the Pact and led the union movement in Mexico City during the Casa's absence.[93] The federation joined together organizations from virtually every sector, from restaurant workers to highly skilled craft workers, and deliberately sought to organize women workers and to address consumer issues of particular concern to women.[94] Perhaps the most notable absence were domestic servants, who were extremely difficult to organize. The federation helped to build a citywide class perspective on issues of both work and consumption. By mid-1916 the federation claimed a membership of 90,000, almost a third of the city's labor force, making it the largest and most unified labor organization in the nation up to that date.[95]

A second aspect of this cycle was escalating conflict between union leaders and the new provisional government of First Chief Carranza. Only ten days after the Constitutionalists took definitive control of the city, the Electricians Union, which had prospered under the Convention government, launched a strike against the Mexican Light Company, a strike that darkened the city.[96] The next year was punctuated by constant strikes led by both newly formed and experienced unions, though their degree of success varied depending on the strategic position of the strikers within the industry or urban economy, the degree of solidarity among other workers in the city, or the willingness of the military authorities to intervene on workers' behalf. But the Constitutionalist attitude toward workers was no longer one of consistent support as it had been in the fall of 1914, when the split with the Convention forces loomed large. The provisional government's attitude was clear from the following message sent by the head of Carranza's Labor Department to striking workers in the spring of 1915: "Strikes were more or less justified in the time of Generals Díaz and Huerta," he said, "but now are absolutely inappropriate and inconvenient given that the Constitutionalist authorities support the working class."[97] In the face of the electricians' support for strikes in the state of Mexico, Pablo González, the general in charge of the Federal District, denounced the "professional agitators" and declared to the press that "if the Revolution had combated capitalist tyranny, it can not avoid sanctioning proletarian tyranny, and that is the tyranny to which workers aspire."[98]

Organizational bonds among workers on the one hand and conflicts with employers and officials on the other were both furthered by the difficult situation in Mexico City. Agricultural production plummeted during the years of worst fighting. A report commissioned by Carranza in 1915 reported that the amount of corn and wheat production reaching markets was less than 10 percent of the levels of 1910, a situation worsened by damage to the railroad system and the continued diversion of much of railroad stock to military use.[99]

In such a situation of scarcity, many large landowners, merchants, and millers profited enormously by cornering limited supplies of foods.[100] Speculation was facilitated by the tremendous concentration of ownership and distribution networks in the city, a tendency that seems to have increased during the years of the revolution. The milling of flour and the baking of bread was controlled, directly or indirectly, by three firms, the largest being the Compañía de Manufacturera de Harina. Likewise, *masa* for corn tortillas was almost exclusively in the hands of the Compañía Mexicana Molinera de Nixtamal.[101]

Constitutionalist officers were quick to condemn these merchants publicly and impose relatively ineffective price controls. But military officers also controlled the train stations of the capital and further raised the price of food through deals and extortion. General Pablo González, while alternately menacing the popular classes of Mexico City and of Morelos, made a considerable fortune through his control of the grain trade in the capital.[102] The situation for urban workers was further worsened by the fact that virtually every revolutionary faction financed war and government by printing its own currency, unbacked by any bank or gold guarantee. When the Constitutionalists definitively retook Mexico City in August 1915, the paper peso had dropped from its 1910 value of fifty U.S. cents to seven U.S. cents.[103] The repeated printing of unbacked new currencies was an invitation to speculate, something soldier and shop owner alike were ready to do.

Material hardship was a fundamental motivation to riots, confiscations, and strikes, but unions meanwhile continued to push for long-standing demands such as recognition of unions and control over arbitrary treatment and firings and to defend the public participation they had achieved since 1910.[104] As conditions worsened throughout the spring of 1916, the federation responded by organizing a series of successful strikes to force employers to recognize unions and grant wage and other demands, but these gains proved short-lived, as long as the Constitutionalists failed to guarantee regular shipments of food or to create a stable currency.

Workers also took initiatives aimed specifically at consumer problems. The Casa-affiliated bakery workers union set up alternative bakeries and over forty distribution points in the poorer areas of the city, using hospital and prison ovens and wheat sold to them by City Hall. In addition they provided work to the unemployed as street vendors of Casa-baked bread.[105] This filled an urgent need that neither military authorities nor businesses were able to meet and at the same time strengthened workers' ties to the poorer neighborhoods they served. This endeavor survived efforts by the big bakeries to control all of the ovens in the city as well as a crisis with City Hall when the Casa attempted to organize a strike among city hall workers themselves.[106]

Such efforts by the Casa and the new federation ended any good will from First Chief Carranza. The final break between workers' organizations and military leaders came in June when Carranza imposed yet another paper currency, the so-called *infalsificables*, which immediately traded at half its announced gold backing of twenty centavos; during July the new *infalsificable* peso again lost half its value.[107] The introduction of this new currency coincided with the elimination of price controls on food in the city. Workers were paid wages in the new paper money at face value, but food prices were posted in gold equivalents.

In late July the Casa and the federation made a series of demands to employers, the most important an insistence that wages be paid according to the same standard of hard currency that shops demanded for payment of goods. The federation demands can be interpreted in two ways. First, they should be seen—as the leadership later explained—as a response to pressure from rank-and-file members and workers in many unskilled sectors, since these were the groups least able to independently push their wage demands to keep up with the currency devaluation.[108] Second, even though worker demands were ostensibly made to employers, the real audience was clearly the military government, since such a standard could only be imposed on a citywide scale by government authorities. Tactics now led inevitably toward direct confrontation with the government. In May the federation had given ample public warning of plans for a general strike, allowing the government time to impose a short-lived agreement with factory owners and merchants. In late July, by resorting directly to the general strike without the explicit warnings and deadlines given on previous occasions, the Casa and the federation made clear their final break with the Constitutionalists.[109] When they received no answer, the labor movement was forced to act. First, the commercial workers' union unilaterally called a strike against key shop owners.[110] The federation responded to this initiative by declaring a general strike on July 31, 1916. At four o'clock that morning, the electrical workers' union cut off power, effectively closing down all production, transport, and commerce.

Mexico City awoke to a general strike. By midmorning thousands of working people had gathered near the city center to celebrate their unity and their ability to bring the city to a stop. The strike committee itself was in many ways a microcosm of the working class of Mexico City. Its ten members included two women and represented the unions of seamstresses, hat makers, carpenters, waiters, printers, commercial employees, and, of course, the electrical workers, who had initiated the strike by turning off electrical power in the city.[111] The linking of work and consumer issues was clear in the strike and served to unite working people across skill and gender lines.

The general strike was a remarkable if short-lived challenge to the new dominant forces of the revolution. General Carranza responded by inviting the strike committee to negotiate and then immediately court-martialed them for treason. Martial law further denied workers the streets and meeting halls. Characteristic of two postrevolutionary trends were Carranza's attitude toward women strikers and his invocation of nationalism: He suggested that the women on the strike committee were "overly influenced by the agitators" and ordered them released. Esther Torres, the head of the seamstresses' union, responded: "Sir, we women have the same representation and same responsibility in the strike as our comrades." Carranza answered by jailing and court-martialing them all. His comments anticipate the "protected" status that the postrevolutionary state would confer on women. Meanwhile, the official press referred to the eight men as *huelgistas* (strikers), whereas the two women on trial were simply "*mujeres complicadas*" ("confused or caught up").[112]

In addition, in his public decree of martial law, Carranza made the unlikely claim that the strikers had "responded to the instigations of North American labor unions and foreign capital."[113] Thus he invoked the nationalism and anti-imperialism that would repeatedly be used by postrevolutionary governments to demand unity from all Mexicans and especially workers.

The federation conceded defeat three days after the general strike began, as the army restored electricity and streetcar service, as other working-class leaders were rounded up by police, and as the popular support that had fueled the strike collapsed. The Casa was dissolved by a combination of direct force and armed persuasion (while a military court deliberated, Álvaro Obregón, now provisional war minister, convinced the Casa leadership to suspend all functions), and the activities of the federation were reduced for much of the next year to solidarity with the prisoners.[114]

A few months later, while a constituent assembly hammered out the country's new constitution, Mexico City was still under martial law and the Casa permanently closed. As military delegates to the Constituent Assembly debated the social charter of the constitution, they made frequent references to the July general strike and its challenge to public order. The Constitution's labor provisions, grouped under Article 123, were among the most progressive in the world at the time. They went far toward recognizing the right of workers to organize, toward regulating work conditions, and toward restricting abuses of workers by employers, but at the same time they established restrictions on any union activities that might threaten public order and put the government at the center of all negotiations between labor and capital.[115]

The labor provisions of the 1917 Constitution, the product of the alliance between the government and workers, arose in part out of the conflict between Mexico City workers and the new revolutionary leadership and reflected a cautious acknowledgment by the revolutionary elite of the previous cycle of mobilization and the relative independence of urban labor in this period.

A brief glimpse at the Mexico City rent strike of 1922 suggests the continued prominence and limits on worker and popular mobilization in Mexico City in the postrevolutionary period. The rent strike emerged from material conditions and the political context of the revolution.

The political context of 1922 was very different from that of 1916. After the dissolution of the Casa del Obrero Mundial, the working people of Mexico City began again to rebuild the union movement and assert themselves in municipal and national politics. With the legal right to organize, unions multiplied, and membership soon greatly exceeded the levels of 1916.[116] But in this effort they would have to negotiate the growing determination of the new government to mediate the social contradictions between classes.

The gap between skilled and unskilled, strategic and nonstrategic workers reemerged. Most of the textile workers in the Federal District and many skilled and strategic workers, such as the members of the Electricians Union and the streetcar workers, reorganized in anarchist and independent unions. For these workers, issues of control and participation in the workplace remained paramount. Outside the workplace, they struggled to organize autonomously from the consolidating revolutionary elite, in solidarity with other unions and occasionally around consumer issues. Many of their unions formed the Great Central Corps and then in 1921 the General Confederation of Workers (CGT), which fiercely rejected alliances with the government.[117]

By contrast, unskilled and casual workers and their leaders were more inclined to seek out political alliances. For these workers, whose position within the labor market was relatively weak, stability and regulation in the terms of employment was a fundamental concern and one of the clearest rewards of joining unions that embraced the political strategies of "multiple action." Many of Mexico City's unskilled workers made the transition to the ranks of the Mexican Confederation of Regional Workers (CROM), which was formed in 1918 under the leadership of former electrician Luis Morones and with support from federal and state political leaders. Although the CROM was truly a national confederation, its base was clearly in Mexico City.[118]

Competing factions within the revolutionary elite, particularly the tension between President Carranza and Álvaro Obregón, furthered the influence of unions that embraced political strategies. Carranza and CROM leaders remained wary of each other, but the latter were quick to embrace the upstart presidential campaign of Alvaro Obregón, even creating their own Labor party for that purpose. When

Obregón assumed the presidency after a successful military coup, the CROM leadership was in a privileged position to incorporate the majority of unions in the Federal District, mostly in the Federation of Workers' Unions of the Federal District, and to assert itself in the workplace as well as in municipal and national politics. Indeed, the prominence of labor leaders in the 1920s in appointed and elected political positions was unprecedented, and the frequency of strikes belies any description of the labor movement in this period as one of docile dependence, though many of the conflicts were between workers associated with the different confederations.[119] This was the political context that shaped the 1922 rent strike.

The dismal housing conditions in Mexico City that characterized the prerevolutionary period only worsened in the immediate aftermath of the revolution. The cost of a single room in a tenement, the typical accommodations of much of Mexico City's working population, had more than doubled from 1914 to 1921 as continued postwar inflation, a doubling of the population in Mexico City in the decade after the Mexican revolution, and a shift of capital from investments in industry and agriculture to urban real estate all increased the pressure on limited housing stock.[120] The 1921 census indicates that only 4 percent of Mexico City residents owned urban property, suggesting a high concentration of property among a city primarily of renters.[121] Conditions and potential conflicts led the Labor Department to periodically issue descriptions of the deplorable crowding, disrepair, and faulty hygiene of Mexico City tenements to newspapers, identifying the names of the landlords in hopes that embarrassment would lead them to remedy these conditions.[122]

During the revolution, provisional governments had flirted with the regulation of rents. The Convention government in Mexico City imposed a moratorium on all housing rents during the spring of 1915. In 1916 the Constitutionalist forces had imposed emergency rent freezes and limits on evictions of tenants in Mexico City and forced landlords to accept the paper currency that merchants refused. But as public order and a solid currency were restored, these measures were removed, and a series of reform measures brought before Congress were defeated. As under Porfirio Díaz, rents and housing conditions were left to the determination of the market.[123]

Mobilization of the population came in two forms. In a flurry of organization in 1916, a Renters League was formed, and over the next years it repeatedly turned to an unsympathetic judicial system to prevent evictions while fruitlessly pushing for laws in Congress to regulate the terms of low-income rentals.[124]

The radicalization of tactics of the renters movement came during the term of President Obregón. In February 1922 the Renters League transformed itself into a Renters Union and soon after moved from a legalistic approach to direct action.[125] This was primarily owing to two factors: first, the inspiration that came from the success of the renters strike that had been initiated in Veracruz one month earlier, and second, the organizational direction that came from the Communist Youth, affiliated with the recently formed Mexican Communist party (CP). The CP had participated in the formation of the anarchist CGT confederation one year earlier but soon fell out with them. With no real affiliated unions beyond the bakers' union and a segment of the railroad workers' union, the CP turned to the renters for its social base.[126]

The CP found the right issue at the right time. In addition the Communist Youth possessed an extraordinary group of inspired and indefatigable organizers. Within a month the Renters Union had 8,000 members, and by early May, over 30,000. The primary demands of the Renters Union did not differ much from earlier legal projects: They sought a decrease in rents by 25 percent; an end to security deposits; improved hygiene, plumbing, and repairs; and the creation of oversight committees to assure these conditions. What was new was their willingness to go beyond legal channels and their determination to force landlords to negotiate as a group, independent of state intervention.[127]

On May 1 the Renters Union began a rent strike, with approximately 35,000 members throughout the Federal District refusing to pay their rent. This was backed by a network of committees at the level of each tenement, block, and finally each of seven districts whose primary activities were to collectively prevent evictions by landlords. Typically as many as 5,000 angry renters would turn police evictors away or reinstall someone who had recently been evicted. In coordination with the Carpenters Union, the Renters Union used a portion of the withheld rent to implement badly needed repairs in many of the tenements. In addition, they took possession of a series of empty buildings, including a former convent, which they used as headquarters.

Participants in the rent strike were working class in the broadest sense of the word. Most participants were probably workers. This is confirmed by the level of their rents: More than 80 percent of those on strike paid less than twenty pesos a month in rent. Similarly, the greatest concentration of striking tenants was in the working-class tenement districts near the train stations, by the factory districts in the south, and east of the central plaza.[128] In spite of the clearly working-class nature of the movement, participants identified with their community rather than with their place of work. Unions themselves were only partially integrated, and although a number of anarchist unions as well as the railroad union and the Public Employees Union supported the strike, the federations they belonged to did not. The anarchist CGT considered the Renters Union to be an instrument of the Communist party and so withdrew their support during the first month of the strike. The officialist CROM federation resented all rival social groups and so after a month of uncertainty formed a Union of Renters of their own.

Another characteristic of the movement, one that further indicates ties to community rather than to work, is the role of women. The vast majority of those who attended meetings in tenements and marches in public plazas and who mobilized on a daily basis to prevent evictions were women, a pattern similar to that of the food riots and confiscations of the decade of military struggle. At the same time, the leadership of the movement was tightly held in the hands of its Communist leadership, only one of whom was a woman.[129] The CGT accusation that the Renters Union was becoming an instrument of the Communist party was justified. In spite of the apparently decentralized structure of the union, the Communist leadership tightly controlled all funds and all strategic decision making.

From May to mid-June the number of rent strikers rose to over 50,000, and the movement remained relatively united. But property owners were soon joined into a single organization dominated by the largest landlords and putting considerable pressure on the government to enforce their property rights. President Obregón, the supreme political juggler, referred the matter to local authorities, who in this case was the presidentially appointed governor of the Federal District, Celestino Gasca, a stalwart of the CROM federation and the Labor party.[130]

This differs from Carranza's response to the general strike of 1916 in two ways: In spite of massive participation in the rent strike and the involvement of key propertied interests, the conflict did not have as immediate an impact on the functioning of the city, and therefore intervention or repression was less urgent; moreover, Obregón relied much more than had Carranza on an extensive web of political alliances, and he often, by pleading deference to state jurisdiction (especially since the Federal District governor was appointed by the president), allowed matters to first be played out by local actors.

For example, in close collaboration with Governor Gasca, the rival CROM Union of Renters began to negotiate separate short-term deals with landlords, while a series of purges of key leaders of the CP furthered the distance between the leadership and tenant members in the Renters Union. In July simultaneous with the repression of the movement in Veracruz, Governor Gasca began to heavily reinforce police carrying out evictions. This forced the Renters Union into a defensive legality, as they began depositing their unpaid rents in a bank and pressing once again for a law regulating rents. By September the renters movement had virtually collapsed.[131]

The reluctance of the state to respond in an institutional fashion to renters' demands, after such an extensive mobilization, is curious and very different from the state response to labor mobilization, which was essentially to simultaneously establish guarantees and mechanisms of control and negotiation between capital and labor. Ultimately the momentum of the Renters Strike was undermined by its failure to develop clear links to unions and by the distance between its popular base and Communist leadership.[132] On the one hand, the sectarian divisions between Anarchists and Communists (echoing events in Moscow) undermined the most obvious organizational alliance among renters. On the other, the outcome of the conflict further tightened the institutional ties between the Obregón government and the CROM federation through its political arm, the Labor party.

In the aftermath of the strike, rents and housing conditions in Mexico City remained essentially unchanged.[133] Government housing policy instead turned toward sponsoring specific housing colonies on the outskirts of the city, and the first such partition was completed within a year of the defeat of the rent strike. This policy allowed successive governments to target largesse toward specific groups of organized or federal employees while also furthering the long-standing Porfirian project of restricting low-income access to the high-valued properties of the city center.[134] The demands and participation of the urban poor who lived in tenements and squatter settlements was eventually channeled into the National Congress of Popular Organizations (CNOP), one of the constituent components of the official, dominant party that was formed in 1929 and eventually transformed into the Party of the Institutional Revolution (PRI). A law regulating rents in Mexico City would not be implemented until 1942, when President Avila Camacho attempted to stem protests to war-related inflation by imposing a rent freeze in the historic center of Mexico City.[135]

Conclusion

From the late nineteenth century through the 1920s, Mexico City was transformed twice over. The first was a transformation of population, the space of the city, production, and work. Key characteristics were the dramatic growth of the city's population through migration; a physical expansion of the city that increasingly separated rich and poor; the concentration of production and infrastructure among a small group of foreign and Mexican businessmen; and a structural and cultural dichotomy between skilled and unskilled workers.

The second transformation was the result of the ideological currents, the political openings, and the material conditions of the revolution. Weakened and shifting political authority allowed workers to organize in new organizations and in unprecedented numbers. But Mexico City workers were not revolutionary in the insurrectional sense; instead, their response to the revolution was one of considerable and relatively independent mobilization. Through riots, strikes, demonstrations, and appeals to authorities, working people pursued demands that included respect from foreign bosses, improved work conditions, recognition of unions, and just prices for food and housing. Because of the structure of industry and work, their efforts were particularly significant when they joined skilled and unskilled workers, and these efforts reached beyond the workplace by focusing on consumer demands that echoed those of the popular classes. In this respect, women played an important role in establishing the link between work and community. This pattern of mobilization manifested itself soon after the start of the revolution, culminated in the general strike of 1916, and reemerged periodically afterwards.

In spite of the repression that ended the 1916 general strike, previous and ongoing mobilizations of workers and the urban poor in this period forced the faction that triumphed in the revolution to acknowledge the potential strength of workers and the poor. In addition, regional challenges to and internal rivalries within the postrevolutionary regime made the need for a social base and political allies among workers more urgent and resulted in significant reforms and an unprecedented degree of political incorporation for workers. The gains that workers made and the relative autonomy of their organizations in this period should not be underestimated.

By contrast, extensive mobilizations of urban workers and the urban poor in Brazil and Argentina in the period during and after World War I had very different results: In Argentina strikes led primarily to electoral reforms that gave workers some leverage vis-à-vis political parties; by contrast, in Brazil urban mobilizations led the political oligarchy to close ranks, neither moving toward liberal democracy nor incorporating workers into the state bureaucracy. In both countries, the massive incorporation of urban workers—into the Peronist party in Argentina or through the state bureaucracy in Brazil—would only come in the 1930s and 1940s.[136]

The earlier gains of Mexican workers can partly be explained by the structures of work, which ultimately shaped their mobilizations and political participation, and by the far deeper political crisis that was the Mexican Revolution. But in spite of these very real gains, the unprecedented participation of workers in the postrevolutionary regime tended over time to fragment the organization of working people along previous axes of skill and gender and to separate issues of work and consumption.

The paradigm for understanding this process should not be exclusively one of the manipulation and subordination of working people by the emerging revolutionary state. More appropriate to this period is a framework that takes into account continuous conflicts and accommodation, often rooted in local structures of class and power. In this process, both working people and the state were transformed. Such a framework can tell us much about the formation of an urban working class and the success and limits of political participation and reform in Mexico and in the rest of Latin America as well.

Notes

1. On the political consequences of urbanization in this period, see James Scobie, "The Growth of Latin American Cities, 1870–1930," in *The Cambridge History of Latin America,* vol. 4, ed. Leslie Bethell (Cambridge: Cambridge University Press, 1986), 261–264.

2. This cycle of general strikes is briefly summarized in Michael Hall and Hobart Spalding Jr., "The Urban Working Class and Early Latin American Labour Movements, 1880–1930," in *The Cambridge History of Latin America,* ed. Leslie Bethell, vol. 4 (Cambridge: Cambridge University Press, 1986), 355–359. For a comparative view of these crises of labor incorporation, see Jeremy Adelman, "Working-Class Incorporation and Labor Politics in Argentina, Brazil, and Mexico, 1916–1922," manuscript.

3. Frank Tannenbaum, *Peace by Revolution: Mexico After 1910* (New York: Columbia University Press, 1966); Alan Knight, *The Mexican Revolution* (Cambridge: Cambridge University Press, 1986); John Mason Hart, *Revolutionary Mexico: The Coming and Process of the Mexican Revolution* (Berkeley and Los Angeles: University of California Press, 1987).

The classic revisionist accounts are John Womack Jr., "The Mexican Revolution, 1910–1920," in Bethell, *The Cambridge History of Latin America,* vol. 5, 80; and Ramón Eduardo Ruiz, *The Great Rebellion: Mexico 1905–1924* (New York: Norton, 1980).

4. Adolfo Gilly calls the written pact from which the Red Battalions emerged "the birth certificate of the union 'charros' (cowboys)," using the term that emerged in the 1940s to refer to labor bosses corrupted by government financial or political manipulation; *La revolución interrumpida, México 1910–1920* (Mexico City: Ediciones El Caballito, 1974), 183.

5. A few examples are Rosendo Salazar and José Escobedo, *Las pugnas de la gleba* (Mexico City: Editorial Avante, 1922); Luis Araiza, *Historia del movimiento obrero Mexicano* (Mexico City: Ediciones Casa del Obrero, 1975); Jacinto Huitrón, *Orígenes e historia del movimiento obrero en México* (Mexico City: Editores Mexicanos Unidos, 1984); Marjorie Ruth Clark, *Organized Labor in Mexico* (Durham: University of North Carolina Press, 1934).

6. See important pioneering works by Barry Carr, *El movimiento obrero y la política en México, 1910–1929* (Mexico City: ERA, 1981); Ramón Ruiz, *Labor and the Ambivalent Revolutionaries* (Baltimore: Johns Hopkins University Press, 1976); Rocío Guadarrama, *Los sindicatos y la política en México: la CROM* (Mexico City: ERA, 1981).

7. David Harvey, *Consciousness and the Urban Experience: Studies in the History and Theory of Capitalist Urbanization* (Baltimore: Johns Hopkins University Press, 1985), 165.

8. "Entrevista con la Señora Esther Torres, viuda de Morales, realizado por Maria Isabel Souza y Carmen Nava, los dias 13 y 25 de febrero de 1975 en la ciudad de Mexico," PHO/1/145. Archivo de la Palabra, Instituto Mora; and Jorge Basurto, oral interview published in *Vivencias femeninas de la revolución* (Mexico: INEHRM, 1992), 52–53.

9. Huitrón, *Orígenes,* 73–84.

10. Unless otherwise noted, data in this section on the composition of the workforce are from the three *Censo de Población,* Distrito Federal, 1895, 1900, 1910, and elaborated in John Lear, "Workers, Vecinos, and Citizens: The Revolution in Mexico City 1909–1917," (Ph.D. diss., University of California, Berkeley, 1993), chap. 2, tables 2.2–2.8.

11. Stephan Haber, *Industry and Underdevelopment: The Industrialization of Mexico, 1890–1940* (Stanford: Stanford University Press, 1989).

12. Jorge E. Hardoy, "Two Thousand Years of Latin American Urbanization," in *Urbanization in Latin America,* ed. Jorge E. Hardoy (New York: Anchor, 1975), 46.

13. Gilberto Loyo, "Notas sobre La Evolución Demográfica de la Ciudad de México," *Boletín de la Sociedad Mexicana de Geografia y Estadística* 45 (1933): 211–250. For a discussion of the Porfirian growth of Mexico City as a recovery of colonial predominance, see Alejandra Moreno Toscano, "Patrones de Urbanización en Mexico," *Historia Mexicana* 22:185; and idem. with Enrique Florescano, *El Sector Externo y la Organizacion Espacial y Regional de México (1522–1910)* (Mexico City: INAH, 1974), and Richard Boyer in "Las Ciudades Mexicanas," *Historia Mexicana,* V. 22:142–159.

14. See the background of early leadership in Araiza, *Historia,* vol. 3, 110, 168, 184; Rosendo Salazar, *Lideres y Sindicatos* (Mexico: Costa Amie, 1953).

15. *Censo de Población,* Distrito Federal, 1895, 1900, 1910 and elaboration in Lear, "Workers," chap. 2, table 2.2.

16. Knight, *Mexican Revolution,* vol. 1, 133.

17. Archivo General de la Nación, Fondo Ramo Trabajo (hereafter AGN, RT), "Lista de industrias establecidas en el Distrito Federal, 1921," box 279: Expediente 5; Haber, *Industry,* 50.

18. This pattern of female segregation is discussed in Verana Radkau, "*La fama*" *y la vida: Una fábrica y sus obreras* (Cuadernos de la casa chata, CIESAS, 1984), 28 and confirmed in

data provided in Cuestionario Censo Industrial y Obrero, textiles, AGN, RT, 288:12; tobacco: Cuestionario para el Censo Obrero, La Tabacalera in AGN, RT, 292:13 (1921); and Buen Tono in 211:17 (1920) and 418:4 (1923); "Entrevista con la Señora Esther Torres."

19. From 1895 to 1910, the number of Mexico City artisanal workers dropped from 1,712 to 686 in cigarette production and from 3,530 to 1,638 in weaving; *Censo de Población*, Distrito Federal, 1895, 1900, 1910. During the same period nationally, the number of artisanal cigarette makers dropped from 10,397 to 6,893, and of weavers from 41,000 to 12,000; Haber, *Industry*, 50, 58.

20. Ira Katznelson, drawing examples from the work of William Sewell, makes the point that the divisions between factory and craft workers have often been overstated. Ira Katznelson, "Working Class Formation and the State: Nineteenth-century England in American Perspective," in *Bringing the State Back In*, ed. Peter Evans, Dietrich Rueschemeyer, and Theda Skocpol (Cambridge: Cambridge University Press, 1985), 264. In his study of Guadalajara, Rodney Anderson suggests that "One trade-proletarianization may be another trade-opportunity"; Rodney Anderson, "Guadalajara's Artisans and Shopkeepers," in *Five Centuries of Mexican History*, ed. Virginia Guedea and Jaime Rodriguez O. (Mexico: Instituto Mora, 1992), vol. 2, 286–299.

21. *Censo de Población,* Distrito Federal, 1910. The number of child factory workers is based on a sample of seven textile factories and three tobacco factories in the early 1920s: Textiles: Cuestionario Censo Industrial y Obrero AGN, RT, 288:12; tobacco: Cuestionario para el Censo Obrero, La Tabacalera in AGN, RT, 292:13 (1921); and Buen Tono in 211:17 (1920) and 418:4 (1923).

22. Carlos Illades, *Hacia la república del trabajo: La organización artesanal en la ciudad de México, 1853–1876* (Mexico City: Colegio de México, 1996); Frederick Shaw, "The Artisan in Mexico City," in *El trabajo y los trabajadores,* ed. Elsa Frost et al. (Mexico City: Colegio de México, 1979), 400.

23. Fernando Rosenzweig, "La Industria, " in *El Porfiriato: Vida Economica,* ed. Daniel Cosío Villegas, *Historia Moderna de Mexico*, vol. 7, part 1, 349; Censo Zapatarias, AGN, RT, 290:6, 290:7.

24. "Censo Fabril," *Boletín de industría, comercio y trabajo* 1, no. 2 (August 1918): 9–11.

25. *Censo de Población,* Distrito Federal, 1895, 1900, 1910 and elaboration in Lear, "Workers," chap. 2, table 2.2.

26. Traditional artisanal settings and incipient changes in mid-nineteenth-century Mexico City are analyzed in Illades, *Hacia la república*, chap. 1.

27. *Nueva Era*, 26 January, 1913, reprinted in Araiza, *Historia*, vol. 3, 26.

28. On Mexican Light Company employment in 1924, see AGN, RT, 772:1; Miguel Rodriguez, *Los Tranviarios y el Anarquismo en México* (Mexico, 1980), 11; Nonoalco shop listed in "Censo Fabril," *Boletín de Industría, Comercio y Trabajo* 1, no 2: 9–11.

29. This pattern is best exemplified by workers of the Mexican Light Company. See Victor Manuel Sánchez Sánchez, *Surgimiento del Sindicalismo Electricista* (Mexico City: UNAM, 1978).

30. Lear, "Workers," chap. 2, table 2.4.

31. Julio Guerrero, *La génisis del crimen en México* (Paris: Viudade Che Bouret, 1901), 158–180, reproduced in *Memoria y encuntros, La ciudad de Méxcio y el Distrito Federal,* ed. Hira Gortari Rabiela and Regina Hernandez Franyuti (Mexico: Instituto Mora, 1988), vol. 33, 369.

32. Ayuntamiento report on domestic servants, Archivo Histórico de la Ciudad de México (hereafter AHCM), 3645, ex. 1711.

33. Jorge Basurto, oral interview with Esther Torres, published in *Vivencias femeninas de la revolución* (Mexico: INEHRM, 1992).

34. *El Imparcial*, Nov. 18, 1911; Julio Sesto, *México de Porfirio Díaz* (Valencia: Sempre, 1910), 129, 132.

35. Sesto, *México,* 134; Wallace Thompson, *The People of Mexico* (New York: Harper, 1921), 342, 356–362. On unpaid child labor, see, for example, an inspector's report in 1921 of the factory La Victoria, with 52 children and 296 adults. The inspector was told that the children "son ayudantes quienes acompañan a sus padres o parientes ellas son los que pagan a este grupo"; AGN, RT, Censo Obrero 288:12.

36. Semanario de Historia Moderna, *Estadísticas económicas del Porfiriato: Fuerza de trabajo y actividad económica por sectores* (Mexico City: Colegio de México), 156–157; Rodney Anderson, *Outcasts in Their Own Land* (Dekalb: Northern Illinois University Press, 1976), 64–65.

37. Thompson, *The People*, 361–362.

38. Lanny Thompson, "Artisan Marginals and Proletarians: The Households of the Popular Classes in Mexico City, 1876–1950," in Guedea and Rodriguez, *Five Centuries of Mexican History*, vol. 2, 307–324.

39. Semanario de Historia Moderna, *Estadísticas Económicas,* 108; on job requests and placements, see AGN, RT, 31:4; useful descriptions of the urban labor market can be found in Sesto, *México,* 131; Adolfo Dollero, *México al Día* (Mexico City: Bouret, 1911),12; John Kenneth Turner, *Barbarous Mexico* (Austin: University of Texas Press, 1969), 99.

40. The rural and urban roots are suggested by specific biographies, observers such as Julio Guerrero, *La Genesis*, and a small but suggestive sample of judicial cases for male workers. For example, over 68 percent of bricklayers in these cases were from outside of the Federal District, whereas only 11 percent of electricians were. Of course, not all migrants to the Federal District were from rural areas, and their numbers are high among some skilled groups such as tailors (57 percent). Illiteracy rates in the same sample ranged from 81 percent for bricklayers to complete literacy for printers; based on data from "Noticia de los obreros penados por los jueces de la Ciudad de México," June, July, August, 1913, AGN, RT, 25:5.

41. Huitrón, *Orígenes*, 77, 226.

42. Basurto, *Vivencias*, 18, 54.

43. An example of the importance to women of religious observance is the history of the textile worker Doña Justa, profiled in Radkau, "*La fama*"; the rural setting of the town of Tlalpan may have made rural origins and religious influence stronger, but even in the urban setting of the Buen Tono tobacco factory, which employed mostly women, the factory chapel and religious societies remained important as late as 1922; See AGN, RT, 672:20.

44. Illades, *Hacia la república.*

45. William Sewell Jr., "Social Change and the Rise of Working-Class Politics in Nineteenth-Century Marseille," *Past and Present* 65 (November 1974): 82.

46. These patterns are described and analyzed in John Lear, "Mexico City: Space and Class in the Porfirian Capital (1884–1910)," *Journal of Urban History* (May 1996): 454–492.

47. Miguel Macedo, *La criminalidad en México* (Mexico City: Secretaría de Fomento, 1897), 60.

48. For examples of such measures, see Lear, "Mexico City," 479–481; William Beezley, *Judas at the Jockey Club and Other Episodes of Porfirian Mexico* (Lincoln: University of Nebraska Press, 1987), 112–115, 128.

49. The Porfirian policing of and resistance by Mexico City's popular classes is described in Pablo Piccato, "Criminals in Mexico City, 1900–1931: A Cultural History" (Ph.D. diss., University of Texas at Austin, in process), chap. 1.

50. *México Obrero,* "Por Qué Postulamos al Sr. Gral. Bernardo Reyes," first half of September, 1909.

51. "Flowing Oratory at Bustling Madero Rally," *Mexican Herald,* May 2, 1910.

52. Working-class public demonstrations during the Revolution are discussed more fully in John Lear, "Del mutualismo a la resistencia: Las organizaciones laborales en la Ciudad de México," in *Ciudad de México: instituciones, actores sociales, y conflicto politico, 1774–1931,* ed. Carlos Illades and Ariel Kuri (Mexico: Universidad Autonoma Metropolitana–El Colegio de Michoacan, 1995).

53. On mutual aid societies and their government ties, see Anderson, *Outcasts,* 228–232; David Walker, "Porfirian Labor Politics: Working Class Organizations in Mexico City and Porfirio Diaz, 1876–1902," *The Americas* 37, no. 3 (1981): 257–289.

54. On worker politics and Madero, see Rodney Anderson, "Mexican Workers and the Politics of Revolution, 1906–1911," *Hispanic American Historical Review* 54 (1974): 94–113.

55. "La gran manifestación popular del Viernes," *Juan Panadero,* 28 May, 1911.

56. John Lear, "La XXVI Legislatura y los trabajadores de la ciudad de México (1912–1913)," in *Poder Legislativo en las décadas revolucionarias,* ed. Pablo Piccato (Mexico City: Instituto Nacional de Historia de la Revolución Mexicana, forthcoming).

57. "Agrupaciones Obreras," 1912, AGN, RT, 14:12.

58. On the divisions within the confederation, see Fernando Córdova Pérez, "El movimiento anarquista en México (1911–1921)" (B.A. thesis, Facultad de Ciencias Políticas y Sociales, UNAM, Mexico City, 1971), 18–21; John M. Hart, *Anarchism and the Mexican Working Class, 1869–1931* (Austin: University of Texas Press, 1978), chap. 8; Lear, "Del mutualismo," 14–15.

59. Huitrón, *Orígenes,* 207.

60. "Los monopolios y la huelga," *El Obrero Mexicano,* 24 November, 1911.

61. "A los Canteros de la Capital," reprinted in Huitrón, *Orígenes,* 197.

62. Attempts to create workers cooperatives are discussed in Lear, "Del mutualismo." For examples of representative cooperative projects, on the foundry cooperative, see "El cooperativismo es acogido con entusiasmo entre los obreros del gremio de fundidores y moldeadores," *El Obrero Mexicano,* 3 November, 1911. The proposals for the housing and agricultural cooperatives are outlined in AGN, RT, 41:26 and 78:3, and for the printing cooperative in "Estatutos de la Confederación Tipográfica de México," printed in *El Radical,* 8 July, 1911.

63. The formation of the Casa del Obrero Mundial is best recounted in Hart, *Anarchism*; Córdova Pérez, "El movimiento"; Huitrón, *Origenes*; Salazar and Escobedo, *Las pugnas;* Araiza, *Historia.*

64. The political challenge to Huerta stemmed as much from the collaboration of Casa leaders with opposition members of Congress such as Heriberto Jara as with the specific work-related demands. The organization of the first May Day against the wishes of Huerta is described in Lear, "Del mutualismo."

65. Hart, *Anarchism,* 118–125; Michael Meyer, *Huerta: A Political Portrait* (Lincoln: University of Nebraska Press, 1972), 174–175; Araiza, *Historia,* vol. 3, 42.

66. Víctor Manuel Sánchez Sánchez, *Surgimiento del Sindicalismo Electricista* (Mexico: UNAM, 1978), 139–166; Huitrón, *Orígenes,* 253.

67. AGN, RT, 70:27; 14:12; 86:27.

68. *El Demócrata,* 12 October, 1914.

69. Huitrón, *Orígenes,* 242–254.

70. Ibid., 253–255; see also the same membership reported in *Mexican Herald,* February 12, 1915.

71. Here I refer to the decision in February 1915 by Constitutionalist authorities to end a strike by turning the management of the Mexican Telephone and Telegraph Company over to the Electricians Union; Sánchez Sánchez, *Surgimiento,* 168–183.

72. AGN, RT, 70:14: 6:6; 52:1; 97:2.

73. The eight-hour day was the central demand of the various workers' organizations who participated in the first May Day in 1913; see Huitrón, *Orígenes,* 230; Salazar and Escobedo, *Las pugnas,* 63; Araiza, *Historia,* vol. 3, 39.

74. *La Convención,* March 27, 1915. See, for example, the concern for gaining "*personalidad juridica*" in *El empleado mutualista* Año 6, no. 32 (October-December 1914); "Agrupaciones obreras," (1912), AGN, RT, 14:12; and "Cuestionario a las asociaciones," (1918) AGN, RT, 128:25, 29, 37, 40.

75. Lear, "La XXVI Legislatura."

76. See, for example, worker demands (1913 and 1914) for housing, AGN, RT, 41:26, 78:3, and the purchase of food, AGN, RT, 96:9.

77. "Peticiones de la Casa del Obrero Mundial," *El demócrata,* October 3, 1914; see also the Casa-organized march of the unemployed, "Al pueblo obrero," *El Pueblo,* October 3, 1914.

78. For an influential discussion of women's mobilization in early-twentieth-century Barcelona, see Temma Kaplan, who argues that "female consciousness" is the "consistent defense of their right to feed and protect their communities either with the support of government or without it"; Temma Kaplan, "Female Consciousness and Collective Action," *Signs: Journal of Women in Culture and Society* 7 (1982): 31.

79. On food riots and confiscations, see especially the extensive events recorded in *El Combate,* July 25, 1915; AHCM 3645, ex. 1761. See convention debates on riots in *El Renovador,* July 1, 1915.

80. See union meetings and leaders' speeches on riots in *El Combate,* June 25, 1915.

81. See John Lear, "Women, Work, and Urban Mobilization During the Mexican Revolution" (paper presented at the International Congress of the Latin American Studies Association, Atlanta, Georgia, March 10–12, 1994).

82. The *Mexican Herald* puts the number of workers in the Battalions at 3,000, plus an estimated 2,000 tramway workers, March 2, 3, 1915. Other historians' estimates range from 5,000 (Womack, "The Mexican Revolution") to 7,000 (Barry Carr, "The Casa del Obrero Mundial, Constitutionalism, and the Pact of February 1915," in *El trabajo y los trabajadores en la historia de México,* ed. Elsa Frost [Mexico City: Colegio de Mexico, 1979], 603–633) to a high of 10,000 (John M. Hart, *Revolutionary Mexico* [Berkeley and Los Angeles: University of California Press, 1987], 307).

83. The best account of the circumstances of the signing of the Pact is Carr, "The Casa del Obrero"; see also Adolfo Gilly, *La revolución interrumpida,* 183; Jean Meyer, "Los obreros en la Revolución Mexicana: Los 'Batallones Rojos,'" *Historia Mexicana* 21, no. 1 (1971): 1–37; Sánchez Sánchez, *Surgimiento,* 121–138.

84. John Womack Jr., "Luchas sindicales y liberalismo social," in *Libertad y justicia en las sociedades modernas* (Mexico City: Grupo Editorial Miguel Angel Porrua, 1994), 332–333.

85. Illades, *Hacía la república*, 115–153; Richard Warren, "The Will of the Nation: Political Participation in Mexico, 1808–1836" (paper presented at the Seventeenth International Congress of the Latin American Studies Association, Los Angeles, September 1992).

86. Araiza, *Historia*, vol. 3, 65–67.

87. Carr, "The Casa del Obrero."

88. The strength of Mexico City unions under the Convention is noted in Womack, "The Mexican Revolution," 112, 118. For Convention labor policy, see the debates over the Labor Law pushed through the Convención by Mendez and Diaz Soto y Gama in *La Convención*, March 27, 1915. Strike activity was greatest among textile, telephone, and electrical workers and shop employees, as noted in *La Convención*, May 4, 13, 17, 1915; *El Combate*, June 26, 1915; *El Radical*, March 26–April 29, 1915; Sánchez Sánchez, *Surgimiento*, 167–237.

89. The rivalries between the Casa-organized provincial unions and "*agrupaciones de resistencia*" sponsored by Carranza and the Department of Labor are discussed in Bernardo Garcia Díaz, "Orizaba, 1915," *Historias* 8–9 (January-June 1985): 91–109.

90. On the unification of streetcar workers, see *Ariete*, November 7, 1916. A partial reconciliation between the Casa and the Electricians Union came only in early December 1915, paving the way for the formation of the FOSDF; see *Ariete*, December 5, 1915. Zapatistas welcomed back by the Casa include Luis Mendez and Octavio Jahn; AHCM 3857.

91. "Entrevista con la Señora Esther Torres," p. 22.

92. Interview with Esther Torres in Basurto, *Vivencias*, 58.

93. "Declaracion de Principios de la 'Federación de Sindicatos Obreros del Distrito Federal,'" reproduced in Araiza, *Historia*, vol. 3, 115–116.

94. At this meeting, the Casa also formally offered to help military authorities distribute food in municipal *expendios; El Demócrata*, August 24, 1915.

95. Araiza, *Historia*, vol. 3, 112; Salazar, *Lideres*, 151.

96. Pablo González, *Informe que el general de divsion Pablo Gonazalez, rinde al C. Venustiano Carranza* (Mexico, 1915), 56.

97. Marcos López Jimenez, director of the Department of Labor, to David Galindo (April 16, 1915), cited in Carr, "The Casa del Obrero," 627.

98. *El Demócrata*, January 19, 1916, reproduced in Sánchez Sánchez, *Surgimiento*, 274.

99. Study by Eduardo Fuentes, in Condumex archive, Fondo 21, L 5861, Carpeta 53, p. 22; for a more moderate estimate of production losses, see Womack, "The Mexican Revolution," 86.

100. Fuentes, in Condumex archive, pp. 23–33.

101. AGN, RT, Censo Panaderias (1921), 397:2; 291:16; the Compañía Mexicana Molinera de Nixtamal owned ninety-one mills listed in the 1921 Censo Molinos de Nixtamal AGN, RT, 173:12.

102. Womack, "The Mexican Revolution," 133.

103. Edwin W. Kemmerer, *Inflation and Revolution: Mexico's Experience of 1912–1917* (Princeton: Princeton University Press, 1940), 45–46.

104. Alan Knight argues: "The frequent strikes of these years, at first sight indications of labour militancy, attuned to the 'revolutionary' temper of the times, were in fact desperate attempts to prevent living standards falling too far, even below subsistence"; Alan Knight, "The Working Class and the Mexican Revolution, c. 1900–1920," *Journal of Latin American Studies* 16 (1984): 76.

105. AHCM, 522:65, 3855:30, 3857; Huitrón, *Orígines*, 291.

106. The Casa organized employees of the Ayuntamiento *expendios* of basic foods on April 8, 1916 (these were different from the Casa-run bakeries). See AHCM 3857; 3853:11; 3855.

107. Kemmerer, *Inflation and Revolution*, 94–101, appendix, 147–148.

108. See the military interrogation of the strike committee, Archivo Condumex, fondo 21, 90–91:10100: Araiza describes similar channels of accountability, Araiza, *Historia*, vol. 3, 140.

109. AGN, RT, 75:15; Salazar and Escobedo, *La pugnas*, 200; by contrast to the June strike, the FSODF on July 24, 1916, made vague warnings without specific ultimatums or deadlines, an issue brought up by authorities in the judicial process. Archivo Condumex, fondo 21, 76–89:9953 and 90–91:10100.

110. *El Pueblo*, July 27, 1916, reproduced in Sánchez Sánchez, *Surgimiento*, 338–339.

111. Araiza, *Historia*, vol. 3, 138–172; *El Demócrata*, August 4, 1916; *El Pueblo*, August 3, 1916.

112. Araiza, *Historia*, vol. 3, 144; *El Demócrata*, August 5, 1916.

113. *El Pueblo*, August 3, 1916.

114. Araiza, *Historia*, vol. 3, 38–172; Hart, *Anarchism*, 51–55; *El Demócrata*, August 4, 1916; *El Pueblo*, August 3, 1916.

115. *Diario de los debates del Congreso Constituyente*, 1916–1917, vol. 2 (Mexico City: Ediciones de la Comisión Nacional para la celebración del Sesquincentenario de la proclamación de la Independencia Nacional y del Cinquintenario de la Revolución Mexicana, 1960), 846–858.

116. Marjorie Ruth Clark, *La organización obrera en México* (Mexico City: ERA, 1979), 56.

117. José Rivera Castro, "Le syndicalisme officiel et le syndicalisme revolutionnaire au Mexique dans les annees 1920," *Le Mouvement Social* 103 (1978): 31–53; Mario Camarena, "Disciplina e indisciplina: Los obreros textiles del valle de México en los años viente," *Historias* 7 (1984): 3–15.

118. Morones was unable to bring the Electricians Union into the CROM. On the strength of the Federal District workers within the CROM, see Clark, *La organización obrera*, 50–62.

119. Ibid., 50–62.

120. AGN, RT, 499:4; Moisés Gonzalez Navarro, *Población y Sociedad en México* (Mexico City: Colegio de México, 1974), 188.

121. *Censo de Población*, 1921.

122. AGN, RT, 324:20 and 227:5, 223:10 (June 1, 1920).

123. *El Renovador*, July 9, 1916; Gonzalez Navarro, *Población*, 189.

124. Interestingly, the project was supported by the Partido Nacional Agrarista rather than the rival Partido Laborista; Gonzalez Navarro, *Población*, 189–190.

125. Erica Berra, "La expansion de la ciudad de México y los conflictos urbanos" (Ph.D. Diss., Colegio de Mexico, 1982), 500.

126. Jose Valadés, *Memorias de un joven rebelde*, (Culiacan, Mexico: Universidad Autónoma de Sonora, 1986), vol. 2, 123–126; Paco Ignacio Taibo II, *Los Bolshevikis: Historia narrativa de los orígenes del comunismo en México* (Mexico: Editorial Joaquín Mortiz, 1987), 164.

127. Gonzalez Navarro, *Población*, 189–190; Taibo, *Los Bolshevikis*, 169–170.

128. Taibo, *Los Bolshevikis*, 172.

129. Berra, "La expansion," 526.

130. AGN Ramo Presidentes Obregón-Calles 805-c–318:3; Valadés, *Memorias*, 126.

131. Taibo, *Los Bolshevikis*, 180–181; AGN Ramo Presidentes Obregón-Calles 731-I–5:17.

132. See Taibo, *Los Bolshevikis*, 175.

133. AGN, RT, 601:2 (rents in 1923)

134. Gonzalez Navarro, *Población*, 198.

135. Ibid., 191.

136. Jeremy Adelman, "Working-Class Incorporation and Labor Politics in Argentina, Brazil, and Mexico, 1916–1922," manuscript.

4

Viva La Revolución Social! Postrevolutionary Tenant Protest and State Housing Reform in Veracruz, Mexico

Andrew Grant Wood

Together with the great irregularities charged against the misgovernment reigning in Veracruz, which seriously affect the industrial prosperity of the State, we must note others, however, which deal with actual anarchy, and which signify an insult, not only for Veracruz, but for the Republic. We refer to the scandalous abuses committed in the Port. That singular and queer syndicate of renters established there, does not limit itself to not paying rent; it has organized itself into a State within a State.

—*El Universal, July 23, 1923*

Only the red city, red as always, kept its aggressive spirit awake.

—*José Mancisidor*

After a visit to the port of Veracruz in mid-1923, *New York Times* reporter Mildred Campagne Moore wrote: "Two years ago, occupying a little house in Veracruz with his wife, his mother and two children, [Herón Proal] became dissatisfied with living conditions, and declared that he was paying too much rent." Proal's landlord, she continued,

> refused to lower the rent or to make certain repairs that Proal demanded, whereupon Proal stopped paying rent. About the same time, a man, who, I am told, was a stevedore for the Ward Line, a young man of 30, met Proal and agreed with him that housing conditions were bad and the rents too high. The two shouted their grievance to a ready audience throughout Veracruz with the result that the stevedore is today the Mayor of the city and the tailor is the leader of 45,000 revolutionists who have

> banded themselves into a society for what they call "The Ideal Socialism for the Betterment of the Working Man." Red flags fly today from hundreds of windows and when a house is not dignified with windows, the occupants display the crimson banner on the roof or at the door.[1]

Moore's account, though celebrating the bold actions of residents in the port, raises two main questions: Under what historical conditions did such an urban protest take shape, and what positive influence, if any, did the mobilization achieve?

The Veracruz rent strike got its start in early 1922 when a small group of angry prostitutes in the La Huaca neighborhood quit paying rent.[2] They quickly found thousands of other tenants throughout the city, many of them women, willing to join a strike. Coming out of the crowded Veracruz neighborhoods and off the waterfront docks where workers had been informed by the radical tradition of *magonismo*, renters soon founded the Revolutionary Syndicate of Tenants, led by charismatic anarchist Herón Proal.[3] As thousands refused to pay their landlords, they started a social protest that quickly spread to several other cities in the state, including Orizaba (as well as nearby towns of Río Blanco, Santa Rosa, and Nogales), Córdoba, Soledad de Doblado, Minatitlán, Puerto México (Coatzalcoalcos), Tierra Blanca, Tuxpan, and the capital, Jalapa.

Regularly parading through the Veracruz city streets, protesters shouted slogans of "pro-communism," "anarchism," and "death to the Spanish landlords," all the while hanging red and black flags in their wake. During the height of the movement, they kept a keen watch on the actions of landlords, rent collectors, police, and politicians. The impassioned speeches of tenant leaders captured the attention of the nation. Despite several attempts to repress the movement, including a violent confrontation between strikers and federal forces in the port of Veracruz on July 6, 1922, renters continued to press local, regional, and national elites for urban reforms.

Across Mexico, tenants also organized strikes in Mexico City, Guadalajara, Puebla, San Luis Potosí, Mazatlán, Monterrey, Tampico, Torreón, Durango, Aguascalientes, and Ciudad Juárez. Strikers interfered with landlords' evictions, participated in marches, and attended dramatic open-air meetings. At this time, tenant action constituted an autonomous cycle of urban protest that challenged the idea that national leaders had produced the kind of progressive changes promised in the 1917 Constitution. Tenant action in several Mexican cities in the early 1920s constituted an urban rebellion against the new revolutionary order.

Renters in Veracruz distinguished themselves as the only grassroots protest to help bring about the passage of significant state housing reform in Mexico during the 1920s. Although the Gulf states of Campeche and Yucatán had approved similar measures a few years prior to the Veracruz reform, these initiatives had been decreed "from above" rather than being influenced by statewide urban protest.[4] Tenant achievements in Veracruz are also unique in that residents in other urban areas complained of similar problems in rental housing and saw comparable (although less sustained) kinds of mobilization but encouraged little or no legislative action resulting in reform.[5]

From Moore's description, it appears as if the tenant strike began almost spontaneously, as if protest represented the necessary consequence of poor housing conditions and high rents. Yet though housing in the port certainly left much to be desired, a focus on emerging political opportunity rather than on accumulated grievances helps explain why tenant protest took shape in Veracruz when it did. Critical to an understanding of tenant mobilization is the influence of Veracruz governor Adalberto Tejeda and his political allies. After taking office in late 1920 Tejeda attempted to gain legitimacy and popular support independent of Mexico's central government by courting labor, tenant, and peasant groups in the state.[6] The Veracruz protest took shape, in other words, not simply because of grassroots activism but in conjunction with new political opportunities shaped by the Tejeda administration.[7] Explaining the fact that the Veracruz state government sponsored legislative action meant to realize urban housing reform must necessarily focus on the relationship between Tejeda and tenant organizing. Here the interaction between political elites and popular groups in 1920s Veracruz tells us much about the institutionalization of the Mexican Revolution. Contrary to the picture painted in official histories that sketch a unified, more democratic Mexico under the administrations of Álvaro Obregón, Plutarco Elías Calles, and later Lázaro Cárdenas or in revisionist interpretations that paint the rise of a postrevolutionary Leviathan state cynically unresponsive to peasants and workers, the Veracruz tenant movement stands as a case where a protracted negotiation between elites and popular groups took place.

To understand the way tenants mobilized in the 1920s, one must first appreciate the urban development of Veracruz and the formation of a new working class who came from neighboring rural areas, towns, and overseas to the city's popular neighborhoods around the turn of the century. Those drawn to the port at this time gradually established a complex web of new social relations. Critical in this process was the establishment of *patios de vecindad* (tenements) in Veracruz.

Birth of the *Patio*: The Rise of the *Porteño* Popular Classes

Until the last third of the nineteenth century, Veracruz was a relatively small town despite its status as Mexico's premier port. Vulnerability to epidemic disease (especially yellow fever) and foreign attack created a particularly difficult physical environment. Only those required to realize specific commercial, bureaucratic, or military tasks lived there. Most quickly escaped the port's challenging environment and made for higher ground.[8]

Economic development during the Porfiriato (the period of the Díaz administrations: 1876–1880, 1884–1911) marked the beginning of a new chapter in the

TABLE 4.1 Population of Port of Veracruz, 1878–1930

Year	*Source*	*Population*
1878	H.W. Bates[a]	10,000
1880	N. Wineburgh[a]	15,000
1882	Charles W. Zaremba[a]	16,720
1882	Lorenzo Castro[a]	20,000
1890	National census	18,200
1900	National census	29,164
1910	National census	48,633
1921	National census	54,225
1930	National census	67,801

[a] Estimated

SOURCES: Keith A. Davies, "Tendencias demográficas urbanas durante el siglo XIX en México," *Historia Mexicana* 21, no. 3 (January–March 1972); National Census, 1921, 1930.

city's history. In 1873 officials inaugurated the recently completed Mexico City–Veracruz railroad, opening Veracruz to new social, political, and cultural forces. Activity in textile and sugar production led to considerable economic dynamism in the region.[9] Growing commercial activity in the port attracted a variety of migrants from inside the state. According to civil registry records, many came from rural areas along the coast and from the neighboring cities of Jalapa, Orizaba, and Córdoba as well as from the smaller towns of Tlacotalpan, Soledad de Doblado, Medellín, and Alvarado.[10] Many of the port's new residents also came from overseas, particularly Spain.

The establishment of the Compañia Transatlántica Española in 1886 helped make Veracruz Mexico's most popular residence for Spaniards after Mexico City.[11] At this time many other foreigners, including a number of Germans and Cubans, settled in Veracruz. (See Table 4.1.)[12]

Between 1877 and 1910 the population of Veracruz increased nearly fivefold, making it one of the Mexico's fastest-growing cities during the Porfiriato.[13] As migration stimulated a demand for urban land, Veracruz rapidly expanded its city limits. In the mid-1880s residents demolished the wall that had once marked the outer boundary of the Spanish town, and rapid urbanization took place toward the southeast and northeast borders of the city. In particular, popular neighborhoods that had once existed outside the city wall, such as La Huaca and Caballo Muerto, filled with many recent immigrants.

The demographic boom in the late nineteenth century gave rise to what would become the most common form of tenement housing in Veracruz: the *patio de vecindad*. Similar to the *casa de vecindad* in Mexico City, the *conventillos* of Buenos Aires and Santiago, or the *corticos* of Rio de Janeiro and São Paulo, *patios* consisted of a number of small rooms centered around a common courtyard where basic cooking and bathing facilities were located. Although the exact number is uncertain, by 1910 dozens of these tenements dotted the Veracruz landscape.[14] Known by names such as La Industria, San Antonio, La Angelita, La Palma, El Paseo, La Lima, and San Salvador, *patios* represented the meeting places for a complex regional network of social, cultural, and political life. From the *patios* and popular neighborhoods of the port would emerge a number of important local developments during the early twentieth century, including the Cuban-derived music of *danzón*, the revival of Carnival, and the Veracruz tenant movement.[15]

Like many cities in a process of rapid expansion, Veracruz soon experienced a housing shortage. Tenements in the city's popular neighborhoods became increasingly crowded. Because of these conditions, many in the city, including the inhabitants themselves, referred to the *patios* as *cuchitriles* (hovels) or *pocilgas* (pigsties). Most of these structures had been slapped together with old wood, tin, stone, and other found materials. Often rooms lacked doors and flooring. Some of the larger *patios* housed as many as 200 men, women, and children; on average, sixty or seventy people shared limited bathing and cooking facilities.[16] To make matters worse, frequent bouts with epidemic disease in the port added to the already abysmal condition of the *patios*.[17]

In early November 1920, for example, the port's conservative daily newspaper, *El Dictamen*, printed an editorial that offered an intimate portrait of the living conditions during the yellow fever epidemic that year. Clearly, their discussion of the epidemic expressed a distinct fear of contagion emanating from the tenements. "The *patios*," the author began, "primarily found in the neighborhoods outside the city center . . . do not only leave much to be desired in terms of public health . . . some of them are downright uninhabitable."[18] The author then offered additional details describing the lack of sanitation in the tenements:

> Inhabitants make use of toilets that are old-fashioned at best or simply holes dug in the ground. Urinals are unknown. Dirty water from cooking or washing is simply thrown into the courtyard or the street, where waste from the toilets also drains. Since the garbage is collected infrequently, unwanted materials tend to accumulate inside the patio, thereby creating a dangerous health environment for residents and neighbors. . . . (I)n sum, the hygienic condition of the city's tenements is miserable.[19]

A similar exposé printed around the same time reinforces the perception that the condition of the *patios* represented a dangerous threat to city residents. This article asserted that "the sanitation of the tenements is the most important issue of public health in the city."[20] Unsanitary conditions, the editorial stated, arose from the fact that landlords charged inflated rents and did little to maintain their properties. Tenants, the author charged, only seemed to make deplorable conditions worse.[21]

Not only did the physical condition of the *patios* infuriate tenants and shock observers, but rates charged by landlords and often collected by paid administrators served as a major source of tenant grievances. Between 1910 and 1920 the cost of housing in Veracruz had increased sharply. A room that was priced at ten pesos in 1910 rented for thirty to thirty-five per month in 1922.[22] In addition to housing, prices for basic goods in the port had soared during the revolution.[23] Given an average laborers' salary of two to five pesos per day in 1920, making ends meet proved to be increasingly difficult. Part of the problem lay in the fact that during the revolution the national economy had suffered a major currency crisis, high inflation, and skyrocketing housing rates.[24] A 1919 study conducted by the Mexican Labor Department that compared the cost of worker housing in Mexico, the United States, and some European countries found urban rents in Mexico to be excessive.[25] Yet despite the condition of rental housing, depredation alone did not lead to tenant protest. Critical to the emergence of tenant organizing in Mexico were changes in the nation's political leadership during the revolution.

The "Legalistic Phase" of Tenant Organizing

During the years of the Constitutionalist government of Venustiano Carranza (1914–1920), a small group of tenants in the port of Veracruz organized to try to persuade state and national officials to enact housing reforms. In this period, renters in several Mexican cities worked closely with organized labor and directed their efforts primarily through legal and political channels. The call to organize urban renters came shortly after a December 15, 1916, decree by President Carranza that ordered reductions in urban rents in an attempt to stabilize a growing housing problem throughout the Republic.[26] The first stirrings of tenant organizing in Veracruz came on December 19, 1916, when conflict between tenants and landlords motivated residents to issue a call to "defend the interests of the public" against local landlords.[27]

An article printed in *El Dictamen* proposed the formation of a tenant organization. Many property owners, the authors claimed, "were foreigners." Readers received notice that "all tenants in Veracruz" should be made aware of their rights that had helped to "lessen the crushing weight of past injustices. . . . Thanks to the Revolution and the Constitutionalists . . . the humble and suffering people of Veracruz" now were capable of fighting against men whose conservative spirit had made them the main enemies of the Revolution: "Allow us to make a call to all tenants in Veracruz and in particular, all those affiliated with organized labor. . . . together we shall form the Great Tenant Union of Veracruz to defend our sacred rights, which are being disregarded by a majority of property owners in this heroic city."[28] This statement, representing the first rallying cry to city tenants, was signed "union, equality and justice, various renters."

On December 25, 1916, residents in the port officially founded a tenant union to organize for lower rents and improved housing conditions and to lobby the state government for housing reform legislation. Under the auspices of the Workers Syndicate of the Mexican Republic, C. Agustín Arrazola, Julían López, Joaquín Correa, and Epigmenio Sánchez presided over the gathering. Arrazola made a presentation in which he encouraged tenants to organize immediately, given the urgency of the housing situation in the port. Renters, he claimed, had been victimized by the abuses of a majority of landlords and tenant administrators in Veracruz. Organizers called upon the state government to name a commission dedicated to evaluating rental rates and the housing situation in general. They quickly developed a program of action. Late in December 1916, they petitioned the governor for housing reform. Tenants argued that given the rise in rents and deteriorating conditions, state officials should dispatch a commission to investigate the situation in the port. On November 28, 1917, Governor Cándido Aguilar signed new reform legislation that attempted to keep the cost of popular housing under control.[29] This appeared to neutralize many of the tenants' demands for a time. After the legislature passed the new rent control law, public discussion concerning popular housing turned to problems of sanitation, prostitution, and rapid urbanization.

The Aguilar Rent Law remained in effect until July 1920. That summer, the housing issue became a matter of heated public debate in Veracruz when acting governor Antonio Nava reversed the 1917 rent control laws. Nava defended his action by asserting that the "causes that had previously motivated [housing] reform now had disappeared."[30] Contrary to Nava's claim, however, the condition of housing in Veracruz had steadily deteriorated. As residents in the city struggled during the recession of 1919–1920, there appeared to be little hope for relief. In late 1920, however, the election of Adalberto Tejeda as the state's governor soon provided new political opportunities for tenant organizing.

New Political Opportunities

During the early 1920s the various areas within Mexico enjoyed a relatively high degree of regional political autonomy. In state and local affairs, President Obregón often "preferred to avoid direct involvement," granting state and local leaders greater freedom to pursue their own agenda.[31] This situation also helped to create expanded opportunities for popular organizing.

Tejeda represented a new breed of political leader. After taking office, he moved to build a broad political base by courting the support of labor, tenant, and later peasant groups in the state.[32] Tejeda, like other revolutionary *caudillos* at the time (Francisco Múgica in Michoacan, Satunino Cedillo in San Luis Potosí and Felipe Carrillo Puerto in Yucatán), developed new techniques and programs in the early 1920s that the official national party would soon adopt to reconsolidate federal power.[33] Greater toleration of popular organizing by Tejeda's administration represented a process of mutual empowerment both for Tejeda and for many popular groups in the state.[34]

Tejeda's reputation as a populist has been maintained by a number of Mexican scholars. As one historian has commented: "The arrival . . . of Tejeda began a [new] era of dramatic and desperate popular struggles—the only of their kind in the history of Mexico."[35] With his first legislative efforts, the new governor attracted both popular support and sharp criticism from certain political and commercial elites. Controversy over Tejeda's policies encouraged a division of the Veracruz political scene, a division that provided new opportunities not squandered by popular organizers.

Tejeda's most powerful appeals to popular groups came through legislative action. In late 1920, for example, Tejeda granted greater protections to labor by revising the 1918 state labor law drafted by former Veracruz governor Cándido Aguilar.[36] Then, on December 25, 1920, only five days after taking office, he sent to the Veracruz legislature a bill (Ley de Utilidades) that proposed profit sharing for employees.

Despite Tejeda's persistent defense of the bill, opposition in the press mounted during the spring and summer of 1921. By the end of the year, approximately 126 injunctions (*amparos*) had been granted by the Supreme Court, thereby successfully frustrating Tejeda's first major populist initiative. In other ways, however, Tejeda's efforts represented a successful appeal to popular groups. Soon the governor would take up another controversial issue in the hope of solidifying his base of political support: popular housing.

In early 1922 support for popular mobilization at the local level received significant encouragement when residents elected well-known labor organizer and stevedore Rafael "El Negro" García mayor of Veracruz. Under the banner of the Veracruz Worker party, the victorious García took the stage in the port's Teatro Principal for the inauguration ceremony. As hundreds packed inside the building to watch, they saw the new mayor take the national flag, receive the keys to the city, and proclaim the "victory of the working people of Veracruz." He called on *porteños* to join together and stand up for their rights as patriotic citizens. "We are charged with the spirit of the revolution to combat the problems the city has struggled with for so long," García declared. "Too many times have we been deceived by those who claim to represent us. . . . now we have demonstrated our power with incomparable force. . . . (T)he working people of Veracruz have won . . . and, if we continue to be well organized, we will never lose power." "*Veracruzanos*," the new mayor proclaimed amidst the red and black banners in the theater, "are not a conquered people."[37]

García's address had a powerful appeal. His promise to work as a loyal and patriotic servant of the people under the law inspired many in the city to view their local government in a different light. The government was no longer seen as the instrument of the bourgeoisie, in cahoots with *gringos* and *gachupines* (derogatory terms for North Americans and Spaniards); residents would soon witness, as one journalist later put it, the raising of a "Red Flag over City Hall," signifying an important shift in the politics of local government.[38] For the first time in Veracruz, the election of a public official helped to create a political environment in which ordinary working men and women were being heralded as true patriots embodying the values of Mexican citizenship.[39] With the rise of these populist leaders, tenants gained new access to the institutions of state and local power.

The Origins of Militant Protest

Noting progressive measures undertaken in the neighboring states of Campeche and Yucatán as well as the early initiatives of governor Tejeda, Veracruz militants felt encouraged to initiate a new phase of tenant organizing in early 1922.[40] Revitalized tenant organization in Veracruz as well as a number of other Mexican cities did not arise spontaneously, however. It came, in part, as the result of tireless efforts on the part of militant organizers. Labor organizing, in other words, served as the social foundation for tenant protest.

For a time since its founding in Saltillo in the spring of 1918, the Mexican Federation of Labor (Confederación Regional de Obreros Mexicanos, CROM) served as one of the most important organizations for Mexican labor. Under the leadership of Luis M. Morones, CROM took a decidedly reformist approach to the problems of Mexican labor, and by the spring of 1919 several members, dissatisfied with the union, had left to form a number of competing factions.[41] In 1920 workers in the port of Veracruz founded the Workers Federation of the Port of Veracruz (Federación de Trabajadores del Puerto de Veracruz).[42] They soon allied themselves with a new national labor organization, the rival General Confederation of Workers (Confederación General de Trabajadores, CGT), which had been established by delegates assembled at the Radical Red Convention in Mexico City in February 1921.[43] Of the seventy representatives who attended the conference sponsored by the Communist Federation of the Mexican Proletariat, twenty came from areas outside of the Federal District. They pledged themselves to an ideology they called "libertarian communism," which endorsed the ideas of class struggle, direct action, and the emancipation of workers and peasants.[44] In September 1921, members of the CGT met in Mexico City for their First National Workers Congress. During the meeting, the CGT pledged itself to the betterment of the Mexican proletariat, both rural and urban. In this strategy, the organization also sought to promote tenant unions.

Communists in Mexico gained inspiration from events in Russia as well as from a group of North American radicals (including Frank Seaman, Linn Gale, and others associated with the International Workers of the World) who had traveled south to organize Mexican workers.[45] After a Socialist Congress in August and September, members officially founded the Mexican Communist party on November 24, 1919.[46] The first national gathering of the party took place December 25–31, 1921, in Mexico City. Delegates agreed to form a "united front" to intervene in labor politics. Although many Communists were only mildly interested in agitating on behalf of urban renters, a handful of radicals from Veracruz, headed by Herón Proal, left the capital full of enthusiasm for the idea.[47] Proal had been among a small group of nonparty members invited to attend the meeting. After reports from local delegates, the fiery anarchist took the convention floor and argued that the urban housing problem represented one of the most urgent issues to be addressed in the nation. If Communists wanted to unite the Mexican proletariat, Proal suggested, addressing the problems of urban tenants would surely be the place to start.[48]

Herón Proal. El Dictamen *(Veracruz, Mexico). Courtesy Archivo General de la Nación.*

Herón Proal, son of Victor Proal and Amada Islas, was born in Tulancingo, Hidalgo, on October 17, 1881.[49] Proal's father was originally from France, and his mother was born in Mexico City, where Proal lived during his youth.[50] At age thirteen he began working in a *casa de cambio* (money exchange) and then worked for a time in a *changarro* (small shop), where he began to read books and various publications of the day. In 1897 he enlisted as a sailor in the Mexican Navy, in which he served as an artillery foreman until 1903. Following this Proal began a career as a tailor in Veracruz, producing uniforms and hats for the government.[51]

Proal first took an interest in labor organizing in 1906. According to his friend and collaborator during the rent strike, Porfirio Sosa, the young tailor benefited from the counsel of a Peruvian activist named Montova, who lived with Proal at the time.[52] Because of his politics, Montova had been expelled from Venezuela, Cuba, and other countries before arriving in Veracruz. There he and Proal worked together on a small newspaper that circulated in the port. This association with Montova encouraged Proal to develop his political interests.

During the next ten years, Proal continued to build a reputation as a labor organizer in Veracruz, especially among the port's maritime workers. On January 7, 1916, he spoke at a meeting in the port's Olimpia Theater commemorating the ninth anniversary of the 1907 Río Blanco strike, in which workers and government troops had engaged in bitter conflict.[53] He attended subsequent labor meetings held under the auspices of the Confederation of Trade Unions of the Mexican Republic in February and March.[54] Among the many themes discussed at these meetings were land reform, the eight-hour day, class consciousness, the world war, and a topic moderated by Proal himself titled "the truth about religion." In February 1916, at age thirty-five, Proal attended the First Preliminary Workers Congress in the port, where delegates selected him to serve on the executive committee.[55] Here Proal began to mature as a political thinker. The Mexican Region Confederation of Labor (Confederación del Trabajo de la Región Mexicana, CTRM), founded during this meeting, espoused a mixture of anarchist and socialist thinking. In its declaration of principles one sees some of the basic ideas, such as class struggle, direct action, and an aversion to formal political participation, to which Proal and later many Veracruz tenants would adhere.[56] Although it is uncertain to what degree Proal endorsed anarchist thinking at the time of the conference, there is little doubt that he, along with a number of his Communist colleagues of the time, had been attracted by radical social thought brought to Mexico by a number of immigrants (particularly Spaniards) over the past few decades.[57]

In the port many workers, including Proal, had become affiliated with the local Chamber of Labor founded by Spanish radical José Fernández Oca. Other Spaniards, particularly Pedro Junco, sponsored anarchist groups in the area. A small group of militant residents of the port also participated in a reading group known as Antorcha Libertaria founded by Communist Manuel Díaz Ramírez in 1921.[58] Months before, Díaz Ramírez had served as one of the executive committee members of the Communist Federation, which organized the founding meeting of the CGT.[59] Many who would soon go on to shape the course of regional history in important ways participated, including Rafael García, peasant organizers Manuel Almanza García, Sóstones Blanco, Úrsulo Galván Reyes, and Herón Proal. In their discussions members created an ideology that "was a strange mixture of Proudhon, Bakunin, Kropotkin and Max Nordan."[60] Indeed, the uniqueness of the Antorcha Libertaria gave the Veracruz tenant protest a distinctive character. Despite their growing political consciousness and organization, grassroots militants could not rely solely on the strength of their ideological conviction. Effective protest would have to wait for an opportune moment.

The Strike Begins

Despite considerable labor unrest, tenant organizing remained on the margins of the public discourse between 1920 and early 1922. Instead, residents concerned themselves with battling a yellow fever epidemic in 1920–1921. In mid-January 1922, however, representatives of the dock workers' union helped to return the idea of housing reform to the public spotlight. In a letter to city hall, they urged Mayor García to do something about the "truly disagreeable conditions of the *pa-*

tios."[61] Their communication stated that "abuses of *patio* administrators could no longer be tolerated."[62] Following this, concern over popular housing grew as tenants and health officials registered a number of complaints regarding various tenements in late January. At the same time, landlords increased the number of evictions throughout the city.

On January 29, 1922, *El Dictamen* printed an article that suggested the beginning of a major tenant protest in the port. The report stated that landlords made a handsome profit by charging prostitutes extremely high rates for their rented rooms. It went on to say that women living in the port's red-light district had presented complaints against their landlords to Mayor García at a meeting held two days earlier. The women argued that the rents the landlords demanded were extremely high, between four and six pesos daily. The women also charged that landlords and their administrators had made a common practice of using extortion to collect their payments. In response, the mayor declared that landlords would be advised to lower their rents as soon as possible and warned that strict measures would soon be taken by the city government if property owners refused to take action.[63]

On February 2, the housing issue took center stage in Veracruz politics. That morning, a headline in *El Dictamen* announced: "Efforts to do something about the problem of high rents and poor housing conditions are being undertaken today with a general meeting of tenants in the Biblioteca del Pueblo [People's Library]."[64] The paper reprinted a handbill circulating throughout the city that stated: "All tenants in the port have long been victimized by innumerable abuses committed by usurious landlords who have increased—to a shocking degree—rents of the pigsties we occupy." Organizers encouraged tenants to attend the meeting to be held that night. "All Veracruz," the text read, "can testify to the fact that it is impossible to pay such high rents!"[65] Having framed tenant problems in terms that strongly suggested that landlords' actions constituted a clear case of social injustice, the stage was set for dramatic action.

That evening, approximately 600 gathered at the People's Library. First Nicolás Sandoval, a member of the Sailors and Stokers Union, spoke to those assembled. Sensing that the time had come for housing reform, Sandoval mentioned recent legislation enacted in Yucatán and Campeche and suggested that Veracruz should adopt similar laws. Dr. Reyes Barriero, a noted reformer in the port, informed the crowd that

> in Yucatán there has been socialist legislation to protect workers. . . . an energetic campaign needs to be started here in the press and everywhere against the excessive prices for these uninhabitable pigsties. . . . We renters, who make up approximately 90 percent of the city's residents, must defend ourselves . . . against the fierce cruelty of the landlords. . . . we must organize a tenant union [*liga de resistencia de los inquilinos*] to fight their abuses. . . . It is not fair that they, who live more than comfortably on what we are forced to give them, gather in their offices to pass off another increase in the rent of the deteriorated tenements we live in.[66]

With a chorus of voices encouraging his criticism of the port's propertied residents, Reyes Barriero testified that in his work as a doctor he had seen many die in the port as the result of poor sanitation. Improved health conditions in the poor districts of the city has never been realized, he charged, "because of the selfishness of the rich."[67] The doctor's oratory provoked a tumultuous response from the audience. The next to address the assembly, Cayetano Huerto, accused the meeting's organizers, including the mayor, of too much talk and too little action:

> . . . we don't want sermons . . . the organizers here have paraded speaker after speaker that offers us empty promises and flashy phrases. Even the mayor has spoken but suggested nothing practical for us to follow. Besides, he already lives in a comfortable room and earns a fabulous salary of eight-hundred pesos. With that kind of money, he could live in an even better house if he wanted![68]

Huerto's criticism provoked an immediate response from the audience. People began yelling "actions, not empty phrases" and other criticisms at the organizers. Eventually, the room grew quiet and someone proposed that Reyes Barreiro be appointed as president of a new renters' organization. The physician quickly accepted and then returned to the podium to express his commitment to fight for the tenant cause.

In the next few minutes, however, Herón Proal came up to the speakers' table holding a stack of newspapers under his arm. Seeing him about to address the gathering, some in the audience shouted "Sit down, sit down!," denying Proal the opportunity to speak. In response Proal stormed out of the room, calling on the crowd to follow him. Outside he railed against Veracruz landlords as well as local politicians, who, he suggested, had convened the meeting with the goal of manipulating the frustrations of tenants for their own ends. "Things don't have to be this way," Proal argued; "open your eyes and see who is trying to use you."[69] Proal then called for the creation of an alternative Red Syndicate. The meeting of this group, Proal declared, would be held "in the shadow of the statue of Don Benito" in the port's Juárez Park the following evening. Although opinions varied about how the problem of popular housing in the port should be resolved, Proal seized the opportunity to act quickly and decisively. Many, fed up with landlords' abuses and steep rents, followed him. However, moderates who disagreed with Proal's militant politics kept their distance.

On February 3, 1922, approximately 600 people assembled in the park for the first of what would soon become daily open-air meetings. Proal and almost twenty other speakers exhorted those gathered to go on strike until the "bourgeois dogs" lowered local rents to 1910 levels.[70] According to the report the following day in *El Dictamen*, Proal then went on to electrify his audience with charges against local landlords and arguments in favor of a rent boycott:

> Let us protest and reclaim our rights. The time has come for us to throw off the infernal yoke of these bourgeois dogs because the bourgeoisie, some of whom are pigs, vipers, and scorpions, . . . should be destroyed! Now what all the city's poor should

> do is agree to not pay their rents. Why should we pay our rent? Why should our money help make the bourgeoisie fatter? No, we won't pay our rents and when the landlord asks for it, tell him to ask for it in writing.[71]

Proal then continued with a rambling commentary suggesting that politicians cared only about the people's vote, not their social condition. The legislature and city council, Proal remarked, were "a useless bunch of cream puffs!" and that only direct action would "achieve revolutionary change." Sensing that the time had come for a full-scale confrontation with the city's elite, Proal left the meeting to begin planning for the following day.[72]

On February 4 organizers informed tenants that a rally would be held the next day beginning in Ferrer Guardia Park. The meeting would then be followed by a march to the Principal Theater. That morning, renters gathered. After parading through the city's central streets they discovered that the police had sealed off the theater, preventing Proal and his fledgling organization from conducting their business inside. Surprised by a significant show of force on the part of the police, many who had joined the march from the park grew frightened and dispersed. Not to be discouraged, Proal directed the remaining individuals towards Juárez Park. Once assembled, he criticized *El Dictamen*:

> They make me out to be crazy, a public disgrace. . . . what's a shame is that there should be four, maybe five thousand people here. . . . didn't we make a commitment to work toward our goal, to establish the tenant union? Then why did so many run away like a bunch of scared old women? Because the reactionaries sent the police to guard the building?[73]

Proal then made an impassioned call to his audience, encouraging them to strengthen their commitment:

> Let us go to the theater and take it by force if we need to. If, when we arrive, the police try to stop us, we will, with stones, sticks, pistols, and whatever else is available, take it because the theater is ours, it is the people's! There we will hold our meeting, no matter what intrigue and controversy the bourgeoisie may stir up, there we will form our tenant union![74]

After Proal's speech, Oscar Robert (originally from Campeche) outlined the plan to begin the strike. Each *patio* in the city, he suggested, should organize itself and decide to stop paying rent. "Let's see," he asked his listeners, "what the landlords will do. . . . If the authorities throw us out," the speaker reasoned, "they will have committed a great injustice." Robert then echoed Proal's fierce determination to bring the issue to the public's attention through direct action. Robert promised that if tenants were evicted, protesters would occupy the major streets of the city, blocking traffic and interrupting business.[75] Organizers agreed that rents would not be paid until public officials and landlords recognized Proal's Red Syndicate as representative of the city's tenants. They also demanded that individual contracts between landlords and tenants be annulled, that landlords reduce rates to 1910 levels or 2 percent of the property (*catastral*) value, and that all tenements be sanitized.[76] After a number of other speeches, the group finally decided to elect a provisional directorship; Herón Proal, Oscar Robert, José Olmos, Julián García, Porfirio Sosa, Mateo Luna, Miguel Salinas, Pío Aguilera, and Francisco Prieto were all named to leadership posts.[77] By the end of the meeting, *porteños* had officially founded the Veracruz Revolutionary Syndicate of Tenants.[78]

Syndicate members soon began coordinating the establishment of strike committees in *patios* throughout the city. Organizers informed tenants of the guidelines set by the central committee: Individuals would agree to pay rents if reduced to 1910 levels; otherwise landlords and administrators would receive nothing. In the event of an attempted eviction, tenant leaders told strikers to immediately alert their neighbors, who would first employ passive resistance. If this failed, force might be required.[79] With militants busily preparing renters for grassroots protest during February, many residents in Veracruz anticipated the first acts of popular resistance.

"The Movement . . . Was the Work of the Women"

In the early months of 1922 *porteños* increasingly heard complaints that associated the exploitation of prostitutes with the problem of tenement housing. This connection was nothing new in Veracruz or in many other urban areas at the time. Efforts to control and regulate prostitution in Veracruz began during the first decade of the century. In addition to general public health measures undertaken before the revolution to combat problems of disease, crime, and other "urban pathologies," local officials had contracted entrepreneur José González Bueno to establish a special area in the southeast corner of the city designated for sexual commerce.[80] Despite the elaborate plans made for such an endeavor, however, civil war prevented the project from being realized.

During the U.S. (1914) and Constitutionalist occupations (1914–1915), business flourished. Sex workers conducted their business in several of the city's popular neighborhoods, including the La Huaca area, located on the city's southeast side. As the port's unofficial red-light district, this neighborhood was the most obvious target for urban reformers, who associated immorality, uncleanliness, and criminality with the urban poor. For tenant organizers such as Herón Proal, the area also represented an important source of popular and particularly female participation during the strike because of the difficult bind in which many poor women found themselves.

On the afternoon of February 27, 1922, Proal visited the El Bosque cantina, proposing to a number of prostitutes that a meeting be held in the nearby *patio de la Vega*. Soon almost eighty women had gathered in the tenement to listen to him. "Dearest *compañeras*," he began, "the hour of social vindication is here, and for you it is the time of liberation. You are great citizens," he continued, "and I am here, sisters, to tell you to burn these filthy hovels where you are being miserably exploited by the bourgeoisie." Encouraged, he elaborated further: "You need to burn these houses and destroy the bourgeoisie. . . . All of you are energetic women who do not have to stand for this exploitation."[81] Proal finished his speech and departed. When the women returned to the street, they encountered their rent collector, José "El Chato" Montero. Inspired by Proal's incendiary discourse, they pelted Montero with stones.[82] After this, word of a growing resistance spread rapidly throughout the port's popular neighborhoods. By the time a group of prostitutes threw mattresses and other furniture into the street and declared themselves on strike during the night of March 6, almost everyone in the city knew that a major confrontation was about to erupt.

Acting independently, measures taken by the women of San Salvador *patio* marked the first major case of popular resistance against local landlords.[83] The following day *El Dictamen* reported that "many of the prostitutes [had taken] their rented mattresses, chairs, and other furniture into the street with the idea of starting a giant bonfire." Having received a tip about the women's plans, the police managed to intervene at the last minute.[84] Although the police had eventually succeeded in restoring order, they could not prevent the news from spreading across town. A few days later, *porteños* heard of several other tenements who had declared themselves on strike and had joined Proal's union.[85] Soon, *El Dictamen* registered the protest of tenants from El Perfume, La Hortaliza, El Aserradero, Vallejo, La Providencia, La Josefina, San Bruno, Ni me olvides, Paraíso, Liébano, La Conchita, and 21 de Abril *patios*.[86] According to the paper, representatives of the renters' union had established themselves in each of these *patios* and were working to coordinate the action. By mid-March thousands of the city's tenants had joined the rent boycott, and well over 100 *patios* were on strike.[87]

As renters came together to make their grievances known, *patio* inhabitants and *propagandistas* of the union hung hundreds of red banners outside their homes to signify their willingness to join the strike. Posters declaring "Estoy en huelga y no pago renta! [I am on strike and not paying rent!]" could be seen tacked on doors, fences, and outside walls of the *patios*. Despite differences that varied according to gender, occupational, and ethnic interests, these expressions testified to a growing solidarity among the city's tenants. One of the first major demonstrations, which revealed the growing magnitude of the strike, took place on the evening of March 12, 1922.

After congregating in Juárez Park, the crowd took their red flags and banners in hand and marched to the offices of the Cangas brothers, probably the most notorious foreign (Cuban) landlords in the port. At the corner of Palma and 1 de Mayo streets, protesters shouted "Death to the Cangas, down with the bourgeoisie" and "Death to the exploiters of the people" and set off a number of firecrackers; they then moved to the city's central square. There, militants Proal, Sosa, and Olmos gained access to a balcony room in the Hotel Diligencias facing the plaza. Standing above the crowd, Sosa encouraged his audience to unite in the renters' struggle; Proal specifically took the opportunity to honor the women of San Salvador *patio:*

> Dear *compañeras* . . . you deserve a vote of confidence from the strike committee and all the inhabitants of Veracruz because you were the first to declare yourselves part of a strike that today has taken on gigantic proportions. You are true heroines for having placed the first stone in this gigantic edifice that we are now building. . . . you were the first. . . . The Red Syndicate . . . opens its arms and welcomes its dear sisters.[88]

When some of the men in the crowd scoffed at Proal's use of the term "sisters," he quickly responded:

> Yes gentlemen, don't laugh, these poor and despised women not only are our *compañeras,* but also our sisters. . . . they are flesh and blood just like us. There is no reason to exclude them from our struggle, especially when you consider that they are the exploited flesh of the bourgeoisie.[89]

With this declaration, however patronizing, Proal openly acknowledged the importance of women's contribution to the movement.

In their actions, these women sought political and social change. They carried out many of the day-to-day tasks of the Syndicate, maintaining various strike committees within the *patios* and filling the ranks of innumerable demonstrations, marches, and other gatherings. Over the years, they constituted the majority of rank-and-file participants.

Female participation in the anarchist practice of direct action revealed their importance in the movement. Basically the direct action strategy derived from the belief that the legal and political system represented bourgeois interests and therefore could never be trusted.

From the first days of the strike, militant female residents had banded together to form an action committee known as the Libertarian Women. United under the syndicate's creed, which stipulated that if a renter was in danger of being evicted, a general alarm (usually a loud whistle) would be sounded, these women regularly challenged housing administrators, police, and other tenants unfriendly to the union. One of their favorite tactics was "giving the horse" (*denle al caballo*) whereby an individual would be apprehended by a group of women, lifted by each limb, and violently shaken. They often installed homeless persons in vacant buildings, publicly scorned landlords and rent collectors, and generally enforced the terms of the strike. Furthermore, tenant women directed their attention to local markets, where they encouraged female servants working for middle-class and elite households to organize a union and strike for higher wages. The strong presence of women in the Veracruz protest during these years often encouraged some observers, including the editors of *El Dictamen*, to imagine that Proal had cast some kind of seductive spell, "conquering [them] with his strange theories."[90] Proal himself reconfirmed the importance of women in the protest thirty years later when he said: "el movimiento . . . fué obra de las mujeres [the tenant move-

Members of the tenant syndicate, 1923. Courtesy Archivo General de la Nación.

Members of the tenant syndicate, 1923. Courtesy Archivo General de la Nación.

ment was the work of the women]."[91] Others, including tenant activist and local historian Arturo Bolio Trejo, later referred to the strike as the *rebelión de mujeres* (the women's rebellion).[92]

The Massacre of July 5–6, 1922

Regular confrontations between renters and landlords, rent collectors, market salespeople, police, and politicians created a wild social environment in the port. Demonstrations held in Juárez Park involved hundreds of men, women, and children. By the end of May approximately 30,000 *porteños,* or nearly half the city's population, had stopped paying rent.[93] Tenant activities beginning in May included the establishment of the port's first workers' neighborhood (*colonia comunista*) on the edge of town, newspaper publication (*El Frente Único* and *Guillotina*), networking with other tenant and peasant organizations in the region, and an increased effort to lower the cost of basic goods in the city. In late May and early June members of the Veracruz union initiated a boycott of general stores in the port, protesting high prices and demanding immediate price reductions.[94] On June 13 tenant women launched a drive to organize domestic workers in the city.[95] The protest, in other words, not only targeted landlords and state politicians in an effort to stimulate change in urban housing but also sought to affect many other consumer-related aspects of Veracruz society.

Action on the part of the city's renters paralleled a new wave of social protest brought on by Tejeda's populist politics and the efforts of grassroots organizers. Throughout 1922 and 1923 unions in the port—ranging from those of dock workers to the many bakers', printers', cigar makers', restaurant employees', electricians', and streetcar operators' unions, as well as organized market vendors, domestic servants, and others—all were well aware if not actively involved in the tenant protest.[96] On June 12, 1922, port workers had initiated a general strike that lasted three days. A number of other organized groups, affiliated with the Chamber of Labor, also quickly joined the effort. Efforts to paralyze business in the city began shortly after labor leaders declared the general strike. Around two o'clock that afternoon, a delegation visited the streetcar station to bring service to a halt. In accordance with the conditions of the protest, a number of ships in the harbor went unserviced or left the port. Strikers ordered cantinas and restaurants to close or to offer only limited service. Bakers promised to work Saturday but not Sunday. *El Dictamen* reported that "hotels and bars were closed, restaurants were without services, and the streets were devoid of trolleys, cars, and much activity of any kind."[97] Although the strike lasted only a short time, the protest had brought almost all business in Veracruz, with the exception of emergency medical care, to a standstill. To some observers, including president Obregón, the city appeared to be on the verge of total chaos.[98]

The activities of the syndicate gained notoriety in the state and throughout Mexico. Earlier in March tenants in neighboring Córdoba and Jalapa had asked

Proal if he would be willing to help them organize similar actions.[99] In April renters in Orizaba had established a tenant union and began protesting for lower rents.[100] In the rest of the state, the influence of tenant activities could also be seen in the smaller cities of Nogales, Santa Rosa, Río Blanco, Tierra Blanca, Minatitlán, Soledad de Doblado, and a few other towns where renter organizations had been created. At the national level, major rent protests also erupted in Mexico City and Guadalajara. Tenants also began organizing in Monterrey, Puebla, San Luis Potosí, Mazatlán, Tampico, Aguascalientes, Ciudad Juárez, Durango, and Torreón during this time. By early summer, organized urban tenants, to the chagrin of landlords, city treasurers, and politicians, enjoyed unprecedented social power.

In June 1922, however, some within the movement became increasingly dissatisfied with Proal's leadership of the Revolutionary Syndicate of Tenants. At the same time, the Veracruz tenant movement began to break apart. From the beginning, several factions, including members of the Mexican Communist party in the port, had fought for control. The dominant authority, however, rested in the hands of Herón Proal despite the fact that Communists such as Porfirio Sosa, Mateo Luna, José Olmos, Úrsulo Galván, Sóstones Blanco, and Manuel Almanza had all served as leaders during the spring of 1922. For their part, Communists increasingly sought to direct tenant loyalties toward political involvement in local and national campaigns. Proal, in maintaining his adherence to anarchist principles, which advocated no participation in formal politics, was not willing to allow the syndicate to come under control of any political party. In late June these and other differences within the movement provided a pretext for federal repression of the tenants.

In late June, after members of the renters' union had charged Proal with financial mismanagement, a rival faction emerged under the leadership of José Olmos. In his own defense, Proal argued that the organization should maintain its "revolutionary, antipolitical and genuinely communist" orientation.[101] After a period of heated debate, the confrontation between the two leaders came to a head on July 5. That night, members of Proal's group met in the city's Ferrer Guardia Park. Proal vigorously denounced Olmos; he and his followers then made their way to Olmos's house. Not finding him there, they proceeded to his sister's residence. When Olmos refused to meet with the crowd, several of Proal's group managed to enter through a nearby *patio* door. Cornering Olmos, they beat him with sticks and clubs. A group of soldiers soon arrived, eventually forcing Proal's group to retreat to the park. Shortly thereafter, reinforcements under the command of Colonel López Manzano engaged the protesters in a violent confrontation that resulted in the death of one officer (Lieutenant Valtierra) and a number of injuries. During the commotion, many of the protesters left the scene, gradually finding their way back to the syndicate headquarters.

Later that night, federal forces received orders for the apprehension of Proal. When troops arrived outside the union office, strikers resisted. Shooting broke out, and after an uneven exchange several tenants lay dead or seriously injured.

Accused of homicide and sedition, Proal eventually turned himself in to officials. Police also arrested approximately ninety men and fifty women, including future syndicate leader María Luisa Marín, and sent them to the city's Allende Jail.[102] Although Proal and the tenant union's newspaper, *El Frente Único*, later stated that close to 150 individuals had died that night, official reports counted four dead and twenty-two wounded.[103] Other accounts suggested that numerous dead bodies had been seen throughout the city, with others "mysteriously appearing" over the course of the following week.[104]

Toward State Housing Reform

Popular protest, as well as pressure from Mexico City, pushed the Tejeda administration and their allies to resolve the conflict in a quick and orderly manner. For Tejeda, interest in housing reform continued to come primarily from his desire to gain popular political support within the state. Dramatic events taking place in the cities of Veracruz during the spring and early summer of 1922 forced politicians to work diligently to negotiate a solution. Although their efforts failed to prevent the bloody confrontation between federal forces and tenants in early July, they would help establish the country's only significant housing reform legislation in the 1920s.

On March 11, 1922, Mayor Rafael García had drafted a housing reform proposal based, in part, on legislation passed in Yucatán and Campeche.[105] The document was discussed by the city council and sent to the state legislature for further consideration.[106] The mayor also shared his ideas with a representative of the property owners' association, Manuel Díaz Cueto, but this meeting had produced no positive results.[107]

On March 25, after prompting from García, the state legislature repealed former governor Antonio Nava's revisions of the 1917 rent control law. On March 27, García sent a letter to Tejeda informing him that "tenant protests have been orderly . . . but criticism of our administration in the press has grown increasingly bitter."[108] Despite increasing tension, the city council took action in late March. They named a commission to accompany health officials from the local public health office. Together they would conduct an inspection of *patios* in violation of sanitation codes and demand immediate repairs. If landlords did not respond, severe fines would be imposed.[109]

However, exactly how Tejeda hoped to handle the housing situation remained uncertain.[110] In a letter dated March 31, representative Miguel Barranco advised Tejeda that in addition to the repeal of Nava's law, new legal action needed to be taken to resolve the housing crisis. He indicated that a member of the legislature had conducted a brief study of the problem, a study that he would soon make available to the governor.[111] The report stated that though in Yucatán rents had been set at 6 percent of appraised property values, "this was not possible in Veracruz because no similar evaluation had yet been conducted." Some other method for regulating urban rents, the author noted, needed to be determined.[112] Nevertheless, a reform bill that imposed significant rent and sanitation controls, the report advised, could potentially improve the living conditions of thousands, not only in the port but throughout the state. Following these and other suggestions, Tejeda began drafting a new rent control law that he would present to the legislature in early July.[113]

In the meantime, Tejeda dispatched staff members Benigo Mata and Salvador Gonzalo García to the port in an effort to gain greater familiarity with the housing situation. On May 13, they visited the Varidades, San Bernardo, La Vega Grande, Josefita, and Enrique Barrera *patios* on the city's west side as well as San Antonio, owned by the Cangas brothers, in the La Huaca neighborhood. After seeing the appalling condition of these tenements, the commissioners reported back to the governor that the port's rental housing was "shockingly overpriced, overcrowded, and in a pitiful state of disrepair."[114]

Armed with new information on the problem, Tejeda moved quickly to impose a legal solution. Following the suggestions of members of the tenant union, his first offer stipulated that in exchange for new contracts between landlords and tenants that calculated monthly rents at 2 percent of property values (with landlords making provisions for basic water, light, and sanitary services in all *patios*), owners would be guaranteed prompt payment from their renters. Not surprisingly, landlords rejected the governor's proposal.[115]

Although Tejeda continued to mediate negotiations between landlords and tenants, officials in Mexico City grew impatient with the situation. President Obregón, working to gain diplomatic recognition from the United States, felt that Tejeda's politics had encouraged "tumultuous and disorderly" events.[116] This was not the first word of caution from the president. The previous year, Obregón had suggested to Tejeda that an explosive confrontation in the state between workers and business owners "must be avoided at all cost."[117] Responding to reports of growing unrest in the port during the spring of 1922, Obregón put federal forces on alert and urged state and local officials to monitor the situation.

Despite the governor's desire to resolve the conflict, tension between tenants, landlords, and police had increased during May and June 1922.[118] On May 9, for example, landlords and tenants had met with municipal officials. In contrast to their earlier offer to reduce rents in exchange for lower property taxes, however, representatives of the property owners' association now avoided entering into any agreement with renters, claiming that tenant action had become entirely "contemptible."[119] Property owners saw the tenant union as belligerent and uncontrollable. In a move to maintain their influence, landlords soon refused to meet with leaders of the syndicate. Instead, owners stated that they would only negotiate informally with individual tenants.[120]

Finally, after almost three months of preparation, Tejeda sent a housing reform proposal to the state legislature in June 1922. The proposal acceded to many of the tenant demands.[121] On June 11, while lawmakers began to study the proposed legislation, Tejeda received word that Secretary of Government Plutarco Elías Calles wanted him in Mexico City.[122] During his visit, Tejeda hoped to discuss the bill with Calles and then send revisions to Lieutenant Governor Angel Casarín in Jalapa. The confrontation of July 5–6, however, caught many by surprise. With Tejeda still out of town, on July 6 Casarín took it upon himself to declare the immediate "public necessity" of constructing worker housing in Veracruz, Orizaba, Jalapa, Córdoba, Tuxpan, Puerto México (Coatzacoalcos) and Huatusco. The following day, Casarín and the state legislature quickly approved Tejeda's Rent Law.[123]

When property owners throughout the state learned of the legislation, they immediately began organizing in opposition. Article 3 of the Rent Law, which set the percentage at which rents would be calculated, represented one of the main points of contention. Even before the initiative had become law, the press, landlords, and unsympathetic politicians had attacked the reform, suggesting that it could never be successfully applied.[124] Now that it had passed the legislature, many quickly organized to resist the reform. They filed injunctions against the governor, the legislature, and local officials, declaring that the law stood in violation of their constitutional rights. One editorial printed in *El Dictamen* claimed that the measure essentially meant the confiscation of private property: "Expropriation . . . can only proceed when in accordance with Article 27 of the Constitution. This absurd law . . . has no civil precedent and is a flagrant violation of our individual rights."[125] While landlords were calling the law unconstitutional, tenants were insisting on the release of Proal and the other prisoners before they would seriously consider legal reforms; successful application of the law seemed a remote possibility. Given the landlords' hostile response to the law, state leaders quickly began considering possible revisions. Lawmakers called representatives from different property owners' organizations to Jalapa to discuss the issue. On November 30, a group met in the port.[126] Veracruz property owner union president Salvador Campa informed the group of his recent visit to talk to congressmen in the state capital. He suggested that possible revisions to the rent law would increase the percentage at which rents were figured. "Certainly," Campa declared, "nowhere in the world have landlords been required to accept rents this low." It was to be hoped, he added, that tenants would be willing to cooperate.[127]

Efforts by politicians to negotiate a new settlement to the rent strike suffered a major setback in mid-December, however, when landlords in Orizaba accused the governor and state legislature of attacks on private property, violations of the Constitution, and a "politics of expropriation."[128] In an interview printed in *El Dictamen* later in December 1922, Campa further indicated the landlords' position on the reform by suggesting that the law would restrict new investment in housing as well as continue to make rental housing an unattractive business venture. He suggested that "very few people in the state appear willing to comply with the new law."[129]

Despite sharp criticism of the reform, representatives Salvador Gonzalo García, Juan Ochoa Díaz, and Cristoforo Redondo presented a revised proposal to the state legislature on December 26. According to their plan, rents were to be fixed at 6 percent of property values, and tax exemptions would be provided for individuals who constructed new housing.[130] After learning of the proposal, *El Dictamen* echoed the sentiments of many property owners when it criticized the reform as "a law that will resolve nothing and satisfy nobody."[131] With pressure from all sides, the state legislature approved several articles of the revised law by late December. Discussion continued, however, regarding the exact percentage upon which rental rates would be based; when some legislators suggested that rents be set at higher levels, many tenants gathered in the gallery vigorously expressed their disapproval by cheering, shouting, and whistling at the congressmen below.[132]

Men and women from tenant unions all over the state attended the session held on December 31, 1922, where lawmakers read each article of the housing reform. When the politicians discussed a possible end to the rent moratorium, tenants shouted their disagreement: "No, we don't want this. . . . the strike will continue!"[133] Representative Ochoa Díaz, one of the members of a special commission assigned to reconsider the measure, then stood and expressed his frustration with the renters in the galleries, who, he claimed, had not shown any previous interest in the law. He stated that property owners had asked for rents based on 12 percent of the property value, claiming the need to pay utility costs, but he then acknowledged that they would be willing to settle for 8 percent. When the audience heard this, they again shouted their disapproval. Immediately the sound of crying children, banging chairs, and shouts erupted inside the assembly. After several minutes of confusion, legislators restored order. Amid shouts from the crowd, Ochoa Díaz again took the floor and again sharply criticized the tenants:

> These people do not represent the interests of all *veracruzanos*. . . . Our society is not simply composed of working-class elements. . . . the middle class are the ones who will suffer and we need to take them into consideration. If the representatives do not study the problem carefully . . . this law will simply be detestable and resolve nothing. With rents based at 6 percent, there will be no businessman in the entire republic who would be willing to build houses in our state. The bill will become a dead letter . . . [and] is basically only a measure that confiscates property and nothing else. With the growing population here in Veracruz . . . the situation is only going to get worse.[134]

Taking offense to these remarks, Congressman Jiménez Bravo responded:

> The working class has made a tremendous sacrifice in the last few years only to be faced with rents that have doubled between 1915 and 1919. . . . No state authority has attempted to do anything about the problem, and for this reason we find ourselves involved in the present conflict. I am not proposing the destruction of capital, but the people have to eat. Six percent . . . is fair.[135]

Hearing this, tenants in the assembly cheered, confident that the revised law would be soon passed. On January 2, 1923, renters again visited the capital, hoping to influence the legislature. After some discussion, lawmakers approved the article, which set rents at a rate of 6 percent of the property value.[136] As the legislature moved to approve the bill before sending it to the governor for review, protesters left the building and assembled across the street, where they displayed their black-and-red banners on the cathedral. That afternoon tenants celebrated in the streets of Jalapa.

Renters paraded through the central district of the city, setting off firecrackers and shouting popular slogans in celebration. Meanwhile, in the port, militants distributed a special edition of *El Frente Único* that commented on the activities of the delegates and announced that they would arrive the following day. When members of the syndicate later returned to the port, renters organized a demonstration outside the railroad terminal to welcome them. After a number of speeches, they left the station area and made their way toward the union headquarters shouting "Viva Proal" along the way. Organizers announced a meeting to be held later that night "to celebrate the tenant victory."[137] Beginning at eight o'clock, tenants gathered in the city square, again raising banners and shooting off fireworks. Then, with tremendous enthusiasm, renters marched through the streets of Veracruz, happily marking the occasion with more shouts and singing.[138]

In late March final deliberations over Tejeda's Rent Law took place. On April 1, with the galleries again filled, tenants loudly applauded the testimony of Congressmen Pérez Cadena and Serrano. In their speeches, the two lawmakers had disagreed with Ochoa Díaz, who persisted in attempting to increase the percentage at which rents would be set. One representative countered by arguing that "workers already had plenty of rights" and that rents based on 6 percent would prevent both new construction and the proper maintenance of existing properties. Yelling "sellout" and other criticisms at the politicians, protesters caused such a commotion that legislators ended the session. The following day, some representatives asked that police be prepared to intervene in case tenants decided to try and interrupt the proceedings again.

Landlords, who considered the housing reform unconstitutional, rallied in opposition. On April 8, 1923, *El Dictamen* printed an editorial by Manuel Díaz Cueto. He commented that certain aspects of the new law only favored irresponsible tenants. "If government is not willing to take our needs into account," Díaz Cueto suggested, "then landlords are capable of fighting back."[139] Indeed, his words represented the feelings of many property owners in the state. When landlords met on April 8 to discuss the new law, they considered undertaking their own brand of "direct action" by refusing to pay city taxes. In an attempt to appease the landlords, Governor Tejeda again met with property owners on April 11. He tried to reassure them that if any "deficiencies" in the law were found when it was implemented, certain adjustments would be attended to.[140] However, his efforts did little to quiet them. Moving against the revised rent law, landlords from Orizaba, Jalapa, Córdoba, and the port met again on April 22. After a heated discussion, they decided that reassurances from the governor meant nothing. Upset over a detail in the new law that granted tenants rent concessions in case of illness, they pledged to "match tenants' direct action with their own," suggesting that many had now decided to withhold their tax payments in protest.[141] Two days later, property owners discussed their differences with Governor Tejeda. They advised him to expect difficulties in applying the new law. In exchange for tabling the bill, landlords offered to pay higher state taxes to fund the construction of popular housing.[142] Taking their position into consideration, Tejeda raised the rate at which rents would be based to 9 percent.[143] Soon thereafter, members of the legislature approved the bill. A few days later, following the popular celebrations of May Day throughout the state, Tejeda declared the new law in effect.

As the most significant housing reform in Mexico during the 1920s, the Veracruz Rent Law reduced rents to slightly more than 1910 levels, donated land for the construction of new housing, and provided for the supervision of relations between landlords and tenants. Important gains also included the dedication of new areas for the construction of popular housing. The intransigence of property owners, however, prevented housing reform in Veracruz from being fully realized. As they had the previous year with his profit-sharing law, landlords and others opposed to Tejeda's politics again organized their resistance. Many filed injunctions in local courts during the spring and summer of 1923, indicating their determination to block the application of the law. In the meantime, however, many in the port anticipated the freeing of Herón Proal and the other members of the renters' union.

Twilight of the Tenant Movement

In the years that followed the passage of the rent law, members of the Revolutionary Syndicate worked to see the full measure of the reform applied. At the same time, they also continued to agitate for more radical social change. As part of their efforts, tenants managed to negotiate the establishment of several new popular settlements (*colonias*) in the port and in other cities in the state.[144] In September 1922 renters organized the first of several tenant conventions to be held in the state.

Shortly after Tejeda issued the rent law, word spread throughout the *patios* regarding the possible release of Proal and the other jailed tenants. Upon hearing the news, *porteños* sympathetic to the renters' cause decorated the fronts of their houses with banners and organized dances to celebrate. On May 11, 1923, officials allowed the prisoners to walk free.[145] In leaving the Allende Jail, tenants celebrated in their usual flamboyant manner. In groups of ten, the men exited first. The women then followed, dressed in cream-colored dresses and straw hats with red ribbons. Well-wishers jubilantly set off firecrackers, applauded their peers, sang songs, and shouted slogans. Finally Proal and a group of his most intimate *compañeros* came out last. They announced that a demonstration would be held in Juárez Park that night. After this, renters loudly paraded through several of the city's main streets, eventually arriving at the offices of the tenant union. Although they celebrated their release that day, Proal and his followers expressed significant dissatisfaction with Tejeda's last-minute revisions to the law. In an interview given shortly after leaving jail, Proal suggested that the union would continue its street activities to press for revolutionary change as they had before: "We will restart our open-air cultural conferences, demonstrations, and public meetings," he proudly asserted, "and of course, our commitment to direct action."[146] Although Proal's announcement followed state legislation that had responded, in part, to their demands, the Veracruz tenant movement continued to fight for radical social change. Despite their fierce dedication, the political tide began to turn against them. In fact, Governor Tejeda had already begun to direct his attention more to the organizing of rural peasants than to the plight of the urban poor.[147]

In late 1923 a major revolt led by Adolfo de la Huerta forced Tejeda to defend himself (as well as the administration of President Obregón) against powerful military forces. In the wake of these developments, tenant organizing gradually grew more fragmented. A bitter fight soon erupted over control of the tenant movement between Proal's followers and a new faction. In a conflict during the spring of 1924, the splinter group simply called the Tenant Organization (Organización Inquilinaria) was led by Proal's former partners Porfirio Sosa and Arturo Bolio.[148] Disagreements over how tenants would approach local and regional politics as well as the management of lands granted by the state led to a new round of public confrontations. At the same time, changes in the national political leadership contributed significantly to a social climate much less receptive to their cause.

The inauguration of Plutarco Elías Calles to the presidency on December 1, 1924, marked the beginning of the end for the tenant movement. On December 18, after a boisterous tenant demonstration and a fight in a *patio* that left several injured and one person dead, President Calles ordered Proal arrested and brought to Mexico City. Two days later Proal was formally charged with rebellion and jailed.[149] In his place María Luisa Marín and later Inés Terán took over leadership of the union. Under their guidance, tenants throughout the state continued to organize, monitoring the signing of new rental contracts, maintaining the network of patio committees, and initiating direct actions against uncooperative landlords.[150] They also devoted a great deal of time and energy to seeking Proal's release. Despite their petitions, however, he would remain in jail for the remainder of President Calles's term.[151]

Several important figures in the Veracruz tenant movement eventually abandoned the city, frustrated in their effort to achieve more significant social reforms. Úrsulo Galván and others affiliated with the Mexican Communist party, financed in part with money from the Tenant Syndicate, turned to organizing rural workers in the region under the banner of the Veracruz Peasant League (Liga de Comunidades Agrarias) sponsored by Tejeda.[152] Some, including Herón Proal, gradually resigned themselves to a life outside the political limelight after struggling for years against the strong-arm tactics of President Calles.[153] Vehemently opposed to Tejeda's legislation, landlords throughout the state continued to lobby against the rent law.

Conclusion

Despite the dramatic rise and gradual decline of the Veracruz tenant movement, collective action taken by renters, in conjunction with efforts on the part of cooperative political elites, made new housing reforms in Veracruz possible during the early 1920s. The Veracruz law proved to be the most significant housing reform of the period. It reduced rents to slightly more than 1910 levels and provided for the supervision of relations between landlords and tenants. Probably the most tangible concession, however, came in the form of land reform.

Tejeda's reform made provisions—granted through Article 27 of the Constitution—for expropriation of urban lands for the purposes of housing construction. In addition to his May 1922 offering of the Pocitos y Riviera or Colonia Comunista area to Proal and his followers, residents in 1926 saw the establishment of the new Adalberto Tejeda, Francisco I. Madero, Alberto Pastrana, and Vicente Guerrero worker settlements. These areas came under the supervision of the Unión Cooperativa de Colonias Obreras 22 de Marzo.[154] On May 7, 1931, state officials finally expropriated the Collado y Boticaria property (known to *porteños* as Colonia Flores Magón) from Spanish businessman Antonio Revuelta for the construction of additional worker housing.[155]

As in the port of Veracruz, tenants in Jalapa continued to strike between 1926 and 1930. Records from the municipal archive show considerable activity on the part of organized renters about the time local officials established a property evaluation board (*junta calificadora*) in February 1929.[156] During 1929 and 1930, residents of the Escojido, Ferrer Guardia, Cuauhtémoc, Sabino, San Roque, and Patio 15 *patios*, among others, complained of landlords who refused to comply with Tejeda's rent law. Some registered their payments with local authorities, sometimes at the Tenant Department in City Hall.[157] Records from other Veracruz cities also indicate that the law remained an everyday matter of contention for tenants, landlords, and government agents.

In Orizaba, tenants took note of revisions to Tejeda's rent law in 1926 and later organized a convention in February 1928. At that time, the local paper *La Prensa* announced:

> Difficulties between landlords and the Tenant Syndicate as well as a number of evictions carried out in the last month have suggested the need for a renters' convention. Representatives from both tenant and landlord organizations will take part under the supervision of authorities from the Labor Chamber. . . . Those invited from each group say they welcome the opportunity to resolve the much debated question. One of the primary recommendations already mentioned is that renters continue to comply with the state law, paying rents and thus avoiding any cause for eviction. Unfortunately, observers have noted that some tenants, members of the Agrupación de Inquilinos, are refusing to cooperate. Their actions have led to the present troubles.[158]

Thus, although Tejeda's housing reform looked good on paper, successful enforcement proved to be extremely difficult.

Information on the outcome of tenant protest in Córdoba presents a similar picture. By the end of 1925, a Tenant Department had been formed to help mediate relationships between landlords and tenants. Between 1926 and 1931, staff members of the department considered numerous cases, often negotiating tenement values, payment rates, eviction requests, and related issues. During this time, the Federación Inquilinaria del Estado de Veracruz served as the official organizing association for tenants, and the Revolutionary Syndicate continued its activities. In 1926 residents saw the establishment of a new worker neighborhood called the Colonia Aguillón Guzmán.[159] In April 1928 residents selected Moíses Lira, Rutilo Cruz, Antonio Rebgolledo, Benjamin Salazar, and Maure Zamora to form the Córdoba red union's new Executive Committee. During this time, many tenants in the city signed new agreements as tenant organizers continued to negotiate with landlords. The formation of new *colonias* in each of the state's major cities offered temporary relief for tenants while at the same time serving to help legitimate revolutionary governments. Despite many difficulties, Tejeda's 1923 Rent Law remained on the books until Governor Miguel Alemán repealed it in 1937.[160]

The tenant movement also helped introduce a new type of actor to the postrevolutionary political stage. As other studies of community organizing have also shown, women in the rent protests played a key role in defining urban popular resistance to revolutionary rule.[161] During the protest, tenant leaders Herón Proal and María Luisa Marín expressed a strong desire for gender equity, economic justice, political representation, and personal dignity in new ways during the 1920s. From an examination of tenant publications, petitions, and letters, as well as newspaper accounts of their activities, one can see that these individuals imagined new kinds of social relationships based on egalitarian concepts concerned not simply with class but with gender as well.[162] Although many may have initially taken to the streets in "defense of community," they soon developed new perspectives on local, regional, and national politics. For example, in the Veracruz tenant newspaper *Guillotina* of July 19, 1923, Estela V. Magón contributed an article entitled "La Esclava del Esclavo" that encouraged women to "wake up" and "demand your rights. . . . It is time [men] see women as [their] equal[s], as . . . sister[s]," she argued. "Remember," she told her male readers, "if you are fighting to better your life, your dreams will never be realized until women are thought of as equals. . . . without their help, your struggle against your enemies will be met with defeat." The emancipation of women, the author concluded, was intimately linked to the goals of the Revolution: "Emancipadla; y entonces para ambos hombre y mujer, será fácil ganar más pronto TIERRA Y LIBERTAD [Emancipate her, and in so doing it will be easier for both men and women to more quickly gain LAND AND FREEDOM]."[163] This article suggests that significant changes were taking place in consciousness about gender in 1920s Mexico.

Not coincidentally, as the rent protest came to a close, residents also revived the age-old celebration of Carnival. Carnival had originated in the *barrios negros* located just outside the city wall in the sixteenth century. Following the destruction of the wall in the mid-1870s, the popular celebration spread throughout the city. Hundreds of revelers, as they do today, participated in daily costumed parades (*desfiles*), dances, and general *mal humor* in anticipation of Ash Wednesday. Although the celebration waned during the years of the revolution, *porteños* living in the *patios*, particularly those of La Huaca *barrio*, revived the ritual in the mid-1920s. Many of those who paraded through city streets, enacting public ritual in a variety of ways, had also participated in the rent strike. Had rent protest spawned the revival of one of the city's most popular public rituals? The numerous parallels are certainly suggestive.

In Mexico, as in many other areas of the world, securing a home has often proved difficult, not only recently but over the course of the last century.[164] Given the degree to which those who rented houses engaged in collective action during the 1920s, there is little doubt that the emergence and process of protest and the range of results seen during the movement illustrate the tremendous capacity of citizens to pursue the goals of improved housing and social justice. Their protest cannot be dismissed as strictly local, as "premodern," or as characteristic of "old" social movements. Instead, tenant organizing took place at a national level and forced federal, state, and local leaders to respond.[165] Yet although residents in Veracruz, Orizaba, Jalapa, Córdoba, Mexico City, Guadalajara, and elsewhere proved themselves highly capable of coordinated action, political circumstances, rather than economic or moral frustration, largely determined protest trajectories.

From below, residents tended to mobilize when they believed they had a political opportunity to do so. Each neighborhood, city, and state provided a different context to be appraised in this regard. In cases in which citizens "read" political circumstances as impractical and inopportune, they tended to remain silent or possibly to engage in different, lower-profile (everyday) forms of resistance. In cases in which they thought the time was ripe and were wrong, they saw protest repressed by local authorities. When municipal leaders such as Veracruz mayor Rafael García urged residents to bolster their feelings of local and national pride, residents responded. Encouraged by similar populist appeals issuing from the governor's office in Jalapa, *veracruzanos* in several cities took action. The informal political alliance these leaders forged best explains why the Veracruz tenants achieved a mighty force as compared to similar but less successful efforts elsewhere. Not only did the Veracruz tenant movement prove to be an "early riser," leading the way for other protests, it also sustained itself the longest.

During the course of the protest, however, the structure of political opportunity changed in Veracruz, in part because property owners opposed to the tenant protest asserted themselves. Combined with resistance to the administrations of Obregón and Tejeda by other disgruntled elites, this opposition caused political opportunities and toleration for urban protest to decline significantly after the first five months of the strike. Although the Veracruz protesters survived federal repression, unlike their cousins in Mexico City and Guadalajara, the movement was increasingly divided from within. Noting this, officials then turned to a second strategy, which involved working to isolate Proal and his followers while negotiating a deal with other tenant leaders.

In this chapter I have tried to show how tenant protest in Veracruz came, first and foremost, because of political opportunity. Although housing conditions were equally bad in most cities, alliances and divisions that emerged after the revolution between national, regional, and local elites set the stage for tenant protest. Apparent national support, coupled with appeals for social justice at the local level, led grassroots organizers to decide to engage in collective action. In the end, national leaders disappointed tenants everywhere in Mexico, with the possible exception of Veracruz. There, state intervention in the housing market offered at least the promise of significant reform, even if it was never fully realized. Although tenant mobilization in Veracruz produced some important gains for state residents, its historical significance is that the tenants' actions today can be interpreted as an early "wake-up call" for a more democratic Mexico after the revolution. Just as tenant protest in Mexican cities during the 1920s marked the beginning of the consolidation of one-party rule, one can hope that more recent organizing among the urban poor will contribute to the dissolution of such rule.

Notes

Support for research in Mexico was provided by a 1993 University of California Mexus Dissertation Grant and the University of California, Davis, History Department. For a full treatment of the Mexican tenant movement, see Andrew Grant Wood, "The Making of *El Movimiento Inquilinario*: Tenant Protest and the State in Postrevolutionary Mexico: 1870–1927" (Ph.D. diss., University of California, Davis, 1997). Thanks to Arnold Bauer, John Walton, Charles Walker, Michael Johns, and Monica Barczak for their support. I also benefited from the advice of John Womack, Heather Fowler-Salamini, and Barry Carr, who commented on earlier versions of this chapter.

1. "Veracruz Tenants Rebel: Capture City Government," *New York Times*, July 8, 1923.

2. Barry Carr notes that for some writing in the 1980s, Alcozauca in the 1930s represented the first "red municipality" in Mexico. Though the port of Veracruz did not have a mayor and city council officially affiliated with the Communist party in 1922, the administration of Rafael "El Negro" García did exhibit significant pro-worker sympathies while tolerating, for a time, the more radical activities of labor and renter groups in the city. See Barry Carr, "The Fate of the Vanguard Under a Revolutionary State: Marxism's Contribution to the Construction of the Great Arch," in *Everyday Forms of State Formation: Revolution and the Negotiation of Rule in Modern Mexico*, ed. Gilbert Joseph and Daniel Nugent (Durham and London: Duke University Press, 1994), 326–352.

3. Ricardo Flores Magón and his brother Enrique founded the radical newspaper *Regeneración* in 1900. Under the banner of the Mexican Liberal party (founded in 1906), they created their own blend of anarchist and communist ideology (anarchocommunism) while advocating workers' rights and resistance to the regime of Porfirio Díaz. On the tradition of *magonismo,* see Arnaldo Cordova, *La ideología de la revolución mexicana: La formación del nuevo régimen* (Mexico City: Ediciones Era, 1973), 173–187; as well as W. Dirk

Raat, *Revoltosos: Mexico's Rebels in the United States, 1903–1923* (College Station: Texas A & M Press, 1981).

4. Campeche enacted housing reform in June 1921. The *Ley de Inquilinato* in Yucatán was approved on January 7, 1922. For a copy of the law, see *Diario oficial del gobierno socialista del estado libre y soberano de Yucatán*, April 12, 1922. For a discussion of reforms carried out under governors Salvador Alvarado and Felipe Carrillo Puerto, see Gilbert. M. Joseph, *Revolution from Without: Yucatán, Mexico, and the United States, 1880–1924* (Durham, N.C.: Duke University Press, 1988), 111–227. On the history of Campeche, see Jose Alberto Abud Flores, *Campeche: Revolución y movimiento social (1911–1923)* (Mexico City: Instituto Nacional de Estudios Históricos de la Revolución Mexicana, 1992); and Roger Elías Cornelio Sosa, *Historia del movimiento obrero de Campeche, 1540–1990* (Campeche: Federación de Trabajadores de Campeche, 1990).

5. Paco Ignacio Taibo II, *Bolshevikis: Historia narrativa de los origenes del comunismo en México, (1919–1925)* (Mexico City: Joaquín Mortiz, 1986), 176. Ignacio Taibo notes that a housing reform bill was introduced in the national Cámera de Diputados in September 1922. However, President Alvaro Obregón, with the support of other representatives, defeated the measure. For Obregón's response to the tenant syndicate, see Paco Ignacio Taibo II, "Inquilinos del D.F., a colgar la rojinegra," in *Anuario* 3 (Jalapa, Mexico: Centro de Estudios Históricos/Universidad Veracruzana, 1983), 125. With respect to tenant protest in Guadalajara, Jaime Tamayo observes that politicians passed no housing reform legislation during the 1920s; see Jaime Tamayo, "El Sindicato Revolucionario de Inquilinos y la huelga de rentas de 1922," in *Jalisco desde la Revolución: Los movimientos sociales, 1917–1929* (Guadalajara: Gobierno de Jalisco/Universidad de Guadalajara, 1988), 129–140. For information on tenant protest and housing conditions in Mexico, see Moisés González Navarro, *Población y sociedad en México, 1900–1970* (Mexico City: UNAM, 1974), vol. 1, 143–227; Manuel Perlo Cohen, "Política y vivienda en México, 1910–1952," *Revista Mexicana de sociología*, 41, no. 3 (July-September 1979): 769–835.

6. "State" is defined here as "the complex of administrative, extractive, and coercive organizations coordinated by an executive authority that claims compliance from the population within a delimited territory and supports this claim with superior control over the means of force, as well as those individuals who at any given time exercise formal control over this apparatus"; Kevin Middlebrook, *The Paradox of Revolution: Labor, the State, and Authoritarianism in Mexico* (Baltimore: Johns Hopkins University Press, 1995), 9. Cycles of protest can be understood as "heightened conflict, broad sectoral and geographic extension, the appearance of new social movement organizations [as well as] the empowerment of old ones, the creation of new, "master frames" of meaning and the invention of new forms of collective action as the main "elements of cyclicity" that constitute significant waves of protest; see Sidney Tarrow, "Cycles of Collective Action: Between Moments of Madness and the Repertoire of Contention," in *Repertoires and Cycles of Collective Action*, ed. Mark Traugott (Durham, N.C., and London: Duke University Press, 1995), 92.

7. For an earlier discussion of the rent strike that views this history through the lens of dependency theory and gives only slight attention to political process, see Manuel Castells, "The Dependent City and Revolutionary Populism: The Movimiento Inquilinario in Veracruz, Mexico, 1922," in *The City and the Grassroots: A Cross-Cultural Theory of Urban Social Movements* (Berkeley and Los Angeles: University of California Press, 1983), 37–48.

8. Pierre Chaunu, "Veracruz en la segunda mitad del siglo XVI y primera del XVII," *Historia Mexicana* 9, no. 4 (April-June 1960): 521–557. For travel accounts of the port during

the nineteenth century, see Alfred H. Siemens, *Between the Summit and the Sea: Central Veracruz in the Nineteenth Century* (Vancouver: University of British Columbia Press, 1990).

9. Sugar production expanded by a factor of six between 1900 and 1910 and then six times again between 1911 and 1921; Ricardo Corzo Ramírez et al., "Balance sobre la investigación de la formación de la clase obrera veracruzana, ca. 1850–1932," in *75 años de sindicalismo* (Mexico City: n.p., 1986), 192. The petroleum industry, much of it located in the region's rich Huasteca region in the north, experienced a significant boom between 1906 and 1921.

10. Bernardo García Díaz, *Puerto de Veracruz: Veracruz. Imágenes de su historia* (Jalapa, Veracruz: Archivo General del Estado de Veracruz, 1992), 95–98.

11. Ibid., 104.

12. For information on the growth of Veracruz and other Mexican cities during the nineteenth century, see Keith A. Davies, "Tendencias demográficas urbanas durante el siglo XIX en México," *Historia Mexicana* 21, no. 3 (January-March 1972): 481–524.

13. John Hart, *Anarchism and the Mexican Working Class, 1860–1931* (Austin: University of Texas Press, 1978), 85. By 1920 the port had emerged as Mexico's seventh-largest population center after Mexico City, Guadalajara, Puebla, Monterrey, Mérida, and San Luis Potosí; see Luis Unikel, *El desarrollo urbano de México: Diagnóstico e implicaciónes futuras*, 2nd ed. (Mexico City: Colegio de México, 1976).

14. On popular housing in Mexico City, see Moisés González Navarro, "La Raíz de Mal," in *Historia moderna de México, El Porfiriato, la vida social*, ed. Daniel Cosio Villegas (Mexico City and Buenos Aires: Editorial Hermes, 1957), 82–102; Taibo, "Inquilinos del D.F.," 103–106; Manuel Perlo Cohen, "Política y vivienda en México, 1910–1952," in *Revista Mexicana de Sociología* 41, no. 3 (July-September 1979): 769–835; and González Navarro, *Población y sociedad en México,* vol. 1, 143–227. Literature on popular housing and tenant organizing for other cities in Latin America include James Scobie, *Buenos Aires: From Plaza to Suburb* (New York: Oxford University Press, 1974); James Baer, "Tenant Mobilization and the 1907 Rent Strike in Buenos Aires," *The Americas* (January 1993): 343–368. On Chile, see Vicente Espinoza, *Para una historia de los pobres de la ciudad* (Santiago de Chile: Ediciones Sur, 1988). For Sao Paulo, see Lúcio Kowarick and Clara Ant, "One Hundred Years of Overcrowding: Slum Tenements in the City," in *Social Struggles and the City: The Case of Sao Paulo*, ed. Lúcio Kowarick (New York: Monthly Review Press, 1994), 60–76. On rent strikes and related popular organizing in New York City, see Ronald Lawson, *The Tenant Movement in New York City, 1904–1984* (New Brunswick, N.J.: Rutgers University Press, 1986).

15. On the history of *danzón* see Jesús Flores y Escalante, *Imagenes del danzón: iconografía del danzón en México* (Mexico City: Asociación Mexicana de Estudios Fonográficos, 1994); and Antonio García de Leon, "Los patios danzoneros," *La Jornada Seminal* 223 (September 19, 1993): 33–40. On Carnival in Veracruz, see Martha Cortés Rodríguez, "Bailes y carnaval en Veracruz, 1925," *Horizonte: Revista del Instituto Vercruzano de Cultura* 1, no. 1 (March-April 1991): 19–25. For accounts of the port's rich cultural history, see Roberto Williams García, *Yo nací con la luna de plata: Antropología e historia de un puerto* (Mexico City: Costa-Amic Editores, 1980); and Anselmo Mancisidor Ortiz, *Jarochilandia* (Veracruz: Author's edition, 1971).

16. For descriptions of the *patios,* see González Navarro, *Población y sociedad en México,* 181; and Cortés Rodríguez, "Bailes y carnaval en Veracruz," 20. For reports on popular housing conditions in Mexico City (January and February 1922) and Veracruz (June 1922)

published by the national department of labor, see *Boletín mensual del trabajo*, June 1922. For a general description of living conditions and public health issues in Mexico City around the turn of the century, see Alberto Pani, *La higiene en México* (Mexico City: J. Ballesca, 1916).

17. Though sanitation officials had begun to bring the port's legendary public health problems under control during the first two decades of the new century, Veracruz again experienced outbreaks of bubonic plague and yellow fever in 1920–1921. For a discussion of the Rockefeller Foundation's role in the public health of Veracruz, see Armando Solorzano, "The Rockefeller Foundation in Revolutionary Mexico: Yellow Fever in Yucatán and Veracruz," in *Missionaries of Science: The Rockefeller Foundation in Latin America*, ed. Marcos Cueto (Bloomington: University of Indiana Press), 52–71. Earlier improvements in the port's sanitation had come, in part, as a result of the U.S. invasion in 1914. For a description of cleanup activities during the occupation see Robert Quirk, *An Affair of Honor: Woodrow Wilson and the Occupation of Veracruz* (New York: Norton, 1962), chap. 4. Other North American impressions of the city can be gleaned from *New York Times* accounts (e.g., "The Peril in Germs That Infests Mexico," April 26, 1914; "(Funston) Cleans Veracruz in Seventeen Hours," May 15, 1914) or Jack London's jingoistic "Stalking the Pestilence," of June 13, 1914, reprinted in King Hendricks and Irving Shepard, eds., *Jack London Reports: War Correspondence, Sports Articles, and Miscellaneous Writings* (Garden City, N.Y.: Doubleday, 1970), 160–172.

18. "Los Patios de Vecindad 'En Su Tinta,'" *El Dictamen*, November 4, 1920.

19. Ibid.

20. "Los Patios de Vecindad y El Departmento de Ingenieria Sanitaria," *El Dictamen*, November 5, 1920.

21. Ibid.

22. Erica Berra-Stoppa, "Estoy en huelga y no pago renta!," *Habitación* 1, no. 1 (January-March 1981): 37; and González Navarro, *Población y sociedad en México,* 181. Robert Quirk notes that during the North American invasion, "(t)he thorniest problem dealt with by the legal department was that of rent disputes. During the period of anarchy which accompanied the revolutions against Díaz and Madero and now against Huerta, many of the Mexican tenants had deferred paying their rents as long as possible, and they were now months or even years in arrears. Nearly six thousand cases involving nonpayment of rent were brought before the informal American courts"; Quirk, *An Affair of Honor,* 142.

23. In 1914 the price of an average dinner amounted to around one peso in Veracruz. In 1922 a *porteño* would pay two and one half pesos for the same meal; Berra-Stoppa, "Estoy en huelga y no pago renta!," 37. Worker incomes, of course, varied considerably. On February 1, 1922, *El Dictamen* reported that workers of the Compañía Termial de Veracruz S.A. (the terminal company that was responsible for the transportation and storage of the import-export trade) had complained about the fact that stevedores earned 7.50 pesos per day (eight hours) whereas they received 4.90. For information on cost of living in Mexico for 1920–1921, see monthly reports prepared by the Department of Labor housed at the Archivo General de la Nación (hereafter AGN), ramo trabajo, boxes 184–189 (1920) and 245–247, 252–255 (1921).

24. On the crisis see Berta Ulloa, "Moneda, Bancos y Deuda," in *Historia de la revolución mexicana, 1914–1917* (Mexico City: Colegio de México, 1983), 159–178; and Diego G. López Rosado, *Historia del peso mexicano* (Mexico City: Fundo del Cultura Economica, 1987), 70–100.

25. Berra-Stoppa, "Estoy en huelga y no pago renta!," 37. By 1920 many agreed that rents in the port "had risen terribly, to the point where it [was] almost impossible for any employee of an average business to find adequate housing." "In the port," observers noted, "housing, as well as the cost of living in general, has always been higher than many other places in Mexico, but now rents are simply out of control"; "Son muy altas las rentas de casas," *El Universal*, August 1, 1920. For reports on worker housing and cost of living in Mexico City, see "El trabajo de sastrería y sus asimilares en México D.F.; Labor a domicilio." *Boletín mensual del Departamento de Trabajo*, January 1922; and "Higiene de la habitación: La habitación obrera en México, D.F." *Boletín mensual del Departamento de Trabajo*, February 1922.

26. Octavio García Mundo, *El movimiento inquilinario de Veracruz, 1922* (Mexico City: Sep-Setentas, 1976), 45.

27. *El Dictamen*, December 19, 1916.

28. Ibid.

29. Ibid., December 30, 1916. Aguilar had passed mild reforms on July 10, 1915, but Provisional Governor Miguel Aguilar reversed these a year later on November 18, 1916. *El Dictamen* reprinted Cándido Aguilar's new *Ley de Inquilinato* on December 1, 1917. See also García Mundo, *El movimiento inquilinario de Veracruz*, 44–45, 46–47.

30. Quoted in García Mundo, *El movimiento inquilinario de Veracruz*, 46.

31. For a discussion of Obregón's approach to state politics, see Ronald G. Hansis, "Alvaro Obregón, the Mexican Revolution, and the Politics of Consolidation, 1920–1924" (Ph.D. diss., University of New Mexico, 1971), 54–56.

32. Heather Fowler-Salamini, "Revolutionary Caudillos in the 1920s: Francisco Múgica and Aldalberto Tejeda," in *Caudillo and Peasant in the Mexican Revolution*, ed. D. A. Brading (Cambridge: Cambridge University Press, 1980), 190–191.

33. Ibid. On the emergence of mass politics in Mexico, see Thomas Benjamin, "Laboratories of the New State, 1910–1929," in *Provinces of the Revolution: Essays on Regional Mexican History, 1910–1929*, ed. Thomas Benjamin and Mark Wasserman (Albuquerque: University of New Mexico Press, 1990), 71–90.

34. For a history of Tejeda's political career, see Romana Falcón and Soledad García Morales, *La semilla en el surco: Adalberto Tejeda y el radicalismo en Veracruz, 1883–1960* (Mexico City: Colegio de México, 1986); and Olivia Domínguez Pérez, *Política y movimientos sociales en el Tejedismo* (Jalapa: Universidad Veracruzana, 1986).

35. He goes on to suggest that "(t)his is not to say the governor was the promoter of these radical explosions: The phenomena of extremism in Veracruz was the culmination of a process that had been developing in Mexico since the beginning of the century as a dialectic reaction of the Mexican people against thirty years of Porfirian repression"; Mario Gill, "Veracruz: Revolución y Extremismo," *Historia Mexicana* 2 (1952–1953): 618.

36. On Cándido Aguilar, see Ricardo Corzo Ramírez, José G. González Sierra, and David A. Skerritt, . . . *nunca un desleal: Cándido Aguilar, 1889–1960* (Mexico City: Colegio de México/Gobierno del Estado de Veracruz, 1986).

37. *El Dictamen*, January 2, 1922.

38. "Veracruz Tenants Rebel: Capture City Government," *New York Times*, July 8, 1923.

39. In his memoirs, García mentions tension between worker party propagandists and the local police during the 1921 campaign; Rafael García Auli, *La unión de estibadores y jornaleros del Puerto de Veracruz: Ante el movimiento obrero nacional e internacional de 1909 a 1977* (Veracruz: Author's edition, 1977), 44–45.

40. On the connections between workers in the Gulf ports, Gilbert Joseph says: "By 1921 there was, practically speaking, a Gulf union of dockworkers, although never formalized"; *Revolution from Without,* 225. Materials at the AGN on port workers in Campeche (especially in the Laguna de Carmen and Ciudad del Carmen areas) from the spring and summer of 1922 also suggest a developed network of well-informed and highly politicized workers.

41. As a consequence, CROM membership dropped to about 7,000; Hart, *Anarchism and the Mexican Working Class,* 158–159.

42. García Mundo, *El movimiento inquilinario de Veracruz,* 61.

43. Barry Carr, "Marxism and Anarchism in the Formation of the Mexican Communist Party, 1910–1919," *Hispanic American Historical Review* 63, no. 2 (February 1983): 289; Hart, *Anarchism and the Mexican Working Class,* 159–160; Taibo, *Bolshevikis,* 113–118.

44. Hart, *Anarchism and the Mexican Working Class,* 160.

45. Barry Carr notes that circulation of ideas regarding the Russian Revolution came, in part, through the Spanish radical press. Various articles from *Tierra y Libertad*, an anarchist paper from Barcelona, appeared regularly in the Mexico City paper *Luz* between 1917–1920; see Carr, "Marxism and Anarchism," 290. The periodicals collection at the Internationaal Instituut voor Sociale Geschiedenis in Amsterdam offers a rich variety of labor history materials for the period 1880–1940.

46. Taibo, "Inquilinos del D.F.," 101.

47. Ibid., 101–102.

48. García Mundo, *El movimiento inquilinario de Veracruz,* 15.

49. Arturo Bolio Trejo, *Rebelión de mujeres: Versión historica de la revolución inquilinaria de Veracruz* (Veracruz: Editorial "Kada," 1959), 26.

50. Ibid.

51. García Mundo, *El movimiento inquilinario de Veracruz,* 51.

52. Ibid., 53.

53. *El Dictamen*, January 8, 1916.

54. See, for example, reports in *El Dictamen* of February 13, 20, 1916.

55. Jesus Silva Herzog, *Breve historia de la revolución mexicana,* Quoted in García Mundo, *El movimiento inquilinario de Veracruz,* 54.

56. For the CTRM declaration of principles, see Rosendo Salazar, *La casa del obrero mundial* (Mexico City: Editorial Costa Amic, 1964), 194. Quoted in García Mundo, *El movimiento inquilinario de Veracruz,* 54.

57. On the history of socialism, communism, and anarchism in Mexico see also Gastón García Cantú, *El socialismo en México, siglo XIX* (Mexico City: Ediciones Era, 1969); Arnoldo Martínez Verdugo, ed., *Historia del comunismo en México* (Mexico City, Barcelona, Buenos Aires: Ediciones Enlace/Grijalbo, 1985); and Barry Carr, *Marxism and Communism in Twentieth-Century Mexico* (Lincoln: University of Nebraska Press, 1992).

58. Fowler-Salamini, *Agrarian Radicalism,* 29.

59. Hart, *Anarchism and the Mexican Working Class,* 160.

60. Fowler-Salamini, *Agrarian Radicalism,* 30.

61. *El Dictamen,* January 18, 1922. An editorial printed in the paper on December 28, 1921, pointed out that the housing crisis had not been resolved in the country. The author, Antonio Escobar, then went on to describe recent housing reforms in New York, Pittsburgh, Germany, and Canada.

62. Ibid.

63. Ibid., January 29, 1922.
64. Ibid., February 2, 1922.
65. Ibid.
66. Ibid., February 3, 1922.
67. Ibid.
68. Ibid.
69. Ibid.
70. Ibid., February 4, 1922.
71. Ibid.
72. Ibid.
73. Ibid., February 6, 1922.
74. Ibid.
75. Ibid.
76. Mario Gill, "Herón Proal," in *México y la revolución de octubre (1917)* (Mexico City: Biblioteca del Militante, 1975), 70.
77. Many of these men were also affiliated with the fledgling Mexican Communist party. For a discussion of the founding of the Mexican Communist party, see Carr, "Marxism and Anarchism," 277–305, as well as Harry Bernstein, "Marxismo en México, 1917–1925," *Historia Mexicana* 7, no. 4 (April-June 1958): 497–516.
78. *El Dictamen*, February 6, 1922. On the leadership of the union, see also Bolio Trejo, *Rebelión de mujeres*, 78; Rafael Ortega, *Las luchas proletarias en Veracruz* (Jalapa: Editorial "Barricada," 1942), 72.
79. *El Dictamen*, February 6, 1922.
80. Various documents dated July-December, 1912, in file titled *Barrio para las prostitutas*, exp. 50, letter c, Gobernación, 1912. Archivo General del Estado de Veracruz (hereafter AGEV).
81. *El Dictamen*, February 28, 1922.
82. Ibid.
83. Ibid., March 7, 1922.
84. Ibid.
85. Ibid., March 8, 1922.
86. Ibid., March 9, 1922.
87. García Mundo, *El movimiento inquilinario de Veracruz*, 86.
88. *El Dictamen*, March 13, 1922.
89. Ibid.
90. Ibid. See also Bolio Trejo, *Rebelión de mujeres*, 90.
91. Quoted in Mario Gill, "Veracruz: Revolución y Extremismo," *Historia Mexicana* 2 (July 1952–1953): 624.
92. On the presence of women in the movement, see also Mario Gill, "Veracruz," 622–624; Castells, "The Dependent City and Revolutionary Populism," 32; García de Leon, "Los patios danzoneros," 36.
93. Berra-Stoppa, "Estoy en huelga y no pago renta!," 35.
94. *El Dictamen*, May 25, 1922. On early connections to the growing peasant movement in the state, see Fowler-Salamini, *Agrarian Radicalism*, 25–47; and Romana Falcón, *El agrarismo en Veracruz: la etapa radical, 1928–1935* (Mexico City: Colegio de México, 1977), 32–43.
95. *El Dictamen*, June 14, 1922.
96. Many of these individuals were affiliated with the Federación Local de Trabajadores de Veracruz (FLTV). For information on the port's many labor unions, see Gema Lozano y

Nathal, *Catálogo del archivo sindical del Puerto de Veracruz; "Miguel Angel Montoya Cortés"* (Mexico City: Colección Fuentes, I.N.A.H., Instituto Nacional de Antropología e Historia, 1990), as well as Gema Lozano y Nathal, "La negra, loca y anarquista Federación Local de Trabajadores del Puerto de Veracruz," *Antropología* 30 (April-June 1990): 10–19.

97. *El Dictamen*, June 17, 1922. The following year, on September 8, 1923, workers again would organize a general strike in the port. This time the action began against the Electric Light Power and Traction Company. A few days later, the conflict spread throughout the city. For several weeks it was virtually impossible to obtain bread, milk, butter, ice, fresh fruit, vegetables, and other basic necessities. By the time it ended, the strike had left the port in ruinous condition. A few months after Tejeda left office in late 1923, the price of consumer goods had risen by almost 25 percent. Garbage filled the streets, while a lack of police encouraged a new wave of robberies and assaults; Falcón, *El agrarismo en Veracruz*, 34–35. For a detailed discussion of the streetcar and electrical workers' role in the strike, see María Rosa Landa Ortega, "Los primeros años de la organización y luchas de los electricistas y tranvarios en Veracruz, 1915–1928" (Licenciado en Sociología, Universidad Veracruzana, 1989). For a brief summary of the general strike and excellent historical photos, see García Díaz, *Puerto de Veracruz*, 210–214.

98. *El Dictamen*, April 30, 1922. According to the paper, Obregón indicated in a telegram to García that the *jefatura de la guarnición* had orders to prevent any kind of civil disorder in the port.

99. Ibid., March 14, 1922.

100. Ibid., March 15, 1922. For details on the founding of the Orizaba renters union, see the Orizaba paper *Pro-Paria*, April 9, 1922.

101. *El Dictamen*, June 30, 1922. See also Hart, *Anarchism and the Mexican Working Class*, 169.

102. *El Dictamen*, July 6–7, 1922. See also Bolio Trejo, *Rebelión de mujeres*, 142; and Ortega, *Las luchas proletarias en Veracruz*, 86.

103. González Navarro, *Población y sociedad en México*, vol. 1, 182.

104. Bolio Trejo, *Rebelión de mujeres*, 142; Ortega, *Las luchas proletarias en Veracruz*, 86; Taibo, *Bolshevikis*, 178–179.

105. *El Dictamen*, March 11, 1922.

106. Veracruz city council records from March 9, 1922. Feedback from local landlords was heard on March 23, 1922. *Veracruz Actas de Cabildo*, 1922, Book 101 (February 16–July 19), Archivo Municipal de Veracruz (hereafter AMV), 57–59, 78–82. During this time, the city council also discussed ways to encourage private initiatives in the building of worker housing; see, for example, *El Dictamen*, March 16, 1922.

107. Property owners had proposed a deal to public officials, including President Obregón, in mid-March suggesting that rents would be reduced if federal taxes were lowered. The paper noted that such action would have to be approved first by municipal and state governments; see *El Dictamen*, March 13, 1922.

108. García Mundo, *El movimiento inquilinario de Veracruz*, 100.

109. *Veracruz Actas de Cabildo*, March 30, 1922, AMV.

110. Later Tejeda issued an official statement on the tenant protest in his address to the state legislature in mid-September 1922; see *Memoria que rinde el Ejecutivo del estado libre y soberano de Veracruz-Llave, a la H. XXIX Legislature del mismo . . .*, in *Estado de Veracruz: informes de sus gobernadores, 1826–1986*, ed. Carmen Blásquez Domínguez, vol. 10 (Jalapa: Estado de Veracruz, 1986), 5480.

111. García Mundo, *El movimiento inquilinario de Veracruz,* 103.

112. Letter to Tejeda from Miguel Barranco, March 31, 1922, AGEV, Gobernación, box 676, 1922.

113. On April 24, Tejeda communicated to Secretary of Government Calles that his administration had been working with local officials to deal with the tenant protest; Tejeda to Calles, April 24, 1922, Archivo Tejeda, vol. 89, 1922. Quoted in García Mundo, *El movimiento inquilinario de Veracruz,* 112.

114. *El Dictamen,* May 14, 1922.

115. García Mundo, *El movimiento inquilinario de Veracruz,* 117–118. Renters had suggested rents based at 2 percent.

116. Ibid., 18. For a discussion of Obregón's relationship with the United States as related to the oil issue, see Lorenzo Meyer, *Mexico and the United States in the Oil Controversy, 1917–1942* (Austin: University of Texas Press, 1977), as well as Linda Hall, *Oil, Banks, and Politics: The United States and Postrevolutionary Mexico, 1917–24* (Austin: University of Texas Press, 1995), chap. 7.

117. García Mundo, *El movimiento inquilinario de Veracruz,* 18.

118. See *El Dictamen,* May 7, 1922. At this time, an area named Pocitos y Rivera just outside the city had been given to tenants to colonize.

119. *El Dictamen,* May 10, 1922.

120. Ibid., May 28, 1922.

121. It stipulated that rents would be reduced to 1910 levels plus 10 percent or, in cases where significant modifications or new construction had taken place after 1910, 9 percent of the property value. It granted other protections to renters against unauthorized evictions and potential landlord abuses. The legislation set guidelines for landlords to register their rental contracts with city officials, make repairs, and follow strict procedures regarding evictions. The bill also gave tenants a four-month moratorium, after which they would be expected to resume payment. See García Mundo, *El movimiento inquilinario de Veracruz,* 154.

122. Calles to Tejeda, June 11, 1922, Archivo Tejeda, quoted in Romana Falcón and García Morales, *Semilla en el surco,* 140. The same telegram indicated that President Obregón had instructed Veracruz military commander Guadalupe Sánchez to "not tolerate any act of violence or disorder initiated by the tenant Syndicate."

123. *Gaceta Oficial: Organo del Gobierno Constitucional del Estado de Veracruz-Llave,* July 11, 1922, pp. 1–3; *El Dictamen* printed the text of the law on July 14, 1922, but incorrectly dated the law's passage as July 5, 1922. See also González Navarro, *Población y sociedad en México,* 182–183 as well as Falcón and García Morales, *Semilla en el surco,* 142.

124. See editorials in *El Dictamen,* July 1–2, 1922.

125. Ibid., July 26, 1922. As another way to resist the new law, many property owners also continued to neglect tax payments. After a grace period during July, local officials began to prosecute these violations. In an article published on August 1, 1922, for example, *El Dictamen* claimed that landlords Manuel Cangas and Francisco Ruiz Murillo each owed three months of back taxes.

126. Ibid., December 1, 1922.

127. Ibid.

128. Ibid., December 12, 1922.

129. Ibid.

130. Ibid., December 27, 1922.

131. Ibid., December 28, 1922.

132. Ibid., December 31, 1922.

133. Ibid., January 1, 1923.

134. Ibid.

135. Ibid.

136. Ibid., January 3, 1923.

137. Ibid., January 5, 1923.

138. Ibid.

139. Ibid., April 8, 1923.

140. Ibid., April 12, 1923. During the first months of 1923 initial moves to establish worker housing in the port had been undertaken including a teachers neighborhood and other constructions. See also *El Dictamen*, April 26, 1923, for requests by customs house employees for city lots.

141. *El Dictamen*, April 23, 1923.

142. Ibid., April 29, 1923.

143. Gill, "Herón Proal," 74; Domínguez Pérez, *Política y movimientos sociales en el Tejedismo*, 62; Taibo, *Bolshevikis*, 183.

144. During 1926, the new worker settlements Adalberto Tejeda, Francisco I. Madero, Alberto Pastrana and Vicente Guerrero were organized under the banner of Unión Cooperativa de Colonias Obreras 22 de Marzo. *Veracruz Registro Público de la Propiedad*, October 7, 1926. The property Collado y Boticaria, long the site of informal popular settlement in the port (known by residents as the Colonia Flores Magón), was eventually expropriated from Spanish businessman Antonio Revuelta for the construction of additional worker housing on May 7, 1931; *Veracruz Registro Público de la Propiedad*, December 15, 1932, AGEV.

145. *El Dictamen*, May 12, 1923.

146. Ibid.

147. On the connections between urban and rural organizing, see Fowler-Salamini, *Agrarian Radicalism*, as well as Victor Hugo Valencia Valera, "La influencia del movimiento urbano (los inquilinos) en la organización campesina: Veracruz, 1923," *Antropología* 32 (October-December 1990): 14–21.

148. Former members of the Revolutionary Syndicate Arturo Bolio and Porfirio Sosa formed the Organización Inquilinaria on April 5, 1924. For documents stating their principles, see AGEV, Gobernación, box 792, file 308, letter U.V.

149. *El Dictamen*, December 19–22, 1924. Although tenants dedicated themselves to securing Proal's return to Veracruz, their efforts were not successful. For examples of their communications to federal officials, see letters (with well over 100 signatures each) from members of the syndicate dated January 14, 1925; September 3, 1926; October 4, 1926; AGN, *Suprema Corte de Justicia*, vols. 2018–2034.

150. On the activities and leadership of María Luisa Marín, see an editorial printed in *El Dictamen* in early February 1925 that stated: Upon her arrival in the port she wasted no time in beginning her "agitation in the *patios*, aggressive commentaries among organized tenants against the authorities, shooting off firecrackers, and a host of other activities that have resulted in the notorious demonstrations remembered with horror by the suffering residents of this city"; "El Buen negocio de Proal," *El Dictamen*, February 7, 1925.

151. Berra-Stoppa, "Estoy en huelga y no pago renta!," 39.

152. For accounts of this history see Fowler-Salamini, "Orígenes laborales," 235–264.

153. Herón Proal died on January 29, 1959.

154. *Veracruz Registro Public de la Propiedad*, October 7, 1926.

155. Ibid., December 15, 1932.

156. Archivo Municipal de Jalapa (AMJ), packet 28, file 69.1.

157. Mention of the Sindicato Evolutivo de Inquilinos Federados in letters of January 9 and August 10, 1929, suggests they remained one of the most important tenant organizations active at the time; ibid. See also files 69.2–12, and packet 26, files 69.12–16.

158. *La Prensa*, February 2, 1928.

159. Beatriz Calvo Cruz, "El Movimiento Inquilinario en Córdoba, Veracruz" (Bachelor's thesis, Universidad Veracruzana, n.d.).

160. Gill, "Herón Proal," 630.

161. For accounts of women confronting tax collectors, obstructing evictions, and carrying out other acts of resistance similar to those of the urban women in the 1920s, see Carlos Vélez-Ibañez, *Rituals of Marginality: Politics, Process, and Cultural Change in Urban Central Mexico* (Berkeley and Los Angeles, University of California Press, 1983), 119–122.

162. In considering the ways in which gender analysis intersects with popular protest, historian Temma Kaplan argues that "the collective drive to secure [certain traditional] rights . . . sometimes has revolutionary consequences insofar as it politicizes the networks of everyday life." These consequences sometimes lead to the observation not only that the networks of everyday life become politicized but that men and women may even "transcend the purposes" for which these networks were originally intended. Kaplan writes that some women who "in the course of struggling to do what women in their society and class were expected to do . . . became outlaws"; Temma Kaplan, "Female Consciousness and Collective Action: The Case of Barcelona, 1910–1918," *Signs: Journal of Women and Culture* (Spring 1982): 545, 567.

163. *Guillotina*, July 19, 1923.

164. Two recent contributions to the literature on Latin American housing are Alan Gilbert, *In Search of a Home: Rental and Shared Housing in Latin America* (London: UCL Press, 1993); and Alan Gilbert and Ann Varley, *Landlord and Tenant: Housing and the Poor in Urban Mexico* (London and New York: Routledge, 1991). Both books advance our understanding of the politics of housing in new directions by mapping the range of options available to residents (housing types, ownership versus renting, etc.), following up and revising earlier studies, comparing the impact (or lack thereof) of government policies as well as considering relations between landlords and tenants.

165. See Teresa Meade's argument against neighborhood- and consumer-based protest being considered as premodern in Teresa A. Meade, *"Civilizing" Rio: Reform and Resistance in a Brazilian City, 1889–1930* (University Park: Pennsylvania State University Press, 1997), 177–192.

5
Buenos Aires: Housing Reform and the Decline of the Liberal State in Argentina

James A. Baer

Buenos Aires presents one of the most dramatic examples of urban growth through immigration among Latin American cities. The creation of a national government with Buenos Aires as its capital and the success of economic and political policies instituted by landowning elites brought significant changes to the city. Between 1869 and 1910 its population expanded from 177,000 to more than 1.2 million, and by 1910, 46 percent of "*porteños*," as the residents of Buenos Aires were called, had been born abroad. The city's population continued to grow during the second decade of the twentieth century, even with the immigration decrease due to World War I, and numbered 2 million by 1930. These immigrants became an important part of the labor force and brought with them experience in labor unions and knowledge of socialist and anarchist ideologies that would challenge the liberal, free market–oriented state fashioned by these elites.

Buenos Aires experienced many serious problems due to rapid urban growth. This chapter will focus on one crucial aspect: housing and its link to working-class struggles for better living conditions. The urban working class of Argentina, steadily increasing through continued immigration, acted both as consumers and as producers in demanding government assistance to improve its standard of living. Not only through labor unions but also by the sheer number of its members, the working class would exert a powerful force that would eventually lead to reforms by land-owning elites who hoped to forge a multiclass alliance to ensure control of political offices. Expensive, overcrowded, and unhealthy housing provided a focal point because it signified the inability of market forces to improve the lives of the largely immigrant working class. This tension between economic development and working-class challenge is central to the concept of collective consumption as described by Manuel Castells and David Harvey.[1] They use the term "collective consumption" to refer to housing, transportation, health care, and even access to open spaces that are shared by different groups within cities and may lead to reform coalitions in response to problems of urbanization. In Argentina the Radical party attempted to take power away from entrenched elites, beginning with an uprising in 1890 and continuing political challenges into the twentieth century. Legislation to reform the political process and laws to alleviate some of the worst housing problems encountered by the working class in Buenos Aires stemmed in part from the rivalries between the Radicals and these elites. This chapter will show how an active working class, whose demands had been articulated through labor unions, newspapers, and tenant associations, found new, if temporary, allies among contending political parties seeking power.

Concerns about housing conditions and costs were expressed by a variety of groups in Argentina during the first decades of the twentieth century. Anarchist unions and members of the working class believed that the capitalist system, with its reliance on private property, was incapable of providing adequate shelter. Catholic reformers were especially troubled by overcrowding, which they thought led to a decline in morality and the degradation of the lives of workers. Finally an increasing number of representatives in Congress, conservatives, and, after 1912, Radicals as well as Socialists saw housing reform as a way to obtain political support from a growing electorate. This convergence of interests in housing issues played an important but largely ignored part in the decline of the liberal state in Argentina. The culmination of postwar political change in Argentina was the 1921 rent law, a dramatic example of state intervention in social and economic policies, which signaled a more active state that would later be called "populist." Historians have identified the inability of conservative and Radical administrations to bring political stability in Argentina as a "failure of democracy."[2] But in a broader sense it was also a failure of liberalism, especially with regard to the provision of low-cost housing, a critical need among Argentina's working class.

Housing was more than an important consumer issue; it was a nexus for economic, social, and political forces that helped shape modern Argentina.[3] Economically, housing represented opportunities for capital accumulation through speculation and investment by property owners, it provided employment and profits for construction firms and their subcontractors and suppliers, and it affected the cost of living. Socially, housing encompassed the living conditions of individuals and families, questions of public health and hygiene, and a growing sense of identity among tenement dwellers who shared common problems. And politically, housing-related issues included tax policies, building and health codes, and state financing.

The origin of the interventionist state in Europe and North America has been linked to pressures from World War I. State control and intervention in the economy and in society exceeded what had been accepted and became the norm. One crucial area in which government response changed was housing problems. D. C. M. Platt compared housing circumstances in Australia, Argentina, and Canada and found that housing reform proceeded from an interest of private charities to a government responsibility.[4] "Churches, private charity and self-help developed (under the twin pressures of rising population and urbanization) into municipal care; once the expense had become unmanageable, it was transferred to the State."[5] But circumstances in Argentina were different from those of Australia, Canada, the United States, or England. All these countries had been participants in the Great War. England, in 1915, passed a Mortgage Reduction Act because "sharply rising rents were causing widespread discontent in areas of war industry, and especially in Glasgow where a rent strike threatened to take on revolutionary overtones."[6] But Argentina had remained neutral during the war. If it was not direct participation in the war itself that produced a change in the state in Argentina, what were the pressures that caused its government to become actively involved in housing reform?

A crisis in housing costs and conditions, especially among the working class, had existed for decades and led to a massive rent strike in Buenos Aires in 1907.[7] Conditions continued to deteriorate during the war years. Eventually, several different groups came to realize that state intervention was necessary because housing problems had defied solutions available within the liberal tradition under which Argentina had otherwise prospered. This liberal tradition had been implemented by an oligarchy that sought economic growth through market forces and the protection of private property and that sought political stability through manipulation of the electoral system. When challenged by the Unión Civica's rebellion in 1890 and by increasing labor unrest fomented by anarchists and socialists, these traditional elites, whose wealth and power stemmed from control of land and the export economy, permitted changes that allowed elected representatives in Congress to debate possible solutions to housing and other social issues. While agreement emerged among many groups about the need for reform, there was less agreement regarding the scope of intervention and the specific policies that should be implemented. But the passage of a rent law in 1921, which gave the state power to limit rent, was a dramatic shift and the first of many interventions by the federal government in Argentina regarding housing.[8]

The research presented in this chapter synthesizes statistics on population growth and housing conditions that depict the daily struggle of working-class tenants in the period between 1870 and 1930 and show how they responded actively to these problems. Their strategies reflect a sense of cohesion and solidarity that has heretofore only emerged in studies of labor unions. Tenant leagues, a rent strike, and ongoing, if ad hoc, organization demonstrate the ability of these working-class tenants to pursue their goals purposefully and collectively.[9]

The economic environment of a port city influenced by export cycles must be taken into account because it has an impact on the timing of events, as other chapters in this book indicate. Buenos Aires shared many of the problems of rapid urban growth that Montevideo and Rio de Janeiro experienced, suggesting that the economic patterns of immigrant port cities created similar circumstances for their inhabitants. These port cities developed as centers for the export trade and controlled much of their respective countries' wealth. As centers of populations, they were affected by diseases and on occasion epidemics. And as national capitals they generated the bureaucratic cadres that controlled government offices and helped allocate resources. However, the examples of Veracruz and Valparaiso also indicate that secondary cities experienced many of the same problems without the political and economic power of the capital. Finally, the response of landed elites is linked to political reforms that created the opportunity for a coalition among forces whose divergent interests are partially masked by common concerns for housing problems.

Housing Issues and the Liberal State, 1870–1910

Beginning in the 1870s Argentina experienced a continuous crisis caused by the lack of low-cost housing. The situation was especially serious in Buenos Aires, the country's capital and largest city. President Domingo Faustino Sarmiento's policies of encouraging immigration and economic expansion through open market trade with Europe represented the triumph of liberalism and assisted the social and economic transformation of Argentina. The resultant changes transformed the city of Buenos Aires after midcentury, although its architecture and size still reflected its colonial heritage.[10] The muddy banks of the Rio de la Plata forced ships to unload far from the town, and goods were brought to shore on large wagons or lighters, much as they had been in the 1700s. The resolution of civil wars, the Constitution of 1853, and the stable government presided over by liberal thinkers who wished to follow the path of Europe and North America toward economic and political liberty for the individual brought dramatic change to Argentina and Buenos Aires. Port facilities were improved and railroads were constructed, largely with foreign investments. Refrigerator ships allowed increased exporting of beef to Europe, and imports of luxury goods rose. The city of Buenos Aires began to grow in size, and immigration fueled this rapid increase in population.[11]

Population growth outpaced available housing, causing overcrowding and high rents. Although many workers chose to seek land on the edge of the city on which to construct their own small homes, others remained in the central districts of the city in *conventillos*, or tenements. These were usually older, large, colonial-style buildings that housed many families in small rooms off a central courtyard. In some *conventillos* increasing density had an impact on health conditions and became a concern of authorities during the 1871 yellow fever epidemic. And rent increases, according to Department of Labor statistics, averaged 10 to 12 percent per year between 1907 and 1912.[12]

The first attempts to address housing problems were promoted by municipal authorities and private charities, reflecting the liberal belief that social issues were

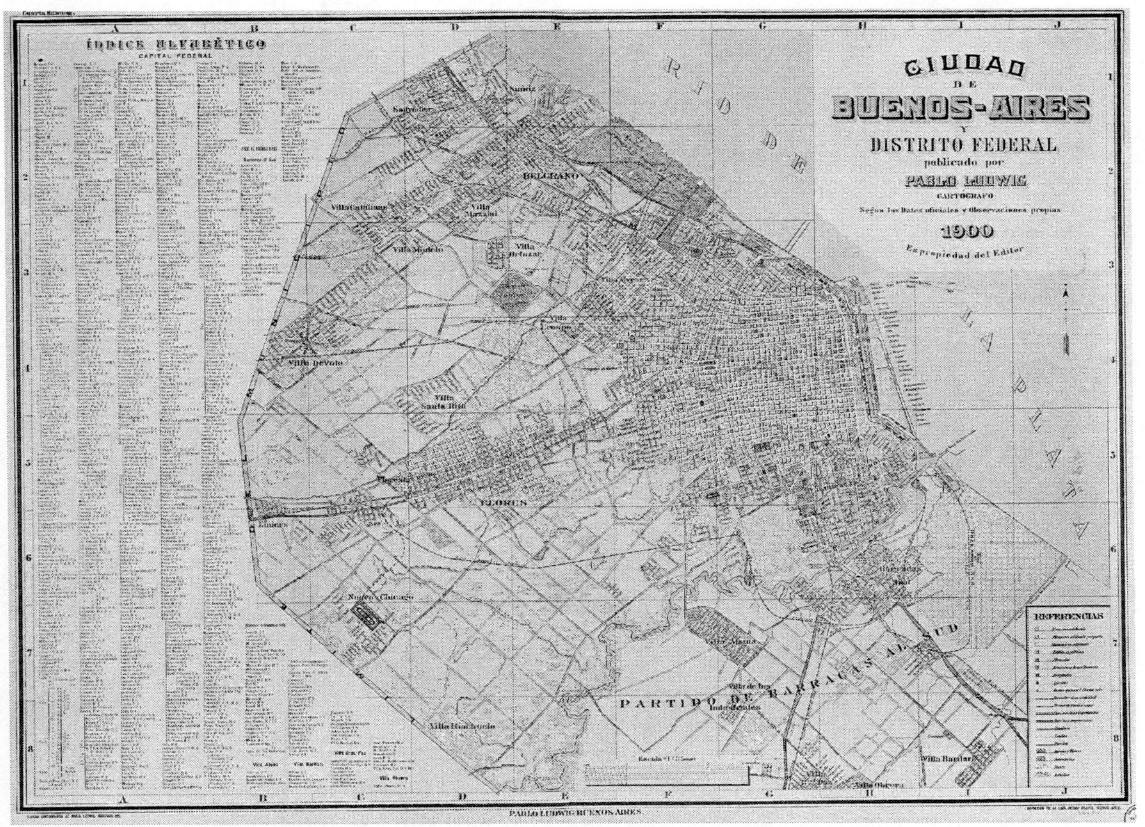

MAP 5.1 Buenos Aires, Argentina, 1900. Reproduced from the collection of the Library of Congress.

to be addressed locally and privately. In 1887 the mayor of Buenos Aires proposed building public housing for workers (*casas de obreros*). The project was built at the north end of the city. A Catholic group, the Saint Vincent de Paul Society, constructed ninety-six two- and three-room houses and rented them for twenty-five to thirty pesos per month. The Socialist party's El Hogar Obrero, organized as a cooperative to provide funds for the construction of worker homes, built thirty-two apartments downtown at the intersection of Bolívar and Martín García Streets. A few private companies also built low-cost housing for their employees. A knitting factory, Establecimientos Americanos Gaty, constructed a group of two- and three-room houses near the factory. The Compañía General de Fosforos, a match company, and Ferrocarril Sud, the Southern Railroad, also built houses for their employees.

The federal government, however, did not pass housing legislation until 1905, when the national Congress passed Law 4824, Casas para Trabajadores (Housing for Workers). This legislation did not represent direct government intervention. Instead, it authorized the municipality of Buenos Aires to collect 25 percent of the receipts of the Thursday races at the Jòckey Club to be used for public housing. Other proposals for direct state intervention in funding or building working-class housing failed to pass.[13] This legislation eventually led to the construction of seventy-four houses on land donated by a wealthy woman, Azucena Buteler, and 116 additional houses on municipal land with 2 million pesos from the city government in 1907. The project was to be directed by a Catholic charity, the Sociedad de la Sagrada Familia—Protectora del Obrero, whose board of directors included women from the most prestigious families in Argentina.[14] Although the original plans for the housing project were drawn up in July, the land had not yet been donated, and the project was not begun until November of that year, when the city was in the throes of a prolonged rent strike initiated by working-class tenants.

Working-Class Response to Housing Problems: Direct Action

Argentina's working class was largely made up of immigrants. They sought work in the port, on construction sites, or in the growing number of factories and workshops in Buenos Aires. They tended to congregate in the center sections of the city, close to jobs and where the majority of the city's *conventillos* were located. High rents, poor conditions, and avaricious landlords were issues that transcended union membership, gender, or ideology and led to tenants' mobilization.[15]

Working-class tenants created tenants' leagues to oppose high rents with the support by both anarchist and socialist unions. The first reported housing league was created in 1893.[16] In 1896 the socialist newspaper, *La Vanguardia*, did a study on housing problems, estimating that rent consumed 25 to 30 percent of a worker's wages.[17] In 1905 another league, the Liga de Inquilinos, sought a 50 percent reduction in rent.[18] The sixth congress of the anarchist Federación Obrera

Regional Argentina (FORA) voted to support a tenant strike movement in 1906 as a new tenant organization, Liga Contra Alquileres e Impuestos (League Against Rents and Taxes), was formed.[19]

Tenants in the city's *conventillos* reacted to rent increases of up to 45 percent with a rent strike in August 1907.[20] Tenants blamed these rent increases on their landlords. *Conventillo* owners were called robbers by the anarchist newspaper *La Protesta.* Rental agents were "a parasitic industry," according to the conservative *La Prensa,* and the socialist *La Vanguardia* referred to the "insatiable greed of the landlords."[21] Representatives from the tenant's committee met with Mayor Marcelo Torcuato de Alvear and asked him to declare a halt to evictions of those renters who participated in the strike by refusing to pay their rent.[22] The mayor promised to look into the matter and met with the minister of the interior of the national government to propose that federal taxes on property be reduced because recent tax increases had been cited by property owners as the reason for rent hikes. Later the mayor pursued this plan with the property owners, suggesting a proposal to institute a form of rent control in return for tax reductions and tax increases for those property owners whose profits exceeded an acceptable amount. The property owners rejected the mayor's plan, and nothing came of municipal intervention.[23] By early 1908 the strike had achieved only limited success and was called off. Rents began to rise again, increasing from twenty-five pesos per month in 1907 to twenty-nine pesos per month in 1912, on average.[24]

In the second decade of the twentieth century immigrants continued to arrive in Buenos Aires, straining the already-inadequate supply of available housing. In 1912 alone, a net total of 206,121 immigrants was added to Argentina's population of fewer than 8 million. World War I would lead to significant changes in the composition and the nature of Argentina's working class, however. The war years, 1913–1917, were ones of depression. Poor harvests and reduced foreign investments in 1913 were followed by a near cessation of foreign trade at the beginning of hostilities in 1914. Trade resumed on a small scale the following year, but exports plummeted. Wheat exports fell from nearly 3 million to less than 1 million metric tons. This affected other branches of the economy; unemployment hovered between 16 and 20 percent during the war. (See Table 5.1.) Immigration turned to exodus as 63,000 more people left the country than entered in 1914. (See Table 5.2.)

The effects of this wartime depression were felt by the working class, which saw its cost of living increase more than 16 percent between 1914 and 1916. (See Table 5.3.) Reduced immigration and lower urban property values brought a decrease in rent in 1915 and 1916. But the average cost of rent rose after 1916, from twenty-nine pesos in 1912 to thirty-two pesos in 1919.[25] As real wages declined between 1917 and 1921 due to inflation, working-class Argentines were becoming worse off. Housing conditions deteriorated, and crowding in the *conventillos* increased from 3.8 persons per room in 1913 to 4.5 in 1917.[26]

In 1913 there were 138,000 people crammed into 2,462 *conventillos;* 70 percent of working-class families in Buenos Aires were living in one-room dwellings.[27] De-

TABLE 5.1 Unemployment Percentages: Argentina, 1912–1918

Year	%
1912	5.1
1913	6.7
1914	13.7
1915	14.5
1916	17.7
1917	19.4
1918	10.8

SOURCE: *Revista de Economia Argentina,* year 2, vol. 4, no. 20 (February 1920): 106.

TABLE 5.2 Emigrants in Excess of Immigrants per Year: Argentina, 1914–1918

Year	*N*
1914	63,363
1915	66,169
1916	40,358
1917	32,931
1918	10,379

SOURCE: Alejandro Bunge, *Revista de Economica Argentina,* year 1, vol. 2, no. 7 (January 1919), 43.

TABLE 5.3 Cost of Living, Rent, and Real Wages: Argentina, 1910–1922

Year	*Cost of Living (1910 = 100%)*	*Rent (1910 = 100%)*	*Real Wages of Workers (1929 = 100%)*
1910	100	100	—
1911	101	107	—
1912	106	114	—
1913	108	117	—
1914	108	101	68
1915	117	94	61
1916	125	88	57
1917	146	90	49
1918	173	117	42
1919	186	152	57
1920	171	—	59
1921	153	—	73
1922	150	—	84

SOURCES: Cost of living: David Rock, *Argentina from 1516 to 1987* (Berkeley and Los Angeles: University of California Press, 1987), 195; rent: *Revista de Economia Argentina,* year 2, vol. 4, nos. 23–24 (May-June 1920), 352; and real wages: Samuel L. Baily, *Labor and Nationalism* (New Brunswick N.J.: Rutgers University Press, 1967), 31.

TABLE 5.4 Strike Activity and Participation: Argentina, 1910–1917

Year	Number of Strikes	Number of Strikers
1910	296	18,803
1911	102	27,992
1912	99	8,992
1913	95	23,698
1914	64	14,137
1915	65	12,077
1916	80	24,321
1917	138	135,062
1918	196	133,042
1919	397	308,967
1920	206	134,015
1921	86	139,751
1922	116	4,737

SOURCE: Department of Labor figures in Ruben Rotondaro, *Realidad y cambio en el sindicalismo* (Buenos Aires: Editorial Pleamar, 1971), 98.

partment of Labor figures indicated that in 1915, 55 percent of all working-class families lived in one-room dwellings, and about 40 percent lived in two-room homes.[28] In 1920 Alejandro E. Bunge commented on conditions in the *conventillos* and the continual crisis in housing: "Ever alarming, always denounced as a national sore, always combated with words and plans, but never overcome."[29] Bunge's statistics reveal how little had changed over the years: By 1920 there were 140,000 to 150,000 working-class families living in *conventillos,* 80 percent in one-room homes, 3 percent with nine or more persons per room, 12 percent with seven to eight persons per room, and 45 percent with three or four persons per room. These workers found it impossible to accommodate increases in rent, which ranged from 19 percent of wages in 1914 to 30 percent in 1918, because they were already sharing space in order to reduce rental costs.[30] Argentina's working class was being squeezed during the war years figuratively and literally. By the time economic recovery began in 1917 workers were anxious to make up for losses, and a spate of strikes ensued. (See Table 5.4.)

Increased labor agitation was also the result of continued industrial growth. Between 1895 and 1914 the number of industrial establishments had doubled. Many of these industries were related to agriculture: dairy products, sugar refining, and meat packing. Most manufacturing establishments were small, averaging about fifteen workers each. Nevertheless, union activity increased with the addition of workers in industry and as a result of deteriorating economic circumstances among workers.

There was also a shift taking place at this time in the labor movement. The anarchist FORA, which had advocated militant direct action on the part of workers and tenants, had lost much of its power since the outburst of strikes prior to 1910.

Many anarchist militants had been deported, and with the decline in immigration due to the war, their ranks had not been renewed. Instead, with the growing numbers of second-generation Argentines and increasing diversification of skills among the workers, syndicalism became the more dynamic movement. Syndicalists, like anarchists, opposed state control but focused less on the messianic revolutionary general strike and more on union organization to bring about the new order. The distinction between these two groups led to a split in the hitherto anarchist FORA at its ninth congress in 1915. The syndicalists emerged in control of the worker federation, and the anarchist unions withdrew, keeping the name FORA but adding "of the V Congress," referring to the 1905 congress, which had stressed the principles of anarchocommunism. This division among anarchists would lead some to support labor and housing legislation in the early 1920s that resulted in the 1921 rent law.

Housing and the Catholic Social Movement

The Catholic church was another important group that sought reforms and a solution to the ongoing housing crisis. By the end of the nineteenth century, Catholic reformers were becoming increasingly critical of a liberal state that maintained that social issues were largely outside the scope of government action. The First National Assembly of Argentine Catholics was organized in 1884 to encourage a Christian response to social questions. The assembly issued an eight-point statement entitled "Catholics and Social Issues." On housing, it said: "High rents, large families in tenement houses, rooms small and unhealthy, all conspire against the health, the dignity, and the morality of the working-class family."[31] In 1892 the Círculo Obrero (Worker's Circle) was created specifically to address working-class problems raised by Pope Leo XIII, whose 1891 encyclical *Rerum Novarum,* although upholding the principle of private property, criticized capitalism for its inability to overcome the poverty and debasement of the working class. In 1905 the Catholic newspaper *Voz de la Iglesia* published a series of articles on the Catholic response to social questions. In the October 18 edition, a page-one article appeared under the headline "The Question of Rents"; it referred to housing as one of the most serious problems facing the working class.[32] The paper blamed greedy property owners and high property taxes for the problem. Although sympathetic to workers' difficulties, the Catholic movement was reluctant to support reforms that would emphasize class distinctions. In late October 1905 *Voz de la Iglesia* criticized the concept of working-class neighborhoods being built as housing projects. It thought workers' housing ought to be spread throughout the city so that workers would have opportunities to learn a better way of life from their social superiors.[33]

In October 1907 the Second National Congress of Argentine Catholics met in Buenos Aires during the rent strike. Catholic reformers, however, were more concerned with helping workers purchase their own homes. Juan F. Cafferata introduced the following proposal, which typified the rationale and approach of the Catholic reform movement: "Making a property owner out of a worker is one of the best ways to save him from anarchism or other ideas that disturb the social order. Ownership of a clean, healthy, and moral home is one of the greatest benefits for a worker."[34] He called on (1) governments to provide low-cost housing for workers, (2) the wealthy to donate funds for this purpose, and (3) Catholics to assist with these efforts.

Cafferata, an obstetrician from Córdoba, also served as a delegate to conferences of the Círculo Obrero and introduced motions for action in the face of increasing housing problems for the working class. Continuing to press for housing reforms, Cafferata began his political career in Córdoba, where he was elected first to the city council and then in 1911 to the provincial senate. In 1912 he became a national deputy and returned to Buenos Aires to serve in Congress. Although Cafferata was elected to local office as an independent, he was sympathetic to the traditional conservative party and was elected to Congress as a member of the Constitutional party. In September 1912 Cafferata sponsored legislation in the Chamber of Deputies to provide low-cost housing for workers. "Private enterprise," he said to fellow deputies, "has accomplished much. But by itself, it is incapable of solving the (housing) problem. Therefore, we need to encourage collective responses in the form of cooperatives and savings and loans."[35] Although not specifically calling for state intervention, Cafferata wanted the government to encourage and facilitate collective action to address the housing problem.

Cafferata was unable to obtain support for legislation in a Congress dominated by conservative delegates who accepted the concept of limited government intervention. *La Nación*, the Buenos Aires daily newspaper founded by Bartolomé Mitre, one of the creators of the liberal state in Argentina, reported one official as saying: "Here, no one is poor permanently," indicating the belief that individual initiative would lead to social mobility. The article continued: "To build worker housing, either single-family houses or apartment buildings, is to create working-class neighborhoods. And this will lead to an organization of a separate social order, set apart, suffering under a fatalistic sense of class."[36]

Cafferata introduced legislation again in January 1913 and May 1914, citing statistics showing that the average monthly cost of rent was twenty-eight pesos for one room and up to sixty pesos for larger apartments. Because of these high rents, 70 percent of all working-class families in Buenos Aires were living in one-room accommodations. This was, he thought, unbefitting individuals of the working class, who ought to be raised to a higher station in society. Cafferata claimed that "state intervention does not exclude municipal or private initiatives. On the contrary, each one complements the other in this humanitarian and social effort."[37] Unwilling to abandon completely his notion that individual effort and market forces could help resolve the housing crisis, Cafferata accepted a form of governmental partnership. As a Catholic reformer, Cafferata genuinely desired better living conditions for working-class families so that their morals would not be degraded through indiscriminate mixing of men, women, and children in crowded tenements.

Politics and Housing Issues

The political events that would eventually lead to housing legislation began with electoral reforms in Argentina, reforms named for President Roque Sáenz Peña. In 1910 Sáenz Peña, candidate of the ruling oligarchy, was elected president of Argentina. He set out to reform the electoral system by increasing the size of the electorate and guaranteeing a secret ballot.[38] In 1912 these electoral reforms had become law, and the dynamics of political and class relations came to reflect the recognition that housing had become both a class issue and a political opportunity.

Economic depression due to war and union discord over ideology weakened the power of members of the working class to press for improvement in their circumstances. However, after the Sáenz Peña voting reforms and with the increasing presence of Socialist party and Radical party deputies in Congress, working-class grievances were openly debated, especially in the lower chamber. Socialist deputy Alfredo Palacios, who had earlier served in Congress, was returned in 1912 and served, along with the party's leader, Juan B. Justo. In 1913 and 1914 voters from Buenos Aires elected more Socialist deputies and one Socialist senator. Housing costs were among the problems listed by the Socialists in their 1913 campaign literature.[39] Nevertheless, in spite of continued pressure for social legislation throughout the war years, including calls for a rent freeze, the Socialists would be challenged for working-class support by the Radicals.

Congress was slow to respond to the housing crisis. Even though Mayor Manuel J. Guiraldes of Buenos Aires had said in 1912 that construction of low-cost housing units was insignificant in the face of the 40,000 workers with families and the 100,000 workers without families in need, many of the members of the Chamber of Deputies believed that municipal authorities should take care of housing problems. If additional units were needed, they reasoned, they should be provided by private enterprise or private charities, not the government. The municipality had already approved the construction of low-cost housing by a charity, and President Sáenz Peña supported 1913 legislation that authorized loans for the construction of housing for public employees (the Ley de Préstamos para Edificación y Construcción de Inmuebles para Empleados Públicos, September 29, 1913). As a further incentive for private enterprise, Law 9471 in 1914 exempted construction firms under contract to build working-class housing from paying customs duties on imported construction materials. Despite these measures, private enterprise and charities were proving incapable of solving the problem.

In anticipation of elections in 1916, the first presidential contest since electoral reforms had been implemented, and in response to increasing housing costs, President Victorino de la Plaza submitted a proposal to Congress. This bill, entitled "Casas para Obreros" (Housing for Workers), would reflect the liberal antipathy to state involvement. It sought to direct the municipal government of Buenos Aires to fulfill its obligations under earlier legislation (specifically the 1908 Law 7102, which appropriated a percentage of receipts at Thursday races at the elite Jockey Club in order to raise funds) for worker-housing to be built on municipal land. These housing units would be either sold or rented to workers who could both demonstrate need and prove themselves to be of acceptable morality. There were to be guidelines for rent and mortgage payments, a requirement that the buyer pay for mortgage and fire insurance, and a stipulation that four months' arrears in either mortgage or rent payments would invalidate the contract.[40] These requirements would severely limit the number of individuals eligible and would have had little impact on the residents of *conventillos,* many of whom did not have stable wages.

This initiative was more effective as an attempt to take housing as a political issue away from the Socialists and the Radicals. Socialist deputies were hoping to increase their voting strength by appealing to the concerns of renters. And the Radical party had become effective in establishing neighborhood committees with *caudillos de barrio* (ward bosses), who would become very active before elections, handing out food along with party propaganda.[41] These *caudillos* used housing as a means to influence voters. David Rock suggests they helped voters secure housing since landlords often required references: "They had some control over the allocation of housing, for example, through their association with the owners of tenement blocks."[42]

The strategy of de la Plaza, therefore, was to deflect the issue of housing away from the national arena, where it could work to the ruling party's disadvantage, and toward the municipal venue. Municipal politics could be well regulated since the mayor of Buenos Aires was a presidential appointee and members of the city council were chosen by a very limited electorate. Nevertheless, municipal resources were insufficient, and Congress began to discuss an alternate housing bill.

If President de la Plaza's goal had been to preempt the housing issue, then the proposal by Deputy Cafferata, which was passed into law one month after the president's bill had been submitted, presented an enormous change of emphasis. The debate in 1915 in many ways presaged the arguments for and against state intervention in 1921. In their book *Vivienda: Ideas y contradiciones (1916–1956),* Ramón Gutiérrez and Margarita Gutman give examples of the participants and their arguments for this bill. Ambrosio Nougués, deputy from Tucumán representing the Unión Popular, had once served as president of the Sugar Producers Association. His conservative background notwithstanding, Nougués supported Cafferata's legislation, saying: "What is important in the question of worker housing is that, whether owned or rented, it be healthy and inexpensive."[43] Marcelo Torcuato de Alvear, deputy from the capital and later president of Argentina, supported Cafferata's bill because it encouraged a mixture of public and private expenditures. Enrique Dickmann, a Socialist deputy from the capital, also supported the bill. But Dickmann argued that the government should fully support all measures that would reduce the cost of housing, including changes to municipal zoning regulations that encouraged speculation. He cautioned that low-cost housing was only a patch for a much larger problem. Finally, Nicholas Repetto, another Socialist deputy from the capital, urged support for cooperatives in addition to Cafferata's bill. Radicals, conservatives, and Socialists all shared the same general goal: clean, affordable housing for workers. The legislation proposed by Cafferata was a compromise that they could agree upon.

The Cafferata Law (Law 9677) passed in 1915 and established a National Commission for Affordable Housing (Comisión Nacional de Casas Baratas). This commission was charged with promoting construction of affordable housing for the nation's workers through private construction or cooperatives by means of prizes or awards, reduction of taxes, and reduction of import duties on construction materials. In many respects this law paralleled that of President de la Plaza. Workers must prove good conduct—a way of excluding labor leaders or militants—as well as need. Housing units could be rented or sold, but as with many earlier measures, the goal was to assist thrifty laborers to purchase their own property and thus to become honest, productive citizens, resistant to debaucheries or radical ideologies. The Cafferata Law sought the same basic goals of labor discipline and moral compatibility with the middle class, but its significance lay in its application of a national response to housing reform.[44] In its first meeting, in November 1915, the commission members, doctors Marcelo T. de Alvear, Gregorio Araoz Alfaro, and Carlos Coll and engineers Juan Ochoa and Eduardo M. Lanus, spoke of their goals. "I understand that [the commission's] objective," said Juan Ochoa, "is to assist the tendency of the working population to acquire its own small property through individual effort. . . . The concrete objective of this law is to stabilize the worker, helping him form the habit of saving and of order, which draws him away from rebellion."[45] This commission did not advocate direct government intervention, but it did provide a mechanism for government action, and this would have political ramifications. Future administrations would have the machinery in place to discuss housing, although little of substance was done until the end of the decade.

The composition of the government changed with the election of Hipólito Yrigoyen as president in 1916. This first Radical party administration presented Yrigoyen with a challenge. Heretofore, his role had been first as an intransigent opponent of conservative oligarchic regimes and then, after 1905, as a source of constant pressure for electoral reform. Now as president, his articulation of specific policies was very different from his earlier vague pronouncements about the "Cause," as Yrigoyen had referred to Radical party goals. He needed to build the broadest possible coalition for electoral support. In 1917, for instance, electoral reforms in Buenos Aires enlarged the municipal franchise from about 4,000 voters, and in the 1918 elections more than 200,000 voters turned out to elect equal numbers of Socialist and Radical members to the city council.[46] As David Rock suggests, Yrigoyen's Radical party had to go beyond the middle class and "include in its project of political integration a new relationship between the State and the urban working class."[47] Under Yrigoyen May 1 became Labor Day, reform laws passed in 1918 regulated working hours, and arbitration and collective bargaining were permitted as of 1919. This new relationship was tested as labor agitation increased after World War I, and Yrigoyen turned to housing reform as one way to increase Radical influence with the working class. A special fund for the construction of housing for city employees was created in 1919 and paid for by a 25 percent tax on the income of foreign-owned trolley lines.[48]

After the war Argentina's economy began to recover. Exports rose, and one domestic industry, textiles, increased output. Employment was generally slow to improve, and the cost of living continued to climb. This contributed to labor unrest, and strikes by port and railroad workers broke out in 1917 and 1918. President Yrigoyen tried to win support from the working class. The strikes were settled by government intervention with some support for labor. The Radical party was rewarded in the polls in 1918 and defeated the Socialists in congressional elections. But there was a price to pay, and a conservative reaction ensued, led by a business association and the newly formed Liga Patriotica, a conservative, nationalistic organization that sought to defend Argentina against a feared immigrant-inspired Bolshevik revolution.

Yrigoyen's administration felt housing reform to be both a recognition of the increasing cost of rent and a way to provide support for the working class on an issue on which, albeit for different reasons, there was a growing consensus for some form of government action. The Tragic Week (Semana Tragíca) of January 1919, in which a general strike led to violence and the deaths of workers at the hands of the police, shattered what hope the Radicals might have had for a multiclass coalition. Nevertheless, by 1920 there were numerous attempts at housing reform, acknowledging both the dramatic increase in rent costs and the power of organized labor, whose membership reached approximately 700,000 in 1920.[49] The Valentin Alsina apartment building, with seventy apartments housing 322 persons, was built in 1920 by the commission; and in 1921 two projects, the Bernardino Rivadavia apartment building, with forty-one apartments, and the Juan F. Cafferata neighborhood, with ninety-seven houses of two, three, or four bedrooms, housed a total of one thousand persons. However, with tens of thousands of people in need of shelter these numbers were not impressive, and Congress would begin to look to other measures, including a rent freeze.

The 1921 Rent Law

Yrigoyen's administration faced intense labor agitation and growing opposition in a postwar economic slump. Joel Horowitz, in an article on the general strike of 1921, argued that that year was critical for Yrigoyen's relations with labor.[50] Looking toward the 1922 presidential elections, Radicals and Socialists felt the need to address the problem of incessant rent increases. Several bills were introduced in

Congress, and the debate over state intervention was unprecedented. Deputy Rodolfo Moreno proposed a bill in Congress attempting to limit rent increases in 1919, and in 1920 Deputy Carlos J. Rodriguez proposed legislation to construct low-cost housing, as did Juan Tierney; José Tamborini sought limits to rent increases, and Deputy D. del Valle proposed legislation to stop evictions in progress.[51]

At issue was the fear that rapidly rising rent would lead to working-class action. The anarchist daily newspaper, *La Protesta*, focused on housing problems and the cost of rent. In November 1919 it referred to the creation of a National Association of Tenants, organized to combat high rents.[52] This association's tactics would change from stridently antagonistic of government intervention to support for a national campaign to pass the rent bill, revealing a willingness on the part of the working class to threaten direct action in order to pressure the government to act. The association originally called for collective action by tenants who suffered from voracious landlords. Its petition demanded

1. reduction of rents for houses, workshops, stores, and *conventillos* to 6 percent of the total value of the property;
2. complete abolition of rent deposits;
3. return of deposits to tenants;
4. payment of rent at the end of the month as long as tenant's payments are up-to-date;
5. abolition of back-dated receipts by landlords;
6. the right of couples with children to rent;
7. one year's grace before eviction.[53]

The meetings and activities of this tenants' association reflected both the renewed hope that legislation would be passed to resolve the housing crisis and the fact that the association's focus was on the government as the agent of change. It proposed that tenants should cease payment of rent, but such collective action could only be successful with sufficient consciousness and organization.[54] To that end, on August 1, 1920, the tenants' association organized a march from Plaza Once down Rividavia Avenue toward the Congress, but the marchers were forcibly dispersed by the police from the Plaza del Congreso.

The threatened rent strike did not occur. Instead, during the congressional debate over the rent bill, the tenant organization joined the national campaign for a reduction of rents as well as for government action to lower the price of sugar. Socialist Deputy Augusto Bunge, speaking to a rally seeking lower rents, claimed that the debate on the issue demonstrated that a fundamental change in the character of the state was needed. The governing class must realize, he said, that "the collective interest is above individual interests in the use and abuse of the right of property" and that these reforms were "a small step toward the only way, under current circumstances, that will resolve the housing problem: that is the progressive socialization of housing."[55]

Socialists sponsored meetings and rallies throughout the city to push for legislation to lower the cost of rent. On August 31 and September 1 meetings were held in nearly half the districts of the city.[56] Speakers included national Deputies Antonio de Tomaso, Federico Pinedo Jr., Fernand de Andreis, and City Councilman Adolfo Dickmann. The Socialists claimed that there were thousands in attendance at rallies. "What was, until now, an inchoate mass of workers is taking shape as a conscious protest, thanks to the constant efforts by the Partido Socialista to clarify the issues among the masses."[57] The secretary general of the Socialist party, Alfredo L. Spinetto, declared that "the best title for property is the need of the people."[58] Tellingly, a similar phrase would later be used by President Yrigoyen as he lobbied for passage of the rent law after the Senate balked and the Supreme Court questioned the constitutionality of the law. "Public need constitutes the highest law," said Yrigoyen, trying to steal some of the thunder from the Socialists.[59]

In September 1920 the Congreso de la Habitación (Housing Congress) met at the Museo Social Argentino, an agency that sponsored moderate social reform. The delegates to this congress represented a group that was very different from the Socialists but that was equally concerned about the growing crisis in housing. Father Gabriel Palau, S.J., professor of sociology at the Pontifical Seminary, gave a talk on the "Mansion Popular" concept as undertaken in Lille, France. Enrique Ruíz Guiñazú, president of the Museo Social Argentino, in his opening remarks said: "Always, gentlemen, here and throughout the world, one's own house, the possession of a family home, has been the center of life, because it protects the individual as the key element of society." The distance between the president of the Museo Social Argentino and the majority of Argentina's working-class tenants was revealed in a comment by Guiñazú in an article entitled "El alza de los alguileres" (Rent Increases), in which he said that "the majority of the *conventillos* were owned by former workers of foreign extraction" who had specialized in this role as slumlord.[60] This antiforeign bias betrayed the rising fear among many upper- and middle-class Argentines that the still largely foreign working class, with its socialist and syndicalist dogma, was an enemy, although these same upper and middle classes sympathized with the mass of workers who suffered from increasingly high rents. Housing costs created an overlapping of interests among otherwise antagonistic groups.

Throughout Argentina in 1920 the argument over government action to reduce rents encompassed Socialists, Catholics, Radicals, and conservatives. The focus of marches, rallies, congresses, and speeches was the congressional debate on housing legislation. One proposal was submitted by Victor M. Molina, elected in 1920 from the federal capital.[61] Molina's bill charged the mayor of Buenos Aires to create arbitration commissions to return rent to the level of January 1, 1920, to protect against future rent increases, and to establish fair rental rates. Although Molina accepted the validity of the laws of supply and demand, the foundation of the economy of the liberal state, he believed that the need for legislation arose from an emergency situation. His bill was designed to protect the middle class and the working class from unheard-of rent increases caused largely by greedy landlords. If the laws of supply and demand ensured individual liberty, he asked, then where was the liberty of the worker who found himself unable to afford a place to live? "We can't let them live in tents like gypsies. My bill will ensure that this temporary crisis will not cause great suffering."[62]

The bill was sent into committee, revised, and eventually passed by the Chamber of Deputies, only to be voted down by the Senate. The Senate, responding to pressure from the property-owners' association and resisting efforts by the Radical administration and Senator Joaquín V. González, who earlier in his career had supported Argentina's first labor legislation, raised questions about the constitutionality of the law. The Supreme Court, headed by conservative ex-president José Figueroa Alcorta, did not look favorably on the legislation. Finally, a joint committee of the two houses met in June 1920 to iron out a compromise. Deputy Antonio de Tomaso, a Socialist from Buenos Aires, demanded that the bill be brought out of committee and debated by the full chamber. The major provisions of the legislation sought to freeze rents at levels of January 1, 1920; to outlaw discrimination against families with children; to declare that all leases in good standing as of April 1921 could be continued without increase until July 31, 1922; to limit the rental on sublets to no more than 20 percent over the original rent; and to fix the minimum length of a lease at two years.

Opponents of the bill argued that it violated constitutional guarantees to the right of property and its free use.[63] Deputy Tomaso responded that the intent of the bill was to protect tenants, not to curb property rights. Arturo Bas, deputy from Cordoba, agreed. He felt that this bill would stop abuses, help tenants in an emergency, and ultimately stimulate more housing construction, thereby benefiting both property owners and tenants in the long run.[64]

The legislation, Law 11,157 (Ley de Alquileres), passed in June 1921, froze rents at the rate in effect on January 1, 1920, and halted all eviction proceedings if back rent were paid within fifteen days.[65] It represented a major break with the past because it initiated active intervention by the federal government in a social question. The rent freeze continued in effect for two years, but the succeeding Radical administration of Torcuato de Alvear saw this as an emergency measure, and it was allowed to lapse in 1923. The law fixing lease terms was renewed in 1923 and 1924 but was then declared unconstitutional by the Supreme Court in 1925.[66]

Conclusion

The liberal state in Argentina faced serious challenges in the aftermath of World War I. Political reforms and a changing labor movement altered the relationship between the working class and the government; economic and social changes produced a postwar crisis; and various groups looked to the state to act in the emergency. Argentina's liberal regime, like governments in wartime North America and Europe, faced pressure to intervene in the economy. Unlike the governments of these other countries, however, Argentina's government was responding to a failure of market forces, private charities, and limited municipal action to resolve several long-standing crises, including the need for low-cost housing for the working class.

Tenant associations, beginning in the 1890s and continuing into the 1920s, sought better conditions and lower rents. The 1907 rent strike reflected the anarchist-dominated labor movement's strategy of direct action by the working class. After World War I, however, the focus became government action, and tenant committees lobbied for the 1921 rent law.

Catholic reformers also moved from early attempts to assist cooperative efforts to pressure for state intervention. Juan F. Cafferata, who served both Catholic agencies and in Congress, spearheaded the effort to pass housing legislation. The National Commission for Affordable Housing emerged from his legislative efforts and became a permanent agency through which housing needs were implemented. This commission oversaw efforts to build public housing units and although its efforts were paltry compared to the need, it did make the government a participant in resolving housing issues.

Radical and Socialist deputies saw in housing an issue that could bring them the support of the working class. They introduced several bills to address housing problems. By far the most important was the rent law of 1921, in which the federal government intervened to freeze rents and altered the economic relationship between tenants and landlords. This had a profound impact on Argentina because it represented a break with the liberal traditions that had guided earlier administrations, traditions, argued some, that supported fundamental freedoms for property owners.

The crisis environment of 1919 and 1920 helped convince many who were philosophically opposed to government intervention that some immediate relief was needed. When the crisis seemed to pass, legislation freezing rents was allowed to expire and later a Supreme Court decision declared provisions of the rent law unconstitutional. The Radical party had needed to reach out to the working class through housing reform. But it went further in recognizing that consumer problems, especially housing costs and conditions, were class issues, and it sought to forge a multiclass electoral alliance through housing reform and through labor legislation, creating the seeds of populism in Argentina. Government action to resolve housing problems became accepted by a variety of groups and would lead later administrations to consciously use housing policies as a way to solve important problems and to elicit support for the regime.

The National Commission for Affordable Housing continued to build housing projects: The Guillermo Rawson neighborhood was started in 1928; the América apartment house was started in 1937 and the Patricios apartment house, in 1939. Debate in the 1930s centered on the relative merits of apartment buildings as opposed to single-family housing, not on the need for state intervention. Said one speaker at a Rotary Club conference in Buenos Aires in 1936: "On the whole, I believe that the state is the only organization that can accomplish this humanitarian goal, and [it] should build special housing projects for those most in need."[67]

Government intervention increased in response to serious economic and social problems throughout the 1930s. Labor tribunals were created, and a state-run petroleum company was formed. By the 1940s the National Commission for Affordable Housing gave way to the Housing Directory (Dirección de Vivienda), which became the National Council for Housing (Consejo Nacional de Viviendas). In June 1945 the military government, by decree, passed Law 11,157 establishing the National Administration of Housing (Administración Nacional de Vivienda). Juan Perón, in his speech to the nation on May 9, 1952, would brag about the nearly 10,000 buildings constructed by his government between 1945 and 1952. He would conclude: "I realize that all this is but a grain of sand in the efforts of the nation to provide every Argentine with his own home . . . as befits a citizen of the New Argentina."[68]

Perón's populist government emerged out of the decline of the liberal state. His program of public housing far surpassed what all earlier administrations combined had accomplished. Indeed, one could argue that the key to Perón's entire economic policy was the stimulation of a growing consumer economy through increased real wages for the working class. The construction of housing and the provision of homes to workers were two important elements of his program. Perón's populist policies signaled a transformation in the relationship between the state and its citizens. In Perón's New Argentina, the state would house its people.

Perón did not solve the problems of urbanization; nor have any of the subsequent administrations. His ultimate failure also serves as a reminder that unresolved urban problems, such as housing, continued to provide a rallying point for urban workers confronting the state. Today, *villas miserias* ring Buenos Aires and surround many other Latin American cities. Whereas an important part of the failure of liberalism was its inability to resolve housing problems without state intervention, the failure of populism has been its inability to deliver on the promises it made in order to obtain the support of urban workers. Current economic policies show few signs of resolving continuing housing problems. Actions by tenants in Buenos Aires, who in 1993 took over vacant apartments and demanded government assistance for those without shelter, demonstrate that neoliberal reliance on market forces may not be successful in bringing economic and political stability unless the perennial crisis in housing is resolved.

Notes

1. See Manuel Castells, *City, Class, and Power* (New York: St. Martin's Press, 1978), and David Harvey, *Consciousness and the Urban Experience: Studies in the History and Theory of Capitalist Urbanization* (Baltimore: Johns Hopkins University Press, 1985). Here, however, I want to stress that the conditions of as well as the response to collective consumption is distinct for each group and that we must recognize the dynamic nature of alliances among these groups over questions of consumption.

2. David Rock, *Argentina from 1516 to 1987* (Berkeley and Los Angeles: University of California Press, 1987), and *Politics in Argentina, 1890–1930* (Cambridge: Cambridge University Press, 1975).

3. Oscar Yujnovsky, *Claves políticas del problema habitacional argentino* (Buenos Aires: Centro Editor Latinoamericano, 1985), chap. 1, provides a detailed discussion of the elements that make up the issues related to housing.

4. D. C. M. Platt, ed., *Social Welfare 1850–1950* (London: The Macmillan Press, 1989).

5. Platt, *Social Welfare,* 10.

6. John Burnett, *A Social History of Housing, 1815–1985* (New York: Methuen, 1986), 221.

7. See James A. Baer, "Tenant Mobilization and the 1907 Rent Strike in Buenos Aires," *The Americas* 49, no. 3 (January 1993): 343–368.

8. Although much governmental activity focused on specific housing projects during the 1920s and 1930s, another dramatic shift occurred after the 1943 coup and during Juan Perón's presidency. One of the first acts of the military government after the 1943 coup was a rent freeze, and Perón's policies placed housing within a broader framework of income redistribution to increase the standard of living of Argentina's workers and "shirtless ones."

9. This question is pursued in James A. Baer, "Housing and the Working Class in Buenos Aires: Consumer Issues and Class Identity," in *MACLAS Latin American Essays*, vol. 4 (selected papers presented at the Eleventh Annual Conference of the Middle Atlantic Council of Latin American Studies at Rutgers University, April, 1990), ed. Robert J. Alexander, Juan Espadas, and Vincent Peloso (Collegeville, Pa.: MACLAS, in cooperation with Ursinus College, 1990), 135–145.

10. James Scobie, *Buenos Aires: From Plaza to Suburb 1870–1910* (New York: Oxford University Press, 1974), describes the dramatic growth of Buenos Aires after 1870 in great detail, although his dichotomy between "Gran Aldea" and metropolis may be somewhat overstated, as the city grew continuously throughout the nineteenth century. I wish to thank Karen Robert at the University of Michigan for raising this point about the extent of change in Buenos Aires throughout the nineteenth century.

11. Censo de la ciudad de Buenos Aires, 1887. The net increase in population was about 65,000 per year.

12. Departamento del Trabajo, *Boletín*, no. 21 (1921).

13. See "Acción parlamentaria: Leyes sancionadas," in *Revista de Economia Argentina,* year 2, vol. 4, nos. 23–24 (May-June 1920): 417.

14. Executive Board: Honorary President (the Argentine First Lady was always given this honorary position until Eva Perón was refused the honor) Sra. Susana R. de Quintana (wife of the former Argentine president); President, Sra. María Adela Atucha de Guamajo; Treasurer, Elina P. de Devoto; Members, Carolina L. de Pellegrini, Condesa de Sena. Listed in Honorable Consejo Municipal, *Barrio Obrero "Buteler"* (Buenos Aires: Talleres Gráficos "Optimus," 1910), 19.

15. See Baer, "Tenant Mobilization."

16. *Voz de la Iglesia* (Buenos Aires), June 3, 1893.

17. *La Vanguardia* (Buenos Aires), November 21, 1896.

18. For more information on the Liga and its program, see James A. Baer, "Tenant Mobilization," 353–354.

19. Diego Abad de Santillán, *La FORA: Ideologia y trajectoria,* 2nd. ed. (Buenos Aires: Editorial Proyección, 1971), 147–148.

20. See Baer, "Tenant Mobilization," 343–368, and Juan Suriano, *La huelga de inquilinos de 1907* (Buenos Aires: Centro Editor de América Latina, 1983).

21. *La Protesta*, October 6, 1907; *La Prensa*, September 24, 1907; *La Vanguardia*, September 14, 1907.

22. *La Prensa* (Buenos Aires), September 22, 1907.

23. Ibid.

24. For 1907, see República Argentina, Departamento Nacional del Tabajo, *Boletín*, no. 4 (1907) and no. 21 (1912).

25. The 1912 figures are from Department of Labor, *Boletín* (Buenos Aires, 1912): 409; for 1919, from Museo Social Argentino, *Boletín*, nos. 85–91 (January–June 1919): 226.

26. Figures for 1913 and 1914 are from Museo Social Argentino, *Boletín* 5 (1920): 142; for 1915 and 1917 from Museo Social Argentino, *Boletín*, nos. 85–91 (January–June 1919): 225, 276.

27. Figures quoted by Juan F. Cafferata in his speech to the Chamber of Deputies on May 29, 1914. Juan F. Cafferata, *Labor parlamentaria* (Buenos Aires: Imprenta y encuadernación de la honorable camara de diputados, 1928), 31–32.

28. Reported in Museo Social Argentino, *Boletín*, nos. 85–91 (January–June 1919): 276.

29. Alejandro E. Bunge, *Los problemas económicas del presente*, vol. 1 (Buenos Aires: n.p., 1920), 231.

30. Bunge, *Los problemas*, 231.

31. José Elian Niklison, Inspector Nacional del Trabajo, "Acción Social Católica Obrera," in República Argentina, Departamento Nacional del Trabajo, *Boletín* (Buenos Aires, 1920), 55.

32. *Voz de la Iglesia* (Buenos Aires), October 18, 1905.

33. Ibid., Oct. 30, 1905.

34. Departamento del Trabajo, *Boletín*, 1920: 95.

35. Maria I. Piñero de Cafferata. *Un hombre y una vida: Juan F. Cafferata* (Córdoba, Argentina: J. F. Cafferata, 1961), 129.

36. Quoted in *Boletín Mensual del Museo Social Argentino* (Buenos Aires: Imprenta y Casa Editora Di Coni Hermanos, 1912), 175.

37. Ibid., 133.

38. Richard Walter believes that Sáenz Peña's willingness to enact political reforms was due to the influence of the Radicals; Introduction, *The Province of Buenos Aires and Argentine Politics, 1912–1943* (Cambridge: Cambridge University Press, 1985), 10. I believe it helpful to understand the inability of liberal economic policies to resolve the continuing housing crisis, as well as increasing labor unrest during the centennial, as additional reasons for Sáenz Peña's interest in seeking reforms.

39. The Socialist list of principles and programs for 1913 is reprinted in Hobart Spalding, *La clase trabajadora argentina* (Buenos Aires: Editorial Galerna, 1970), 278.

40. For the full text of the bill, see *Revista de Economia Argentina*, year 2, vol. 4, nos. 23–24 (May–June 1920): 430–432.

41. See David Rock, *Politics in Argentina*, 55–60.

42. Rock, *Politics in Argentina*, 56.

43. Ramón Gutiérrez and Margarita Gutman, *Vivienda: Ideas y contradiciones (1916–1956)* (Buenos Aires: Instituto Argentino de Investigaciones de Historia de la Arquitectura y del Urbanismo, 1988) contains much information on the Comisión de Casas Baratas and other housing legislation.

44. For the complete text of the bill, see *Revista de Economia Argentina*, year 2, vol. 4, nos. 23–24 (May–June 1920): 421–426. Article 3 defines the duties of the commission: (1) investment of funds for the construction of hygienic, inexpensive houses in Buenos Aires and throughout the country by private companies or individuals, to be sold or rented to workers with low wages, (2) intervention on behalf of private construction firms who will build these homes, (3) stimulation of construction through prizes or rewards, (4) proposing of organization of cooperatives or other credit institutions to build directly or loan money for construction of such housing, (5) other activities to encourage construction of low-cost housing. Article 4 defines the responsibilities of eligible workers: The commission will sell such houses, through lotteries and at cost, only to workers "whose proof of good conduct and lack of resources can be documented"; 417.

45. República Argentina, Ley no. 9677 y reglamentación Ley no. 10.479, *Comisión nacional de casas baratas* (Buenos Aires: Talleres Gráficos Moldes, 1927), 11.

46. Guy Bourdé, *Urbanisatión et Immigratin en Amérique Latine* (Paris: Editions Aubier-Montaigne, 1974), 100.

47. Rock, *Politics in Argentina,* 117.

48. Buenos Aires, Consejo Deliberante, *Digesto Municipal de la Ciudad de Buenos Aires* (Buenos Aires: Establicimiento Gráfico "Fermi", 1929), 1043.

49. Rubén Rotondaro, *Realidad y cambio en el sindicalismo* (Buenos Aires: Editorial Pleamar, 1971), 100–101.

50. Joel Horowitz, "Argentina's Failed General Strike of 1921: A Critical Moment in the Radical's Relations with Unions," *Hispanic American Historical Review* 75, no. 1 (February 1995): 57–79.

51. *Revista de Economía Argentina* (May-June, 1920), "Acción parliamentaria," 417.

52. *La Protesta* (Buenos Aires), November 9, 1919.

53. *La Vanguardia,* May 11, 1920.

54. "Pro rebaja de los alquileres," *La Protesta,* November 25, 1919. The statement said, "Aunque sin cifrar mayores esperanzas, porque sabe muy bien que los hombres que nos gobiernan pertenecen en su casi totalidad a la clase capitalista, ha agotado todos los recursos a su alcance solicitando la sanción de leyes que protegieran a los inquilinos de la voracidad de propietarios y locadores al solo efecto de justificar su actitud futura que ha de consistir en la cesación colectiva del pago a los alquileres, cuando las víctimas hayan adquirido conciencia de la justicia que les asiste y tengan la organización necesaria."

55. *La Vanguardia* (Buenos Aires), September 6, 1920.

56. Ibid., August 31 and September 1, 1920.

57. Ibid., September 6, 1920.

58. Ibid.

59. Silvano Santander, *Yrigoyen* (Buenos Aires: Editorial La Fragua 1965), 107.

60. *Revista de Economia Argentina,* year 2, vol. 4, nos. 23–24 (May-June 1920): 375–376. "La Comisión de Casas Baratas ya mencionada, ha afirmada en documento público, que la mayoría de los conventillos son propiedad de ex obreros de procedencia extranjera, afincados entre nosotros con esa especialidad."

61. República Argentina, Congreso, Cámera dediputados, *Diario de Sesiones*, vol. 1 (April 6–June 17, 1920) (Buenos Aires: Imprente del Congreso nacional, 1920), 315–316.

62. Ibid.

63. See República Argentina, Congreso, Cámera dediputados, *Diario de Sessiones* (June 9, 1921) (Buenos Aires: Imprente del Congreso nacional, 1921), 477–487.

64. Ibid., 477–487.

65. *Revista de Economia Argentina,* year 4, vol. 7, no. 20 (October 1921): 331–333.

66. The Supreme Court in *Mango v. Traba* said: "This emergency measure, which had a fundamental impact on property rights, has been tolerated in juridical decisions only in consideration of the extreme economic circumstances of tenants due to the absence of one of the factors that regulates the cost of rent, that is the lack of available housing"; Antonio de Tomaso, "Las Leyes Argentinas de Alquileres y el Contracto de Locación," *Almanaque del Trabajo* 9 (1926): 152.

67. Antonio U. Vilar, "Consideraciones sobre el problema de la vivienda económica," *La Habitación Popular* (Buenos Aires), no. 14 (January 1938): 22.

68. Juan D. Perón, "Mensaje a la Nueva Argentina, 6 años de gobierno de Perón," Buenos Aires, May 9, 1952. "Yo sé que todo esto es un grano de arena en el esfuerzo que debe realizar toda la Nación para que cada argentino tenga su propia casa . . . , nueva y digna de la Nueva Argentina"; 137.

6

Civilizing the City of Kings: Hygiene and Housing in Lima, Peru

David S. Parker

In contrast to Rio de Janeiro or Buenos Aires, Lima did not do a terribly good job of modernizing itself. Try as they might, and try they did, neither mayors nor presidents succeeded in turning South America's former colonial capital into the clean, healthy, ordered, elegant city they wished it could be. One problem, of course, was the eternal shortage of funds for basic services and infrastructure. But Peruvian officials continually complained, decade in and decade out, that the greater obstacle was an "ignorant" and "backward" people, who doggedly refused to change their uncultured and unsanitary habits. Urban reform, therefore, was not just a matter of paving streets and connecting water mains: It also involved educating the masses, "improving the race," and molding behavior to the new demands of a modern, cosmopolitan city.

This chapter looks at the ambiguities of that civilizing project. On the one hand, the public health officials who spearheaded Lima's modernization were genuinely concerned with epidemic disease, infant mortality, and the health of all Peruvians, rich and poor. Their preoccupation with hygiene and sanitation led them to study the abysmal living conditions of the poor, and their recommendations prompted a host of novel initiatives, from public housing to the regulation of industrial working conditions. On the other hand, these so-called *higienistas* were inevitably constrained by the medical and ideological orthodoxies of their time. All too frequently they attributed the unhealthy conditions in which the poor lived to the inherent characteristics of the poor themselves, and they could not imagine reforming one without simultaneously reforming the other. The policies that arose from these assumptions, although rooted in altruism and aimed at promoting social change, were typically authoritarian in practice, frequently tinged with racism, and almost always doomed to failure.

Popular responses to the modernizing project were equally contradictory. It was certainly not too hard to find examples of resistance to a "civilization" defined by others and imposed by force. In thousands of uneventful, everyday ways, poor Peruvians resisted efforts to change their familiar customs and habits, thwarting public health officials in the process. At the same time, however, surprisingly large numbers of artisans and workers did just the opposite: They actively promoted the ideology of progress and devoted their energies not just to ameliorating their own working and living conditions but equally to "improving" themselves and their peers. Labor unions, for example, organized extension classes in personal hygiene and campaigned against alcoholism. Those workers who embraced the civilizing ideal were by no means uncritical of the wealthy and powerful; their idea of "progress" differed from that of the men who governed them and often included radical demands for material well-being and political inclusion. But ultimately the culture of self-improvement and moral reform could not help but distance organized workers, moderate and radical alike, from the many thousands of other Peruvians who did not wish to abandon their traditional lifeways in order to become "civilized." Sharply diverging responses to modernization thus drove a wedge through the heart of Lima's popular classes, reinforcing ethnic conflict and impeding the emergence of a unified working-class alternative.

The Dream of Progress

Lima had been the center of Spain's empire in South America, but independence seemed to bring little but decadence and decline. When *limeños* in the 1860s compared their home to bustling Buenos Aires or Santiago, the contrast was anything but flattering. Trapped inside now-useless defensive walls, the "City of Kings" was not much of a city, nor was it particularly kingly. With a population of barely 100,000 and less than 1 percent annual growth since 1812,[1] Lima appeared to most travelers to be a fading relic of a bygone age, its dusty streets bisected by fetid open sewers, its crumbling adobe walls silently mocking the exquisite wooden balconies that had once been the symbol of the city's colonial splendor.[2]

Efforts to shake off Lima's "backwardness" began in earnest in the mid-1860s. José Balta, who became president in 1868, engaged U.S. engineer Henry Meiggs to tear down the colonial walls and to replace them with two broad promenades inspired by Georges Haussmann's Paris. The Palace of the Exposition, built by Meiggs in 1872, rivaled any public building on the continent for its combination of Italianate Renaissance beauty and modern Yankee functionality. Peru's engineers and architects drew up a host of other equally ambitious plans for urban reform, impelled not by the press of demographic growth but by the elites' desire to see Lima join the "cultured," "civilized" capitals of the world.[3] However, a series of tragedies dashed all hope that this shimmering future might soon become a reality. By the mid-1870s Peru's guano export economy had fallen into visible decline, bankrupting a treasury dependent on customs revenues. Far worse was the disastrous loss to Chile in the War of the Pacific. The Chilean occupation from 1879 to 1882 plunged Lima into an unprecedented crisis: Public buildings were looted, the economy was destroyed, and private fortunes were lost virtually overnight. Nor did the city's troubles end with the departure of the foreign invader: Violent civil conflict continued, on and off, until the victory of Nicolás de Piérola, who became president in 1895. The final quarter of the nineteenth century, years of phenomenal growth and change in Buenos Aires, Santiago, and Rio, were thus lost years for Lima, whose population in 1900 was unchanged from 1876 and whose physical extension was scarcely greater than that of 1650.[4]

After 1895, as the economy recovered and political stability was restored, Peru's leaders rediscovered and dusted off those earlier development projects. President Piérola took an especially active interest in the modernization and embellishment of Lima. Between 1895 and 1899, he passed several laws facilitating urban expansion, and upon leaving office he made a career as a real estate developer, building the elegant downtown avenue known as La Colmena. Like others of his generation, Piérola saw a city's architecture as the measure of its culture and explicitly linked urban renewal to national progress. Lima, in his eyes, was thus an embarrassment and a disgrace:

> Our buildings, in terms of solidity, hygiene, and of course comfort and beauty, are truly deplorable, giving very sad account of our advancement. No one here, not even the wealthy, strives to build a solid, healthy, and dignified roof under which to live. Even if they tried, they would not find the means to achieve it, creating the often offensive contrast between the luxury of the furniture and the baseness of the building in which it is installed. It is as if we were just passing through, temporary guests in our own land. . . . This has enormous impact on our customs and national character, on the vitality and power of the country, and it urgently demands an effective solution.[5]

As elsewhere in Latin America, the solution called for the demolition of the old Spanish-style adobe homes and their replacement with modern, multistory, French-style palaces of brick and concrete; for the opening of broad avenues and parks in place of the narrow checkerboard streets of the traditional colonial center; for paving stones, streetcars, public lighting, and water mains; and for decisive, immediate action, since Lima had fallen so far behind its neighbors and so desperately hoped to "catch up." Nonetheless, by the first decade of the twentieth century the march of Lima's urban progress was seemingly back on track. New mansions first began to appear along the Paseo Colón west of the Palace of the Exposition and later on La Colmena, whose initial section was opened in 1907. Electric streetcars started running in 1904. Each passing year saw the fanfare-filled inauguration of streets, statues, plazas, parks, and public buildings and the less-publicized construction of water mains, sewers, and homes.[6]

Public works, however, were only one facet of the larger drive to make Lima a modern, dignified, "cultured" capital. Broad avenues might beautify an urban landscape, but as elite critics increasingly lamented, they could not civilize a people. Writer and journalist Pedro Dávalos y Lissón, for example, marveled at Lima's recent material progress but despaired of the habits of its populace.

> At night, when I cross [the bridge over the Rímac] and see it all illuminated by bright street lamps, animated by the streetcars that majestically pass up and over, I seem to be in a city more populous than Lima, and of superior rank. . . . I look at [the new avenue on the other side of the bridge] and imagine how beautiful this esplanade will be once the trees have grown and the paving and sidewalks are completed, when my nerves are assaulted by an acrid, fetid, intolerable odor of urine. . . . I turn my head and see, with the greatest clarity, in full view of a policeman and of all the people passing by, a man in indecent posture, adding his liquid waste to the thousand and one others that accumulate at all hours of the day in that filthy spot. Do the police authorities have the order to promote this uncultured and uncivil practice, which is not seen even among the savage Indians of the Ucayali? Doesn't the Direction of Public Health know that all the streets of the city have been turned into public urinals? . . . Haven't the women of Lima considered that their decency could be unfavorably judged by the foreigner who for the first time visits the city and watches, stupefied, this indecent custom?[7]

For Dávalos y Lissón and others of like mind, the authorities had a duty to educate the masses in the customs of the civilized world, using the police when necessary to repress public urination and other social ills such as swearing, spitting, smoking, and talking in the theater.[8] The well-traveled Dávalos was perhaps a bit more fastidious than most, but he was hardly exceptional. Built into the drive to modernize was a constant effort to emulate the more advanced, more "cultured" cities of the Atlantic world, from Paris to London to New York to Buenos Aires. Implicit in that effort was the need to meet European standards of civilization, the need to attract European immigrants, and the need to refashion both public institutions and private habits along European lines.

The idea of civilizing an entire society, no small task anywhere, was perhaps especially quixotic in turn-of-the-century Lima. For one thing, it was difficult to imagine just who was supposed to be doing the civilizing, given the weakness of the Peruvian state and the general fragmentation of authority. Lima's municipal government had long exercised regulatory power over a range of activities but suffered from a constant shortage of funds. The national government, somewhat better off financially, had trouble entering areas of traditional municipal competence. Assistance to the poor remained in the hands of the church and the private Sociedad de Beneficencia Pública. The concentration of power in such traditional institutions rendered the state virtually impotent as a vehicle for behavioral reform. And the idea that the police might serve as a force to repress bad manners was laughable, as Dávalos himself realized, given the institution's low level of professionalism and the scant formal education of its members.

Nor were *limeños* terribly realistic in their hopes of civilizing the city by importing racially "superior" Europeans. At a time when opportunities for immigrants abounded in Argentina, Uruguay, Brazil, the United States, Canada, and elsewhere, distant Peru held comparatively little attraction. Indeed, the number of Italians, French, Spanish, English, and Germans living in Lima peaked sometime in the 1860s or 1870s and declined significantly thereafter, no doubt because of the crises of the last quarter century.[9] Despite the fact that Peru made the same efforts as did other Latin American nations to attract European workers, few came.[10] Instead, the 1908 census classified the majority of Lima's urban working class as either native-born whites, mestizos, blacks, or Indians.[11] Within that working class were further divisions: Skilled artisans and factory workers were overwhelmingly mestizo or white, and many saw themselves as respectable members of society, even if the upper class did not always share the same view.[12] Lima's indigenous population, in contrast, remained heavily concentrated in unskilled labor, domestic service, agriculture, and the military. Maligned, patronized, or more typically ignored by other workers, they did not figure significantly in the nascent labor movement. It was not until the 1940s and 1950s that massive migration from the highlands to the capital would begin to change this situation.

Lima also had an important population of Asian immigrants, victims of a hatred far more intense and violent than anything faced by the city's other ethnic groups. Somewhere around 100,000 Chinese indentured laborers arrived between 1849 and 1874, primarily to work on the sugar and cotton plantations of the Peruvian coast. Significant numbers moved to Lima upon completion of their contracts, and by the 1870s a sizable Chinatown had formed in the streets surrounding the Central Market.[13] A second wave of Chinese and Japanese immigrants, some 30,000 in all, began arriving around the turn of the century.[14] The Asians who made their home in Lima, undercounted at 5,487 in the 1908 census,[15] carved out an important niche in small commerce and certain service occupations yet remained extraordinarily unwelcome. Most other Peruvians saw them as a degraded, inferior race, intrinsic enemies of Lima's "civilization."[16] As we will see, racism against Asians revealed a dark underside to the dream of progress.

Doctors, Epidemics, and the Discovery of the Poor

The hope of Peru's modernizing elite—that their capital and its population might be remade in the image of Europe—was in some ways absurd. Lima was, after all, a tiny white enclave in a vast Andean nation. Yet the drive to develop, to emulate the *países cultos* (cultured nations), to "improve" the race, and to "civilize" the people dominated official thinking and drove public policy for generations. As Europeans themselves were becoming disillusioned with the fruits of modernity, as Argentines questioned the benefits of immigration, Peruvian elites held fast to the idea of importing "civilization" and lamented each setback on the road to progress. The civilizing imperative underlay government action in everything from factory regulation to census taking and played an especially important role in issues of public health and housing.

The key figures in the effort to make Lima a more salubrious and progressive capital were the so-called *higienistas*, physicians trained in the increasingly influential fields of epidemiology and sanitation. As they diligently waged war against epidemic disease, these reform-minded medical experts attacked the unhealthy conditions in which the majority of Lima's population lived. Public health and hygiene provided a powerful rationale for urban reform, and many of the advances of the Balta years had been justified in the name of the fight against yellow fever, typhoid, and other contagious diseases. Indeed, many late-nineteenth-century thinkers argued that health was the key to national progress and that Peru's backwardness, not to mention its recent military defeat, could be attributed primarily to its poor hygiene and high mortality rates. In the words of the radical weekly *Germinal*:

> Because of our lack of hygiene, are we not perhaps witnessing our physical decadence? . . . Either stunted, stooped, and feeble, or overflowing with fat, we are rapidly becoming true caricatures of Homo sapiens. . . . The conquests of civilization have never been the product of organisms nourished by impure and miserable blood. Our sickliness: This is the origin of our ills. It brings lack of character, mediocrity of intelligence, cowardly compromise with evil, inconstancy in our loves and hates, and incurable sloth, which has led to our defeat in every struggle for life.[17]

Still, in spite of these arguments, the *higienistas* generally fought a losing battle throughout the nineteenth century. They constantly lacked the resources and authority they needed, in part because of the economic crises of the era and in part because public health fell into the gap between national and municipal jurisdiction. In 1903, however, an outbreak of bubonic plague and the resulting call for a decisive response significantly strengthened their hand. No previous epidemic had set off the kind of panic that came with the bubonic plague: The plague was a new and exotic disease in Peru, the scourge of fourteenth-century Europe, a sickness spread by rats, leading in many cases to a painful, ugly, horrible death. While many Peruvians (including several doctors) initially refused to believe the official diagnosis of plague, others threw themselves into a panicked frenzy, firing servants, denouncing slovenly neighbors, and dousing their walls and floors daily with disinfectant.[18] In the face of a widespread clamor for action, public health officials found that they could finally implement measures that they had advocated fruitlessly for decades. Lima's city council organized a new Institute of Hygiene, and the national government established the Dirección de Salubridad Pública. Together they carried out an ambitious program of inspections, disinfections, and quarantines unprecedented in Peruvian history.

During the peak of the plague, so-called sanitary police went door-to-door inspecting the health conditions of each home, ordering garbage removed, spraying disinfectant, taking household objects away to be sterilized or destroyed, lifting floorboards to search for rats to kill, and ordering rodent holes to be plugged with cement. All the while they recorded exhaustive statistics about the location of each case of disease and of each rat found dead.[19] For a while they published the addresses of infected homes in the papers, and some people complained that they subjected individuals with suspicious illnesses to the indignity of a medical exam right on the street, in full view of their neighbors.[20] Most controversial of all, however, were the mandatory requirements that doctors and family members report all cases of infection to the authorities and that patients be forcibly removed to *lazaretos* (quarantine hospitals) on the outskirts of town.[21] Over time, public health officials became more selective in their interventions, inspecting homes only when a contagious disease had been positively diagnosed, when a landlord or resident requested disinfection, or when neighbors raised a complaint. But they retained the power to inspect private dwellings when necessary, penetrating even Lima's cloistered monasteries in search of rats and other dangers to public health.[22]

This intrusion of government power into the most intimate private sphere marked an extraordinary break with Lima's deep patriarchal tradition, and it did not occur without opposition. The inspectors were authorized to call on the police in order to ensure that people allowed them into their homes.[23] In one case, even a member of the Callao municipal council proved uncooperative when an official insisted upon inspecting not just his sitting room but his interior rooms as well.[24] The most common form of resistance, however, was the refusal to report cases of infection in order to avoid the forced relocation of the patient or family members to the *lazareto*. Hospitalized patients would provide an incorrect home address to safeguard their loved ones' freedom. The wealthy and middle class (at times paying a bribe for the service) had their family doctors issue false or vague death certificates. Some poorer patients fled before the authorities arrived, and in one instance residents barricaded a street and threw rocks to keep the municipal health employees out of their neighborhood.[25] For a time, public officials were forced to give a reward for each denunciation of plague.[26]

Ultimately, however, health inspectors were aided by the panic that surrounded the disease. Reward or no reward, many fear-stricken citizens proved more than willing to denounce their local "*focos de infección*" ("centers of infection"). Both the municipality and the newspapers became accustomed to receiving neighbors' complaints about a clandestine garbage heap or guinea pig farm, as each new outbreak rekindled a middle- and upper-class phobia about microbes, dust, and foul smells. With all the fervor of recent converts, the "respectable people" called on the state to instruct the masses in the new religion of hygiene, and critics lashed out at those who continued to throw household garbage onto their roofs or into their back patios.[27] At the peak of the epidemic, in April 1904, the clamor reached such a pitch that the exasperated mayor of Lima felt the need to remind people that the municipality was incapable of policing the interior of each and every home. "Soon they will ask me why I don't send a brigade to clean, bathe, and soap everyone who doesn't wash!" he complained.[28]

As with most crises, the bubonic plague brought out the best and the worst in people. On the one hand, upper- and middle-class fears of contagion fueled a palpable desire to segregate the poor. Newspapers seriously discussed the forced relocation of Chinatown to a site across the Rímac river, and some public officials seemed to care about slum eradication only when those tenements stood uncomfortably close to the homes of "respectable people."[29] On the other hand, the door-to-door campaign against the plague also provided the first sustained opportunity for health-minded government reformers to investigate the actual living conditions of the poor. The experience profoundly marked a generation of young medical students, many of whom had their first up-close view of poverty as volunteers in the sanitary police. The Dirección de Salubridad Pública became a permanent and influential arm of the state, increasingly turning its attention to tuberculosis, typhoid fever, infant mortality, syphilis, alcoholism, and a host of other medical and social problems. Epidemiology and hygiene became the vehicle by which government reformers began to investigate the "social question" and to propose solutions that bypassed the church, the Sociedad de Beneficencia, and the tradition of private charity.

The historical significance of this official discovery of the poor cannot be stressed enough. For the first time, urban social problems became the focus of systematic, scientific study by an increasingly interventionist central government. The dictates of public health increasingly reigned in the private power of landlords and employers, once nearly absolute. In the process, a genuinely reformist impulse was able to gain a firm foothold within the apparatus of the state, promoting an agenda that would go far beyond hygiene and sanitation to include such issues as workplace accidents, public housing, Sunday rest, and the eight-hour workday. As *higienista* Carlos Enrique Paz Soldán put it:

> Because social assistance [is] a work of national solidarity, and no longer just a pious act of charity, . . . its exercise in a democracy should be inspired principally by high ideals of patriotic fraternity and social justice. It is through social reforms, broadly conceived and implemented, that the countries that march in the vanguard of civilization have resolved the essential issue of public assistance: the struggle against misery and pauperism.[30]

Social reform, in other words, was the keystone of progress and civilization; for Paz Soldán and other public health officials, the struggles against epidemic disease, endemic poverty, and national backwardness were inseparable.

At the same time, however, the *higienistas*' vision of social reform was constrained and distorted by the orthodoxies of the time, including ideas of race that dominated thinking in the scientific community. The perceived connection between race and disease was unshakable in Peru, as it was throughout the Western world in this era of social Darwinism and eugenics.[31] Despite the lack of conclusive evidence about the origin of the bubonic plague, experts and laymen alike assumed that the epidemic had come from the Far East and that the Asian immigrant was a prime vehicle of its propagation. One newspaper critic wrote:

> From the nations of the yellow race, where civilization has not yet penetrated, there comes to spread throughout the world . . . the most devastating plague that has ever afflicted humankind. With the unsuitable mixing of degenerate races that immigration inevitably brings, they carry [from China] the constant threat of the dissemination of plague throughout the rest of the world.[32]

Few public health experts doubted that the high mortality of Asians and indigenous peoples was both a function and proof of their inherent racial weakness. This weakness also made them a danger to others, because the epidemic diseases they so easily contracted could then be passed on to the population at large.[33]

Interestingly, although most *higienistas* accepted the "scientific" racism of their age, that did not make them any less reformist or any less conscious of the need to improve the living conditions of the majority. Quite the opposite: In fact, eugenics in Peru, as in the rest of Latin America, made little distinction between heredity and environment. As Nancy Stepan has noted, Latin American eugenicists were less influenced by Darwin than by Jean-Baptiste Lamarck, the early-nineteenth-century French naturalist who championed the idea that biological characteristics acquired over an organism's lifetime could be passed on to subsequent generations. As a result, Peru's experts believed that the racial stock of their nation could be improved not only by means of biological mixing with "superior" races but also through the amelioration of living conditions, the defense of public health, and the aggressive struggle against the "degenerative" forces of alcoholism and vice. In contrast to northern European social Darwinism, which often viewed any state intervention on behalf of "inferior" races as counterproductive, eugenic ideology in Latin America served the cause of reform, giving scientific support to the civilizing imperative.[34] In Peru physicians explicitly employed eugenic ideas to justify the battle against tuberculosis, campaigns against alcoholism, demands for factory legislation, the construction of workers' housing projects, and much more.[35]

However, because of the neo-Lamarckian tendency to make little distinction between heredity and environment, Peru's public health experts also made little distinction between the conditions in which people of different races found themselves and the intrinsic characteristics of those races. As a result, the crudest stereotypes assumed the guise of scientific knowledge and at times formed the basis for public policy. Asians, for example, appeared even in official reports as inherently filthy, ignorant of hygiene, congenitally addicted to opium, and sexually deviant.[36] Indians were unhygienic, indolent, resentful, and prone to alcoholism.[37] Both races were alleged to be natural targets of tuberculosis, plague, syphilis, and a host of other diseases, and most health officials could not imagine disaggregating the biological, cultural, and socioeconomic factors that made them so. The experts duly noted that most Indians and Asians were poor but rarely gave special importance to the fact; poverty simply joined the list of characteristics that, along with ignorance, contributed to their high mortality. Even the few writers who downplayed the importance of race argued that cultural level, not income, was the crucial predictor of one's susceptibility to epidemic disease.[38] In the end, no attempt to determine cause and effect could escape this neo-Lamarckian circularity: sickly, degenerate races were more likely to contract disease, yet disease itself debilitated its victims and their offspring, thereby weakening the race.[39] Indians were allegedly predisposed to alcoholism, yet alcoholism was assumed to be the reason why Indians had become a degraded race in the first place. One medical student, preparing a hygiene curriculum for use in primary schools, had to wrestle with whether or not to talk about the supposed genetic heritability of alcoholism: On the one hand, students should know the dire consequences of drinking, but on the other hand, the children of alcoholics should not be deprived of hope.[40] In short, Lima's public health experts were captives of an explanatory paradigm that had the great virtue of turning scientific racism into a rationale for social reform but that at the same time blamed the victims for their plight, or more accurately, saw victim and plight as inseparable, as one and the same thing.

Housing Reform and Social Conflict

The issue of housing provides a unique window onto the contradictions of a reformist project that was both progressive and racist, genuinely concerned with the well-being of the poor yet unwilling to confront poverty itself. Government intervention in housing had begun as an emergency measure during the antibubonic campaign of 1904–1905, when thousands of homes were disinfected and several hundred thousand rats were exterminated.[41] Over time, however, Lima's endemic tuberculosis, rather than the plague, became the primary rationale for housing reform. Drawing on the writings of European authorities, Lima's health care professionals cited insufficient light, lack of ventilation, dust, humidity, filth, and overcrowding as essential factors promoting transmission of the Koch (tubercular) bacillus.[42] Poor housing was also alleged to contribute indirectly to disease by fomenting alcoholism, immorality, and a sense of fatalism, all of which weakened workers' resistance.[43]

Beneath the veneer of medical objectivity, the *higienistas* seemed to dwell inordinately on the lurid details of filth and degradation in Lima's tenements, vividly describing the sights and smells with a mixture of disgust and fascination.[44] Rarely, however, did these Dantesque portraits distinguish in any significant way between miserable buildings and miserable tenants. While official reports and journalistic exposés did criticize the greedy or negligent landlords who refused to invest in the upkeep of their properties, they nevertheless betrayed the assumption that filthy, unsanitary homes were caused primarily by filthy, unsanitary people:

> All the preventable diseases, endemic or not, ravage [these tenements] because there they find a favorable environment in which to seethe: subjects debilitated by alcoholism, by misery, by life in an infected environment; individuals in complete physical decadence and no less moral decadence, influenced by stupid prejudices, crass ignorance, and the most complete indolence.[45]

Overcrowding itself was cast in the same ambiguous terms. Public health experts constantly described lower-class housing as a hazard to both health and morality, citing the "promiscuity" with which fathers, mothers, children, and even non–family members shared a single room and sometimes a single bed. But just as often, the reports left the impression that the relaxed morals of the poor predisposed them to live that way, or at least made them oblivious to the fact that they were violating every principle of "civilized" life.[46] Race, as usual, dominated the equation: "Uncivilized" races by definition lacked an understanding of cleanliness and hygiene, so the fact that disproportionate numbers of Indians and Asians lived—and died—in Lima's worst, most unsanitary dwellings confirmed not their oppression but their backwardness. According to one report:

> It is an inveterate custom among individuals of the common people [*sujetos del bajo pueblo*], principally among those of the Indian race, to live in shocking promiscuity with all the domestic animals, those who with their excrement dirty the pavement and the furniture and contribute, in no small part, to the unhealthiness of the home. Dogs, cats, pigs, guinea pigs, chickens, etc., are inseparable companions of these individuals of the lowest social class.[47]

Rarely if ever did the *higienistas* voice the possibility that unsanitary habits like raising animals in the home or immoral habits like sleeping many to a bed might be a response to economic necessity.[48] And once again prejudice was most apparent against the Chinese. This is how the popular weekly *Variedades* described the Callejón Otaiza, a tenement in the heart of Lima's Chinatown:

> With a motley full-time population of nearly 500 vice-ridden and abject Chinese, and a transient population no less in number, with its dark and asphyxiating opium dens, clandestine motel rooms, abominable dives, gambling dens—all working together to produce the greatest possible degradation and filth—that *callejón* was an affront to Lima and a school of immorality and corruption for the social dregs.[49]

Demographers gave scientific support to this caricature, establishing (with a statistical rigor matched solely by their lack of imagination) that members of the yellow race lived too closely together and too many to a room.[50] The only question left was whether this proven tendency toward overcrowding was a cause or a product of Asians' alleged moral degeneration.[51]

A modern reader may see the early-twentieth-century *higienistas*' ideas as hopelessly confused and therefore assume that the *higienistas* were incapable of formulating a coherent program to confront the problem of unsanitary housing. Actually, quite the opposite was true. Housing policy simply had to satisfy two different objectives at the same time: On the one hand, it had to provide the poor with clean, spacious, well-ventilated buildings that would resist the incubation of microbes; on the other hand, it had to educate the poor in cleanliness, hygiene, childrearing methods, savings, and temperance. In the eyes of Lima's *higienistas*, these goals were not only harmonious but mutually dependent: Low-income housing that did not also serve a civilizing purpose was a waste of time. The chosen solution, following precedents in England and France, was to attempt to turn workers into the owners of their own single-family homes, encouraging them to invest their wages in mortgage payments instead of rent.[52] Elite reformers considered self-evident the benefits of turning workers into proprietors: Not only would workers live in sanitary homes and no longer be at the mercy of landlords, but they would also develop the habit of saving (rather than spending their paychecks on drink) and by becoming homeowners would supposedly learn the joys and responsibilities of domestic life.[53] The worker-proprietor model had other advantages as well. For one thing, private entrepreneurs could build houses and provide credit at little cost to government, which needed only to cede the land and provide loan guarantees.

Alongside plans to civilize workers by turning them into homeowners, government officials enacted a range of other measures designed to teach sanitary habits, control threats to public health, and elevate the "cultural level" of the masses. Courses in hygiene were brought up to date and taught more aggressively in elementary schools. Adults were targeted with a blitz of instructive flyers on the symptoms, prevention, and treatment of such diseases as plague, tuberculosis, and syphilis. Doctors and medical students taught extension courses on personal cleanliness and the evils of alcohol. Around 1912 the government established a School of Domestic Education designed to teach poor girls the art and science of home economics, cooking, cleaning, sewing, and hygiene. "Experience shows us," wrote President Guillermo Billinghurst (1912–1914), "that domestic education, when it penetrates the [lower] social classes, is the best defense against tuberculosis and alcoholism, the great plagues that afflict the human species."[54] In 1916 antialcohol education was made compulsory in elementary and middle schools, and a year later the government banned the sale of alcohol on Saturdays and Sundays.[55] Prostitution also came under closer scrutiny by health officials. In addition, concern with public health (and defense of the race) contributed significantly to Peruvians' early efforts to regulate labor conditions, including a 1911 law on workplace accidents and 1918 laws on Sunday closing and the limitation of child and female labor.[56] Although each of these measures arose in its own unique circumstances, they all owed a common debt to the civilizing imperative, to the elites' desire to improve the poor, to promote public health, and to foster national progress by adopting the advanced legislation of the world's "civilized countries."[57]

Scores of laws were written during these years to regulate the construction and renovation of rental properties in an attempt to rid the city of its old tenements and prevent the building of new ones. A string of measures passed in 1911 prohibited the construction of large rental units without prior approval of their building plans, mandated a sanitary inspection before every change of tenants, and banned the use of clay in the construction of rental housing, among other things.[58] Tenants' behavior was also regulated more and more closely: One ordinance, for example, prohibited the raising of domestic animals inside the home, while another made it illegal to hang washing from balconies that overlooked the street.[59]

These measures, designed to improve public health, reduce mortality rates, and bring Lima into the "modern" world, failed on virtually every count. To begin with, the few workers' housing projects that got beyond the planning stage did little to lessen, much less solve, the problem of unsanitary dwellings. Much of the difficulty could be traced back to the effort to use housing policy to "civilize" the masses. Despite the experts' attempt to study what a worker could afford, the homes built to their meticulous specifications proved entirely beyond the reach of the truly poor.[60] More important than sheer cost was the difference between payment of rent and commitment to a mortgage. Rents in most of Lima's tenements were paid weekly rather than monthly, and the process of collection was highly informal and ad hoc. This was a necessary response to the situation of a huge segment of Lima's poor, who lacked permanent jobs and steady incomes but who could still manage to scrape up a bit of money here and there when they needed to. If circumstances turned so dire that they could no longer keep the landlord at bay, relocation to another place was not the end of the world, and in most cases of delinquency, eviction was the exception rather than the rule. Worker-proprietor plans, in contrast, demanded that potential homeowners sign contracts, provide letters of reference, take out life insurance policies, and make large regular monthly payments.[61] Limits on the number of people allowed to occupy each home prevented owners from realizing the economies that went with sharing a dwelling. These inconveniences compounded the basic problem that private developers did not see workers' housing as a safe investment and government plans were always woefully underfunded.[62] Ultimately, instead of becoming the magic formula for housing, instructing, and civilizing the poor, the few "workers' houses" actually built ended up in the hands of well-off artisans and white-collar employees, people who already enjoyed stable, comfortable incomes and a degree of social respectability.[63]

Not only did the fantasy of workers' housing fail to materialize in a significant way, but public officials also continued to confront ever-greater numbers of overcrowded slum dwellings in horrible states of repair and worse states of hygiene. Builders and owners routinely disregarded the flood of codes and regulations, and municipal officials were frequently unable or unwilling to enforce the law. More often than not, inspectors reported the unsanitary conditions in this or that building, made radical recommendations for demolition or remodeling, and then waited years for action. When faced with owners' refusal to comply, the municipal council took the path of least resistance, allowing the landlords of condemned buildings to renovate instead, permitting superficial disinfections instead of structural improvements, and charging fines they knew would never be paid.[64]

The poor also resisted efforts to reform their behavior, despite the fact that public health officials could be extraordinarily coercive in their dealings with social "inferiors." During the 1904 plague epidemic, for example, the sanitary police virtually invaded Chinatown's Callejón Otaiza, tore down the partitions that subdivided the building's hundred or so rooms into hundreds more, ordered the number of tenants limited to about 300, and hired a night watchman to control who entered. Most tenants did not look favorably upon this new discipline, imposed ostensibly for their own good. The watchman became the target of enormous hostility, died within the year, and was not replaced. In 1908 inhabitants of the *callejón* even refused to cooperate with census takers, who achieved their objective only by bringing in police to surround the building in a surprise nighttime raid.[65] Distrust of authority was endemic in Lima and was by no means restricted to the Chinese: Census officials reported that renters refused to disclose how much they paid, fearing that providing the information would cause their rents to go up.[66] Nor were poor tenants necessarily pleased even when landlords sought to make their lodgings more habitable. One owner went to the sanitary authorities and complained that his tenants refused to let him install kitchens in their apartments. He asked for the city's help to evict them temporarily until the work was done.[67] The *higienistas* generally attributed such behavior to the ignorance and indolence of the poor, failing to comprehend people's legitimate fears that their rents would rise, that they would be compelled to follow new and onerous rules, or that they would be evicted. Tenant resistance often played into the hands of unscrupulous landlords who refused to keep up their properties, but popular opposition to slum eradication was understandable all the same. No bylaws or education campaigns could stop the majority of poor *limeños* from sleeping several to a bed, raising animals in their rooms, hanging laundry out over the street, or urinating in public as long as the alternatives remained costly and impractical or carried no visible benefit. Given the distance between the reformers and the masses they hoped to reform, given the eugenic assumptions of health experts, and given the official disregard for basic questions of poverty, any other lower-class response should surprise us even more.

Workers and the Civilizing Imperative

Nevertheless, a significant segment of Lima's lower classes did in fact respond differently, embracing rather than rejecting the elite reformers' discourse of health, hygiene, and progress. Indeed, what is so surprising in the Peruvian case is the fact that opponents of the civilizing impulse appear so *infrequently* in the public record. Their resistance, as we have seen, is revealed in the complaints of elite reformers, but the people's own voice is rarely heard. Instead, even in the so-called working-class press, the advocates of progress dominate entirely. Almost without exception, Lima's mutual aid societies and nascent labor unions took great pains to promote the "culture" and "moral improvement" of their members. They established libraries, promoted workers' theater and poetry, invited university students to teach extension courses in their meeting halls, and denounced the evils of alcoholism and vice in their newspapers. And although this ideology of culture and self-improvement was typical of the politically moderate workers who dominated Lima's major mutual aid societies prior to 1919, it was hardly theirs alone. Anarchists were even more aggressive civilizers, arguing that education of the worker was the key to winning his emancipation from clerical indoctrination and superstition. "Civilization," wrote the anarchist newspaper *Los Parias* in 1905, "is not just material progress; civilization is also illustration, truth, justice; civilization is patriotism, abnegation, truth; civilization is nobility of spirit and sentiment."[68] As late as the 1920s, pro-APRA[69] and even communist unions repeated the same rhetoric. Nearly all labor organizations, be they anarchist, syndicalist, or conservative, joined the fight against alcohol, gambling, and other vices; the more radical the organization, the louder its criticism of the government's failure to act more aggressively.

In the area of housing, Lima's mutual aid societies were strong proponents of the worker-proprietor model and agreed wholeheartedly with the idea that housing policy should contribute to the moral improvement of the worker. A few mutual aid societies actually worked to implement home finance and construction plans of their own, responding to members' sincere aspirations to home ownership. And significantly, as they called for more extensive government intervention in the building of workers' housing, some artisans went so far as to echo the ideas of elites like Piérola and Dávalos y Lissón, arguing that Peru's pride as a nation was undermined by its failure to provide decent housing for all. *La Verdad*, the organ of the Confederación de Artesanos Unión Universal, wrote in 1917:

> The date of our Centennial approaches, and it would be a national embarrassment if we offered for the contemplation of the foreigners who will visit us at that time—as the housing of the working classes of Peru—infected pigsties, some of which are not even fit for the lowest beings on the zoological scale. This is a disgrace. . . . it is something that diminishes our standing as a civilized people.[70]

This is not to say, however, that artisans and other organized workers sought "progress" and "civilization" on exactly the same terms as elites did. Within the boundaries of consensus on general principle, the devil was always in the details, and conflict could be intense. In 1917, for example, the government offered to sell private developers an expanse of public land on the Avenida Grau for the purpose of building workers' housing. Debating the project, one senator opposed its location, arguing that the Avenida, being the continuation of the Paseo Colón, "has a brilliant future and should be the location of public buildings of greater importance."[71] As an alternative, he proposed building the homes on the other side of the Rímac, between a centuries-old slum and a recently reclaimed garbage dump. Incensed, *La Verdad* attacked the senator in an article dripping with sarcasm: "Our attention is drawn to the low estimation [the senator] seems to have for those poor men, whom he must suppose are not on the same social plane as he, given that he would banish them to some suburb or other zone outside the city limits, just as they do with gypsies and other vagabonds, whose contact is noxious to the rest of mankind."[72] At issue here, clearly, was not just a matter of location but, rather, a far more basic question: whether or not workers themselves were to be treated as full and equal members of society. In essence, Lima's literate organized workers were appropriating the reformers' discourse of progress, civilization, and respectability in order to assert their basic rights as Peruvian citizens, rights that many conservative elites were unwilling to grant them.

The radicalism of that claim is undeniable, but it did not come without a price. In a deeply stratified, caste-bound society like that of turn-of-the-century Lima, it was perhaps impossible for artisans and organized workers to successfully claim their rightful place in society without inevitably distancing themselves from the illiterate majority. As they criticized liquor, games of chance, cockfighting, and other traditional diversions of the poor; as they established libraries and theaters for workers; and as they published newspapers and held public assemblies, they were in effect telling elites that they deserved consideration as equal human beings.[73] But in embracing self-improvement and temperance as the means to a better life, organized workers could not help but accept the gulf that separated them from the thousands of other poor Peruvians who drank, who gambled, and who did not share their ideals. Evidence of this gulf can be seen, for example, in organized workers' insistence upon calling themselves *obreros* (workers), in order to emphasize their special skills and to distinguish themselves from the common *péon* (peon) or *jornalero* (day laborer).[74] Evidence can also be seen in the support that organized workers gave to housing plans designed to transform workers into respectable property owners. On the one hand, the dream of home ownership was both sincere and powerful. But on the other hand, as we have already seen, worker-proprietor plans were extraordinarily ill-suited to the needs of the truly poor. In fighting for the worker-proprietor model, organized workers closed off other options—the subsidized construction of large rental units, for example—that might otherwise have been considered.

The ideology of hygiene, cleanliness, and public health, including its undercurrent of "scientific" racism, cropped up frequently in the writings and speeches of Lima's artisans and organized workers. Working-class papers were no less diligent than their middle- and upper-class counterparts in denouncing those unseemly and unhealthy tenements that threatened the health of Lima's residents. On the one hand, the workers' press was far more likely than the elite press to denounce the owners of those buildings, to complain about high rents, and to support tenants' interests, even to the point of advocating rent strikes in 1914 and 1919.[75] But on the other hand, working-class papers were not entirely immune from the confused causal thinking that attributed unsanitary dwellings to the ignorance and poor hygiene of their tenants.[76] And like the upper and middle classes, artisans and organized workers were most likely to blame the victim for unsanitary housing when that victim was Asian. "We knew very well," wrote *La Verdad*, "that the rooms of the Chinese were true rabbits' dens, filthy and ramshackle, inside of which one encountered only misery and putrefaction, no matter what the economic conditions of the occupants, who were generally many to a room."[77] The same paper went on to describe the dwellings of Asians as "nauseating sewers" and "centers of filth," while elsewhere it denounced Asians themselves as "these yellow microbes, incubators of all the physical and moral ills that destroy the vitality of peoples."[78]

Fear of contagion was not the only, or even the primary, cause of racism against Asians in Lima. Workers in unstable precarious jobs justifiably believed that immigrants would flood the labor market and drive down wages. Artisans in particular had long complained of being undercut by lower-cost goods from Chinese and Japanese competitors.[79] Consumers criticized a host of alleged abuses by Asian shopkeepers. But time and time again, these economic arguments were conflated with a discourse that emphasized Asians' alleged sickliness, filth, moral turpitude, and racial degeneration. The phrase "*inmundo chino*" ("filthy Chinaman") was so often repeated that one word didn't seem complete without the other.[80] Racism has been expressed throughout history in a language of cleanliness versus filth, or "purity and danger," as Mary Douglas famously put it,[81] but it is still worthwhile to emphasize the extent to which the campaigns of Peru's public health experts legitimated and shaped working-class race hatred. Asian merchants, it was argued, were able to undersell native artisans because of their racial predisposition to live and work in unsanitary conditions that would offend the dignity of even the humblest Peruvian. "Modest native-born ice-cream sellers," argued *El Obrero Textil*, "are being replaced by nauseating Japanese *raspadilleros* of cadaverous complexions and slanty eyes, with black fingernails, swarming with flies."[82] In addition, Asians supposedly thwarted the efforts of honest native workers to improve themselves because they owned the bars and gambling houses that preyed upon human weakness.[83] The ideology of progress and civilization underpinned each and every criticism of the Asian worker, adding weight to the arguments against their importation.

In addition, some of the acts of hostility that Asians suffered at the hands of other poor Peruvians seem almost bizarre unless we look for their explanation somewhere other than the labor market. Why, for example, did people in 1909–1910 pelt Chinese street sweepers with rocks, often with such violence that the sweepers were forced out of their neighborhoods?[84] Competition for miserable sanitation jobs was not at issue, according to contemporary observers.[85] Instead, it appears that the rock throwers were motivated by the belief that the street sweepers, instead of contributing to urban hygiene, were making things worse. Many public health experts had long criticized garbage-removal methods in Lima, arguing that sweeping with dry brooms actually contributed to typhoid and tuberculosis by raising microbe-laden particles into the air.[86] Although attributing motives is a game of speculation, it is not unreasonable to believe that even the poor identified the street sweepers as agents not of sanitation but of infection, especially at a moment when the re-emergence of bubonic plague had raised fear of contagion to near-panic levels. Marching through the streets in a cloud of foul-smelling dust, themselves covered with the filth they were charged with removing, the Chinese laborers symbolized contagion, disease, and death.

Guillermo Billinghurst, as mayor of Lima in 1909–1910, certainly perceived a connection between the ideology of health and hygiene and working-class violence against Asians. In May 1909, a political demonstration by the artisan-led *Partido Obrero* (Worker's party) degenerated into the worst anti-Asian riot seen in Lima to that date. Yelling "death to the Chinese," an enraged mob smashed the windows of Asian-owned stores and workshops, sacked and destroyed merchandise, and tried to set at least one establishment on fire. Asians who were unlucky enough to be on the street were assaulted and several were seriously injured, though no one was reported killed.[87] What was Billinghurst's response to the riot? Two days later he issued an order to demolish the Callejón Otaiza, the tenement in Lima's Chinatown that had long been denounced by health officials as a source of contagion.[88] Disregarding the protests of the building's Italian landlord, Billinghurst sent a crew of workers to carry out the destruction, which was completed in a matter of hours. *Variedades* described the scene with undisguised satisfaction:

> Once the *callejón* was taken, as if by assault, there began a veritable exodus of Chinks [*macacos*]; swarming like ants, they emerged like frightened rabbits, leaving fearfully in single file, hugging the wall, rapidly filling the street like mice whose nest had been flooded. . . . The job continued amidst all this, and minutes later Mr. Billinghurst, like a new Columbus, could cry "land!" upon seeing the adjoining street through the now-perforated *callejón*. There, where the filthy tenement once stood, a clean and decent street worthy of bearing the mayor's name will be opened up.[89]

By all accounts, workers witnessing the demolition shared the reporter's enthusiasm and cheered Billinghurst.[90] No one cared about the unfortunates who, as ironic recompense for their earlier victimization by rioters, were thrown into the street with two days' notice and no place to go.[91]

The demolition of the Callejón Otaiza speaks volumes for the two-edged nature of urban reformism in Peru. Of all the important politicians in early-twentieth-century Lima, few were more dedicated than Billinghurst to the cause of workers. As president in 1912–1914, he threw the full resources of the government behind a plan for workers' housing, supported regulation of the price of basic necessities, and granted the eight-hour day to stevedores. Some historians have thus considered Billinghurst a "populist precursor" and an enemy of the traditional elite, which in many ways he was.[92] But on closer inspection the question arises: What distinguished Billinghurst's reformism, rooted in considerations of public health, hygiene, and the improvement of the working class, from the civilizing imperative of aristocratic figures like Dávalos y Lissón? Billinghurst's housing plan, for example, explicitly followed the worker-proprietor model, and had it ever been completed, it would have done nothing for the truly poor. His aggressive attack on tenements owed primarily to the desire to eliminate alleged centers of contagion. In the end, nothing in Billinghurst's rhetoric or behavior indicates that his ideas differed in any significant way from those of the *higienistas*, with their eugenic fear of racial degeneration and their inherent failure to address the issue of poverty itself. Yet Billinghurst was undeniably a man of the people with a genuine working-class base.

How can this paradox be explained? First of all, we cannot escape the fact that workers, like all other Peruvians, were deeply divided by race and racism. The scapegoating of Asians was an ugly but comprehensible reaction to unstable employment, intense competition, and—perhaps most important—the omnipresent fear of disease in a notoriously unhealthy urban environment. Second, the literate, organized workers who spearheaded Lima's early labor movement and dominated the workers' press were in some ways victims of their own discursive strategies. As we have already seen, these workers embraced the ideology of hygiene and civilization as a way to stake a claim to respectability and hence a radical claim to citizenship. Just as important, by echoing the *higienistas*' assertion that Peru's "progress" as a nation depended upon raising the cultural, moral, and material level of the average worker, they mounted a powerful and convincing argument for higher wages, shorter hours, better working conditions, improved housing, and a host of other genuine economic gains. In so doing, however, it became extraordinarily difficult for those workers to also maintain an effective solidarity with the many other poor Peruvians who showed little interest in becoming more like the "respectable people."

Finally, it is essential to remember that there *were* fundamental differences between the ideology of hygiene, race, and progress as understood by elites and the formulation of those same ideas in the minds of Lima's organized workers. What is fascinating about working-class ideology in Lima is the extent to which the civilizing imperative and even anti-Asian hatred fueled a coherent and quite radical critique of the Peruvian elite itself. "If gambling and alcoholism exist here," wrote *El Obrero Textil,*

> it is because the very people charged with enforcing these laws violate them and allow them to be violated. The workers in general . . . petitioned authorities for a complete ban on the elaboration of alcoholic beverages in the country, and if these requests have been ignored, it is because it serves the interests of capitalism and the bourgeoisie to have the masses living in a state of lethargy, made dull and stupid for their eternal exploitation.[93]

We have seen that workers' organizations campaigned against vice, but they differed from most *higienistas* in that they never lost sight of the elites who either profited from that vice or, at any rate. showed scant interest in its repression.[94]

Workers similarly enlisted the racial ideas of public health reformers in a biting critique of Peru's most powerful landowning families. "Everywhere else the Chinese are thrown out," complained the militantly antigovernment and anticlerical paper *Fray K. Bezón* in 1907, "but they are brought to Peru, because otherwise, the haciendas of Messrs. Pardo and Leguía would suffer greatly. What does it matter to Messrs. Leguía and Pardo that the Chinese deform and destroy the race of our people?"[95] Workers, in other words, excoriated elites for putting their personal interest in securing a low-wage workforce above the general interest in "improving" the nation's racial stock. This argument was extremely radical in some ways, describing Peru's leaders as lackeys of an egoistic and utterly antinational landholding elite. It resonated deeply with an emerging popular nationalism that accused

Peruvian landowners (and their Chinese workers) of collaborating with Chile in the War of the Pacific. But in denouncing elite self-interest and hypocrisy, workers tacitly embraced the very beliefs that those elites professed but allegedly ignored, including the idea that Peru's national progress depended upon its racial improvement and that Europeans were in fact superior.[96]

Reform, Discipline, and Failure: Final Reflections

By 1930 Peru's leaders had made great strides in the "hygienization" of Lima, but much remained unaccomplished. Between 1919 and 1930 President Augusto B. Leguía dedicated substantial resources to the city's improvement, bringing in U.S. technology to satisfy the need for pavement, sewers, and potable water in the urban center. Brick and cement finally began to replace adobe as the building material of choice. Bubonic plague ceased to appear in the city, although tuberculosis, typhoid fever, and other diseases persisted. The most significant change in the 1920s was the increasing conversion of the downtown core into a strictly commercial center and the exodus of the elite and middle class to suburban neighborhoods such as Santa Beatríz, Jesús Maria, and later San Isidro. Much more slowly, the poor, too, began to leave the city center, but for them the change was not always for the better. Lower-class suburbs like La Victoria were settled without the provision of basic services, as the municipality and developers fought for years over who should pay. Tenements sprang up even in new neighborhoods, reproducing all the health and hygiene problems of the traditional urban core. And around 1930 Lima saw the emergence of its first shantytowns, foreshadowing what would eventually become the typical residence of the city's poor majority.

In 1945 an urban planner named Luis Ortiz de Zevallos continued to voice a familiar lament: "If we *limeños* have something to be ashamed of, it is the unhealthy housing of our city. Few places in the civilized world are marked by such an ignominious blemish, which belies Lima's cultured and humanitarian tradition."[97] Apparently little had changed in the fifty years since Nicolás de Piérola had written virtually identical words. Indeed, Ortiz de Zevallos, like the *higienistas* of a generation earlier, pointed to Lima's unsanitary housing as the main source of tuberculosis, "radiating centers of the white plague, from whence the terrible illness spreads to more comfortable and luxurious residences."[98] While Ortiz de Zevallos differed from the *higienistas* of the early 1900s in his appreciation of the importance of poverty, he nonetheless continued to emphasize that reform could not succeed without the education of the masses, or in his words, "trying to make Lima's less advanced social groups enter into our Western way of life."[99] On the one hand, Ortiz de Zevallos was talking specifically about recent indigenous rural migrants, not about the lower classes as a whole. This was a significant change from the situation at the beginning of the century. But on the other hand, his perception that Lima's urban problems could only be solved by giving the masses a good dose of Western culture demonstrated both the persistence of the civilizing imperative and the perception that past efforts had been in vain. Despite the strides made in hygiene education, Lima remained a city where every vacant lot soon became a garbage dump, where street vendors prepared food with waste-water, where all kinds of domestic animals ran free in the patios and interiors of homes, where men urinated in the street in plain view of police and passers-by. The modernizing elites' efforts to educate, discipline, and change the habits of the poor had largely failed.

What do we make of that failure? It is not unreasonable to argue that urban reformism in fin-de-siècle Lima was, among other things, an authoritarian effort to sanitize the poor in order to protect "respectable people" from contagion and give them the illusion of residence in a cultured, civilized capital. It is easy to see the blindness and racism of a reformist project that blamed poor housing on the tenant, "solved" overcrowding simply by ordering people to live fewer to a room, and tore down slums without making provisions for relocation. If this is our view, then the failure of reform in Lima is a triumph of popular resistance. Poor people refused to change their way of life, escaped eviction far more often than not, and retained the freedom to drink, gamble, have sex, spit, and urinate as they pleased. But it is just as reasonable to argue that urban reform, despite the limitations of its advocates, was a humanitarian effort to prevent children from dying before their first birthday, to prevent adults from living inhuman lives in inhuman surroundings. It is impossible to ignore the enthusiasm with which so many organized workers embraced the ideology of progress, temperance, and hygiene in an effort both to improve the quality of their lives and to claim their place as equal citizens in a society that called itself democratic. If this is our view, then no one can claim victory in Lima's frustrated struggle for civilization.

Notes

Research for this chapter was supported by a grant from the Social Sciences and Humanities Research Council of Canada, administered through the Advisory Research Council of Queen's University. I also wish to thank Aldo Panfichi, the Pontificia Universidad Católica del Perú, Eduardo Zimmermann, and especially Marcos Cueto, who knows more about this topic than anyone else.

1. Juan Bromley and José Barbagelata, *Evolución urbana de Lima* (Lima: Ed. Lumen, 1945), 79, 90.

2. See, for example, Manuel A. Fuentes, *Estadística general de Lima*, 2nd ed., vol. 1 (Paris: Ad. Lainé et J. Havard, 1866), esp. 57–59.

3. Julio Llosa Málaga, "Estructura económica, clases sociales y producción arquitectónica: Lima 1900–1930" (B.A. thesis, Universidad Nacional de Ingeniería, 1979), 9.

4. Juan Günther Doering and Guillermo Lohmann Villena, *Lima* (Madrid: Editorial Mapfre, 1992), 227.

5. *Boletín de "La Colmena," sociedad anónima de construcciones y ahorros* 1, no. 1 (July 2, 1900): 5 (Nicolás de Piérola Archive, Biblioteca Nacional, Sala de Investigaciones, Lima).

6. *El siglo XX en el Perú a través de "El Comercio,"* vol. 1 *(1901–1910)* (Lima: Empresa Editora "El Comercio," 1991), 53–58, 88–91; Bromley and Barbagelata, *Evolución urbana de Lima*, 93–101; Günther and Lohmann, *Lima*, 227–245.

7. Pedro Dávalos y Lissón, *Lima en 1907* (Lima: Lib. e Imp. Gil, 1908), 51–52.

8. Dávalos y Lissón, *Lima en 1907*, 81–84.

9. Giovanni Bonfiglio, "Los Italianos en Lima," in *Mundos interiores: Lima 1850–1950*, ed. Aldo Panfichi and Felipe Portocarrero (Lima: Universidad del Pacífico, 1995), 44–45; Bromley and Barbagelata, *Evolución urbana de Lima*, 90–92, 99.

10. Carlos Contreras, *Sobre los orígenes de la explosión demográfica en el Perú: 1876–1940* (Lima: Instituto de Estudios Peruanos, Documento de Trabajo #61, 1994), esp. 13–17; Mario del Rio, *La inmigración y su desarrollo en el Perú* (Lima: Sanmartí, 1929); Peru, Ministerio de Fomento, *Memoria presentada por el Director de Fomento Dr. Carlos Larrabure i Correa, 1907–1908*, vol. 2 (Lima: La Opinión Nacional, 1908), cxli–cli.

11. Peru, Ministerio de Fomento, Dirección de Salud Pública, *Censo de la Provincia de Lima (26 de junio de 1908)*, vol. 1 (Lima: Imp. de "La Opinión Nacional," 1915), 90–95, 910–927. Racial categories were notoriously vague and subjective, reflecting a combination of self-identification, physical appearance, socioeconomic position, and cultural patterns.

12. Cynthia Sanborn, "Los obreros textiles de Lima: Redes sociales y organización laboral, 1900–1930," in Panfichi and Portocarrero, *Mundos interiores*, esp. 188–193.

13. Humberto Rodríguez Pastor, *Hijos del celeste imperio en el Perú (1850–1900)* (Lima: Instituto de Apoyo Agrario, 1989), 221.

14. Peter Blanchard, "Asian Immigrants in Peru," *North/South: Canadian Journal of Latin American Studies* 4, no. 7 (1979): 61.

15. Peru, *Censo de 1908*, 95. The total population for the Province of Lima in 1908 was 140,884.

16. Blanchard, "Asian Immigrants," esp. 66–67.

17. "Regeneración por la higiene," *Germinal* 1, no. 1 (January 1, 1899).

18. Juan B. Agnoli, "Inspección de higiene: Memoria del Inspector," in *Memoria de la Municipalidad de Lima 1904* (Lima: Lib. e Imp. Gil, 1905), v–vii. On the climate of panic, see *El Comercio*, May 21, 1903 (m.); May 25, 1903 (m.); April 2, 1904 (m.). (On Mondays through Saturdays, *El Comercio* came out in two editions, morning [m.] and afternoon [a.].)

19. Marcos Cueto, "La ciudad y las ratas: La peste bubónica en Lima y en la costa peruana a comienzos del siglo veinte," *Histórica* 15, no. 1 (July 1991): 5–10; Juan B. Agnoli, "Informe que eleva a la Presidencia de la Junta Directiva de la campaña contra la peste bubónica en la Provincia de Lima," *Boletín del Ministerio de Fomento, Dirección de Salubridad Pública* (hereafter cited as *BMF/DSP*) 2, no. 2 (February 28, 1906): 20–56; Agnoli, "Inspección de higiene," xii–xxxvi, l–lvi.

20. *El Comercio*, April 4, 1904 (m.); April 15, 1904 (m.); April 13, 1904 (a.).

21. Cueto, "La ciudad y las ratas," 14–16.

22. Carlos B. Cisneros, *Provincia de Lima: Monografía del Departamento de Lima* (Lima: Lit. Tip. Carlos Fabbri, 1911), 190.

23. *El Comercio*, May 15, 1903 (m.).

24. *Ibid.*, May 13, 1903 (a.).

25. Cueto, "La ciudad y las ratas," 10–14. For the case of an alleged bribe for a false death certificate, Archivo Histórico del Consejo Provincial de Lima (hereafter AHCPL), Ramo Higiene 1909–1913, Expediente #890–297–1–1911, September 1, 1911. On the rocks and barricades, *El Siglo XX*, vol. 1, 70.

26. Agnoli, "Inspección de higiene," viii–x.

27. Jorge Spero, "Reflexiones higiénicas," *El Comercio*, May 4, 1903 (m.).

28. "Con el Alcalde de Lima," *El Comercio*, April 2, 1904 (m.).

29. See especially the campaign to demolish the Callejón de Petateros, a narrow passage of cheap bars and shops that bordered Lima's central plaza; *Variedades* 4, no. 2 (March 14, 1908): 65–68; 4, no. 3 (March 21, 1908): 97–100; *Prisma* 2, no. 17 (July 1, 1906): 27.

30. Carlos Enrique Paz Soldán, *La asistencia social en el Perú: Tesis para el doctorado* (Lima: Imp. del Centro Editorial, 1914), 38.

31. Nancy Leys Stepan, *"The Hour of Eugenics": Race, Gender, and Nation in Latin America* (Ithaca: Cornell University Press, 1991); Eduardo A. Zimmermann, "Racial Ideas and Social Reform: Argentina, 1890–1916," *Hispanic American Historical Review* 72, no. 1 (February 1992): 23–46.

32. "La peste bubónica," *El Comercio*, May 10, 1903.

33. *Germinal* 1, no. 1 (January 1, 1899).

34. Stepan, *"Hour of Eugenics,"* chap. 3; Robert A. Nye, *Crime, Madness, and Politics in Modern France: The Medical Concept of National Decline* (Princeton: Princeton University Press, 1984).

35. A few examples of many: J. Antonio Escarena, "La tuberculosis bajo su aspecto médico-social" (B.A. thesis, Universidad Mayor de San Marcos, 1914); Germán Flores, "Higiene en la mujer en cinta" (B.A. thesis, Universidad Mayor de San Marcos, 1913); Carlos Enrique Paz Soldán, *La medicina social: ensayo de sistematización* (Lima: Imprenta SS.CC., 1916).

36. Cisneros, *Provincia de Lima*, esp. 263–265. See also Enrique León García, *La razas en Lima: Estudio demográfico* (Doctoral thesis, Facultad de Medicina, Universidad Mayor de San Marcos, 1909), esp. 61, 63.

37. These arguments persisted even into the 1950s; Carlos Enrique Paz Soldán, *Lima y sus suburbios* (Lima: Instituto de Medicina Social, 1957), 60–61, 251.

38. Abel S. Olaechea, "Estado actual de los conocimientos relativos a la tuberculosis," *BMF/DSP* 4, no. 6–7 (June 30, 1908): 129–131.

39. Escarena, "La tuberculosis," 10; Olaechea, "Estado actual," 134–135.

40. Carlos A. Campos, "Informaciones sobre la higiene escolar en Lima," *Anales de la Universidad Mayor de San Marcos de Lima* (Lima) 30 (Año escolar de 1902): 98.

41. Agnoli, "Informe que eleva," 49–56; "Desinfectorio Municipal de Lima: Resumen de las desinfecciones practicadas durante el segundo semestre de 1904," *BMF/DSP* 1, no. 1 (July 31, 1905): unpaginated.

42. Olaechea, "Estado actual," esp. 100, 114–124. AHCPL, Ramo Higiene 1909–1913, Informe del Inspector de Higiene y Vacuna al Alcalde de Lima, December 31, 1910.

43. Enrique León García, "Alojamientos para la clase obrera en el Perú," *BMF/DSP* 2, no. 1 (January 31, 1906): 57–58; Carlos Enrique Paz Soldán, *La medicina social (ensayo de sistematización)* (Lima: Imp. SS.CC., 1916), chaps. 9–10. See also Diego A. Armus, "La tuberculosis en el discurso libertario argentino," in *Salud, cultura y sociedad en América Latina: Nuevas perspectivas históricas*, ed. Marcos Cueto (Lima: IEP, Organización Panamericana de la Salud, 1996); and David S. Barnes, *The Making of a Social Disease: Tuberculosis in Nineteenth-Century France* (Berkeley and Los Angeles: University of California Press, 1995).

44. Juan Antonio Portella, "La higiene en las casas de vecindad; necesidad de construir casas higiénicas para obreros" (B.A. thesis, Universidad Mayor de San Marcos, 1903), 15–19; Santiago Basurco and Leonidas Avendaño, "Higiene de la habitación: Informe emitido por la

comisión nombrada por el gobierno para estudiar las condiciones sanitarias de las casas de vecindad de Lima," *BMF/DSP* 3, no. 4 (April 30, 1907): esp. 108–112. Two newspaper articles of this genre are reproduced in *El Siglo XX*, vol. 1, 63–66. On French reformers' preoccupation with the foul odors of the poor, see Alain Corbin, *The Foul and the Fragrant: Odour and the French Social Imagination* (London: Macmillan/Picador, 1994), chap. 9.

45. León García, *Las razas en Lima*, 35. For similar arguments, see Mariano Pagador Blondet, "Contribución al estudio de la fiebre tifoidea en Lima," *BMF/DSP* (2nd trimester 1917): 82; Luis A. Chaves Velando, *Higiene de la habitación* (Arequipa: Tip. Medina, 1909), 3–4.

46. *Memoria que presenta al Supremo Gobierno Juan E. Rios, Prefecto del Departamento de Lima, 1904–1906* (Lima: Imp. La Industria, 1906), 38. Also see Paz Soldán, *La medicina social*, chap. 9.

47. Basurco and Avendaño, "Higiene de la habitación," p. 110.

48. Cueto, "La ciudad y las ratas," 9; Peru, *Censo de 1908*, 178.

49. "El callejón de Otaiza," *Variedades* 5, no. 63 (May 15, 1909).

50. Peru, *Censo de 1908*, 177 n.; León García, *Las razas en Lima*, 35.

51. Cisneros, *Provincia de Lima*, 263.

52. See esp. Ann-Louise Shapiro, *Housing the Poor of Paris, 1850–1902* (Madison: University of Wisconsin Press, 1985), 90–95.

53. Peru, Senado, *Diario de los debates, Congreso Ordinario de 1917*, 289–290, 306, 325. Cisneros, *Provincia de Lima*, 197–200.

54. Guillermo Billinghurst, *El Presidente Billinghurst a la nacion: Primera parte* (Santiago, Chile: Lima Imprenta Diener, 1915), 56.

55. Daniel E. Lavorería, *Prontuario de legislación sanitaria del Perú*, vol. 1, *1870–1920* (Lima: La Equitativa, 1928), 243, 341, 394.

56. Lavorería, *Prontuario*, vol. 1, 203–214, 436–441, 444–446.

57. David S. Parker, "Peruvian Politics and the Eight-Hour Day: Rethinking the 1919 General Strike," *Canadian Journal of History/Annales canadiennes d'histoire* 30, no. 3 (December 1995): 422–426.

58. Lavorería, *Prontuario*, vol. 1, 243–254.

59. AHCPL, Ramo Higiene 1909–1913; see the many "expedientes de multas"; Lavorería, *Prontuario*, vol. 1, 48.

60. Alberto Alexander Rosenthal, "Los problemas urbanas de Lima y su futuro" (Part 3), *Ciudad y Campo y Caminos* (December 1927), 5; Mariagrazia Huaman Bello and Manuel Ruiz Blanco, "Las casas de obreros de la Sociedad de Beneficencia Pública de Lima, obra de Rafael Marquina" (B.A. thesis, Universidad Nacional de Ingeniería, 1990), 1.

61. *Ley Regional #319: Reglamentación, bases, y cuadros demostrativos de la construcción de casas para empleados y obreros del Callao* (Callao: Tip. Mundial, 1924), esp. 12–16; *Boletín Municipal* 10, no. 476 (February 12, 1910): 3729; Cisneros, *Provincia de Lima*, 199.

62. Peru, Senado, *Diario de los debates, Congreso Ordinario de 1917*, 334–335; Alberto Alexander Rosenthal, *Estudio sobre la crisis de la habitación en Lima* (Lima: Torres Aguirre, 1922), 54.

63. Peru, Senado, *Diario de los debates, Congreso Ordinario de 1917*, 309, 323–324. The same thing happened in France; Shapiro, *Housing the Poor of Paris*, 99–104.

64. A few of many examples: Agnoli, "Informe que eleva," 44; *Boletín Municipal* 10, no. 471 (January 8, 1910): 3690–3691; *Variedades* 4, no. 2 (March 14, 1908): 2; AHCPL, Ramo Higiene 1909–1913, "Informe sobre la casa llamada 'del Pescante,'" August 31, 1911; Julio Pflücker de la Fuente, #770 fol. 257 ser 1 1911.

65. Peru, *Censo de 1908*, 177 n.

66. Ibid., 169.

67. AHCPL, Ramo Higiene 1909–1913, letter from Pascual Castagnola, October 29, 1928.

68. "Ecos," *Los Parias* 2, no. 16 (August 1905).

69. APRA (Alianza Popular Revolucionaria Americana) was the populist, reformist, and ostensibly anti-imperialist movement founded in 1924 by Víctor Raúl Haya de la Torre. APRA had enormous influence within Peru's labor movement between the 1920s and 1960s.

70. "El techo obrero," *La Verdad* 2, no. 94 (October 20, 1917).

71. Peru, Senado, *Diario de los debates, Congreso Ordinario de 1917*, 33–34.

72. "Casas para obreros," *La Verdad* 2, no. 84 (August 11, 1917).

73. See, for example, the printed circular from the secretary of the Asamblea de Sociedades Unidas, March 1, 1906, in Federación de Obreros Panaderos, "Estrella del Perú," Correspondence Received Folder 5, pp. 156–157; Pontificia Universidad Católica del Perú, Deapartamento de Ciencias Sociales, Centro de Documentación.

74. "Aclaremos," *La Verdad* 2, no. 67 (April 14, 1917): 527; *El Obrero Textil* 1, no. 10 (May 15, 1920): 2.

75. "Vida obrera," *El Comercio*, August 1, 1919 (m.).

76. See, for example, "Querer es poder," *La Verdad* 3, no. 121 (April 27, 1918).

77. "Pobre Lima," *La Verdad* 2, no. 64 (March 24, 1917): 505.

78. "La inmigración," *La Verdad* 2, no. 94 (October 20, 1917): 743.

79. Augusto Ruíz Zevallos, "La multitud y el mercado de trabajo: Modernización y conflicto en Lima de 1890 a 1920" (M.A. thesis, Pontificia Universidad Católica del Perú, 1993), esp. 134.

80. Ruíz, "La multitud y el mercado de trabajo," 106.

81. Mary Douglas, *Purity and Danger: An Analysis of Concepts of Pollution and Taboo* (New York: Praeger, 1966).

82. "El peligro amarillo," *El Obrero Textil* 1, no. 2 (December 6, 1919), 4. (*Raspadilleros* were vendors of a sweet frozen snack similar to a snow cone.)

83. Oscar F. Arrús, *Las razas china e india en el Perú* (Callao: Imp. de "El Callao," 1906), 22–23.

84. *Boletín Municipal* 10, no. 482 (March 26, 1910).

85. Arrús, *Razas china e india*, 15.

86. *Germinal* 1, no. 4 (January 21, 1899): 27; "De higiene," *La Crónica Médica* 27, no. 524 (October 31, 1910): 249; Cisneros, *Provincia de Lima*, 291–292.

87. Ruíz, "La multitud y el mercado de trabajo," 105–110.

88. *Boletín Municipal* 9:439 (29 May 1909), p. 3432. Humberto Rodríguez P., "La Calle del Capón, el Callejón Otaiza y el barrio chino," in Panfichi and Portocarrero, *Mundos interiores*, pp. 420–426.

89. "El Callejón de Otaiza," *Variedades* 5:63 (15 May 1909).

90. Ruíz, "La multitud y el mercado de trabajo," 111.

91. Rodríguez, "La Calle del Capón," 425.

92. Peter Blanchard, "A Populist Precursor: Guillermo Billinghurst," *Journal of Latin American Studies* 9, no. 2:251–273.

93. "Peligro amarillo," *El Obrero Textil* 1, no. 4 (January 13, 1920): 4.

94. See also "Ecos," *Los Parias* 2, no. 16 (August 1905).

95. *Fray K. Bezón* 2 (February 2, 1907): 5. José Pardo y Barreda was president of Peru from 1904 to 1908 and from 1915 to 1919. Augusto B. Leguía was president from 1908 to 1912 and from 1919 to 1930.

96. Letter from "Amigo del Pueblo," in Federación de Obreros Panaderos, "Estrella del Perú," Correspondence received, Folder 5, pp. 83–84.

97. Luis Ortiz de Zevallos, "Consideraciones sobre el problema de la vivienda insalubre en Lima," *Historia* 3, no. 10 (April-June 1945): 252.

98. Ibid.

99. Ibid., 257.

7
Public Health Care in Valparaíso, Chile

Ronn Pineo

"There are two kinds of political problems—those that have no solution and those that solve themselves."

—attributed to Ramón Barros Luco, president of Chile, 1910–1915

Chile has long enjoyed a reputation as one of the most prosperous and enlightened of the Latin American republics during the nineteenth and early twentieth centuries. To many, Chile was a nation noteworthy for its fabulous mining riches, verdant central valley, and sturdy old democracy. To many, Chileans were the "English of South America."

This chapter examines public health conditions in Valparaíso, Chile, between 1870 and 1930, assessing the extent of government commitment to social progress. Great advances in medical knowledge came during the years at the turn of the century, enabling public authorities everywhere to attack scientifically the problems of urban sanitation and health conditions. Government action could improve, indeed save, the lives, of its citizens. Nothing a government could do for its people could be more important.

Looking back, there is every reason for us to assume that Valparaíso must have led the way in public health care reform in Latin America in these years, that it must have had one of the most humane cases of urbanization. Chile's wealth cannot be doubted; it was the richest nation per capita in Latin America before the turn of the century.[1] Moreover, natural conditions favored Valparaíso, a city set in a pleasant temperate climate. Valparaíso did not have to confront the health challenges of the torrid tropics, regions infamous as virtual petri dishes harboring deadly afflictions. Valparaíso, the prosperous port of a nation rich in mining and agriculture, a city set in a mild climate, certainly should have had one of the best records of urban public health care in Latin America.

Surprisingly, it did not.

As we will see, public health officials in Valparaíso and Chile understood the origins of the problems facing them, made sound recommendations for addressing the major concerns, and spearheaded the call for action. These efforts resulted in some noteworthy successes. Nevertheless, infant mortality rates and death rates in Valparaíso and Chile remained very high, underscoring the limited accomplishments of public health care reform. As we will see, Valparaíso and Chile compared very unfavorably in infant mortality and overall death rates to other cities and nations of this era.

In general, urban health conditions are most shaped by two large forces: the environment, the challenges to health imposed by nature; and politics, the response by government in improving sanitary and public health conditions. The explanation for Valparaíso's poor public health care record can only in small measure be attributed to the environment; it must be attributed primarily to a lack of political will. This was a city and a nation in which people could have expected to enjoy good health conditions but did not. This chapter emphasizes how a uniquely dysfunctional Chilean political system and the class and racial prejudices of the Chilean elite and middle class undercut progress on health care reform in Valparaíso and Chile.

The Setting

Founded in 1536, Valparaíso, or "vale of paradise," is a beautiful, protected deepwater port on the central Pacific coast of Chile, ninety miles west of Santiago. (See Map 7.1.)[2] Long the hub of international commerce for the region, the port of Valparaíso grew with the rising Chilean agricultural export and import trade over the course of the nineteenth century. Port traffic reflected this increase. By 1880 more than 700 large vessels moved in and out of Valparaíso each year, and by 1900 that number had grown to almost 800.

During the late nineteenth century nitrates (a mineral used as a fertilizer and in making gunpowder), mined and shipped from the far north of Chile, became the dominant Chilean export, eclipsing shipments of wheat and copper. For a time Chile enjoyed a monopoly on world nitrate production. But even though Valparaíso was not in the mining zone, in 1901 the city still handled about a third of all Chilean shipments overseas and continued to receive most of Chile's imports, typically taking in about two-thirds of Chile's total. Into the 1920s and after, Valparaíso remained the busiest port on the Pacific coast of Latin America.

The growth of Valparaíso's commerce, especially after the 1888 port improvements carried out by the Kraus Commission, stimulated an expansion of other economic activities in the city. This drew people who came looking for work. Mestizo peasants left conditions of landlessness and poverty in the countryside and made their way to Valparaíso. Men found jobs on the docks, in construction, and in industry; women found work as domestic servants, as cooks, and as seamstresses. Valparaíso blossomed into a modern, vibrant city.

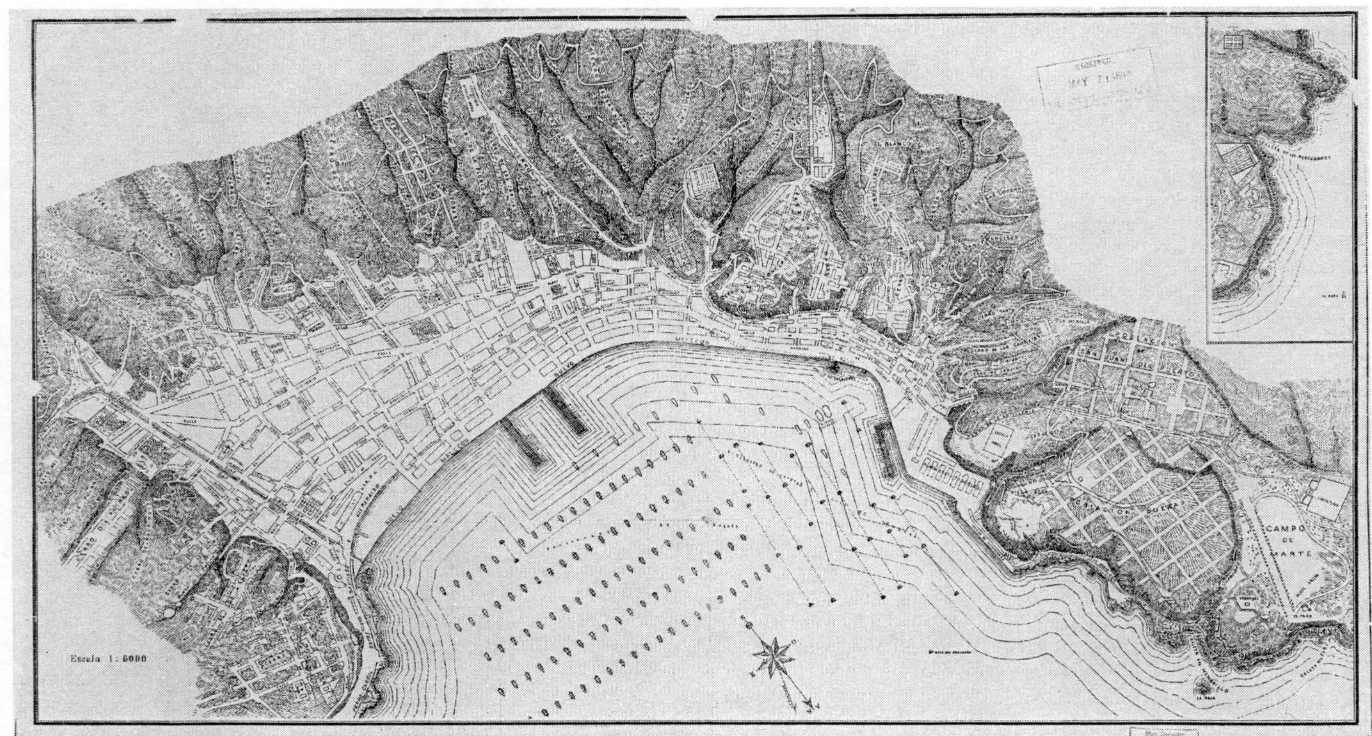

MAP 7.1 *Valparaíso, Chile, about 1894. Reproduced from the collection of the Library of Congress.*

Chile's population rose faster than that of many of the republics of Latin America in these years, although not as fast as those of Argentina, Uruguay, and Brazil, nations that attracted substantial European immigration. Although today it is still widely believed that many Europeans, especially Germans, came to Chile, actually relatively few did. The few thousand Germans who did arrive settled principally in isolated farming colonies in the south. As the 1907 census revealed, immigrants accounted for only about 4 percent of the total population in Chile, and they had made up an even smaller percentage in the preceding years.[3]

As Chile grew it urbanized, but the new city residents were migrant mestizos from the central valley rather than immigrants from Europe. In 1865 there had been only two cities in Chile with populations of 20,000 or more: Santiago and Valparaíso. However, the waves of unemployment associated with periodic economic downturns put countless people in motion in quest of work and wages. Peasants drifted to the cities or to the mining zones and then to the cities. By 1907 there were eight Chilean cities of 20,000 or more, although only the leading two, Santiago and Valparaíso, had 50,000 or more people. "Between 1885 and 1920 the proportion of the population living in cities with over 20,000 inhabitants increased from 14.3 to 27.8 percent."[4] The population of the city of Valparaíso grew from about 70,000 in 1865 to more than 193,000 in 1930, an average annual growth rate of 1.56 percent. In the same period the population of Chile rose from 1.819 million to 4.365 million, an annual average growth rate of 1.35 percent.[5]

Valparaíso's population density was the highest of any urban region in the nation. Population density in Valparaíso reached 755 per square mile in 1920 and in 1925, 799. (In Chile as a whole, population density equaled 8.1 persons per square mile in 1920, and 8.5 in 1925.) Valparaíso was arguably one of the most densely packed cities in the world in this period.[6]

This crowded urban situation was imposed by geography. Valparaíso is set on a thin coastal shelf, at some points as narrow as five city blocks. Ringing the city is a severe escarpment, with deep, sharp gorges cutting between the nineteen hills. As the population of Valparaíso grew, housing became increasingly dense on the coastal shelf. By 1885 most newcomers to Valparaíso moved up into the surrounding hills or set up their dwellings on the sides of the ravines.[7] Valparaíso built *ascensores* (skytrams), which became the city's signature feature, to carry people up and down the steep hills. This situation of extreme crowding would have grave health implications for the people of Valparaíso.

City Services

Valparaíso is very arid. Between 1876 and 1925 the city averaged only twenty-two inches of rain a year, and in some years the city received almost no rain at all; the driest year for the period under study was 1924, when less than two and a half inches of rain fell on Valparaíso.[8] Despite this aridity, in the early 1800s Valparaíso nevertheless had no real need to develop a potable water service. The city was still

A quebrada *in Valparaíso, Chile, 1914. Reproduced from the collection of the Library of Congress.*

so small, uncrowded, and even clean that residents could find enough fresh water in the *quebradas* (ravines). City residents also drew upon freshwater wells. Water workers, called "*aguadores*" or "*aguateros*," brought the water up from the wells and sold barrels door-to-door throughout Valparaíso.

In 1850 Guillermo Wheelright signed a contract with the city to build water lines for Valparaíso. Because other private interests had already claimed the water in the *quebradas,* Wheelright built a new catchment and laid underground pipes. In 1852, at a ceremony at Valparaíso's Plaza Victoria, President Manuel Montt (president 1851–1861) turned on the new public water spigot, inaugurating the potable water service for Valparaíso.

This early system quickly proved inadequate to city needs, and *aguateros* continued to find many customers in the growing city. The water problem had worsened by the 1870s, when many of the city's wells began to fail, pumped dry. Ef-

An ascensor *in Valparaíso, Chile, 1916. Reproduced from the collection of the Library of Congress.*

forts to bring water from the nearby Río Mapocho failed, as did various schemes to gather rain water.

In 1876 Jorge Lyon and Eugenio Kammerer received a city contract to build a potable water service, a project they finished in 1881. In June of that year desalinized water from Estero Salto (a nearby saltwater estuary) began to flow through underground pipes. Nevertheless, the people of Valparaíso continued to find themselves short of water. Part of the problem was that the desalination treatment did not work well; the water from the Estero Salto was still too salty for most people's taste, especially during the drier months of the year. So in 1894 Valparaíso launched another effort to expand city water supplies, but this undertaking failed, as did several other subsequent efforts.

Therefore, even after Valparaíso began to get water from Estero Salto, many city residents still had little choice but to take water from wells, local gathering ponds, or from little waterfalls in the *quebradas,* sources that almost certainly were contaminated with human feces. The water from Estero Salto was also impure; reports in 1896 indicated that people and factories dumped every manner of pollutant into the *estero.*[9] Unfortunately, the city continued to pump water from this source into public spigots and into businesses, homes, and apartments all around Valparaíso. Another concern was that the bodies interred at the city cemetery were not always properly contained, and once underground this decaying organic matter also polluted the groundwater. Meanwhile, the water lines from the *estero* did not remain in good working order very long, and by 1901, a scant twenty years after the lines had been built, most of them had already been corrupted.

So severe was the water shortage that authorities mandated a citywide water rationing plan. As city officials were forced to admit in 1896: "It is a well known fact that Valparaíso lacks an adequate supply of potable water."[10] They recognized that Valparaíso compared unfavorably to important cities in Europe or the United States in supplying potable water. Valparaíso also compared poorly to Santiago. In 1894 Santiago had begun conducting regular chemical testing of city water. Not even Paris had such testing until 1900, and least of all did Valparaíso.

On August 16, 1906, a major earthquake rumbled through central Chile, all but destroying the city of Valparaíso.[11] The earthquake was then followed by a fire. In the end, as many as 5,000 people died in Valparaíso. Although the earthquake had destroyed many of the functioning underground water lines, the disaster actually created an opening for urban renewal. Countless old and ramshackle structures had fallen over or burned; there was now ample open space to build anew in Valparaíso. The city took advantage of this opportunity, its efforts strengthened by an infusion of 57.5 million pesos for reconstruction from the national government. And finally progress came. By 1923 William Alfred Reid could write for the Pan American Union: "The domestic water supply of Valparaíso has been obtained at heavy expense, but is now available in adequate quantities."[12]

Building an adequate sewer system also proved to be a major challenge for Valparaíso.[13] The city completed its first sewer lines in 1883, but by 1896 officials of the city health council admitted that Valparaíso lacked a proper sewer system to serve the many houses, *conventillos* (tenements), and industries in the city. In the hilly section of town there were no sewer lines at all, nor was there any trash pickup. The people who lived there dumped garbage and feces down the sides of the hills, from whence it slid into the *quebradas,* into the streams, and into the city's drinking water.

Several small rivers coursed through the coastal shelf section of Valparaíso, and over the years these had been directed into widened channels. Many businesses and homes along the rivers built illegal drains to discharge raw sewage into the channels. The results were disgusting and dangerous. The open channels served as the focal points of epidemic infection, the city health council correctly reported. (The Valparaíso health council oversaw city health matters. Its members were educated middle-class physicians and public health experts, appointed by the national government.) The channels that ran through the central district of the city had an absolutely "shameful" appearance.[14] As the Valparaíso health council noted in 1897, "this system of channels is what produces . . . the bad smell that . . . is characteristic of Valparaíso, easily recognizable when one enters . . . the city."[15]

For several years the city health council sought to have covers installed over the channels, but progress came very slowly. By 1899 many of the coverings had already developed wide holes, through which people were again tossing garbage and other waste matter. That same year uncommonly heavy winter rains washed sand down into the river channels, blocking their course to the ocean. Everywhere neighborhoods flooded. As the health council reported: "All of the channels in Valparaíso are filled with sand, trash, and filth."[16] This material overflowed the clogged river channels, piling up on streets already caked with sand and mud. As city officials concluded, the heavy rains and flooding had left Valparaíso in a "deplorable state of sanitation, [revealing] the great uncleanliness and neglect that is the condition of the lower-lying areas of Valparaíso."[17]

Street paving was another problem. In 1897 only the major throughways had been paved and were more or less level. City workers cobbled downtown streets using large river rocks. When it rained the spaces between the stones formed countless little pools of water. Street cleaning was evidently a very low priority in Valparaíso, for residents complained that most paved streets were usually coated with a mixture of dried animal manure, trash, and other material. The streets were almost never washed down, although it might have been fairly inexpensive and easy to do it with seawater. As the public health council pointed out in 1897, it would have been simple enough to draw the water up from the ocean with a pump and fill some wagons. The streets that led up into the hills where most city residents lived were not even graveled. During the dry season the city was a whirlwind of dust and dirt kicked up from the many unpaved roads.

As Valparaíso grew more crowded, open places for recreation and for children to play disappeared. The city was becoming more congested, more befouled. An 1881 letter from the city council to Señora Concepción Ramos de Barra, who was refusing to sell her land to make a park, was particularly telling in this regard. In the letter the council explained that past city officials had sought to address the "disgraceful sanitary conditions" in the city. The issue had been studied to death over the years, the council said, and the archives were full of reports on sanitation, "all offering solutions to the grave problem of improving the sanitary conditions and public hygiene of Valparaíso."[18] The council pointed out the need for more public plazas and parks. The national government had passed a law mandating the building of plazas and even specified their size, realizing that otherwise selfish local business interests could refuse to comply or be niggardly in the size of the areas given over. The letter noted that whenever people visited Valparaíso, they commented on the city's crowded housing and old, narrow, ugly, and unclean streets. People needed green, clean, airy, open spaces. As Valparaíso grew, it could offer few such places.

Other urban conditions in Valparaíso were in need of improvement. One clear shortcoming was in the work of food examiners. People in the city lived in constant danger of being poisoned from tainted beverages, one expert observed.[19] Meat was suspect too. In 1877, according to the director of the city slaughterhouse, Fredrico S. Costa, the building was in horrible condition and the water used to rinse off the meat was not reliably clean.[20] Analyses by the city chemical laboratory, founded in 1893, uncovered other problems. In the first half of 1896, for example, fully half the goods tested were found to be unsuitable for human consumption. The worst foods, the laboratory said, were "milk, wine, alcoholic beverages, olive oil, and fats."[21] Unfortunately, city schools also received failing sanitary grades from health inspectors. The city conducted on-site checks of the schools in the mid-1890s, finding a "deplorable state, with respect to sanitation, . . . in some of the public schools in the city."[22] Because of similar concerns over the working conditions at Valparaíso's various workshops and factories, the members of the health council visited a sampling of establishments in the late 1890s. In the words of their report: "Nearly all of these places were unsuitable—dark, poorly ventilated, and cramped."[23] Factory conditions were very dangerous, and many workers had suffered serious injuries, the report found. But most troubling of all, the report concluded, was the sight of pale, sickly, ghostlike children, bending to their endless labor over their workbenches.

Little was done to improve these workplace conditions. The Valparaíso health council had provided the city government with draft legislation on these matters in 1897, but, they noted in despair, "it had not been approved and probably never would be."[24] They were right. For most of the period under study there were no laws regulating factory conditions or the length of the workday for children and women in Valparaíso and Chile.

City officials were not above trying to shift the blame for the wide array of sanitation problems onto the underclass. Health authorities linked the miserable overall state of health of the urban poor to their ignorance, alcoholism, and illiteracy. An 1875 report on hygiene lamented what it saw as a widespread popular indifference to sanitation in urban Chile.[25]

An 1897 report by the city health council continued this complaint against the underclass, asserting that their "total ignorance of even the slightest notion of hygiene was revealed in all aspects of city life"[26] and that "the common people never wash, never bathe, and live in tranquil harmony with all the dogs, cats, and rats in their houses."[27] As another report put it, in 1903 Valparaíso had 1,093 bars, one for every 161 people, but only six bathhouses, or one for every 29,000 people. Moreover, most city health officials believed that the country ways of the common folk were filthy and immoral.[28] City officials noted that other nations were holding congresses, issuing reports, and offering instruction on good hygiene in the public schools. Chile was not. Health officials felt that Chile was sleeping, was in "profound ignorance," while the rest of the world, or at least the developed world, was making steady advances in public health.[29]

In 1897 the Valparaíso health council recommended undertaking a mass education campaign to get common people to understand the danger of old habits and encourage them to change their ways. The health council called for building free public bathhouses and free gyms and for putting playground equipment in public parks. It even recommended sponsoring prizes for those who took the most baths. The health council also sought the creation of a commission to be charged with inspecting the homes of working-class families and, once in the door, giving the residents free hygiene advice.[30]

The health council of Valparaíso had clearly declared its determination to attack the entire array of unsanitary urban conditions vexing the city. It had pledged to campaign for the closure of drains that poured pollutants directly into city water supplies; clean and paved streets; sewers for the whole city; the destruction of all filthy, substandard *conventillos;* the cleanup of city stables; the improvement of the unhealthy conditions at the city slaughterhouse; the regulation of prostitution and the mandating of periodic medical examinations for all sex-trade workers; and the passage and enforcement of tougher zoning laws.

Over the years addressed here, some improvements did come to Valparaíso. For example, laws regulating *conventillos* came into effect by mid-1897, and soon forty-nine substandard *conventillos* were closed down, although new structures were not built to replace them. City authorities began to pay more attention to food inspection and to fine those who sold unwholesome goods. After 1904 the government began carrying out the disinfecting of homes and businesses. And by the mid-1920s progress had come in supplying potable water to city residents.[31]

In quickly coming to understand and accept new scientific ideas about the source and spread of deadly diseases and to implement solutions, the physicians and public health experts of the city health council demonstrated both courage and wisdom. Clearly the public health officials in Valparaíso cared about the well-being of the people of their city and exhibited a sincere concern about unsanitary conditions. To take just one year as an example, in 1899 the Valparaíso health council met twenty-six times, sent out forty-seven public health messages, and made numerous sound suggestions for improving public health in the city. Public health officials in Valparaíso knew what was wrong and knew how to go about correcting the situation.

Nevertheless, as Dr. Daniel Carvallo of the health council put it, it was "painful" to admit that the council's efforts had done little good. As Dr. Carvallo said: "With only a few exceptions, the administrative authorities in charge of carrying out programs did not welcome our recommendations."[32] If Valparaíso had a poor state of public health, it was not because no one in charge of health care matters knew what to do.[33]

Hospitals and Health Care Facilities

The number of hospitals in Chile increased from 29 in 1865 to 142 by 1930, and the number of patients treated rose from about 54,000 to 206,183 in the same period. (See Table 7.1.) Despite this growth, the patient-to-bed ratio (the ratio of the total number of patients treated each year to the total number of available hospital beds for the same year) grew progressively worse (at least for the period for which data are available), increasing from about ten patients per hospital bed in 1910 to about thirteen per bed by 1930. In hospital construction and expansion, Chile was not

TABLE 7.1 Total Patients Treated and Total Number of Hospitals in Chile, Selected Years 1860–1950

Year	*Males*	*Females*	*Total Patients*	*Hospitals*
1860	—	—	—	27
1865	—	—	53,589	29
1871	—	—	50,781	—
1872	—	—	61,325	—
1873	—	—	51,963	—
1874	—	—	49,990	—
1875	—	—	48,403	42
1885	—	—	58,065	64
1900	—	—	63,151	74
1905	—	—	89,707	80
1910	62,241 (60%)	41,321 (40%)	103,562	98
1911	63,992 (60%)	42,225 (40%)	106,217	98
1912	63,065 (57%)	46,752 (43%)	109,817	99
1913	62,911 (57%)	46,985 (43%)	109,896	103
1915	—	—	110,976	109
1919	—	—	140,039	114
1920	—	—	142,173	117
1921	—	—	145,889	114
1922	—	—	141,474	117
1923	77,239 (52%)	72,403 (48%)	149,642	118
1924	—	—	149,411	117
1925	76,711 (51%)	73,239 (49%)	149,950	119
1930	—	—	206,183	142
1935	—	—	261,262	149
1940	—	—	312,699	161
1950	—	—	434,134	178

SOURCES: Chile, Oficina Central de Estadística, *Quinto censo jeneral de la población de Chile, 1875;* Chile, Oficina Central de Estadística, *Anuario estadístico, beneficencia, medicina e higiene, 1913, 1923, 1925;* René M. Salinas, "Salud, ideología, y desarrollo social en Chile 1830–1950," *Cuadernos de historia* 3 (July 1983): 121–122.

keeping up. Another expression of this is shown by comparing the number of hospital patients against total population. (The lower the ratio the better, indicating that more people received care at hospitals if they needed it.) In 1865 the ratio of total population to patients in Chile was about 33 to 1. By 1900 this ratio had worsened to 46 to 1. With time, however, the situation improved, and by 1930 the ratio had fallen to 21 to 1 and by 1950 to 13 to 1.[34] In other words, by 1930 and certainly by 1950 more Chileans were likely to receive medical care at a hospital when they needed it. Before then, fewer were likely to get such treatment.

In Valparaíso the number of facilities for treating the ill showed some slow growth over this period. In 1860 there had been only three hospitals in the city, including one reserved for French sailors and another one for British seamen. The sole Valparaíso hospital for Chileans was inadequate, leaving many of the afflicted with little option but to seek refuge at a Saint Vincent de Paul Society workshop, a facility neither designed nor intended for treating the sick.[35]

The city-operated quarantine (a medical isolation facility for patients with infectious diseases) was also in very bad condition. In a letter to quarantine officials in 1870, the governor declared: "I can no longer keep quiet about the state of the quarantine facility."[36] The governor reported that there were no beds, sheets, or other basic supplies at the quarantine. The roof leaked, and there were no covers over the windows. Patients were laid out on tables or on old rags or sacks on the floor, the governor said. When it rained the patients were soaked.

Of course, it's probable that few health care facilities of the day were much to boast about, in Chile or anywhere else. For instance, the major hospital for the poor in Santiago in 1875, the Hospital San Juan de Dios, offered such substandard care that it was a commonplace among the Santiago medical establishment to say that the best thing that could be done to improve the hospital would be to level it.[37]

By 1897 in Valparaíso, however, many more treatment facilities had opened their doors. There were five general medical centers, one general surgery center, three children's medical centers, two eye clinics, one gynecological center, one obstetrics center, two dentists, one child hygiene and feeding center, and sixteen drug dispensaries. The leading public charity institutions were the Hospital San Juan de Dios, founded in 1772; the Hospital San Agustín, founded in 1888; the quarantine, founded in 1861; and an *hospicio* (long-term-care facility).

This remained the situation in 1903. The two principal charity hospitals were still the Hospital San Juan de Dios for men and the Hospital San Agustín for women. There were also two private hospitals for foreigners, one for Germans (founded in 1875) and one for British residents and sailors. In 1903 the Valparaíso-area facilities also included the *hospicio*; the quarantine in nearby Playa Ancha (see Map 7.1); two asylums, one for the aged and invalids, the other for orphans; two maternity houses; and numerous medicine dispensaries for working-class families.

By 1913 Valparaíso had five major facilities. The San Juan de Dios Hospital had expanded and now had seventeen sick wards and 370 beds. The five operating rooms there handled 674 operations that year. The Hospital San Agustín, a charity maternity hospital, had seventeen sick wards, 384 beds, and four operating rooms, which handled 861 operations that year. The Británico y Norte Américano private hospital (for U.K. and U.S. patients), which opened in 1913, had thirty rooms, seventy-four beds, and two operating rooms in which they carried out ninety operations that year. The German private hospital had twenty-eight rooms, fifty-seven beds, and three operating rooms. Doctors carried out 461 operations in the German Hospital that year. The charity quarantine in Playa Ancha had nine wards, 201 beds, and three operating rooms and carried out forty operations that year.

Finally, by the mid-1920s Valparaíso had seven principal facilities. The San Juan de Dios charity hospital for men had expanded and now had 405 beds and saw about 4,700 to 5,000 patients a year. The San Agustín charity maternity hospital now had 483 beds and had added a wing for newborns with fifty additional beds; it treated about 3,800 to 4,600 patients a year in the mid-1920s. The El Salvador charity quarantine had 285 beds and was open to females and males. The quarantine saw from 1,500 to 3,000 patients a year in the mid-1920s. The Británico y Norte Américano private hospital had sixty-three beds and treated about 470 patients a year in the mid-1920s. The Casablanca charity quarantine had twenty beds and treated male patients only, handling 125 to 240 patients a year in the mid-1920s. The German private hospital treated about 1,200 patients a year in the mid-1920s.

Throughout this period the leading hospital for working-class men in Valparaíso was the Hospital San Juan de Dios. However, as a 1904 report by the hospital's directors made plain, the hospital faced many challenges, large and small.[38] The X-ray service, the report complained, was unreliable, mainly because of deficiencies in the city's electrical supply. Much of the surgical equipment needed to be replaced, having been worn out through steady use. The facility needed an additional surgery room. Hospital hallways were filthy because patients spit all over the floors. (As a solution, the administration ordered the placement of spittoons every twenty feet.) The hospital needed a separate facility for the chronically ill, especially tuberculosis patients. In addition, officials reported, the hospital needed a proper place to store bodies prior to removal for burial. Patients complained that it was unnerving to be surrounded by so many corpses.

Because the city lacked an adequate ambulance service, those injured in accidents or violence were slow to reach the hospital. By the time they arrived, many patients had already lost too much blood to be helped; had they arrived sooner, doctors could have saved them. Contributing to this situation was the fact that most ordinary people continued to distrust hospitals and refused to go until the very last hours, if not minutes, before death closed in. Said one official: "Our people have an innate aversion to hospitals, and only those with the most extreme cases go to the hospitals."[39] Finally, as facility administrator Dr. Santiago Lyon noted in his 1904 report, the major difficulty the hospital faced was overcrowding. The source of the problem, Dr. Lyon complained, was that "incurable patients were sent by the authorities in the north[ern]" mining districts down to Valparaíso.[40]

Conditions at the dispensary annexes for the poor were particularly bad. The medical assistants there often tried to examine as many as 100 to 200 patients within an hour. Given this patient load, surely only the most manifestly evident symptoms could be recognized and treated. "This system is deplorable," the 1904 hospital report concluded.[41]

Taken together, these problems elevated the hospital's death rates. In 1904 the Hospital San Juan de Dios in Valparaíso treated 5,244 patients, of whom 464 (9 percent) died. Of the 464 who died, 82 did so within twenty-four hours of their arrival at the hospital. Still, the 9 percent patient mortality rate that year represented a marked improvement over the 20 percent mortality reported at the hospital in 1870–1871 or the chilling 30 percent mortality rate reported in 1876–1877.[42]

By 1929–1930 several improvements had come to the hospital.[43] (The facility had since been renamed the Van Buren Hospital to honor one-time director Carlos Van Buren. Van Buren was a generous benefactor to the hospital, and in his will he left enough money for the hospital to open a new eye clinic.) The facility still handled 4,500 to 6,400 patients a year by 1929–1930, but now the hospital was able to save more of these people. In 1928, 332 patients (7 percent) died at the hospital; in 1929, 407 (7 percent) died; and in 1930, 357 (6 percent) died. The facility had been modernized and renovated. The hospital had twenty-two wards with 503 beds by 1929, or twenty more beds than in 1928. The hospital now also offered dental service. Medical chief Dr. Pedro Montenegro A. reported that there was now heat in all of the rooms of the hospital.

However, hospital director Dr. Aurelio Cruzat noted in his 1929 report that there continued to be many remaining problems. The X-ray service was still deficient. The venereal disease lab facilities were inadequate. The triage room was too small. There were not enough hospital gowns for all the patients.

A more serious problem was that sometimes the hospital had to reject patients because there were not enough beds. The hospital took in homeless children, patients from outside the city, and tubercular and other chronically ill patients. The facility was being asked to do too much. As a result, when homeless adults entered the hospital waiting room, the staff usually had to turn them away, despite patients' often-obvious afflictions. In such instances, the hospital would call the police, who would take them back to the police station and from there release them back onto the streets. As the hospital report in 1929 concluded: "No one can deny the urgent need to add to the capacity of the hospital."[44]

Some charities in Valparaíso sought to fill the gaps in patient care left by overcrowded public hospitals. The Asilo de la Providencia de Valparaíso (Providence Asylum) orphanage, for example, opened in 1858 and by 1911 was home to about 300 children. Every year this orphanage took about 100 children off the streets.[45] The Sociedad Protectora de la Infancia de Valparaíso (Infant Protection Society), founded in 1889, provided free meals and baths and generally helped take care of poor children and their mothers. This was a private charity, although the government also contributed a small subvention. The Gotas de Leche de Valparaíso (Drops of Milk), founded in 1919, provided milk to infants in poorer neighborhoods. By 1929 there were several auxiliary health care associations in Valparaíso: the Consejo Superior de Asistencia Social (Superior Council for Social Assistance), the Casa de Santa Ana de Valparaíso (House of Santa Ana), the Casa del Buen Pastor de Valparaíso (House of the Good Shepherd), and the Red Cross, among others.

In general, the poor received treatment for free at Valparaíso and other Chilean health care facilities. By 1897, according to the city health council, "there were in Val-

Milk carriers in Valparaíso, Chile, 1923. Reproduced from the collection of the Library of Congress.

paraíso many totally free medical services, [including] dispensaries, children's hospitals, maternity hospitals, and [even doctor's] house calls."[46] Across Chile, only a minority of hospital patients paid for care. In 1919, 9 percent paid; in 1920, 10 percent paid; in 1921, 11 percent paid; in 1922, 11 percent paid; and in 1923, 11 percent paid. In 1925 in Valparaíso about 17 percent of surgery patients paid at city hospitals, as compared with about 12 percent of surgery patients in Chile as a whole.[47]

Overall, health care facilities made uneven progress in Valparaíso between 1870 and 1930. In 1896 the health council concluded that although they had done a great deal, there remained much more to do. In the end, the council had to acknowledge that all the public and private charity efforts had been insufficient to meet the city's needs.[48] As one authority concluded in a 1911 report: "Public assistance has never met the actual demand for services."[49]

By 1930 there still remained many obvious shortcomings. It is astonishing that a city this size still did not have an insane asylum or a tuberculosis quarantine.[50] Overall, the number of hospital beds available in Valparaíso was still far too small for the growing urban population. Western European nations in 1930 generally had about 12 hospital beds per 1,000 people; in Valparaíso there were usually less than 5 beds per 1,000 people.[51]

Hospital death rates at public charity facilities in Valparaíso were much higher than those in the more commodious private facilities in the city. In the mid-1920s death rates at the two major charity hospitals were from 6.3 percent to 7.9 percent at the Hospital San Juan de Dios and from 6.7 percent to 7.7 percent at the Hospital San Agustín. The death rates during those years at the two major privately funded hospitals were not nearly as high. At the German Hospital the death rate was from 4.4 percent to 5.6 percent, and at the Británico y Norte Américano hospital the death rate was from 2.1 percent to 2.7 percent.[52]

Sickness

When death came to Chileans, doctors were often at a loss to say what had caused it. Data available for Chile from 1903 through 1908 reveal that the cause of death could not be determined in roughly one-third to nearly one-half of all cases. Gradually, however, diagnostic skills improved. From 1909 to 1914 the cause of death remained undetermined for only about one-fifth of all deaths in Chile. After 1913 the cause of death remained unknown in only about one-seventh of all cases in Chile.[53]

Respiratory illnesses, such as pneumonia, whooping cough, and bronchitis, among other afflictions (but excluding tuberculosis, which will be discussed presently), were the leading known causes of death in Valparaíso and Chile in this period.[54] In Valparaíso respiratory illnesses were endemic and usually accounted for 20 to 29 percent of all deaths each year, or roughly 1,000 to 2,000 deaths a year in the city.

Also endemic were a lethal array of digestive illnesses such as dysentery, gastroenteritis, and other intestinal afflictions. However, these diseases posed a comparatively lesser threat in Valparaíso. Deaths attributable to digestive illnesses generally accounted for 1 to 3 percent of all fatalities in the city each year, or roughly 80 to 180 deaths annually. This group of digestive afflictions had a lower morbidity rate—was less deadly if contracted—than were the various respiratory illnesses taken as a group. In Valparaíso Province in 1923 and 1925, for example, hospitals lost about one in five of all respiratory patients but only one of every twenty patients treated for digestive illnesses.[55]

The single leading known cause of death in Valparaíso and Chile in these years was tuberculosis.[56] In Valparaíso tuberculosis usually accounted for 12 percent or more of all deaths in the city each year, or about 700 to 800 fatalities. Tuberculosis was endemic, although some years were much worse than others. In 1897, for example, the 1,322 recorded fatalities due to tuberculosis were one-quarter of all deaths in the city that year.

Because Valparaíso did not have a tuberculosis sanatorium, tuberculosis sufferers were placed in with the general patient population at the main city charity hospitals. Not until January 1896 did the health council even begin to study the idea of segregating tuberculosis patients from others receiving care at the hospitals. By 1905 the Hospital San Juan de Dios finally opened a separate wing for tuberculosis patients, but soon it became congested; the highly contagious tuberculosis patients again overflowed into the general hospital population. The hospital usually lost about one of every three tuberculosis patients they tried to assist.

Syphilis presented another endemic threat in Valparaíso, and many people suffered from this affliction.[57] Weekly medical examinations of legally registered prostitutes in Valparaíso between 1907 and 1910, for example, showed that 2 to 7 percent of prostitutes were infected with syphilis. Military medical authorities reported that 25 percent of all Chilean soldiers had syphilis or some other venereal diseases in 1907, 22 percent in 1908, and 17 percent in 1909. In a modest improvement, by 1910 only about 15 percent of Chilean soldiers suffered from venereal disease. Among Chilean railway workers, venereal diseases accounted for 7 to 11 percent of all illness between 1900 and 1907. Incident rates in Valparaíso, a wild port city, may well have been that high or higher.

Although many suffered from syphilis, relatively few in the city died from it. Usually only a half a dozen to two dozen deaths in the city each year could be directly linked to syphilis. Some additional deaths due to syphilis may have gone improperly diagnosed, however, especially in cases where infants were born with the disease. Nevertheless, even if syphilis did not often kill, it could open one up to fatal infections. As a result, how many may have died as an indirect result of syphilis infections is a larger, if unknown, number.

Violence and accidents were also significant causes of death in the city. Usually about 100 people or more lost their lives each year because of work-related or traffic accidents or as the victims of homicide. (Sometimes it was much worse. In August 1890, for example, over 300 died in one day as police and military responded with violence when rioting and looting broke out in the city during the nation's civil war.[58]) City authorities blamed much of the loss of life from accidents and violence on excessive drinking.[59] Valparaíso probably did have more than its fair share of heavy drinkers; almost every year the city police arrested at least 20,000 people for public drunkenness. Most years authorities picked up twenty or more drunks who had collapsed and died on the streets. Meanwhile, the number of bars in Valparaíso steadily increased. "There were one or more bars per block" in Valparaíso, health officials said.[60]

Other diseases were not present every year but could nevertheless take a huge toll in human lives when they did appear. Not all diseases that caused epidemics visited Valparaíso. Because of the absence of the appropriate mosquito vector, malaria could not and did not take hold in Valparaíso. Yellow fever also never established itself in Valparaíso or in Chile. In 1868 twelve people who had contracted yellow fever in Peru arrived in Valparaíso, but the disease died with them, never spreading to the rest of the population. From 1913 through 1917 seven people in Chile died of yellow fever; all of them had brought the disease in from outside the nation. Bubonic plague came to Chile in 1899, but it hit principally in the north (in the city of Iquique 135 died from the plague in 1903). Valparaíso was largely spared the ravages of the bubonic plague.[61]

Some epidemic diseases would show up only very rarely but could be absolutely devastating when they did. One such affliction was measles, a disease that principally attacks children. Some years no Valparaíso child died of measles; 1887 was such a year. However, the very next year 780 died of measles in the city, one of every ten deaths in Valparaíso that year. In 1889 an additional 307 in the city were lost to the disease. Fortunately, by 1923 measles had only a very small presence in Chile. That year fifty-seven people in Valparaíso province contracted measles and none died. Scarlet fever posed a similar threat in Valparaíso.[62] Most years scarlet fever was not present, but in 1890 an epidemic occurred, killing eighty-three people in the city.

Diphtheria likewise appeared as an epidemic disease in Valparaíso periodically. In 1894, for example, 155 people, mostly infants, died of diphtheria in Valparaíso. Diphtheria was a highly lethal infection; about half of those stricken died.[63] In 1894 the city health council established a disinfection program, but their efforts proved largely ineffectual; mostly sanitation workers sprayed poison haphazardly around some of the *conventillos.* However, the city did at least set up special rooms at the hospitals and a special wing for diphtheria patients at the city quarantine.

Typhus and typhoid fever also struck Valparaíso as epidemics and could sometimes cause as many as 100 deaths or more in a single year. For example, an 1897 typhoid fever epidemic claimed 111 lives in Valparaíso.[64]

Deadly influenza epidemics visited Valparaíso as well. In 1892 the last wave of a global flu pandemic washed over Valparaíso leaving 347 dead.[65] The infamous 1918–1919 pandemic affected the entire nation. During the last half of 1919 the total number of deaths in Chile jumped sharply; Chile lost at least 18,000 more people than might have been expected in typical winter and spring seasons. Most of these additional deaths were due to influenza. Because of influenza's low morbidity rates—usually only around 1 or 2 percent of those afflicted die—these death totals suggest that roughly half of all the people in Chile contracted the flu during this pandemic.

Cholera presented a particularly serious epidemic threat to Valparaíso.[66] Between 1886 and 1888 two deadly cholera epidemics occurred in Chile, the disease coming perhaps from India by way of Argentina. The first cholera epidemic, December 25, 1886, to July 15, 1887, attacked 27,217 and killed 10,585 in Chile. In Valparaíso this first epidemic lasted 106 days; 1,527 were infected and 628 (41 percent) died. In Santiago the epidemic lasted 104 days; 8,463 were infected and 3,481 (41 percent) died. But just when Chileans thought that the danger had passed, cholera reappeared for a second pass. The second Chilean cholera epidemic, October 20, 1887, to May 20, 1888, attacked 56,836 people and killed 23,395 (41 percent). Weekly death totals were higher in Valparaíso than in Santiago, even though the capital was a much larger city. In Valparaíso 3,689 were infected in the second epidemic, which lasted 130 days, and 1,451 (37 percent) died. In Santiago the second epidemic raged for 161 days, infecting 5,399 and killing

1,790 (33 percent). Then, as abruptly as the cholera epidemic had begun, it ended. In 1889 no one in Valparaíso died of cholera. Cholera remained present in Chile, however, although after this time it killed far fewer people. In 1907, 511 people in Chile died of cholera; by 1917, only 76 were lost to the disease.

Chile also fought a long battle against smallpox. As early as 1765 Chile had begun to use variolation—the injection of live pustules from a smallpox victim into the arm of one not yet infected—as a method of inoculation.[67] Thousands received immunization in this fashion during a smallpox epidemic that year and again in 1785 during another epidemic. This method provided protection to those inoculated but also ran the unintended risk of actually spreading the disease by creating other focal points of infection. In general, mortality of those immunized in this manner was about 0.3 to 2 percent, better odds, at least, than for those who refused or did not receive inoculation. The safer cowpox vaccine was first introduced in Valparaíso in 1807.

In 1883 Chile established a nationwide vaccination service. The vaccine became mandatory by 1887, but coverage was very uneven. Chilean health workers administered about 200,000 vaccinations or booster shots a year in the 1870s and about 700,000 a year in the 1880s. After that, however, vigilance slackened, and Chile gave out only about 400,000 smallpox vaccinations a year in the 1890s. Eventually the number of vaccinations and boosters given began to increase again, reaching 600,000 a year in the decade beginning in 1900 and 700,000 a year in the decade beginning in 1910 before leaping to an average of 1.4 million a year in the 1920s.

Without adequate vaccination coverage, smallpox remained a major killer in Chile for most of the period under study: In the 1880s and 1890s smallpox killed over 30,000 a decade; in the decade from 1900 through 1909 it killed over 24,000; during the decade from 1910 through 1919 it killed over 13,000; and in the decade of the 1920s it killed over 11,000 Chileans. The number of annual deaths due to smallpox in Chile fluctuated widely. Peak years came in 1886, when 8,121 died of smallpox; in 1905, when 10,615 died, making it the single leading cause of death in the nation that year; and in 1911, when 4,473 died of smallpox in Chile, accounting for 4 percent of all deaths in the nation that year. The last major nationwide smallpox epidemic in Chile came in 1921–1923. As late as 1923, 428 people died in the Valparaíso smallpox quarantine.

Although it is true that Chile eventually made significant progress with its smallpox vaccination campaign, it is also true that for Chile this was an effort whose success came comparatively late. Most nations in the Western world had tackled smallpox and moved on long before the 1920s. After 1925 Chile finally caught up, and there were almost no further smallpox deaths in Chile. In 1930 only two people in Chile died of smallpox.

Chile operated many quarantines for smallpox victims, but the facilities did little to help patients. During epidemics, many people, distrustful of the authorities and even more distrustful of city hospitals and quarantines, hid their afflicted loved ones rather than send them to city facilities. As a consequence, other household members could be infected. Parents were deeply reluctant to take their infants to dreaded city quarantines and sometimes departed for the hospital only when the children were near death. In some cases they waited until even after that.

Smallpox quarantines were death houses. In 1893–1894, for example, 1,514 people entered the smallpox quarantine in Valparaíso, and 44 percent (672) of them died there. It was no better in other Chilean smallpox quarantines. During the 1909 smallpox epidemic in Santiago, for example, 54 percent of those treated in the quarantine died (2,150 deaths total).

The smallpox epidemic that came to Valparaíso in February 1905 is worth considering in some detail because this event highlighted many of the city's dilemmas in providing health care service for ordinary people.[68] Valparaíso had long cut corners on ordinary city health and sanitation needs, and when this crisis hit, the community was overwhelmed.

As one member of the health council admitted in 1905, they had known for at least eight years that the smallpox quarantine was too small for city needs. Unfortunately, hospital authorities had fallen into the habit of using the smallpox quarantine to house their overflow tuberculosis patients and other incurables. So in 1905, as smallpox cases began to rise, the health council decided to bed smallpox victims at an old diphtheria ward at the San Juan de Dios hospital, a section the junta had earlier ordered razed.

By March 1905, as the smallpox epidemic advanced, the hospital filled beyond capacity. Administrators there refused to take any more patients. Unfortunately, the quarantine was also completely filled with smallpox victims. The search was on for someplace else to put the new smallpox patients. One idea explored but ultimately rejected was that of placing patients in a vacant navy warehouse. Eventually health officials decided to use the quarantine's chapel to house overflow smallpox patients.

As the number of those infected swept ever upward, even the task of arranging for transportation of patients became a nightmare. Because the city had only one ambulance, many smallpox victims had to be shipped to the quarantine on public transport, thus placing all other riders at serious risk of infection.

Dealing with the bodies of the dead proved a dilemma too. Those who died penniless suffered the final indignity of having their body tossed onto an open cart and hauled across town to the cemetery in plain public view. A debate erupted over the best time of day and the best route to take when transporting the dead to be buried. There was some discussion of at least waiting until dark to transport the bodies, but the road to the graveyard, like so many other city streets, still did not have streetlights, and so the hearse wagons could not drive down it at night. Meanwhile, the city was literally running out of space at the cemetery.

By June 1905 the health council had begun to make progress in coping with the situation, normalizing the business of buying coffins and making the various travel arrangements: from home to the quarantine and from there to the cemetery. Now they had five cars to transport bodies to the cemetery. Still, the council admitted that the cars were inadequate to the task.

Conditions at the quarantine were very bad. Short of funds, the council acknowledged that "the [financial] situation was hopeless."[69] Dr. Enrique Deformes of the health council carried out an inspection of the quarantine facility in June 1905. He noted that there were 487 patients and that the facility could offer beds to all but thirty of them. The facility lacked many basic supplies. There were not enough hospital gowns, and since they could not hang the gowns up outside because of seasonal rains, they needed a clothes drier. There were only eight bathrooms for the hundreds of patients and the staff. They needed another kitchen; the one they had could only cook for about 300 people at most, not the sometimes nearly 500 at the quarantine. The staff of doctors, nurses, and assistants was being severely overworked. They needed a wing for recovering patients so that people would not be asked to leave the quarantine while still infectious. Most of all, the facility desperately needed a segregated wing for those who were only suspected of having smallpox, a place where doctors could observe patients for several days. Sadly, some children with measles (a disease far less deadly than smallpox) had been misdiagnosed as having smallpox and had been sent to the quarantine. Some of these children had subsequently contracted smallpox at the quarantine and had died there. At least, Dr. Deformes concluded, the mortality rate at the quarantine was going down, at last inching below 50 percent.

As the crisis swept over Valparaíso, several city health officials just gave up. In April 1905 Dr. Nicolás Anguita resigned as physician at the Hospital San Juan de Dios, and Dr. Deformes quit his post as subdirector of the quarantine. In June Dr. Gonzáles Olate resigned his post as doctor at the quarantine. Dr. Ricardo Donoso replaced him but soon quit. His replacement, Dr. Cruz, quit shortly thereafter.

By September 1905 the health council finally reported that they could begin to cut back on quarantine personnel; the epidemic was subsiding. In the end, the smallpox epidemic had afflicted 11,000 people in Valparaíso, or about 7 of every 100 people. Of those infected, 4,985 (45 percent) had died in Valparaíso in 1905.

Infant Mortality and Death

In the city of Valparaíso and in Chile as a whole the infant mortality rates (the number of deaths of infants age 0–1 per 1,000 live births per year) and the death rates (the number of deaths per year per 1,000 population) were very high compared to what is known about the situation in other cities and nations during this era. Chilean health care authorities acknowledged this. For example, the Valparaíso health council made a special point of noting in its 1897 report "the enormously high mortality rate of children in Valparaíso."[70]

The numbers confirm this judgment. Infant mortality rates in Valparaíso often reached over 300. (See Table 7.2.)[71] In 1911 more than one-third of the children

TABLE 7.2 Infant Mortality in Valparaíso, Selected Years, 1897–1925 (Number of Infant Deaths per 1,000 Live Births)

Year	*Infant Deaths (age 0–1)*	*Infant Mortality Rate*
1897	1,973	322
1898	1,823	306
1899	1,632	278
1909	2,038	313
1910	1,967	300
1911	2,201	362
1917	1,419	209
1921	1,380	207
1925	1,410	241

SOURCES: Valparaíso, Chile, Consejo de Hijiene, *Actas, 1899–1900,* 219; Chile, Oficina Central de Estadística, *Anuario estadístico, movimiento de población, 1911;* Chile, Oficina Central de Estadística, *Anuario estadístico, demografía, 1921, 1923, 1925.*

born in the city died prior to their first birthday. By 1925 fewer Valparaíso infants, about one in four, died in their first year. The situation was roughly the same for Chile as a whole for this period. (See Table 7.3.) From 1885 to 1940 infant mortality in the nation was frequently higher than 300 and was always over 200 per 1,000, even though it was trending gradually downward. From 1890 to 1915 Chile had an average infant mortality rate of 293 per year.

Because the study of the history of public health care in Latin America is just beginning, complete data for all cities and nations are not available. Nevertheless, some comparisons of the infant mortality situation in Valparaíso and Chile to that of other cities and nations are possible. In Guayaquil, Ecuador, for example, infant mortality ranged from a high of 349 in 1907 to a low of 197 in 1914.[72] Valparaíso was generally this bad or worse in this period, despite the fact that Guayaquil is a tropical city and hence was frequently attacked by yellow fever and malaria, afflictions not present in Valparaíso. In his study of the State of São Paulo, Brazil, John Allen Blount reported an infant mortality rate of 155 for the year 1916.[73] The 1917 rate for Valparaíso was 209; the 1916 rate for Chile was 241. In New York City the infant mortality rate was lower and fell much faster than in Chile. In New York City the infant mortality rate fell by two-thirds from 1885 to 1915, from 273 in 1885 to 94 in 1915; in Chile the rate fell by only one-fifth in the same period, from 323 in 1885 to the still very high rate of 254 in 1915.[74]

As a consequence Chilean working-class parents were often utterly fatalistic about the potential loss of their children: If they died they became just another *anjelito al cielo* (little angel in heaven).[75] Parents had no choice but to try to look at it this way. In 1909, for example, more than half of all children in Chile died before they reached age six.

Death rates tell much the same story.[76] In Valparaíso the death rate was usually above 50 per 1,000 prior to 1900. (See Table 7.4.) Thereafter, the death rate stayed

TABLE 7.3 Infant Mortality in Chile, Selected Years, 1885–1950 (Number of Infant Deaths per 1,000 Live Births)

Year	*Infant Deaths (age 0–1)*	*Births*	*Infant Mortality Rate*
1885	—	61,965	323
1890–94 (avg.)	33,433	—	338
1895–99 (avg.)	30,562	—	290
1900	37,917	110,697	343
1901	39,330	115,745	340
1902	31,299	115,813	270
1903	30,467	115,524	264
1904	33,399	116,950	286
1905	29,849	119,650	250
1906	38,321	117,123	327
1907	37,529	126,104	298
1908	41,221	129,733	318
1909	40,767	129,333	315
1910	35,754	130,052	275
1911	44,424	133,468	333
1912	38,836	135,373	287
1913	40,135	140,525	286
1914	34,782	136,550	255
1915	34,744	136,597	254
1916	34,797	144,193	241
1917	40,169	149,161	269
1918	37,151	145,871	255
1919	44,424	144,980	306
1920	38,654	146,725	263
1921	41,151	147,795	278
1922	35,364	147,205	240
1923	42,965	151,805	283
1924	41,297	155,100	266
1925	40,276	156,225	258
1926	40,053	159,611	251
1927	39,047	172,673	226
1928	38,003	179,594	212
1929	39,481	176,030	224
1930	39,714	169,395	234
1940	36,190	166,593	217
1950	28,792	188,323	139

SOURCES: Pedro Lautaro Ferrer, *Higiene y asistencia pública en Chile: Quinta conferencia sanitaria internacional de las repúblicas Américas* (Santiago: Imprenta Barcelona, 1911), 127; Chile, Oficina Central de Estadística, *Anuario estadístico, demografía, 1917, 1921, 1925;* J. D. Long, "El problema sanitario de Chile y su solución," *Anales de la Universidad de Chile* 1 (1926): 791; Markos J. Mamalakis, *Historical Statistics for Chile: Demography and Labor Force,* vol. 2 (Westport, Conn.: Greenwood Press, 1980), 18–19, 40–41; María Angélica Illanes, *"En el nombre de pueblo, del estado y de la ciencia, (...)": Historia social de la salud pública, Chile 1880/1973 (hacia una historia social del siglo XX* (Santiago: La Unión, 1993), 27–28, 121, 145.

TABLE 7.4 Deaths and Death Rates in Valparaíso, Selected Years, 1854–1925

Year	Deaths	Death Rate[a]
1854	2,117	40.4
1865	3,822	52.3
1875	4,275	43.7
1885	5,871	55.9
1886	5,231	48.7
1887	6,455	58.8
1888	8,037	72.3
1889	4,631	41.1
1890	6,167	54.0
1891	6,842	59.2
1892	6,330	54.0
1893	6,326	53.4
1894	6,528	54.5
1895	6,382	52.1
1896	5,357	43.3
1897	5,555	44.3
1898	5,413	42.4
1899	5,385	41.6
1908	6,032	36.8
1909	6,127[b]	37.1
1910	6,703	40.2
1911	6,405	38.1
1917	4,885	27.5
1921	6,012	32.8
1925	4,971	26.4

[a] Death rate = number of deaths per 1,000 population.

[b] Estimated.

SOURCES: Valparaíso, Chile, Consejo de Hijiene, *Actas, 1896–1897,* 112, 116–117, 121–122, 283; Valparaíso, Chile, Consejo de Hijiene, *Actas, 1899–1900,* 219–220; Chile, *Anuario estadístico, movimiento de población, 1911;* Pedro Lautaro Ferrer, *Higiene y asistencia pública en Chile: Quinta conferencia sanitaria internacional de las repúblicas Américas* (Santiago: Imprenta Barcelona, 1911), 133; Chile, Oficina Central de Estadística, *Anuario estadística, demografía, 1921, 1925.*

in roughly the middle to high 30s or low 40s, finally dropping to 28 in 1917 and 26 in 1925. For Chile as a whole, death rates were lower. (See Table 7.5.) Death rates in Chile were generally in the high 20s in the years from about 1860 to the late 1880s, although these numbers probably reflect something of an undercount of deaths, especially among the rural poor. By the late 1880s record keeping had improved and probably offers a more accurate picture even if not an exact count. For Chile from the late 1880s until 1930 or so death rates showed very little change, generally ranging from the high 20s to the mid 30s per 1,000.

TABLE 7.5 Deaths and Death Rates in Chile, Selected Years, 1850–1930

Year	Deaths	Death Rate[a]
1850	23,970	18.8
1851	26,013	20.5
1852	26,147	19.5
1853	31,450	22.9
1854	30,567	21.7
1855	30,410	21.1
1856	33,384	22.7
1857	36,865	24.5
1858	34,151	22.3
1859	39,119	25.0
1860	46,270	28.9
1861	44,164	27.0
1862	40,830	24.4
1863	45,790	26.8
1864	60,236	34.6
1865	52,111	29.4
1866	46,399	25.5
1867	47,374	25.7
1868	43,699	23.4
1869	49,400	26.1
1870	47,402	24.7
1871	49,452	25.4
1872	57,668	29.2
1873	56,329	28.2
1874	55,897	27.6
1875	57,973	28.3
1876	62,817	30.2
1877	62,349	29.4
1878	60,507	28.0
1879	61,108	27.7
1880	70,036	31.2
1881	62,866	27.4
1882	65,425	28.0
1883	61,286	25.7
1884	58,909	24.2
1885	66,818	27.0
1886	67,451	26.7
1887	80,375	31.6
1888	82,260	32.1
1889	83,538	34.7
1890	95,547	36.7
1891	89,422	34.1
1892	99,274	37.6
1893	90,712	34.3
1894	89,799	33.7
1895	84,225	31.4
1896	82,662	30.5
1897	85,956	31.2

(continued)

TABLE 7.5 *(continued)*

Year	*Deaths*	*Death Rate*[a]
1898	81,419	29.1
1899	83,778	29.5
1900	104,312	36.2
1901	108,199	37.0
1902	86,107	29.0
1903	80,300	26.6
1904	86,630	28.3
1905	110,276	35.5
1906	104,890	33.2
1907	96,451	30.1
1908	104,226	32.1
1909	104,707	31.8
1910	106,073	31.9
1911	107,816	32.0
1912	103,905	30.5
1913	107,200	31.1
1914	100,059	28.7
1915	96,716	27.5
1916	99,856	28.0
1917	107,199	29.8
1918	108,667	29.9
1919	137,538	37.5
1920	115,428	31.1
1921	124,197	32.7
1922	108,756	28.4
1923	126,877	32.8
1924	114,172	29.2
1925	108,787	27.8
1926	108,251	29.2
1927	105,553	26.2
1928	101,728	24.7
1929	110,066	26.2
1930	105,140	24.5
1935	112,364	25.0
1940	107,771	21.5
1945	107,064	20.0
1950	91,180	15.0

[a] Death rate = number of deaths per 1,000 population.

SOURCES: Pedro Lautaro Ferrer, *Higiene y asistencia pública en Chile: Quinta conferencia sanitaria internacional de las repúblicas Américas* (Santiago: Imprenta Barcelona, 1911), 126, 306; Chile, Oficina Central de Estadística, *Anuario estadístico, movimiento de población, 1911;* Chile, Oficina Central de Estadística, *Anuario estadístico, demografía, 1923, 1925;* J. D. Long, "El problema sanitario de Chile y su solución," *Anales de la Universidad de Chile* 1 (1926): 788, 790; Markos J. Mamalakis, *Historical Statistics for Chile: Demography and Labor Force,* vol. 2 (Westport, Conn.: Greenwood Press, 1980), 37–38; María Angélica Illanes, *"En el nombre de pueblo, del estado y de la ciencia, (. . .)": Historia social de la salud pública, Chile 1880/1973 (hacia una historia social del siglo XX)* (Santiago, Chile: La Unión, 1993), 77, 145.

Complete comparison on this issue is also hampered by the dearth of research on health care matters in other cities and nations. Nevertheless, it is possible to obtain a general idea of how Valparaíso and Chile compared to the rest of the world. In most years during this period the death rate in Valparaíso was lower than that of Guayaquil, Ecuador, for example. Direct comparison of rates in these two cities is possible for twenty of the forty years between 1885 and 1925. (See Table 7.6.) Valparaíso had a higher death rate than Guayaquil for only five of these twenty years.[77] Death rates in Valparaíso were roughly the same as in Santiago, at least in those years for which data are available. Both Santiago and Valparaíso had death rates that were significantly higher than the national average, offering a rough measure of the increased health risk from urban overcrowding and lack of proper urban sanitation.

Valparaíso compares very unfavorably to the other Latin American cities for which information is available. Direct comparison with São Paulo is possible for five of the twenty-three years from 1894 to 1917. Valparaíso death rates were always higher than those in São Paulo and are usually nearly twice as high. In Bogotá, Colombia, in the 1890s the death rate averaged about 25 per 1,000; in Valparaíso in these years it ranged from 59 to 37. In Paris, France, in 1920 the death rate was about 14; in Valparaíso in 1921 the death rate was 33.[78]

The death rate for Chile as a whole was also higher than that of the other nations for which data are available for this period. (See Table 7.7.) Although the death rates for the Latin American nations of Argentina and Uruguay were similar to those found in the United States, western Europe, Australia, and New Zealand—rates generally in the 10 to 20 range for these years—the death rates in Chile were always in the high 20s or the 30s. Chilean death rates were also higher than those found in the less-wealthy nations of Europe: higher than those of Spain, Hungary, Romania, or Serbia. As Pedro Lautaro Ferrer summed it up in his report on public health in Chile in 1911: "The death rate in Chile is without a doubt exceedingly high."[79]

The Politics of Reform in Chile

Without the natural harbor at Valparaíso there would have been no reason to build a city there. Yet nature also imposed on Valparaíso a geographic setting that made creating a healthy city a serious challenge. As we have seen, until the mid-1920s Valparaíso suffered severe problems in supplying potable water. Population density also developed into an acute concern, especially in the older part of town, where people lived crammed together on the narrow coastal shelf. Just how crowded Valparaíso became was underscored during the 1905 smallpox epidemic, when these cramped conditions not only contributed greatly to the high number of deaths but also made it impossible to find vacant land on which to build a new cemetery to bury the additional dead.

Chile is not a poor country, and this was an era of especially fantastic riches—riches that flowed generously into private hands and that poured into national government coffers. By 1882 Chile had fifty-nine private fortunes of 1 million pe-

TABLE 7.6 Comparative Urban Death Rates, Valparaíso and Selected Cities, Selected Years, 1854–1925

Year	*Valparaíso, Chile*	*Guayaquil, Ecuador*	*Santiago, Chile*	*São Paulo, Brazil*	*Buenos Aires, Argentina*
1854	40	—	—	—	—
1865	52	—	—	—	—
1875	44	—	—	—	29
1876	—	70	—	—	26
1885	56	52	—	—	23
1886	49	57	—	—	24
1887	59	55	—	—	28
1888	72	—	—	—	27
1889	41	80	—	—	28
1890	54	70	52	—	30
1891	59	64	55	—	24
1892	54	52	63	—	24
1893	53	52	57	—	22
1894	55	58	—	28	23
1895	52	63	—	31	22
1896	43	—	—	—	19
1897	44	75	46	23[a]	19
1898	42	46	44	—	18
1899	42	46	44	—	17
1900	—	48	60	—	20
1908	37	44	—	18[a]	15
1909	37	45	55	—	15
1910	40	39	—	—	16
1911	38	41	—	—	17
1917	28	41	—	17	—
1921	33	38	—	—	—
1925	26	40	—	—	—

[a] 1897 = average for 1894–1900; 1908 = average for 1901–1910.

NOTE: Death rate = number of deaths per 1,000 population.

SOURCES: Valparaíso, Chile, Consejo de Hijiene, *Actas, 1896–1897,* 112, 116–117, 121–122, 283; *1899–1900,* 219–220; Chile, Oficina Central de Estadística, *Anuario estadístico, movimiento de población, 1911;* Pedro Lautaro Ferrer, *Higiene y asistencia pública en Chile: Quinta conferencia sanitaria internacional de las repúblicas Américas* (Santiago: Imprenta Barcelona, 1911), 133; Chile, Oficina Central de Estadística, *Anuario estadística, demografía, 1921, 1925;* John Allen Blount, "The Public Health Movement in São Paulo, Brazil: A History of the Sanitary Service, 1892–1918" (Ph.D. diss., Tulane University, 1971), 168–169, 193; María Angélica Illanes, *"En el nombre de pueblo, del estado y de la ciencia, (. . .)": Historia social de la salud pública, Chile 1880/1973 (hacia una historia social del siglo XX)* (Santiago: La Unión, 1993), 85, 98; Ronn Pineo, *Social and Economic Reform in Ecuador: Life and Work in Guayaquil, 1870–1925* (Gainesville: University Press of Florida, 1996), 119–120; Vera Blinn Reber, "Life and Death: Patient Perspectives and the Social Context of Tuberculosis in Nineteenth Century Buenos Aires," paper presented at the 49th Congreso Internacional de Americanistas, Quito, Ecuador, July 1997.

TABLE 7.7 Comparative Death Rates, Chile and Selected Nations, Selected Years, 1876–1925

Year	*Chile*	*Argentina*	*Cuba*	*Uruguay*	*United States*	*Germany*	*United Kingdom*	*New Zealand*
1876	30.2	—	—	—	—	—	—	10.0
1885	27.0	—	—	13.4	—	—	—	—
1889	34.7	16.2	—	—	—	—	—	—
1900	36.2	—	28.4[a]	—	17.2	—	—	—
1908	32.1	19.0	—	14.6	—	—	—	—
1910	31.9	—	—	—	—	17.1	—	—
1911	32.0	—	—	—	—	18.1	14.8	—
1912	30.5	16.1	—	13.6	—	16.4	13.8	—
1913	31.1	—	—	12.0	—	16.0	14.2	—
1914	28.7	15.8	—	11.6	—	16.3	14.4	—
1915	27.5	—	—	12.3	13.2	—	15.6	—
1916	28.0	—	—	14.7	—	—	—	—
1918	29.9	—	—	—	18.1	—	—	—
1920	31.1	—	—	—	—	16.3	—	—
1925	27.8	14.2	15.0	12.0	11.9	—	—	8.3

[a] Year approximate.

NOTE: Death rate = number of deaths per 1,000 population.

SOURCES: Pedro Lautaro Ferrer, *Higiene y asistencia pública en Chile: Quinta conferencia sanitaria internacional de las repúblicas Américas* (Santiago: Imprenta Barcelona, 1911), 126, 306; Chile, Oficina Central de Estadística, *Anuario estadístico, movimiento de población, 1911;* Chile, Oficina Central de Estadística, *Anuario estadístico, demografía, 1917, 1923, 1925;* J. D. Long, "El problema sanitario de Chile y su solución," *Anales de la Universidad de Chile* 1 (1926): 788–790; John Allen Blount, "The Public Health Movement in São Paulo, Brazil: A History of the Sanitary Service, 1892–1918" (Ph.D. diss., Tulane University, 1971), passim; Markos J. Mamalakis, *Historical Statistics for Chile: Demography and Labor Force,* vol. 2 (Westport, Conn.: Greenwood Press, 1980), 18–19, 40–41; María Angélica Illanes, *"En el nombre de pueblo, del estado y de la ciencia, (. . .)": Historia social de la salud pública, Chile 1880/1973 (hacia una historia social del siglo XX)* (Santiago: La Unión, 1993), 77, 145.

sos or more, of which only twenty-four dated from the colonial era; the rest were of recent origin. The rate of increase of private wealth in Chile in the late nineteenth century was faster than that of most other Latin American nations. Overall, nitrate exports had risen from 224,000 metric tons in 1880 to 2.794 million metric tons in 1920. Meanwhile export taxes on the nitrate trade provided vast though sometimes erratic revenues to the national government. The cities in Chile came to rely upon the national government and its nitrate tax revenues for nearly all of their funding. So grand was the windfall in nitrate export tax revenues that the Chilean elite decided that they could eliminate nearly all forms of taxation on themselves, and they did. Therefore it is fair to conclude that the Chilean economy generated ample government resources to pay for reform, money that should have been adequate to the task of overcoming the health care challenges that nature had imposed on Valparaíso.[80]

Urban problems were the province of Chile's national government, and it controlled nearly all funding for urban needs. However, the Chilean national political leadership fell far short of effectively addressing urban public health concerns. Certainly part of the explanation for their failure lies in the famously unusual political situation in Chile: a perpetual structural stalemate. In Chile formal politics were for the elite and loyal members of the middle class only. Political parties there were, but these were all but devoid of meaningful ideological differences. As Karen Remmer aptly put it in her analysis of Chilean political history: "Even contemporaries found it hard to define the differences between the parties in programmatic terms."[81] Chilean parties were primarily competing political patronage clubs.

A tangled web of complexity left Chilean governments in a continual state of inertia; they were incapable of taking almost any action of any type at any time. Throughout much of this era, but especially from 1891 to 1924, Chilean governments were highly volatile, unsettled, and temporary coalitions. Because politics had been drained of nearly all ideological meaning, all potential political allies were utterly faithless; all coalitions, unstable. Governments found themselves almost totally preoccupied with the basic task of staying in power. Yet even with this limited goal they failed. A coalition of three parties was usually required to form a government, and these triangulated politics presented problems in political trigonometry too complex for Chilean political leaders to solve. Government after government dissolved amid back-stabbing and bickering. Between 1891 and 1915 Chile had sixty cabinets, a new one every four months.[82]

After 1891 the Chilean Congress had successfully wrestled most power away from the presidency. Even "a strong-minded president" such as Pedro Montt (president 1906–1910) "could not successfully steer his programs through . . . [the] maze of congressional factions."[83] But just because Congress blocked presidents from doing anything did not mean that Congress put together a coherent policy of its own for governing the nation. The rules of debate allowed for endless filibusters in either chamber, a privilege fully utilized by long-winded Chilean politicians. Some presidents had no energy for the job and saw few programs they would have cared to try to enact anyhow. President Ramón Barros Luco, seventy-five years old when he entered his presidency (1910–1915), took "a siesta" during his turn in office, according to his many critics.

Nearly all of the leading historians of Chile have come to the same judgment regarding the emptiness of Chilean politics in these years. To Harold Blakemore the Chilean parliamentary republic (1891–1924) was a time of political "impasse" when the nation was hamstrung by an "unworkable" system of government. For Fredrick Pike this was a time of "apathetic drifting" for Chile, and Simon Collier and William Sater see it as a time of "political paralysis" and "empt[y]" "sterile debates" in Congress.[84] Karen Remmer concurs, summing it up this way: "Cabinet instability worked against lower-class interest. As long as party leaders were preoccupied with meeting demands for special favors, social reforms of any type were improbable. . . . The main beneficiaries of the parliamentary system were the already privileged: commercial, agricultural, and mining elites who stood to profit most from . . . government inaction and who could buy votes . . . and otherwise use their resources to control electoral outcomes."[85]

But if all this made it difficult for leaders to do anything, it is also true that they did not always try. Government responded to elite interests, and the elite made it plain that they cared very little indeed about what befell the underclass. Class prejudice and racism infected the belief system of the Chilean elite, and that attitude spread into the middle class as well.

Chilean class prejudice and racism were as least as strong or stronger than those of other Latin American nations of the day. White Chileans regarded the mixed-blood Chilean workers as racially inferior. The various schemes to induce "white" European immigration by giving away land was only the most obvious outward confirmation of the internal racism of leading Chileans. A window on these attitudes was provided by Francisco Antonio Encina, arguably the most influential Chilean historian of all time, who insisted in volume after volume of his history of Chile, written during this period, that the key to the nation's problems was the racial inferiority of the mass of Chilean workers.[86] His was a widespread attitude.

The insouciance of the urban elite to the plight of the underclass stemmed also from the fact that the urban poor were recent migrants from the countryside, where their conditions as *inquilinos* or *gañanes* approached feudal serfdom. If people in power had little real regard for the welfare of these people when they moved to the cities, this was merely a continuation of attitudes long held by Chilean elites.

So the elite blamed the poor for high mortality rates in working-class neighborhoods because to the elite way of thinking this situation was caused by the disgusting personal habits of the poor in the first place. These attitudes were laid bare during the 1903 congressional debates over what to do about a bubonic plague epidemic that year. Congressmen blamed the general health care woes of the underclass on what they saw as the inferior racial composition and filthy practices of the *rotos* (the mestizos), the great mass of ordinary Chilean women and men and their families. As the conservative Santiago daily *La nación* opined in 1923, it was probably a bad idea to try to lower the infant mortality rates among the poor anyway. It could only increase the breeding of inferior mixed-blood types who would weaken the Chilean race, the newspaper said.[87]

Senator Rafael Errázuriz Urmeneta put the matter this way: "There must always be ignorance in the world just as there must always be poverty, and to attempt to remove either by legislative process is to try to upset the natural balance of life."[88] Conservative party president Héctor Rodríguez de la Sotta shared this view and added in 1932: "The suffering and mean circumstances which beset the poor and which the sociologists say is wrong, we Christians say is proper."[89] The Chilean elite blamed the victims of poverty for their own living circumstances, and this provided them with all the excuse they needed to neglect the plight of the poor.

Things could have been different. Sometimes, in some places, if fractures opened up within the ranks of the elite, contending elite fractions could reach outside of their inner circle in an effort to recruit new political allies. This could open the political process to other voices and interests and could lead to change or even reform.

This did not happen in Chile. No elite schism developed. In part, what so brought the Chilean elite together was their feeling of enormous self-confidence, even arrogance, especially after Chile's victory in the War of the Pacific (1879–1883). The judgment of leading historians is quite uniform on this point too: The Chilean elite was remarkably solid. As historian Charles Bergquist has put it, there had long been a distinct "community of interest within the dominant class of exporters and importers."[90] Or as Pike notes: "By the turn-of-the-century, . . . urban and rural interests were crossed and crisscrossed to such a degree that the distinction was often meaningless."[91] This sturdy, interconnected elite was highly resistant to change.

Also highly distinctive to Chilean politics of this era was the extent to which the emerging middle class identified with the elite. Economic growth brought significant expansion in the middle class in these years, with jobs in the public bureaucracy, for example, increasing ninefold from 1880 to 1919. Yet the Chilean middle class was not a progressive force for change. Elite "wanna-bes," or in Chilean terminology, *siúticos*, middle-class elements in Chile were eager to fit in and go along.[92] These people were easily co-opted by the lure of jobs in government or by other opportunities in the expanding economy. Nearly all scholars have been struck by the peculiar strength of the middle class/elite alliance in Chile. In a classic piece on Chilean politics and society Fredrick Pike summarized this oft-noted feature of Chilean society: "Almost the only clear middle-class trait has been the tendency to shun the lower mass and to embrace the aristocracy."[93]

The Chilean middle class/new elite/old landed elite alliance was complete. No group needed to reach out to the workers as a potential ally against an entrenched old oligarchy in a struggle for political inclusion. To the middle class in Chile, the fact that they looked less Indian than the working class told them all they needed to know. Like the elite, much of the Chilean middle class felt indifferent to the misery of the masses.

After 1920 and the election of Arturo Alessandri (1920–1924, 1925, 1932–1938), the Chilean elite finally began to give more attention to the social question, frightened as they were by the emerging specter of naked class warfare in the streets of Santiago and Valparaíso. The notion that it might be government's job to do something about social conditions began to get a hearing in Chile. But even as Alessandri contemplated social programs, the collapse of the Chilean nitrate export economy after World War I meant that there was now little money to pay for reforms unless the rich were taxed, and that was politically impossible. Most of elite opinion continued to hold that there was really nothing wrong with Chile the way it was anyway. Reformers, mostly from the middle class, liked the status quo too; they merely felt that something had to be done to lessen the misery of the workers lest this rabble rise up and do serious damage to the whole system. Out of all this concern came much writing; Chilean muckrakers produced an outpouring of treatises on the "social question." However, despite a good deal of hand-wringing, much too little meaningful action followed.[94]

Deep divisions within the Chilean working class undermined their efforts to work together to effectively respond to their situation.[95] With the nitrate economy tucked away in its northern desert enclave, the export workers found themselves unusually isolated and disconnected from other modern workers, such as the factory employees in Santiago and the longshoremen in Valparaíso. Ideological preferences also split the workers: The northern mining districts tended to be socialist, Santiago workers were more likely to be anarchist, and in Valparaíso the International Workers of the World "wobblies" were strongest.

When workers insisted that their voice be heard, the government silenced them. Mounting inflation led to a series of working-class protests in the 1890s, and in Valparaíso dock workers struck. When looting broke out, the government repressed the uprising, killing at least fifty protesters. In May 1903 dock workers again struck in Valparaíso. This time the government killed thirty-two. In October 1905 Santiago workers staged mass cost-of-living protests. The government killed 200 protesters. In December 1907 the government massacred 2,000 nitrate workers and their families at Iquique. When after World War I the nitrate economy fell apart, massive unemployment resulted, sparking an explosion of worker protests from 1918 to 1921. In 1918 workers formed into a grand assembly in Santiago to demand relief from the high cost of necessities, and 50,000 marched in the streets of the capital. The government again responded with repression, the key to controlling the workers of Chile.

Only at the very close of the period under study did the elite in Chile begin to inch toward an accommodation with workers. In 1924 the military government passed a labor reform package, and the 1925 Constitution included labor laws and social provisions. After 1926, President (and strongman) General Carlos Ibáñez sought to co-opt the labor movement. He successfully captured and tamed the labor movement of Chile, at least for a time.

But for the most part government in Chile in this period did not include the voice of workers. Radical party leader Enrique Mac-Iver spoke for many in positions of power when he said in 1888: "The workers do not have the proper culture or sufficient preparation to even understand the problems of governance, let alone to form part of a government."[96]

During this period, Valparaíso and Chile could have achieved far greater progress in health care reform than in fact occurred. The medical knowledge was available to Chile and the rest of the world. Chile had money; it could have afforded the costs of reform. Even as early as the 1870s Chilean medical authorities understood why the more developed nations had better hygienic conditions: They spent more on it. In Chile the government instead spent most of its money on the military and the police—the forces of repression—and on economic infrastructure, railways, port facilities, roads, bridges, and massive government office buildings.[97]

Chile failed in health care reform because its leaders lacked the political will to do anything meaningful about it. Instead, the elite marshaled their resources and united with the middle class to face down a divided underclass. If this meant that public health conditions for ordinary people in Valparaíso were a disgrace, so be it. Chile's leaders did not care.

Notes

I would like to gratefully acknowledge the assistance of John Sanfuentes for his help in the initial stages of research for this chapter. I would also like to thank the following people for their ideas and comments: David Bushnell, Lois Roberts, Fredrick Pike, Jim Baer, Jay Kinsbruner, Larry Clayton, Garry Van Osdell, and David Patterson. Research for this chapter was made possible by a grant from the Towson State University Department of History.

1. Fredrick B. Pike, *Chile and the United States, 1880–1962* (Notre Dame: University of Notre Dame, 1963), 33.

2. This section on the Valparaíso setting is drawn from Luis Aguirre Echiburru, *El libro de Valparaíso* (Valparaíso: Escuela Tipográfica Salesiana, 1946), 9–10, 23, 24, 94; William Alfred Reid, *Valparaíso: The South American Emporium* (Washington, D.C.: Pan American Union, 1923), 1, 2; Alberto Fagalde, *El puerto de Valparaíso i sus obras de mejoramiento* (Santiago: n.p., 1903?), 77, 115, 199; Brian Loveman, *Chile: The Legacy of Hispanic Capitalism* (New York: Oxford University Press, 1988); Harold Blakemore, "Chile from the War of the Pacific to the World Depression, 1880–1930," in *The Cambridge History of Latin America: c. 1870 to 1930*, ed. Leslie Bethell, vol. 5 (Cambridge: Cambridge University Press, 1986); Jay Kinsbruner, *Chile: A Historical Interpretation* (New York: Harper Torchbooks, 1973); Pike, *Chile and the United States.*

3. Pedro Lautaro Ferrer, *Higiene y asistencia pública en Chile: Quinta conferencia sanitaria internacional de las repúblicas Américas* (Santiago: Imprenta Barcelona, 1911), 112, 117, 122, 306. See Carl Solberg, *Immigration and Nationalism: Argentina and Chile, 1890–1914* (Austin: University of Texas Press, 1970), 36, 38. Germans numbered about 11,000 in 1907, or 8 percent of the Chilean immigrant total.

4. Karen L. Remmer, "The Timing, Pace, and Sequence of Political Change in Chile, 1891–1925," *Hispanic American Historical Review* 57, no. 2 (May 1977): 211.

5. Markos J. Mamalakis, *Historical Statistics for Chile: Demography and Labor Force*, vol. 2 (Westport, Conn.: Greenwood Press, 1980), 4, 413–414.

6. Chile, Oficina Central de Estadística, *Anuario estadístico, demografía, 1925.*

7. Valparaíso, Chile, Consejo de Hijiene de Valparaíso, *Actas, 1896–1897,* 150; Adolphe Murillo, *Higiene et assistance publique au Chile,* trans. d'Emile Petit (Paris: Exposition Universelle de Paris, 1889), no page numbers.

8. Chile, Oficina Central de Estadística, *Anuario estadístico, demografía, 1925.* This section on potable water is drawn from: Aguirre Echiburru, *El libro de Valparaíso,* 38–40; Lautaro Ferrer, *Higiene y asistencia pública,* 137–141; Franklin Martin, *South America* (London: Fleming H. Revell Co., 1927), 110; Valparaíso, Chile, Consejo de Hijiene de Valparaíso, *Actas, 1896–1897,* 128, 296–297.

9. Ibid.

10. Ibid., 296.

11. See Lautaro Ferrer, *Higiene y assistencia pública,* 231; Aguirre Echiburru, *El libro de Valparaíso,* 49, 52; Reid, *Valparaíso,* 10.

12. Reid, *Valparaíso,* 13.

13. This section on city sewers is drawn from Valparaíso, Chile, Municipalidad, *Anales, 1870–1872,* 116–117; Valparaíso, Chile, Consejo de Hijiene de Valparaíso, *Actas, 1896–1897,* 113, 123–124, 299–300; *1899–1900,* 201–203; Fagalde, *El puerto de Valparaíso,* 36.

14. Valparaíso, Chile, Consejo de Hijiene de Valparaíso, *Actas, 1896–1897,* 300.

15. Ibid., 299.

16. Valparaíso, Chile, Consejo de Hijiene, *Actas, 1899–1900,* 202.

17. Ibid., 203.

18. Valparaíso, Chile, Secretaría de la Municipalidad, *Documentos, 1880–1881,* vol. 4, to Señora Concepción Ramos de Barra, in Valparaíso, May 3, 1881.

19. Isaac Ugarte Gutiérrez, "Algunas reflexiones sobre el estado de la salubridad pública en Chile," *Anales de la universidad de Chile* 47 (1875): 150.

20. Chile, Ministerio de Interior, *Correspondencia, informes y cuentas relativas a la Intendencia de Valparaíso, 1876–1883,* Fredrico S. Costa, Director of the Public Slaughterhouse, to the Minister of the Interior, March 20, 1877.

21. Valparaíso, Chile, Consejo de Hijiene de Valparaíso, *Actas, 1896–1897,* 287–291.

22. Ibid., 319.

23. Ibid., 301.

24. Ibid., 303.

25. Isaac Ugarte Gutiérrez, "Algunas reflexiones," 151.

26. Valparaíso, Chile, Consejo de Hijiene de Valparaíso, *Actas, 1896–1897,* 303.

27. Ibid.

28. Fagalde, *El puerto de Valparaíso,* 93. Among the worst practices—and certainly one of the most dangerous—was the custom of the *fiesta del velorio* (wake gathering). In this traditional rite, loved ones placed the corpse of the deceased in the room full of mourners, affording ample opportunity for the wide broadcast of deadly microorganisms. In some cases the body was moved from house to house for up to six days.

29. Valparaíso, Chile, Consejo de Hijiene de Valparaíso, *Actas, 1896–1897,* 322–323. Meanwhile, Chilean officials pointed out, since 1892 in New York State in the United States, the law required that children be taught hygiene in the schools.

30. Ibid., 301–305. This section on streets, sanitation, and urban conditions is drawn from: Valparaíso, Chile, Consejo de Hijiene de Valparaíso, *Actas, 1896–1897,* 112, 119–120, 300–301; Aguirre Echiburru, *El libro de Valparaíso,* 44.

31. Valparaíso, Chile, Consejo de Hijiene de Valparaíso, *Actas, 1896–1897,* 287–291.

32. Valparaíso, Chile, Consejo de Hijiene, *Actas, 1899–1900,* 217, 218.

33. Of course, even in the late 1890s, much of the Chilean medical establishment also maintained some belief in the "miasma" theory, the notion that all disease came from "bad air" exuding from putrefying organic matter. Even if most Valparaíso doctors had by this time accepted the germ theory of disease, most had still not quite given up entirely on the old theory of miasmas; Valparaíso, Chile, Consejo de Hijiene de Valparaíso, *Actas, 1896–1897,* 294–296, 299.

34. Chile, Oficina Central de Estadística, *Quinto censo jeneral de la población de Chile, 1875*; Chile, Oficina Central de Estadística, *Anuario estadístico, beneficencia, 1913, 1923, 1925*; René M. Salinas, "Salud, ideología y desarrollo social en Chile 1830–1950," *Cuadernos de historia* 3 (July 1983): 121–122.

35. Aguirre Echiburru, *El libro de Valparaíso,* 52; Valparaíso, Chile, Municipalidad, *Anales, 1870–1872,* 238–243.

36. Chile, Ministerio del Interior, *Beneficencia de Valparaíso, 1870–1872,* J. Ramos Silva, Beneficencia de Valparaíso, to the Minister of the Interior, June 8, 1870, and reply from Minster of the Interior Miguel Luís Amemátegui, June 10, 1870.

37. Isaac Ugarte Gutiérrez, "Algunas reflexiones," 165–168. On city facilities, see Valparaíso, Chile, Consejo de Hijiene de Valparaíso, *Actas, 1896–1897,* 136; Fagalde, *El puerto de Valparaíso,* 33; Chile, Oficina Central de Estadística, *Anuario estadístico, beneficencia, 1913, 1923, 1925,* 3–6.

38. Valparaíso, Chile, Junta de Beneficencia, *Actas y memorias, 1904.*

39. Valparaíso, Chile, Consejo de Hijiene de Valparaíso, *Actas, 1896–1897,* 139.

40. Valparaíso, Chile, Junta de Beneficencia, *Actas y memorias, 1904,* 129.

41. Ibid., 140.

42. Chile, Ministerio Interior, Intendencia Valparaíso, *Informe, 1871–1872*; Chile, Ministerio de Interior, *Correspondencia, informes y cuentas relativas a la intendencia de Valparaíso, 1876–1883,* the Hospital Jeneral de Caridad de Valparaíso, to the Minister of the Interior, April 13, 1877.

43. Valparaíso, Chile, Hospital Carlos Van Buren, *Anuario, 1929, 1930.*

44. Valparaíso, Chile, Hospital Carlos Van Buren, *Anuario, 1929,* 15.

45. Valparaíso, Chile, Consejo de Hijiene de Valparaíso, *Actas, 1896–1897,* 286; Lautaro Ferrer, *Higiene y assistencia pública,* 301, 303; Valparaíso, Chile, *Anuario del Hospital Carlos Van Buren de Valparaíso, 1929,* 7–10; Aguirre Echiburru, *El libro de Valparaíso,* 235, 237, 247; María Angélica Illanes, "*En el nombre de pueblo, del estado y de la ciencia (. . .)*": *Historia social de la salud pública, Chile 1880/1973 (hacia una historia social del siglo XX)* (Santiago, Chile: La Unión, 1993), 97.

46. Valparaíso, Chile, Consejo de Hijiene de Valparaíso, *Actas, 1896–1897,* 313.

47. Chile, Oficina Central de Estadística, *Anuario estadístico, beneficencia, 1923, 1925,* 6.

48. Valparaíso, Chile, Consejo de Hijiene de Valparaíso, *Actas, 1896–1897,* 135.

49. Lautaro Ferrer, *Higiene y assistencia pública,* 290.

50. Chile, Oficina Central de Estadística, *Anuario estadístico, beneficencia, 1925.*

51. Valparaíso, Chile, Hospital Carlos Van Buren, *Anuario, 1930,* 14.

52. Chile, Oficina Central de Estadística, *Anuario estadístico, beneficencia, medicina e higiene, 1925.*

53. Lautaro Ferrer, *Higiene y asistencia pública,* 128–133; Chile Oficina Central de Estadística, *Anuario estadístico, movimiento de población, 1911*; Chile Oficina Central de Estadística, *Anuario estadístico, demografía, 1917*; and adapted from Table 7.4.

54. Valparaíso, Chile, Consejo de Hijiene, *Actas, 1896–1897,* 121–122; *1899–1900,* 219; Chile, Oficina Central de Estadística, *Anuario estadístico, demografía, 1925.*

55. Valparaíso, Chile, Consejo de Hijiene, *Actas, 1896–1897,* 121–122; *1899–1900,* 219; Chile, Oficina Central de Estadística, *Anuario estadístico, beneficencia, 1923, 1925.*

56. Valparaíso, Chile, Consejo de Hijiene, *Actas, 1896–1897,* 121–122, 307–308; *1899–1900,* 219; Lautaro Ferrer, *Higiene y assistencia pública,* 367–370; Chile, Oficina Central de Estadística, *Anuario estadístico, beneficencia, 1923, 1925*; Chile, Oficina Central de Estadística, *Anuario estadístico, demografía, 1925*; René M. Salinas, "Salud," *Cuadernos de historia* 3 (July 1983): 121; and adapted from Table 7.4.

57. Valparaíso, Chile, Consejo de Hijiene, *Actas, 1896–1897,* 121–122, 309; Lautaro Ferrer, *Higiene y assistencia pública,* 378–387.

58. Simon Collier and William Sater, *A History of Chile, 1808–1994* (Cambridge: Cambridge University Press, 1996), 156.

59. Valparaíso, Chile, Consejo de Hijiene de Valparaíso, *Actas, 1896–1897,* 113, 130, 133, 305–306.

60. Ibid., 306.

61. On yellow fever, see Lautaro Ferrer, *Higiene y assistencia pública,* 423; Chile, *Anuario estadístico, demografía, 1917.* On bubonic plague, see Valparaíso, Chile, Consejo de Hijiene, *Actas, 1899–1900,* 143–156, 218; Lautaro Ferrer, *Higiene y assistencia pública,* 415–419; Chile, Oficina Central de Estadística, *Anuario estadístico, beneficencia, 1913*; Salinas, "Salud," 121. See also the chapter by David Parker in this volume.

62. On measles, see Valparaíso, Chile, Consejo de Hijiene, *Actas, 1896–1897,* 121–122; *1899–1900,* 206–208, 219; Chile, Oficina Central de Estadística, *Anuario estadístico, beneficencia, 1923.* On scarlet fever, see Valparaíso, Chile, Consejo de Hijiene, *Actas, 1896–1897,* 121–122; *1899–1900,* 219.

63. Valparaíso, Chile, Consejo de Hijiene, *Actas, 1896–1897,* 121–122; *1899–1900,* 219.

64. Valparaíso, Chile, Consejo de Hijiene, *Actas, 1896–1897,* 121–122, 139; *1899–1900,* 219; Salinas, "Salud," 120.

65. Valparaíso, Chile, Consejo de Hijiene, *Actas, 1896–1897,* 121–122, 139; Chile, Oficina Central de Estadística, *Anuario estadístico, demografía, 1921*; Chile, Oficina Central de Estadística, *Anuario estadístico, beneficencia, 1923, 1925.* For comparison, see Sam Adamo, "Rio de Janeiro," in *The 1918–1919 Pandemic of Influenza: The Urban Impact in the Western World,* ed. Fred R. van Hartesveldt (Lewiston, N.Y.: Edwin Mellen Press, 1992), 198; and see the chapter by Anton Rosenthal in this volume.

66. Valparaíso, Chile, Consejo de Hijiene, *Actas, 1896–1897,* 121–122; *1899–1900,* 221; Lautaro Ferrer, *Higiene y assistencia pública,* 128–133, 421–422; Chile, Oficina Central de Estadística, *Anuario estadístico, movimiento de población, 1911*; Chile, Oficina Central de Estadística, *Anuario estadístico, demografía, 1917*; Salinas, "Salud," 118–119; Illanes, "*En el nombre,*" chap. 4 and passim.

67. This section on smallpox is drawn from Chile, Ministerio del Interior, *Beneficencia de Valparaíso, 1870–1872*; Valparaíso, Chile, Municipalidad, *Anales, 1870–1872,* 62–64; Valparaíso, Chile, Consejo de Hijiene, *Actas, 1896–1897,* 121–122, 137, 139, 140–146, 298; *Actas, 1899–1900,* 204, 219, 221; Fagalde, *El puerto de Valparaíso,* 33; Lautaro Ferrer, *Higiene y assistencia pública,* 128–133, 270, 405–414, 523–524; Chile, Oficina Central de Estadística, *Anuario estadístico, movimiento de población, 1911*; Chile, Oficina Central de Estadística, *Anuario estadístico, beneficencia, 1913, 1923, 1925*; Chile, Oficina Central de Estadística, *Anuario estadístico, demografía, 1917*; J. D. Long, "El problema sanitario de Chile y su solu-

ción," *Anales de la Universidad de Chile* 1 (1926): 799–800; F. Puga Borne, "Reseña histórica de la higiene pública en Chile," in *El cuerpo médico y la medicina en Chile,* ed. René A. Maffet (Santiago: Imprenta Chile, 1939), 422; Enrique Laval M. and René García Valenzuela, "Síntesis del desarrollo histórico de la salubridad en Chile," *Revista del servicio nacional de salud* 1, no. 1 (October 1956): 24; Salinas, "Salud," 103, 119–120, 123–124; "*En el nombre,*" 57, 63, 78–79, 110.

68. Valparaíso, Chile, Junta de Beneficencia, *Actas y memorias, 1905,* 8–114.

69. Ibid., 56.

70. Valparaíso, Chile, Consejo de Hijiene de Valparaíso, *Actas, 1896–1897,* 310.

71. On infant mortality, see Valparaíso, Chile, Consejo de Hijiene de Valparaíso, *Actas, 1896–1897,* 310–311; *1899–1900,* 219; Chile, Oficina Central de Estadística, *Anuario estadístico, movimiento de población, 1911*; Lautaro Ferrer, *Higiene y assistencia pública,* 127; Chile, Oficina Central de Estadística, *Anuario estadístico, demografía, 1917, 1921, 1923, 1925*; Long, "El problema sanitario," 791–792; Mamalakis, *Historical Statistics,* vol. 2, 18–19, 40–41; Salinas, "Salud," 107, 116, 123; Blakemore, "Chile," 528; Illanes, "*En el nombre,*" 22, 27–28, 121, 145.

72. Ronn Pineo, *Social and Economic Reform in Ecuador: Life and Work in Guayaquil, 1870–1925* (Gainesville: University Press of Florida, 1996), 136.

73. John Allen Blount, "The Public Health Movement in São Paulo, Brazil: A History of the Sanitary Service, 1892–1918" (Ph.D. diss., Tulane University, 1971), 175–176.

74. Data cited in Blount, "Public Health Movement," 175.

75. Valparaíso, Chile, Consejo de Hijiene de Valparaíso, *Actas, 1896–1897,* 311.

76. Valparaíso, Chile, Consejo de Hijiene, *Actas, 1896–1897,* 112, 116–117, 121–122, 283; *1899–1900,* 219–220; Chile, *Anuario estadístico, movimiento de población, 1911*; Lautaro Ferrer, *Higiene y assistencia pública,* 126, 133, 306; Chile, Oficina Central de Estadística, *Anuario estadística, demografía, 1921, 1923, 1925*; Long, "El problema sanitario," 788, 790; Mamalakis, *Historical Statistics,* vol. 2, 37–38; Illanes, "*En el nombre,*" 77, 145.

77. Valparaíso, Chile, Consejo de Hijiene, *Actas, 1896–1897,* 112, 116–117, 121–122, 283; *1899–1900,* 219–220; Chile, Oficina Central de Estadística, *Anuario estadístico, movimiento de población, 1911*; Lautaro Ferrer, *Higiene y assistencia pública,* 133; Chile, Oficina Central de Estadística, *Anuario estadística, demografía, 1921, 1925*; Blount, "Public Health," 168–169, 193; Illanes, "*En el nombre,*" 85, 98; Pineo, *Social and Economic Reform in Ecuador,* 119–120.

78. See the chapter in this volume by David Sowell; other data cited in Blount, "Public Health."

79. Lautaro Ferrer, *Higiene y asistencia pública,* 126. For comparative data, see Ferrer, *Higiene y asistencia pública,* 126, 306; Chile, Oficina Central de Estadística, *Anuario estadístico, movimiento de población, 1911*; Chile, Oficina Central de Estadística, *Anuario estadístico, demografía, 1917, 1923, 1925*; Long, "El problema sanitario," 788–790; Blount, "Public Health," passim; Mamalakis, *Historical Statistics,* vol. 2, 18–19, 40–41; Illanes, "*En el nombre,*" 77, 145.

80. Julio César Jobet, *Ensayo crítico del desarrollo económico-social de Chile* (Santiago: Ed. Universitaria, 1955); Collier and Sater, *History of Chile,* 162–163, 169.

81. Karen Remmer, "The Timing, Pace, and Sequence of Political Change in Chile, 1891–1925," *Hispanic American Historical Review* 57, no. 2 (May 1977): 222. See also Blakemore, "Chile"; Charles Bergquist, *Labor in Latin America: Comparative Essays on Chile, Argentina, Venezuela, and Colombia* (Stanford: Stanford University Press, 1986); Fredrick B.

Pike, "Aspects of Class Relation in Chile, 1850–1960," in *Latin America: Reform or Revolution?,* ed. James Petras and Maurice Zeitlan (Greenwich, Conn.: Fawcett Publications, 1968); Pike, *Chile and the United States.*

82. This situation led, in the words of historian Harold Blakemore, to a certain "lack of long-term planning and, above all, a certain discontinuity of government business which led presidents to concentrate on immediate and necessary objectives, such as the passage of the budget or the acquisition of arms, but obliged them to neglect more lengthy measures such as social reform"; "Chile," 534. On Chile's political "anarchy" in these years, see Collier and Sater, *History of Chile,* 194.

83. Jay Kinsbruner, *Chile: A Historical Interpretation* (New York: Harper Torchbooks, 1973), 119–120.

84. Blakemore, "Chile," 524, 527; Pike, *Chile and the United States,* 46; Collier and Sater, *History of Chile,* 146, 162, 197.

85. Remmer, "Timing," 223–224, 228–229. In 1908–1909 Paul S. Reinsch, writing in the *American Political Science Review,* put it this way: "An aristocracy of birth and wealth has unquestioned control of social and political life"; "Parliamentary Government in Chile" (507–508), cited in Collier and Sater, *History of Chile,* 192.

86. See the discussion in Charles C. Griffin, "Francisco Encina and Revisionism in Chilean History," *Hispanic American Historical Review* 37 (1957): 1–28. As Pike has noted: "Middle and upper groups tended . . . to join in a disparaging attitude toward the lower mass. This disparaging attitude contributed significantly to the neglect shown by the ruling class to . . . social problem[s]"; "Aspects of Class Relation," 207. Also see Blakemore, "Chile," 509; and Collier and Sater, *History of Chile,* 195, who note that by 1914 Chile's Congress still had passed only two, largely ineffectual, laws that addressed the "social question."

87. Cited in Pike, *Chile and the United States,* 201. See also Illanes, "*En el nombre,*" 107.

88. Quoted in Pike, *Chile and the United States,* 112.

89. Quoted in ibid., 201. See also Salinas, "Salud," 108; Collier and Sater, *History of Chile,* 146.

90. Bergquist, *Labor in Latin America,* 21–22.

91. Pike, "Class Relations," 209–210.

92. Collier and Sater, *History of Chile,* 172; Pike, "Class Relations," *Latin America,* 211.

93. Pike, "Class Relations," 211.

94. As Pike notes: "Only one thing is more impressive than the volume of writing produced by Chilean exposers of social horrors: the utter failure of this literature to stimulate amelioration of the conditions described"; *Chile and the United States,* 103–104.

95. Jobet, *Ensayo crítico del desarrollo económico-social de Chile,* 102, and passim; Solberg, *Immigration and Nationalism,* 105–106, and passim; Kinsbruner, *Chile,* 121, and passim; Blakemore, "Chile," 529, 533, 539, and passim; Bergquist, *Labor in Latin America,* 29, 61, 75, and passim; Illanes, "*En el nombre,*" 24, 48–49, 96, 132–136, 146, chap. 2, and passim; Collier and Sater, *History of Chile,* 153, 196, and passim.

96. Quoted in Jobet, *Ensayo crítico del desarrollo económico-social de Chile,* 99.

97. Isaac Ugarte Gutiérrez, "Algunas reflexiones," 147; Jobet, *Ensayo crítico del desarrollo económico-social de Chile*; Bergquist, *Labor in Latin America,* 31.

8

The Sick and the Dead: Epidemic and Contagious Disease in Rio de Janeiro, Brazil

Sam Adamo

Rio de Janeiro, the modern-day metropolis long known as the "marvelous city," has not always had such an exhilarating or alluring reputation. The city's beautiful physical setting obscured a host of debilitating and deadly diseases whose adverse health effects all too frequently proved fatal for the city's inhabitants. A potpourri of epidemic and contagious diseases made Rio one of the deadliest cities in the world. Well-known day-to-day maladies like tuberculosis, cancer, pneumonia, and bronchitis were joined by myriad tropical diseases that once made Rio de Janeiro a dangerous place to live and work. By the turn of the century public officials had armed themselves with a growing body of scientific and medical knowledge that they used to combat the deadliest and most lethal maladies attacking the city's residents. However, local, state, and federal officials spent money and time in combating the deadliest diseases from a desire to benefit not the city's toiling masses but the elite. Public services and rudimentary public health measures (for example, vaccinations and environmental controls) had two goals: to protect the middle and upper classes from the deadliest contagious diseases and to reverse the city's deadly nineteenth-century image.[1]

Still, the success of the city's public health campaign overshadowed the struggle's human component. The triumph over diseases like yellow fever and malaria masked day-to-day battles with epidemic and contagious diseases like tuberculosis, diarrhea, and enteritis that continued to claim innumerable lives in the period under scrutiny. Control of these diseases is not as glamorous as the eradication and control of illnesses like malaria and yellow fever, yet deaths from these common maladies served as quiet testimony to the deficiencies in the city's socioeconomic well-being. Many of the ailments that afflicted Rio's turn-of-the century population were diseases of poverty whose levies could have been substantially

TABLE 8.1 Intercensal Population Growth in Rio de Janeiro, 1872–1920

Year	*Population*	*Annual Increase (%)*
1872	274,972	—
1890	522,651	3.6
1906	811,433	2.8
1920	1,157,873	2.5

SOURCES: Directôria Geral de Estatística, *Recenseamento da população do império do Brasil a que se procedeu no dia 1 de agosto de 1872,* vol. 21, 21; Directôria Geral de Estatíca, *Recenseamento do Distrito Federal de 1890* (Rio de Janeiro: Oficina de Estatística, 1901), 36; Directôria Geral de Estatística, *Recenseamento do Rio de Janeiro (Distrito Federal) 1906,* (Rio de Janeiro: Oficina de Estatística, 1907), 13; Directôria Geral de Estatística, *Recenseamento do Brasil, População do Rio de Janeiro 1920 (Distrito Federal)* (Rio de Janeiro: Typografia da Estatística, 1923), 3.

reduced by investment in basic public services. Not surprisingly, these diseases disproportionately affected the city's lower classes and working poor, who had little or no access to the public services that would have impeded or prevented the spread of disease. Rio de Janeiro's tropical climate provided an almost ideal habitat for countless pathogens, and the climate along with the absence of basic utility services and of rudimentary medical care created a deadly triad that made the city a risky place in which to live, especially for the disadvantaged.

Rio's population explosion made it difficult, if not impossible, for government authorities to provide basic municipal services that would have forestalled some of the diseases whose abundance and tenacity were buttressed by the unsanitary conditions prevalent throughout the city. Census data for Rio de Janeiro underscore the city's dramatic fourfold growth in population between 1872 and 1920. (See Table 8.1.) The city's population expanded from almost 275,000 in 1872 to slightly over 1.1 million persons by 1920. Natural increase throughout the period under scrutiny was vigorous, but domestic and international migration was responsible for much of the city's dramatic growth. The migratory streams inundating Rio de Janeiro between 1870 and 1920 were a diverse mixture of European immigrants from Portugal and Italy and poor nonwhites from Brazil's hinterlands. Language, culture, and most important, race distinguished Rio's newest citizens.

The racial and ethnic groups calling Rio home were all exposed to the same pathogens, but they had dissimilar risks of succumbing to the city's medley of debilitating and often deadly diseases. Socioeconomic circumstances played pivotal roles in determining health and well-being. The city's middle and upper classes had access to the basic sanitation and housing that could help guarantee not only the quality of life but life itself. Piped water, sewerage, adequate housing, a steady diet of nutritious foods, and medical care were basic necessities to which the city's working classes and poor had little or no access. Afro-Brazilians were disproportionately represented among Rio's poor, the under- and unemployed, and the working classes; they were the ones most susceptible to the city's countless epidemics and contagious diseases.

This chapter will examine the living conditions of the city's lower classes and consider how these factors contributed to the differential mortality experiences that distinguished Rio's racial groups. Mortality for all racial groups declined between 1870 and 1920, indicating that the overall quality of life improved for all the city's residents. The advancements in housing, sanitation, and nutrition were not, however, equally distributed. The relatively narrow gap that seemed to distinguish whites from nonwhites increased rather than decreased with the passage of time. The mortality data suggest that nonwhites languished on the periphery of Rio's health and sanitation revolutions. The economy, beset by alternating waves of inflation and austerity, was unable to create employment opportunities that would satisfy the thousands of internal migrants and immigrants now calling Rio home. Rio's struggling Afro-Brazilian population also had the burden of color.[2] The nation continued to nurture and fortify its racist ideas and ideologies, which meant that Afro-Brazilians, like their counterparts in the United States, were the last hired and the first fired. The chronically under- and unemployed Afro-Brazilians, unable to afford rudimentary food and housing, paid a toll that was reflected in the city's mortality rates. Two of the more pernicious "diseases of poverty," tuberculosis and diarrhea/enteritis, are highlighted later in the chapter because they illustrate preventable maladies that exacted a heavy toll on Rio's citizenry, especially its Afro-Brazilian component. Substandard housing and inadequate sanitation provided an ideal environment for infectious and contagious diseases.

Housing

Early-twentieth-century newspapers were full of reports linking diseases like malaria, yellow fever, tuberculosis, and typhoid to inadequate housing.[3] Sustained natural increase and immigration created an ongoing and unfulfilled demand for sanitary, low-cost housing. Government officials experimented with various schemes to provide affordable housing for the lower classes in the period under scrutiny. Most of the projects failed because of insufficient funds, poor planning, distance from the projects to work, and neglect. The abysmal failure of affordable housing programs and half-hearted attempts to establish and enforce rent controls gave landlords the power to charge high rents for cramped, overcrowded, and unsanitary quarters. Single-family dwellings were almost exclusively occupied by the middle and upper classes. The working classes generally lived in substandard communal housing known as *cortiços* and *estalagens.* These dwellings were the best housing the working poor could hope to obtain, in contrast to their under- and unemployed counterparts who inhabited the temporary shelter of the *casas de comôdos* (boarding houses), the favelas, or lived in the streets.

The tenement-like *cortiços* and *estalagens* were cheap structures designed to earn quick profits for their proprietors. The main buildings were generally made of unseasoned wood. Large cracks and gaps appeared as the wood dried, opening the superstructure to rain and humidity, which further accelerated deterioration. Termites compounded the effects of environmental decay, further shortening the life span of the fragile structures.[4] Housing pressures were so great that neither susceptibility to fire nor rapid decomposition stayed construction of wooden buildings. Even as late as 1920 engineers defended the wood buildings because they were cheap and easy to construct.[5]

Most of the small apartments or *casinhas* opened to a central courtyard that accessed the street through a single corridor. The more spacious quarters had a small living room, a kitchen, and one or two small bedrooms. The majority of the *cortiços* and *estalagens* were diminutive one-windowed rooms described as "sepulchers" since they allowed in little fresh air or light.[6] Most apartments were so small that one government health specialist, Dr. Agostinho José de Souza, recommended legislation prohibiting construction of communal dwellings unless the rooms were at least three to four meters square.[7] The small cubicles in the *cortiços* housed from six to ten persons, while larger dwellings designed for ten to twelve would accommodate forty to fifty people.[8]

Residents shared a common water tank or fountain and latrines; consequently hygiene was difficult to maintain. Crowded conditions accentuated the inadequate sewerage service, which was frequently interrupted, sometimes for days. The occupants also shared their limited space with an assortment of animals (such as poultry, pigs, and even horses), which were contained in makeshift stalls in the buildings' patios. The agglomeration of humans and animals in cramped quarters without proper ventilation, water, or sewerage made the *cortiços* and *estalagens* breeding grounds for infectious and contagious diseases.[9]

Conditions were equally appalling in the *casas de comôdos* and hostels throughout the city.[10] These structures comprised a series of small rooms that were rented out on a daily basis. Rude burlap screens were often the only division between rooms that, like the *estalagens*, lacked lighting and ventilation. Typically, the only furniture in the rooms were filthy mattresses. The ongoing housing shortage guaranteed proprietors a clientele despite unsanitary and overcrowded rooms sheltering five or six people though intended for one. Most hostels matched the low to nonexistent construction and sanitation standards of *cortiços* but earned reputations as inferior housing as a consequence of the patrons' transitory status. Many hostels were redoubts for gambling, prostitution, and other illegal activities in the city. The illicit activities in hostels earned them fame as dens of "libidinous" behavior.[11]

The impoverished who were unable to afford the exorbitant rents of the *cortiços*, *estalagens*, or hostels lived in the city's infamous favelas. Favelas were squatter settlements established on hills located in and around the center of the city. They provided cheap housing with ready access to the workplaces located in downtown Rio. A small house on the Morro do Santo Antônio could be erected for as little as forty to sixty milreis while the average rent for an apartment in the collective housing unit was forty to eighty milreis per month.[12]

The inexpensive favela housing had serious liabilities that offset any monetary savings accruing to residents. Old zinc plates, flattened kerosene cans, and discarded lumber were the primary construction materials. Most houses were one-room affairs less than two meters tall. The makeshift construction methods meant that homes were stifling in the summer and cold in the winter. Furniture was rudimentary at best, often constructed from discarded materials found in the streets. Limited space and danger from fire meant that kitchens, usually no more than a collection of old pots and pans, were located outside. Families commonly slept together, so the number of persons per household ranged from two to as many as ten.

A distinguishing characteristic of the favelas was the absence of piped water and sewerage. Most residents, like those on the Morro do Santo Antônio, had to carry water to their homes. June Hahner estimates that in the mid-1870s there was approximately one spigot for every 400 residents in the city.[13] Some lucky settlements had piped water, but they were the exception rather than the rule.[14] The unplanned neighborhoods and streets—little more than dirt footpaths—not only complicated efforts to improve sanitation but made it extremely costly as well. Rains turned the streets into quagmires. Homes had no foundations and were in constant danger from mud slides.[15]

Housing for the poor remained an object of public debate throughout the period. The *cortiços*, *estalagens*, and favelas located in the heart of the city were highly visible to foreigners. Middle- and upper-class Brazilians realized such scenes compromised the nation's image abroad and invalidated the nation's motto of "order and progress." Magazines like the glossy *Revista da semana,* which catered to the upper-class readership, described favelas as "parasitic neighborhoods" that "stained" the "magnificent aspects of the great metropolis."[16] The elite felt such housing should be eliminated not so much to enrich the hygienic and health considerations of the residents but to improve the "aesthetics" of the city. The elite believed that elimination of favelas would also restore foreign confidence in Brazilian civilization. Government officials complained that the favelas stood in "violent contrast" to the plans for urban beautification.[17] Pressure by the elites forced the government to undertake action to correct some of the worst abuses in lower-class housing. Officials correctly assumed that improved housing would eliminate the sources for the epidemics that frequently began in the overcrowded neighborhoods inhabited by the poor.

The lack of money, work crews, and material; government indifference; and the immensity of the problem frustrated efforts to improve housing in Rio. As early as 1888 the inspector general of health had proposed the construction of public baths and laundries in order to eliminate breeding grounds for diseases. Unfortunately the suggestion was ignored.[18] Proprietors fought public health regulations with lawsuits asserting their rights as property owners. A local newspaper, the *Gazeta de Notícias,* claimed that lawsuits by landlords were nothing more than a "shield" for owners to avoid local sanitary regulations and laws. The daily observed that a judicial ruling by Judge Godofredo Cunha in which he stated that private property was subject to public health codes failed to stem the ongoing wave of lawsuits by proprietors.[19] The public health department's manpower shortage prevented inspectors from enforcing sanitation regulations in most collective residences. Legislation and enforcement were unable to correct the deplorable conditions in Rio's sordid collective housing.

Affordable housing had been a problem in Rio as early as 1850.[20] The city's exploding population in the latter half of the nineteenth century exacerbated an already woefully inadequate housing situation. The government's primary solution for alleviating the housing scarcity was the construction of cheap, low-cost residences called *villas operárias* (working-class villages). The single-family units had spacious rooms, piped water, and sewerage. Rent controls would be enforced in order to end the high, exploitative fees charged in most private establishments.[21] But the absence of an efficient, affordable system of mass transportation required public housing to be situated as close as possible to Rio's urban core, where most of the jobs were located, and long distances to and from home resulted in the early failure of a village in suburban Marechal Hermes. The expansion of commuter rail service in the late 1910s and 1920s made suburban development more feasible, but transportation remained an important issue.[22]

Neither the housing shortage nor the deplorable conditions in Rio's collective residences assured government expenditures for the villages. Building codes, inspection, and maintenance presented government officials with costly problems that they frequently preferred to ignore. By 1908 the ongoing obstacles convinced Souza Aguiar, a top city administrative official, to recommend that housing construction be left to private initiative.[23] The ability of these projects to reduce residential shortfalls was also hamstrung by rules limiting access to housing to government employees or to middle- and upper-class families with influence in government circles.[24] Newspapers denounced the favoritism inherent in the municipal and federal governments' housing programs because shelter was not made available to the people whom the program was intended to assist.[25] Municipal and federal construction projects continued regardless of the drawbacks and criticism and the failure to alleviate the housing situation.

Unsuccessful government housing projects and regulatory failures gave proprietors tyrannical control over their domiciles. Aside from complaints pertaining to maintenance and sanitation, the most frequent protests concerned the outrageous rents charged by landlords, who as the antigovernment newspaper *Gazeta de Notícias* put it, "lacked scruples, [were] inhumane, exploitative, greedy, and shameful."[26] Discontent was widespread, but residents rarely moved since housing alternatives did not exist.[27] Jurisdictional disputes between the municipal and federal governments also impeded resolution of the pricing problem. Rent control laws were passed that attempted to prohibit owners from raising fees, but landlords found loopholes that made the laws ineffectual, and the upward spiral in rents continued virtually unabated.[28] A study conducted in Rio in the mid-

1930s found that working-class families spent from 25 to 33 percent of their total incomes for substandard housing.[29]

Poor government administration affected city revenues since clandestine residences were not taxed. Illicit residences operated with impunity throughout the city and denied local government an important source of income.[30] Proprietors were so powerful that salary increases granted to public functionaries and military personnel sparked widespread fears of rent hikes.[31] Authorities passed a tenants' rights law in the mid-1920s to protect inhabitants from exorbitant increases, but the local court quickly invalidated the law, leaving owners to do as they pleased.[32]

Inhabitants of the city's substandard housing were primarily immigrants and nonwhites. Afro-Brazilians were particularly prominent in contemporary accounts of the city's favelas. The flood of immigrants meant that many of the newly arrived shared deplorable housing with nonwhites. The rapid assimilation and success of European immigrants into the city's socioeconomic framework enabled them to escape the squalor of Rio's substandard housing much earlier than Afro-Brazilians, who remained trapped at society's lowest socioeconomic levels.[33] Government reports on favelas in the 1940s and the 1950s rarely mentioned immigrants but confirmed the predominance of nonwhites in these neighborhoods.[34] Housing remained one of Rio's most important social questions, an issue whose ultimate solution depended on the "material progress of the capital."[35] Afro-Brazilians, hamstrung by their history of servitude, were unable to escape the shackles that kept them at the bottom rungs of the city's socioeconomic ladder. Labor market saturation, the preference for hiring foreigners, and racial bias all worked to keep nonwhites out of society's mainstream.

Nutrition

Poor nutrition was yet another contributing factor to Rio's mortality rates, particularly among nonwhites, who as a consequence of their socioeconomic status were the most likely to have inadequate nutrition. The city's lower classes lacked adequate knowledge to select proper diets, and their low incomes severely restricted their ability to purchase foods rich in proteins, minerals, vitamins, and fats. Most of the city's working classes labored long hours in grueling, unsafe conditions.[36] The combination of abysmal working conditions and unbalanced diets low in caloric intake made good health difficult, if not impossible, to maintain. Poor nutrition paved the way for many of the diseases that preyed upon Rio's poor and working classes, and the epidemic and contagious diseases endemic to the city exacerbated the effects of poor nutrition, creating a vicious cycle of malnutrition and illness that frequently proved fatal. Low socioeconomic status with little opportunity for upward mobility locked most nonwhites into the vicious cycle, which debilitated the living as well as future generations.

Prior to abolition in 1888 nutrition was worse for slaves and freedmen than for other members of the lower classes. Breakfast was commonly a simple affair of coffee and bread, and lunch and dinner were a combination of beans, manioc flour, and an occasional piece of salted beef or fish. Nonwhites preferred dried meat and fish over the same foods fresh. Many also had to secure their own fresh fruits and vegetables. Free blacks and mulattoes employed as masons, carpenters, stevedores, or in other occupations outside of the household had to buy their own food. Consequently, their diets were frequently worse than those of their bonded counterparts. Haphazard eating habits characterized the diet of free blacks and mulattoes.[37] Nonwhites in Rio were subject to a variety of nonlethal but debilitating diseases, such as scurvy, rickets, ophthalmia, and hemeralopia, all of which were a consequence of poor nutrition.[38] The diet of most blacks and mulattoes seriously affected the newborn, who entered the world with nutritional deficiencies that decreased their chances of survival.

Contemporaries unanimously condemned the dietary habits of the poor while ignoring economic barriers that prohibited the working poor and disadvantaged from maintaining a healthy diet. According to an 1860s study, breakfast was typically light, consisting of coffee or tea with some bread. Lunch was a much heartier meal, at which time small portions of salted or dried beef were consumed along with beans, manioc flour, bread, and fruit (usually oranges or bananas). Dinner was similar to lunch but had in addition soup, vegetables, and more fruit. Fresh meat was a luxury item that rarely appeared on the tables of Rio's working poor, who reserved its consumption for Sundays, holidays, or special occasions. Other sources of meat protein available to the lower classes were codfish and sardines, but expenditures on fish products were rare. Beans were typically cooked with a variety of vegetables that included potatoes, yams, sweet cassava, squash, cabbage, turnips, and okra. The most popular beverages were coffee, tea, chocolate, and alcohol. The absence of refrigeration and transportation facilities precluded the consumption of fresh milk for most city residents.[39]

Scientists made few studies of diet and nutrition, and those that appeared in the 1930s now seem flawed, especially in regard to caloric intake. One of the early pioneers of Brazilian nutritional science, José de Castro, conducted important surveys of nutrition among the working classes of Rio de Janeiro and Recife. His studies confirmed ongoing nutritional deficiencies and imbalances that had been observed by his predecessors in the nineteenth century. Castro claimed that working-class families in Rio received an average of 3,078 calories per day, of which 16 percent were proteins, 57 percent were carbohydrates, and 28 percent were fats. Caloric intake varied by as much as 32 percent and was positively correlated with income.[40] Purchases of milk, eggs, and meats were also highly correlated with income.[41] Expenditures on fruits and vegetables rich in vitamins and minerals varied not only with income but also with the distance to and from the market.[42] The caloric intake for most people in the survey was sufficient to sustain life, but the diet lacked important vitamins and minerals, and the deficits increased as income diminished.[43]

Substandard nutrition was responsible for debilitating deficiencies in vitamins, calcium, iron, and protein, and it caused high death rates from gastroenteritis and pneumonia.[44] The nutritional studies highlighted ongoing problems in the Brazilian diet ranging from improper eating habits to economic barriers that impeded proper nutrition. Rio's turn-of-the-century markets lacked the variety of modern day *feiras* (neighborhood fresh-produce markets), which have large selections of fruits and vegetables. Nor can the economic circumstances of the city's working poor be ignored. Their wages never kept pace with inflation, especially in the second half of the nineteenth century. The shift from food production to commercial agriculture (primarily to coffee), coupled with transportation difficulties and crop failures, wreaked havoc on the budgets of the city's underclasses. For example, food prices tripled between 1889 and 1898.[45] The volatility of food prices coupled with wages that failed to keep pace with the cost of living meant that the food was the first area to be cut back during times of severe economic distress. Consequently, most of the city's working poor were almost always experiencing dietary inadequacies that contributed both to their poor health and to their high mortality rates.

Ignorance of proper diet contributed to the malnutrition that plagued Rio's lower classes; however, the high cost of food proved to be the greatest barrier to adequate nutrition. Descriptions from newspapers and government officials indicate that all basic food prices were unusually high.[46] In 1890 government officials reported that the city was all but totally dependent upon the State of Minas Gerais for its stock of fresh meat. Any interruption in the supply would result in an immediate shortage. The report's release was accompanied by news of a price-fixing plot between Cesário Alvim, the interior minister, and the Companhia Pastoril, the business responsible for the shipment of cattle to the local market. The interior minister granted the company a monopoly to facilitate transportation of cattle and to protect the beef industry in Minas Gerais. Rising meat prices in Rio were allegedly the consequence of a drought that decimated herds in the state. A subsequent investigation revealed that the company was fixing beef prices by controlling the number of cattle reaching Rio's market and using the drought to justify price increases in the city. The importation of foreign beef helped alleviate the meat shortage, and the Companhia Pastoril's plot backfired as its sale of beef in the city plummeted.[47]

This kind of abuse of power was not unusual, nor was it limited to one commodity. Thirty years later the mainstream *Jornal do Brasil* called milk producers "monopolists of commerce" who "extorted" money from the poor, making it impossible for them to purchase the milk necessary for their families.[48] City fathers were aware of the abuses but were hamstrung by laws prohibiting them from immediately punishing offending merchants.[49] Prices were so high that working-class families spent 50 to 75 percent of their total wages on food.[50] Popular outcries for the regulation of food prices went unheeded, leaving the working classes and poor at the mercy of local merchants.[51] Indifference to the plight of the lower classes largely explains the failure of the government to tackle issues associated with food prices and supply. Food, like housing, was something the elite and upper classes could afford; consequently, it was not an issue that concerned government officials.

Aside from price, food quality was marginal at best. Only the middle and upper classes could afford the most expensive domestic and imported foods. Meat, regarded as a necessity by most Brazilians, regularly entered the market in such a pitiful state that it was often dangerous for consumption. Most cattle endured a long, arduous journey in cramped railroad cars that resulted in weight loss and sickness. The animals had no chance to recover from the trip, for they were immediately placed in holding pens without water or grass for twenty-four to forty-eight hours; after which they were slaughtered. All aspects of meat preparation, preservation, and shipment were unsatisfactory. A local newspaper claimed that sanitation at the Island of Sapucala, the city's garbage dump, was superior to that of the city's slaughterhouses.[52] Meat was cut on soiled wooden blocks, wrapped in newspaper, and then shipped without refrigeration to meat markets in Rio. Poorly paid employees had little incentive to maintain sanitary conditions prescribed by law, nor did public health authorities do much to enforce the laws. Tubercular, cancerous, carbuncular, and rotten meats were regularly sold in meat markets throughout the city.[53] The sale of tainted meat exemplified conditions widespread in the food processing industry. As late as the 1930s purchases of milk, meats, fresh fruits, and vegetables often depended upon price and distance from the market.[54] The absence of refrigeration and preservation techniques in all areas of the city made fresh foods difficult to obtain for residents in the suburbs. Proper nutrition was a luxury only the middle and upper classes could afford.

High prices and poor quality foods exacerbated the substandard nutrition that left the disadvantaged more susceptible to the myriad diseases endemic to Rio. Public officials and reporters chronicled the plight of the indigent, who survived only by making "great sacrifices." An observer describing the hardships the lower classes endured during World War I implied that hunger and unemployment were a daily aspect of life for nonwhites in the city.

The government initiated a large-scale public health campaign at the turn of the century. Its primary objective was to improve sanitation and to control the major epidemic and contagious diseases endemic to the city. Water and sewerage services were expanded, swamps were drained, vaccines were given to the poor, insect control began, and public health clinics were started. These and other measures instituted by the government resulted in a dramatic reduction of the death rates in the city. These reforms were enacted, as Jeffrey Needell has shown, not for the betterment of the masses but as part of a larger plan to protect the elite from the worst consequences of epidemic and contagious disease and to modernize what was then the nation's capital. All racial groups in Rio made large absolute improvements in health, mortality declined, and life expectancy increased. However, the benefits from the measures were not distributed equally between whites and nonwhites. The absolute decline in mortality masked large proportional differentials between the races that in fact increased with the passage of time. Both the general and infant death rates were greater for nonwhites than for whites. Mortality among the lower classes was always higher than among the middle and upper classes; nevertheless, the elevated death rates of nonwhites affirm the inferior position of blacks and mulattoes in Carioca society.

Mortality

A monthly summary of mortality published by the city of Rio de Janeiro made it possible to estimate crude mortality for whites and nonwhites in the city.[55] The city's mortality figures suggest relative equality between the races shortly after the turn of the century. The parity evident in the data is probably a result of unreported deaths. The failure to report deaths and births was common among the city's economically disadvantaged, a class in which nonwhites were overrepresented. A 1940 study of natality in Rio conducted by the Instituto Brasileiro de Geografia e Estatística (IBGE) found that registered births among whites had to be adjusted upward by 11 percent whereas those of mulattoes and blacks required adjustment upward by 21 and 66 percent, respectively.[56] Even though Rio was the capital and had better statistical information than most other regions in the nation, underreporting was an ongoing problem, as the 1940 Brazilian study suggests. Despite the data's shortcomings, the figures illustrate fundamental quality-of-life differences between the races. Death and its various causes make the descriptive shortcomings in nutrition and housing quantifiable. The significant gaps separating the races become more disturbing when one considers how much greater mortality would be if unreported deaths were included in the equation, especially for nonwhites. The graph in Figure 8.1 indicates that the quality of life improved for the city's whites; in contrast, nonwhites' mortality rates were not much changed from those recorded near the turn of the century. Rio's public health campaign was successful in that overall mortality declined steadily after the dawn of the twentieth century.

The mortality figures (Figure 8.1) also suggest that nonwhites benefited the least from the public health revolution, for the gap separating whites and Afro-Brazilians increased with the passage of time. Studies of nonwhites in Brazil prior to 1870 found that the death rates of nonwhite bondsmen and women were higher than those of the white free population.[57] The findings provide important insights into the mortality experience evident in Rio at the turn of the century. Mary Karasch discovered that urban slavery, in terms of mortality, did not differ markedly from its rural counterpart. Overall, white freemen and women had much lower death rates (34 per 1,000) than either the slaves (40) or freed men and women (46).[58] Mortality levels were also consistently higher for men of all racial groups than for women. Death rates for free men were 39; for male slaves, 43; and for freed men, 53. These contrasted with lower rates for females: 28 for free women, 36 for slaves, and 41 for freed women. Differential mortality levels such as those described by Karasch did not change markedly in the early twentieth century because Afro-Brazilians remained confined to the bottom rungs of the city's socioeconomic ladder.

FIGURE 8.1 Mortality in Rio de Janeiro, 1904–1939 (per 1,000)

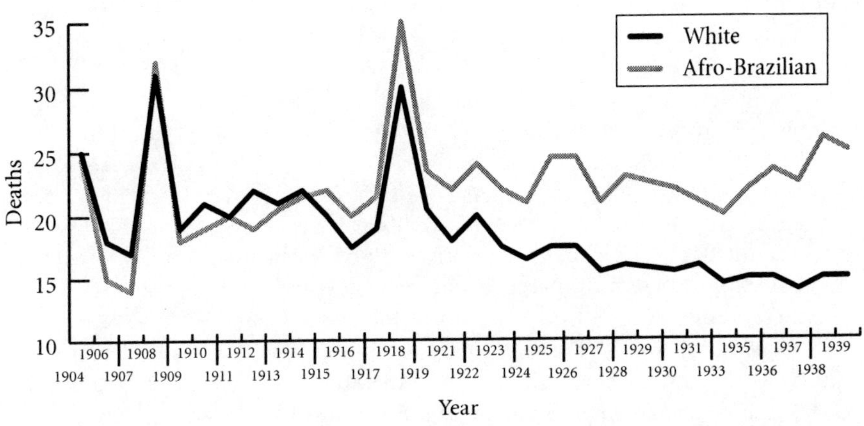

SOURCE: Directoria Geral de Saúde Pública, *Boletim mensal de estatística demografo-sanitária da cidade do Rio de Janeiro* (Rio de Janeiro: Directória Geral de Saúde Pública, 1904–1939).

The trends observed by Karasch in the mid-nineteenth century remained unchanged in the early twentieth century, as Figure 8.1 suggests. The figure also illustrates the problem posed by the undercounting of deaths. Death rates in the century's first decade suggest that nonwhite mortality was less than that observed for the city's white population. Improved reporting showed observable yet contrary trends in the mortality experience of Afro-Brazilians and whites. Mortality for the city's white population showed a clear, consistent decline; in contrast, that of nonwhites increased with the passage of time. Rising Afro-Brazilian death rates were probably not a consequence of deteriorating conditions among the city's nonwhite population but, rather, a function of better reporting. The advances in the public health department's record keeping make it difficult to gauge the extent and the breadth of improvements among the city's Afro-Brazilian population. The figures do indicate that housing, nutrition, and health dividends were much slower to reach Rio's Afro-Brazilian community, thus creating a widening public health gap.

Infant death rates in 1890 highlight socioeconomic disparities between Rio's Afro-Brazilians and whites. The 1890 census tabulated births (both live and stillborn) by race of married couples. Whites had the lowest levels of infant mortality (0–1 years of age) at 397 per 1,000, followed by mulattoes at 407. The white and mulatto levels of infant mortality were high, but they were outstripped by that of blacks at 497 per 1,000. Almost one-half of the black children born died within the first year of life.[59] Infant mortality rates published in the *Annuário estatístico do Distrito Federal* for the years 1937–1939 indicate that the average infant death rates, though greatly reduced, remained high. Infant mortality rates for whites, mulattoes, and blacks were 65, 142, and 322, respectively.[60] The adjusted infant mortality rates for the racial groups in the city showed higher levels for whites and mulattoes at 123 and 241, respectively, whereas those for blacks were substantially lower at 204.[61]

The differential mortality rates that distinguished whites and Afro-Brazilians were linked to their respective socioeconomic circumstances. Nonwhites were more likely to live in substandard housing without potable water or sewerage. These conditions, coupled with diets lacking in calories, vitamins, proteins, and other essential nutrients, make the racial differentials an expected outcome. Two diseases, tuberculosis and gastroenteritis, both of which are linked to poverty, illustrate the quality of life differences between whites and Afro-Brazilians.

Tuberculosis was one of the deadliest of the diseases associated with Rio, yet it did not receive the attention that crusades against either malaria or yellow fever did. That the malady received relatively little attention is probably because the disease is first and foremost a disease of poverty, an affliction that thrived among Rio's poor, a segment of the population in which Afro-Brazilians were disproportionately represented. The city's inadequate public services made tuberculosis the city's deadliest disease. Public health and government officials had long identified tuberculosis as an affliction of the "less favored classes."[62] The Brazilian League Against Tuberculosis recognized that Afro-Brazilians were more likely to contract the affliction than whites.[63] The league's observations were by no means unprecedented, for earlier nineteenth-century studies had indicated that slaves were highly susceptible to the malady.[64] (See Figure 8.2.)

Rio's Afro-Brazilian population was likelier to contract and die from tuberculosis than whites. In 1904 the white mortality rate was slightly over 321 per 100,000; that for nonwhites was 427. The city's seesawing mortality rates roughly parallel the nation's economic fortunes in that death rates for all races rose significantly during the hardships imposed by World War I. White and Afro-Brazilian death rates rose to 361 and 589, respectively, per 100,000 by 1915. The figures represent mortality increases of 11 and 28 percent, respectively. Conversely, death rates declined as economic conditions improved in the 1920s. By 1925 white death rates from tuberculosis had declined to 281 per 100,000, and for Afro-Brazilians, to 473. White death rates had declined to well below their 1904 level; in contrast, that of nonwhites lingered at a relatively high 473 per 100,000. The figures suggest that hard-won gains eroded rapidly during World War I and were slow to recover from the reverses the conflict imposed.

The malady's relationship to socioeconomic status is apparent when death rates from the city's various neighborhoods are examined. Middle- and upper-class locales such as Botafogo, Copacabana, and Tijuca had the lowest death rates from the disorder, while the poorest areas of the city (São Cristovão, Engenho Novo, Piedade, and Madureira) had the highest mortality rates.[65] Nor is it surprising that nonwhites were disproportionately represented in the city's poorest neighborhoods, which lacked sanitation and housing.

FIGURE 8.2 Tuberculosis Mortality in Rio de Janeiro, 1904–1926 (deaths per 100,000)

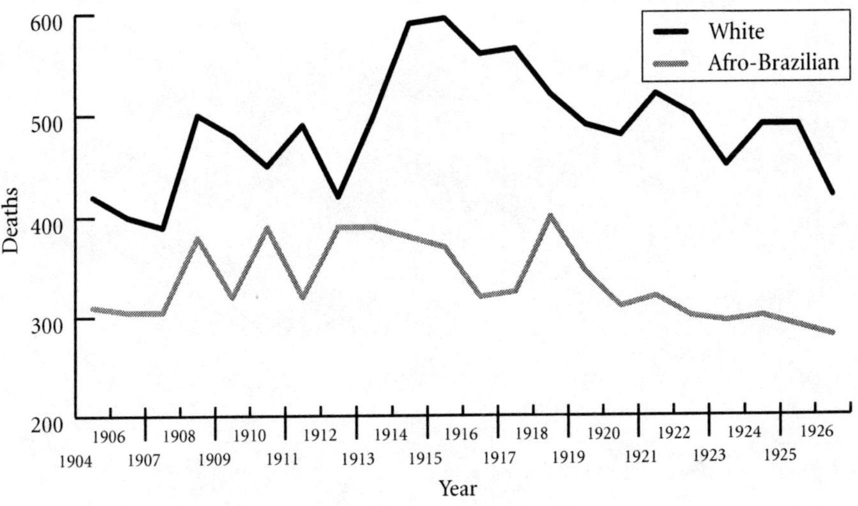

SOURCE: Directoria Geral de Saúde Pública, *Boletim mensal de estatística demografo-sanitária da cidade do Rio de Janeiro* (Rio de Janeiro: Directória Geral de Saúde Pública, 1904–1926).

Gastroenteritis, a seemingly innocuous illnesses, was especially lethal to the city's newest and youngest members, particularly those under two years of age. Unsanitary conditions prevalent in the city's favelas and communal housing exposed the very young to fly- and water-borne infections that produced diarrhea and enteritis. These maladies impede an infant's capacity to absorb food from the stomach, which becomes inflamed. The inability to absorb vital nutrients, especially among the newborn, precipitates malnutrition. Young children who survive the vicious cycle of malnutrition and attacks of diarrhea or enteritis generally develop kwashiorkor (a severe protein and vitamin deficiency) in the second or third year of life.[66]

The mortality rates for children under two years of age (Figure 8.3) remained high throughout the period under scrutiny. It is not difficult to see how potable water and sewerage would have reduced the mortality from these diseases. Once again Afro-Brazilians seemingly had the lowest level of mortality from the disorders. Underreporting undoubtedly plays a part in the comparatively low death rates observed for Afro-Brazilian children. Afro-Brazilian dietary and childrearing practices may also play a role in the mortality rates observed for nonwhites. Karasch found bondsmen and women in Rio often put together more nutritious meals than did free men and women, and bondswomen breast fed their children until the age of two or three.[67] Some of the low Afro-Brazilian mortality rates, especially after the turn of the century, may be linked to the preservation of some Afro-Brazilian childrearing and weaning customs. These African cultural prac-

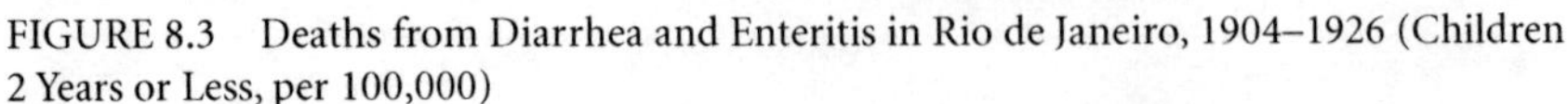

FIGURE 8.3 Deaths from Diarrhea and Enteritis in Rio de Janeiro, 1904–1926 (Children 2 Years or Less, per 100,000)

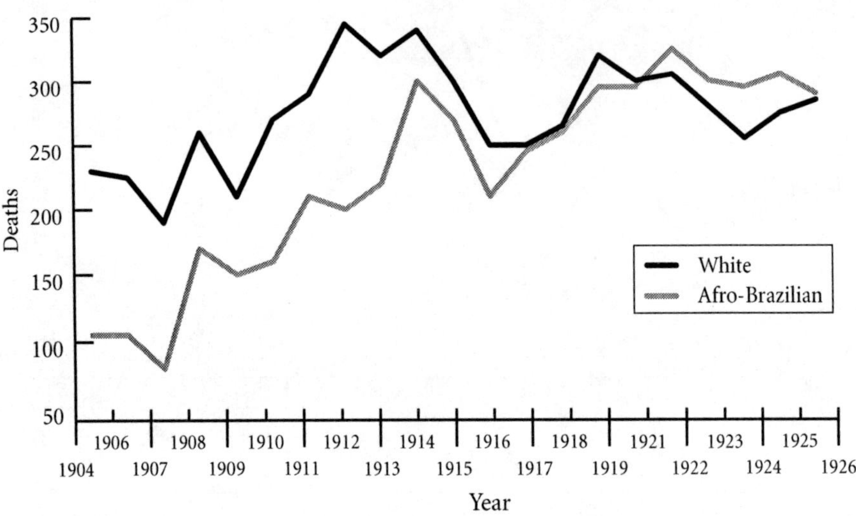

SOURCE: Directoria Geral de Saúde Pública, *Boletim mensal de estatística demografo-sanitária da cidade do Rio de Janeiro* (Rio de Janeiro: Directória Geral de Saúde Pública, 1904–1926).

tices gradually eroded in Rio's urban environment, and they were no longer practiced by the lower classes by the 1950s. Nevertheless, unreported deaths were probably the primary cause of the low Afro-Brazilian death rates. Nonwhite deaths, just like those observed for tuberculosis, increased with the passage of time. The high infant mortality rates discussed earlier also suggest that nonwhite deaths were substantially underreported. The high death rates from gastroenteritis suggest that all of the city's citizens suffered from the disease, but none more than nonwhites.

For the most part, Rio's working classes and poor endured the drudgery and hardships presented by life in the capital. This is not to say that they accepted their lot in life passively. There were frequent outbursts protesting harsh working conditions, inadequate wages, and high rents, all of which were violently repressed by the authorities. The Brazilian masses had a long history of social and economic protest, yet their demonstrations never yielded substantive results as a consequence of the authorities' willingness to use violence to quell any and all disturbances.[68] Only one of these many protests, the antivaccination riot of 1904 (*revolta contra vacina*) was linked directly to public health concerns. The legendary Brazilian physician Dr. Oswaldo Cruz initiated a mandatory smallpox vaccination program that eventually became the lightening rod for a popular outburst and a failed military coup that temporarily placed the nation's capital in the control of the masses.

By November 1904 Rio's population was extremely discontented and volatile. Inflation from the previous decade had dramatically lowered their standard of living. The budding popular discontent was paralleled by the massive public works program of Francisco de Paula Rodrígues Alvez's administration (1902–1906); this program not only modernized Rio's port facilities but also resulted in massive renovation to the city's downtown area. New government buildings, such as the National Library, replaced thousands of *cortiços* and *estalagens,* and the Avenida Central (Central Avenue) became the city's new, thoroughly modern promenade. The massive construction project displaced approximately 20,000 persons among the city's lower classes, leaving them nowhere to go.[69] The city's Afro-Brazilian population had also grown increasingly desperate. Beset by ongoing under- and unemployment, displaced by foreigners from occupations that they had formerly dominated, handicapped by illiteracy and racism, the city's Afro-Brazilians, like many others in the lower classes, were approaching a dangerous flash point.

The government's mandatory vaccination program ignited one of the largest and most frightening riots in the history of the first republic. The populace, already at wit's end, was unwilling to let the city's sanitation police wield what they considered to be unconstitutional and authoritarian power. The city's physicians and public health officials were given the authority to enter peoples' homes unannounced, conduct inspections, condemn their homes, and administer vaccinations. All this proved too much for the city's poor, who finally rose up in protest. Rio's Afro-Brazilian citizens, according to Needell, were in the forefront of the outburst, in which the masses temporarily seized control of the capital. The riot was eventually repressed, but it forced the government to end its mandatory vaccination program. The masses had achieved a small victory in stopping the government's program, but that did nothing to alter their insalubrious environment, which ultimately brought them to an early death.[70]

If anything, the riot's failure typified class relations in urbanizing Brazil. Urbanization and industrialization brought new classes of people into the nation's social and economic framework; businessmen, entrepreneurs, teachers, professionals, government functionaries, and the urban proletariat all began playing important new roles in society. The newly emerging middle and upper classes entered the urban forum deeply imbued with Auguste Comte's positivist ideas, which called for civil liberties, religious freedom, free association, and free speech. These concepts helped bring about the abolition of slavery in 1888 and the emergence of the first republic in 1889. These seemingly progressive and reform-oriented ideas, which were in vogue in late-nineteenth-century Brazil, also embraced Comte's respect for the social hierarchy and his belief that equality was nothing but a myth. The urban elites readily applied these concepts to their urban situation, much as the planter class had done in rural Brazil. The republic's birth represented not so much a break with the past as a continuation of the planter classes' values in an urban setting. Positivist ideas justified both their status and their privileged position in society. Within this context, the working classes were nothing more and nothing less than another resource for exploitation. The elite, if threatened, was able to rely on both the police and the military to maintain the existing social and economic order. The *revolta contra vacina,* like the many protests that preceded it and like those that were to follow, was doomed to failure. The elite's control of legal and political institutions, as well as its monopoly on violence, guaranteed that the working classes and the under- and unemployed would have no voice in the government that shaped their lives.

Rio's working classes were not without power, for the urban milieu provided the working classes with opportunities to organize and communicate with one another; but the ties that bound them together were extremely weak. The glut of labor, ethnic and racial friction, and the economy's incessant boom-and-bust cycles worked against the urban proletariat throughout the period under scrutiny. And furthermore, the new urban elites could always count on the government's repressive powers to quell disturbances, no matter how minor or how great. These onerous circumstances made day-to-day life in Rio a tenuous and often difficult struggle. Rio's under- and unemployed were nothing more than fodder for the emerging industrial society. The undervalued and disdained lower classes worked long hours in dangerous conditions for meager salaries that enabled them to purchase expensive food of poor quality. The resultant poor nutrition, coupled with hard work, led to a life of debilitating illness and finally to death. For most of the city's under- and unemployed, among whom Afro-Brazilians were disproportionately represented, the future held little promise.

The city's bay, beaches, and lofty peaks were a beautiful web that was home to countless epidemic and contagious diseases. The maladies endemic to Rio made day-to-day life in the nation's capital precarious, especially for the working poor and underprivileged who had little or no access to basic public services. This was especially true in the nineteenth century, when knowledge regarding the spread and control of many diseases was still in its infancy. Medicine's rapid evolution in the early twentieth century provided public health officials with a vast new array of weapons that were used to combat many heretofore deadly illnesses. The greatly feared tropical diseases like malaria and yellow fever were successfully managed and controlled. The availability of potable water and sewerage also made significant contributions to mortality's downward spiral in Rio. All segments of the population benefited from the government's public health campaign, albeit at vastly different levels.

The high mortality rates that typified Rio's Afro-Brazilian community in the period under scrutiny were an important indicator of their socioeconomic status, their lack of political power, and the racism that dominated the nation throughout the waning of slavery and the nation's entry into the twentieth century. Afro-Brazilians, who had once occupied a variety of semiskilled and skilled positions in the local economy, were pushed aside by the wave of European immigrants that inundated the city in the latter half of the nineteenth century. Educational and racial barriers made the struggle for life's necessities even harsher. The positivist ideas prevalent among Rio's new urban elite seemed to justify the Afro-Brazilian position on the bottom rungs of society's socioeconomic ladder. Rio's Afro-Brazilians made the ultimate sacrifice for their sordid living and working conditions: They paid with their lives and those of their children.

Notes

1. Details of the elite's policy goals are highlighted in June E. Hahner, *Poverty and Politics: The Urban Poor in Brazil, 1870–1920* (Albuquerque: University of New Mexico Press, 1986). The author makes it clear that public health improvements proceeded for the "benefit of the elite" (1).

2. There are several works that highlight the racial inequities and biases experienced by Brazil's Afro-Brazilian population in the postabolition era; these include Carlos Hasenbalg, *Discriminação e desigualdades raciais no Brasil*, trans. Patrick Burglin (Rio de Janeiro: Edições Graal, 1979); Nelson do Valle Silva, "Côr e o processo de realização socioeconômica" *Revista de ciencias sociais* 24 (1981): 391–409; Nelson do Valle Silva, "O preço da côr: Diferenciais raciais na distribuição da renda no Brasil," *Pesquisa e planajamento econômico* 10 (1980): 21–44; George Reid Andrews, *Blacks and Whites in São Paulo Brazil* (Madison: University of Wisconsin Press, 1991); Sam C. Adamo, "The Broken Promise: Race, Health, and Justice in Rio de Janeiro, 1890–1940" (Ph.D. diss., University of New Mexico, 1983).

3. Some of these articles include *Gazeta de Notícias*, August 11, 1900; October 17, 1908; April 2, 1914; November 18, 1919; *A Notícia*, May 19–20, 1917; July 31, 1940.

4. Conselho Superior de Saúde Pública, *Os meios de melhorar as condições das habitações destinadas as classes pobres* (Rio de Janeiro: Imprensa Nacional, 1886), 3.

5. *Journal do Brasil*, March 23, 1920.

6. Conselho Superior, *Classes pobres*, 11.

7. Ibid., 7.

8. *Gazeta de Notícias*, February 17, 1917; Antônio Pedro Pimentel, *Terceira delegacia de saúde-relatôrio annual apresentado ao Exmo. Sr. Dr. Oswaldo Gonçalves Cruz*, vol. 2 (Rio de Janeiro: Relatôrio da Ministério da Justiça, 1907), 5.

9. Conselho Superior, *Classes pobres*, 22–5; Antônio Martins de Azevedo Pimental, *Estudo de hygiene no Rio de Janeiro* (Rio de Janeiro: Typografia e Lithographia de Carlos Gaspar da Silva, 1890), 184–186.

10. *Casas de comôdos, penções*, and *albergues nocturnais* are included in the hostel category because of their patrons' temporary status.

11. *Correio da Manhã*, October 3, 1910; Pimental, *Estudo de hygiene*, 189–190.

12. The milreis was the basic monetary unit of Brazil; it was superseded by the cruzeiro in 1942. João do Rio, "A cidade do morro de Santo Antônio," *Gazeta de Notícias*, November 5, 1908; Victorino Oliveira, "Babylônias do Rio—a estalagem," *Gazeta de Notícias*, August 23, 1907. Hahner details the effects that periods of inflation and austerity had on Rio's working classes; *Poverty and Politics*, 87.

13. Hahner, *Poverty and Politics*, 31.

14. Contemporary accounts, for example, described the fountain on the Morro da Providência as "primitive," only capable of furnishing a "thin stream" of water. Residents had to wait in long lines for their daily water supply or go to a public fountain; *Gazeta de Notícias*, July 25, 1914.

15. Everardo Backheuser, *Habitações populares* (Rio de Janeiro: Imprensa Nacional, 1906), 111; José Antônio, "Alta da miséria," *Gazeta de Notícias*, August 11, 1907; May 15, 1915. Conditions in favelas improved, and these reforms are noted in the following works even though the authors continue to describe living conditions that are horrid by modern standards: Maria Hortencia do Nascimento Silva, *Impressões de uma assistente sobre o trabalho na favela* (Rio de Janeiro: Gráfica Sauer, 1942); Departamento de Geografia e Estatística, *Censo das favelas, aspectos gerais* (Rio de Janeiro: Serviço de Divulgação do Departamento de Geografia e Estatística, 1949); Carlos Calderaro, *Favelas, e favelados do Distrito Federal* (Rio de Janeiro: Instituto de Pesquisas e Estudos de Mercado, 1957).

16. "A nodoas do Rio-os bairros parasitários dos morros," *Revista da Semana* 17 (January 15, 1916): 48. A similar article describing favelas as "antihygienic and antiaesthetic" appeared in a later edition of the magazine; "Os últimos dias da favela," *Revista da Semana* 28, no. 29 (July 9, 1927): 6.

17. Aloar Prata Soares, *Mensagem do prefeito do Distrito Federal lida na sessão do conselho municipal, 1 de junho de 1923* (Rio de Janeiro: Typographia do Jornal do Comércio, 1923), 28.

18. Rio de Janeiro, *Boletim da illustrissima câmara municipal da corte* (Rio de Janeiro: Typographia Imperial e Constitucional de J. Villeneuve e Companhia, 1888), 16–17.

19. *Gazeta de Notícias*, August 11, 1900.

20. Jeffrey D. Needell, "The Revolta Contra Vacina of 1904: The Revolt Against 'Modernization' in Belle Epoque Rio de Janeiro," *Hispanic American Historical Review* 67, no. 2 (May 1987): 251.

21. Distrito Federal, *Annães do conselho municipal, primeira sessão 6–25 de fevereiro, 1893* (Rio de Janeiro: Typographia do Jornal do Comércio, 1893), 88. Other examples of discussions revolving around the urgent need for the city to provide cheap, hygienic housing can be found in *Annães, 4 novembro de 1893 a 6 de fevereiro de 1894* (Rio de Janeiro: Typographia do Jornal do Comércio, 1894), 102; *Annães, 2 de março a 30 de abril de 1894* (Rio de Janeiro: Typographia do Jornal do Comércio, 1894), 110, 117; Directôria Geral de Polícia Administrativa, Archivo, e Estatística, *Boletim da intendência municipal abril a junho, 1906* (Rio de Janeiro: Typographia da Gazeta de Notícias, 1906), 43–45; *Polícia administrativa, abril a junho 1908* (Rio de Janeiro: Oficinas Gráphicas do Paíz, 1908), 68; Polícia Administrativa, *Boletim da prefeitura do Distrito Federal* (Rio de Janeiro: Oficinas Gráphicas do Paíz, 1911), 48; Alvar Prata Sores, *Mensagem do prefeito do Distrito Federal lida na sessão do conselho municipal de 1 de junho, 1923* (Rio de Janeiro: Typographia do Jornal do Comércio, 1923), 23–25.

22. Conselho Superior, *Classes pobres*, 2–3; Distrito Federal, *Annães 2 de março a 30 de abril 1894* (Rio de Janeiro: Typographia do Jornal do Comércio, 1894), 110; Distrito Federal, Departamento de Geografia e Estatística, *Contribuição para a campanha de extinção das favelas* (Rio de Janeiro: Oficina Gráfica do Departamento do Predios e Aparelhamentos Escolares, 1942), 6–7; Michael L. Conniff, *Urban Politics in Brazil: The Rise of Populism, 1925–1945* (Pittsburgh: University of Pittsburgh Press, 1981), 26–28.

23. F. M. de Souza Aguiar, *Mensagem do prefeito de 2 de abril de 1908* (Rio de Janeiro: Oficinas Gráficas do Paíz, 1908), 12.

24. Polícia Administrativa, *Boletim de intendência, julho a setembro, 1909* (Rio de Janeiro: Oficinas Gráphicas do Paíz, 1909), 58.

25. Jacabino Freire, "Em prol dos pobres, habitações baratas," *Gazeta de Notícias*, July 20, 1919.

26. *Gazeta de Notícias*, November 18, 1919. Newspapers in Rio were not alone in pointing out the absurdity of the rents charged by most owners. Government officials were aware of the unusually high rents levied by landlords, blaming them for the "crisis in habitation." Distrito Federal, *Annães, 2 de março a 30 abril de 1894* (Rio de Janeiro: Typografia do Jornal do Comércio, 1894), 110; Polícia Administrativa, *Boletim, abril a junho 1911* (Rio de Janeiro: Oficinas Gráphicas do Paíz, 1911), 48; Secretária do Gabinete do Prefeito, *Boletim da prefeitura do Distrito Federal, 14 setembro de 1920* (Rio de Janeiro: Typographia do Jornal do Comércio, 1922), 294–295; Aloar Prata Soares, *Mensagem do prefeito, 1 de junho de 1923* (Rio de Janeiro: Typographia do Jornal do Comércio, 1923), 22–24.

27. *Gazeta de Notícias*, November 18, 1919; Gilberto Amado, "O problema da habitação," *Gazeta de Notícias*, April 13, 1920.

28. Needell and Hahner both discuss the adverse effects that inflation and austerity had upon the city's working poor; Needell, "The Revolta Contra Vacina of 1904," 253–254; Hahner, *Poverty and Politics*, 31; *Gazeta de Notícias*, November 15, 1919; *A Notícia*, March 6, 1925.

29. João de Barros Barreto, José de Castro, and Almir Castro, "Inquerito sobre condições de alimentação popular no Distrito Federal," *Arquivos de hygiene* 8, no. 2 (November 1938): 385–386.

30. *Gazeta de Notícias*, November 28, 1917; January 3, 1920.

31. *Gazeta de Notícias*, January 3, 1920.

32. *A Notícia*, July 10, 1925.

33. Backheuser, *Habitações populares*, 108–109; *Gazeta de Notícias*, May 15, 1915; April 2, 1914.

34. Carlos Calderaro, *Favelas e favelados do Distrito Federal* (Rio de Janeiro: Instituto Federal de Pesquisas e Estudo de Mercado, 1957), 18, 31–32; Departamento de Geografia e Estatística, *Contribuição*, 8.

35. Polícia Administrativa, *Boletim julho a setembro de 1907* (Rio de Janeiro: Typographia de Gazeta de Notícias, 1907), 34; Souza Aguiar, *Mensagem do prefeito, 2 de setembro de 1907* (Rio de Janeiro: Typographia do Paíz, 1907), 5.

36. Hahner, *Politics and Poverty*, chap. 6, "The Dimensions of Urban Poverty," highlights the wretched working conditions and inhumane treatment endured by workers in urban Brazil.

37. Antônio Correa de Sousa Costa, *Alimentação que usa a classe pobre do Rio de Janeiro e sua influência sobre a mesma classe* (Rio de Janeiro: Typographia Perseverança, 1965), 35–37. For greater details on the insufficient diets of slaves, consult Alvaro de Faria, "Alimentação e estado nutricional do escravo no Brasil," *Estudos Afro-Brasileiros*, vol. 1 (Rio de Janeiro: Ariel Editora Ltda., 1935), 206–211.

38. Faria, "Alimentação e estado nutricional," 206–211.

39. Costa, *Alimentação*, 33–35; Pimental, *Estudo de hygiene*, 241–243, 245–246.

40. Barreto, Castro, and Castro, "Alimentação popular," 388–389. The study surveyed the dietary habits of 12,106 families, analyzing them by income and place of residence in Rio.

41. Ibid., 391–393.

42. Ibid., 393–396.

43. Similar circumstances appeared among slaves in the United States whose diets were quantitatively satisfactory but qualitatively deficient; Kenneth F. Kipple and Virginia H. King, *Another Dimension to the Black Diaspora: Diet, Disease, and Racism* (Cambridge: Cambridge University Press, 1981), 80–81. Other studies by Castro demonstrated similar

dietary deficiencies in other regions of Brazil that were much worse than those evident in Rio. Poor diets were synonymous with low incomes; José de Castro, *Alimentação brasileira a luz da geografia humana* (Porto Alegre: Edição da Livraria do Globo, 1937), 135–143, 159.

44. Ibid., 304, 306, 308, 313.

45. Hahner, *Poverty and Politics*, 31, 87–91.

46. Consult the following for typical reports pertaining to high food prices in Rio: Polícia Administrativa, *Boletim, outubro, novembro, e dezembro de 1890* (Rio de Janeiro: Typografia de Rodrigues e C., 1890), 11; Soares, *Mensagem, 1 de junho de 1924*, 11; *Gazeta de Notícias*, January 29, 1890; February 2, 1890; October 28, 1899; July 6, 1901; February 9, 1920; *A Lucta*, March 20, 1915; March 18, 1915; *A Notícia*, January 24–25, 1917; *Jornal do Brasil*, June 2, 1920.

47. There was no mention of disciplinary action undertaken against the interior minister or the Companhia Pastoril; Polícia Administrativa, *Boletim, outubro, novembro, e dezembro de 1890* (Rio de Janeiro: Typographia de Rodrigues e C., 1890), 11; *Gazeta de Tarde*, October 28, 1890; November 10, 1890.

48. *Jornal do Brasil*, June 2, 1920; June 4, 1920. The *Gazeta de Notícias*, February 7, 1915, reported price fixing by vendors of fresh fruits and vegetables in the city.

49. Soares, *Mensagem, 1 de junho de 1925*, 18.

50. Barreto, Castro, and Castro, "Alimentação popular," 375.

51. The *Gazeta de Notícias*, February 7, 1915; "O problema da alimentação," *Brazil moderno* 4, no. 90 (July 14, 1917).

52. *Gazeta de Notícias*, November 15, 1919.

53. *Gazeta de Notícias*, January 23, 1890; January 27, 1890; April 11, 1890; July 6, 1901; November 15, 1919; February 4, 1920; *A Lucta*, March 20, 1915.

54. Barreto, Castro, and Castro, "Alimentação popular," 391, 396.

55. The subsequent death rates were calculated upon figures published in the *Boletim mensal de estatística demográfica sanitária da cidade do Rio de Janeiro* and the city's estimated population. Census data from 1890, 1906, 1920, and 1940 were used to generate population estimates for Rio's various racial groups. The analysis focuses on the period after 1904, when race-specific mortality data became available; *Boletim mensal de estatística demográfica sanitária da cidade do Rio de Janeiro* (Rio de Janeiro: Imprensa Nacional, 1904–36). Earlier titles of the periodical are *Boletim quinzenal de estatística demográfo sanitária da cidade do Rio de Janeiro (1893–1901)* and *Boletim trimestral de estatística demográfo sanitária estatística demográfica sanitária da cidade do Rio de Janeiro (1902–05);* all were published by the Directôria Geral de Saúde Pública.

56. Instituto Brasileiro de Geografia e Estatística, "Rectificação da taxa de natalidade, da quota dos nascidos mortos e das taxas de mortalidade infantil para o Distrito Federal," *Estudos de estatística demográfica,* no. 4 (Rio de Janeiro: Serviço Gráfico do I.B.G.E., 1948), 33.

57. Herbert S. Klein, "The Colored Freedmen in Brazilian Society," *Journal of Social History* 3, no. 1 (Fall 1969): 30–52; Pedro Carvalho de Mello, "Estimating Slave Longevity in Nineteenth Century Brazil," *Latin American Workshop Report* 7475–21 (Chicago: University of Chicago, Department of Economics); Robert W. Slenes, "Demography and Economics of Slavery in Brazil," 2 vols. (Ph.D. diss., Stanford University, 1976); Mary C. Karasch, "Slave Life in Rio de Janeiro, 1808–1850" (Ph.D. diss., University of Wisconsin, 1972). The dissertation has been published as *Slave Life in Rio de Janeiro, 1808–1850* (Princeton: Princeton University Press, 1987). High levels of mortality were common in the population at large.

58. All crude and infant mortality rates represent rates per thousand persons.

59. Directôria Geral de Estatística, *Recenseamento 1890*, 258–259.

60. Instituto Brasileiro de Geografia e Estatística, *Annuário estatístico do Distrito Federal, ano 6–1937* (Rio de Janeiro: Serviço Gráfico do I.B.G.E., 1939), 44. Instituto Brasileiro de Geografia e Estatistíca, *Annuário estatístico do Distrito Federal, ano 7–8, 1938–39* (Rio de Janeiro: Serviço Gráfico do I.B.G.E., 1939–40), 43, 58.

61. Adjustments include corrections for unregistered births, deaths, age, and additions made by migrants. Instituto Brasileiro de Geografia e Estatística, "Rectificação," 40.

62. Polícia Administrativa, *Boletim de intendência municipal, julho a setembro, 1902* (Rio de Janeiro: Typographia da Gazeta de Notícias, 1902), 19; Joaquim Xavier da Silveira Junior, *Relatôrio do prefeito do Distrito Federal, 5 de setembro de 1902* (Rio de Janeiro: Typographia do Jornal do Comércio, de Rodrigues e C., 1902), 19.

63. Liga Brasileiro Contra Tuberculose, *Relatôrio da Liga Brasileiro contra tuberculose sobre a gerência de 1910* (Rio de Janeiro: Typographia do Jornal do Comércio, 1911), 35–36. The league estimated that differential mortality from tuberculosis was 2.8 per 1,000 for whites and 9.1 for blacks and mulattoes.

64. Karasch, "Slave Life in Rio de Janeiro," 210–211; blacks in the United States and South Africa are also noted for their susceptibility to tuberculosis; Julian H. Lewis, *The Biology of the Negro* (Chicago: University of Chicago Press), 100–101; Edward E. Mays, "Pulmonary Diseases," in *Textbook of Black Related Disease*, ed. Richard A. Williams (New York: McGraw-Hill, 1975), 417–418; Kenneth E. Kiple and Virginia H. King, *Another Dimension to the Black Diaspora: Diet, Disease, and Racism* (Cambridge: Cambridge University Press, 1981), 146; Jacque M. May, *The Ecology of Human Disease*, Studies in Medical Geography, vol. 1 (New York: MD Publications, 1958), 111; Ida Freiman and Jacob Geefhuysen, "Tuberculosis in Black Children," *South African Medical Journal* 49, no. 39 (September 13, 1975): 1591.

65. José Parancos Fontenelli, *A saúde pública no Rio de Janeiro, Distrito Federal 1937 e 1938* (Rio de Janeiro: Serviço de Saúde Pública, 1939), 171–172.

66. Kwashiorkor is a severe protein and vitamin deficiency disease characterized by any or all of retarded growth, potbelly, or anemia; Derrick B. Jelliffe, *Infant Nutrition in the Tropics and the Subtropics*, 2nd ed. (Geneva: World Health Organization, 1968), 120–121.

67. Karasch, "Slave Life in Rio de Janeiro," 174, 179–180.

68. Many of the late-nineteenth-century and early-twentieth-century protests revolving around long working hours and poor working conditions are documented in Hahner, *Poverty and Politics*.

69. Needell, "The Revolta Contra Vacina of 1904," 257.

70. Ibid., 233–269. Jeffrey D. Needell's excellent article on the "*revolta contra vacina*" provides important details and analysis on the riot and its importance in Brazilian historiography.

9

The Cities of Panama: Sixty Years of Development

Sharon Phillipps Collazos

From the time of the discovery and settlement of the Americas, the passageway between the Atlantic and Pacific Oceans has been the raison d'être of Panama. The port cities at each terminal point of this passageway, Panama and Colon, and the narrow strip of land that runs between them have been the nerve center of the country of Panama throughout its history and have dominated all the important events that have affected Panama's development.

The development of Panama's working class has been inextricably linked with the events that occurred in the passageway. Workers at first were boatmen, carriers, and mule drivers, but by the mid-nineteenth century the labor demands shifted to those of heavy construction. The laborers of Panama were a fluid group that moved back and forth between work camps along the passageway and at its two terminal cities. During the construction period of the mid-nineteenth and early twentieth centuries, the period covered by this chapter, the amount of local labor proved insufficient, and massive numbers of laborers were imported to carry on the work. This foreign contingent also settled either in the port cities or in labor camps and moved around as their labor was required and their health permitted.

My purpose in this chapter is twofold: First I will explore the living and working conditions of the laborers that worked in Panama at the time of the large construction projects and assess their efforts to offer a collective response to these conditions. I will emphasize how the split between native and foreign-born workers in the laboring class hindered nearly all efforts at collective action and show the pervasive role played by the confluence of interests between the Panamanian upper classes and U.S. power in repressing the labor movement. Second, I will map the growth and development of the port cities at each end of the isthmian passageway in relation to the changes brought about by the demands for labor created by the construction projects.

The cities at either side of the Isthmus of Panama played an important role in the history of colonial Latin America because of their strategic location and the role they played in the passage of goods and people between the Atlantic and Pacific Oceans. From the time of the European discovery of the Americas and through the Spanish colonial period, the narrow strip of land used as a transit way between the Atlantic and Pacific Oceans became the nerve center of the territory that later would be known as the Republic of Panama. When Panama first gained its independence from Spain in 1821, it joined La Gran Colombia (Grand Colombia). When this nation disintegrated in 1830, Panama remained a province of Colombia. Although to Colombia Panama was a backward and remote territory accessible only by sea, its importance to countries engaged in mercantile endeavors became increasingly obvious. Soon Great Britain, France, and the United States began vying for the unimpeded use of the transit area and later for the right to build a canal.

It was during the second half of the nineteenth century and the early part of the twentieth century that the narrow isthmus experienced the great changes that had enormous repercussions for the development of the future country. These changes affected in an unprecedented manner Panama's class structure, its politics, and its social fabric. In 1850 a group of New York businessmen funded the construction of a trans-isthmian railroad and imported thousands of laborers to complete it. This was followed by the French effort to build an interoceanic canal in the 1880s and later on by the U.S. venture to complete the French project. For the construction of the Panama Canal, during its two phases, massive numbers of laborers were imported, the majority from the English-speaking Caribbean.[1]

These three construction projects were landmark events in the development of the country and were critical for the cities at each terminal point in the trans-isthmian passage area. These projects irreversibly changed the country. The canal made Panama stand out among the rest of Central American countries, giving it an incalculable economic advantage. The canal also secured for Panama a prominent role in the world of transportation and mercantile endeavors.

Another outcome of canal construction was its effect on the development of the terminal cities, Panama and Colon, and on the evolution of the country's working class. The working class of Panama, roughly between 30 and 40 percent of the population,[2] included a highly fluid group made up of many adventurers and fortune seekers as well as ordinary laborers. This last group was in a constant state of flux, and for some there were great opportunities for social mobility throughout the period.

Many laborers came to seek employment during the construction of the railroad and the canal.[3] The workers were different in race, language, and belief system from the native inhabitants of the isthmus, and this created a situation that had profound implications for the development of the working class. The Caribbean blacks were British subjects and were accustomed to that colonial power's style of governance and set of values. They were Protestants and spoke

English. In contrast, Panamanian natives were Spanish-speaking and Catholic and racially were a mixture of European white, Indian, and black, these last the descendants from former slaves or runaways.

Beyond the racial and cultural differences, another important factor affecting the development of the working class was the economic opportunities afforded each group. After the completion of the canal, Caribbean blacks were by and large unable to return to their islands of origin and remained working for the U.S.-controlled Panama Canal Company. Although their relationship with their U.S. employers was deeply affected by the racism of the U.S. managers, they at least had a shared language, religion, and work ethic. Hence the Americans preferred the Caribbean blacks to the native Panamanians, whom they considered inferior workers. Work in the U.S.-controlled Canal Zone brought far better pay and benefits than did jobs current elsewhere in Panama. The Panamanian working class was segmented, a situation that has prevailed throughout the twentieth century.

Panama and Colon at the Turn of the Century

Panama City has existed since shortly after the discovery of the Americas by Spain. In 1673, after it had almost been razed to the ground by an attack by the pirate Henry Morgan, the city was rebuilt in a new location. The new site made it easier to protect since it was built on an abutment, and strong fortifications were put in place to secure its shores and high walls surrounded it on the land side.

As the city of Panama grew and ran out of space to accommodate newcomers within its gates, new arrivals settled outside. People's social standing was denoted by where they lived. Thus the upper class lived in the "*intramuros,*" the area inside the walls, while the rest, mostly laborers, lived in the "*arrabal,*" the shanty area outside the walls. In the nineteenth century the *arrabal,* by far greater in extension and population, included the neighborhoods of Santa Ana, Calidonia, and Guachapalí.

The year 1852 year saw the demolition of the walls separating Panama City. Also in that year the city of Colon was founded on the Atlantic coast. Before then, Portobelo, located thirty-eight kilometers up the coast, had been the major regional Atlantic coast port. But during the construction of the trans-isthmian railroad, land speculation by Panamanian landholders along the proposed route prompted the railroad company to purchase the small swampy island of Manzanillo to be the Atlantic terminal, which they christened Colon.[4]

From the mid-nineteenth century Panama and Colon were affected by periods of boom and bust as construction projects began or ended in the isthmus or as international events, such as the discovery of gold in California or the two world wars in the twentieth century, affected the use first of the trans-isthmian railroad and later of the Panama Canal.[5] Although the construction of the trans-isthmian railroad was a large enterprise for its time and transit through the isthmus was sustained at a fairly high level until the transcontinental railroad was finished in the United States,

TABLE 9.1 Periods of Economic Boom and Bust in Panama

Years	*Boom or Bust*	*Events*
1852–1868	Boom	Construction of railroad, 33,000 annual passengers to and from California during the gold rush
1868–1880	Bust	Intercontinental railroad built in U.S.
1880–1889	Boom	First attempt by the French to build the Panama Canal
1888–1894	Bust	French fail and go bankrupt
1894–1902	Boom	Second French effort to build the Panama Canal
1902–1904	Bust	French fail in second attempt to build canal
1904–1914	Boom	U.S. takes over construction of Panama Canal
1914–1921	Bust	Canal finished—massive unemployment

SOURCE: Omar Jaén Suárez, *La población del Istmo de Panamá del siglo XVI al siglo XX* (Panama: Impresora de la Nación, 1978), 32–36, 318–334.

it was the efforts to build a canal through Panama that provided the greatest periods of growth and dislocation. Table 9.1 lists these episodes in Panama's history, including the years that each period lasted and the reason for each economic boom or bust. The boom years were 1852–1868, during construction of the trans-isthmian railroad and its use to transport passengers during the California gold rush; 1880–1889 and 1894–1902, when the French attempted to build the Panama Canal; and 1904–1914, the years of U.S. construction of the Canal. The years in between these, as well as the years after 1914, were periods of bust.

So from 1868 when the transcontinental railroad linking the east and west coasts of the United States became operational and until 1880 when Ferdinand de Lesseps began the first French attempt at building the Panama Canal, both Panama City and Colon experienced a bust period. During this time, the cities returned to a somnolent state, with the population of Panama City declining slightly from 10,000 and the population of Colon falling by 50 percent, from 8,000 to 4,090 inhabitants. (See Table 9.2.)

This situation did not change until after 1880, when de Lesseps was successful in forming the Compagnie Universelle du Canal Interocéanique (Universal Company of the Inter-Oceanic Canal) and began construction of the Panama Canal. These economic booms and busts had strong repercussions on the private property available in the cities. Between 1875 and 1880, the last years of the postrailroad depression, the number of private properties decreased in Panama City by 6.3 percent.[6] During the boom period of the first French effort, private property owned by Panamanian landholders increased by 19.3 percent, and by 66.9 percent in the 1885–1890 period.[7] Some of these were houses rented to French engineers and managers, but the majority were tenements rented to the laborers.

Life in both cities was extremely taxing and uncomfortable, although Colon was probably the worse of the two because of its lowland location and its climate, which is far more rainy and humid than Panama City's.[8] Most buildings were constructed out of wood, and devastating fires were common. Colon was ravaged

TABLE 9.2 Population and Population Growth Rates of the Cities of Panama and Colon

Year	*Panama*	*Average Growth (%)*	*Colon*	*Average Growth (%)*
1851	5,000	—	800	—
1856	10,000	13.9	8,000	46.1
1870	9,855	–0.1	4,090	–4.8
1885	30,000	7.4	15,000	8.7
1911	46,500	1.7	20,000	1.1
1920	66,851	4.0	32,952	5.5
1930	82,827	2.1	33,460	0.2
Average Annual Growth 1851–1930		3.6		4.7

SOURCES: Omar Jaén Suárez, *La población del Istmo de Panamá del siglo XVI al siglo XX* (Panama: Impresora de la Nación, 1978), cuadro 4, 32; Panama, Contraloría General de la República, *Censo demográfico 1920,* Boletín no. 1; Panama, Contraloría General de la República, *Censo demográfico 1930,* tomo 1.

by huge fires in 1862 and 1864, and the fire of March 31, 1885, burned down nearly the entire city, sparing only seven buildings. The last big fire of the nineteenth century decimated Panama City in June, 1894.[9]

Coinciding with the boom-and-bust periods, the populations of Panama City and Colon fluctuated as the new projects attracted many people to Panama in search of jobs or financial ventures. By the time the French Canal Project was underway in 1885, the population of Panama City had increased 300 percent and the population of Colon had increased 366 percent above 1870 levels. (See Table 9.2.) This sudden growth provoked great economic tensions and imbalances since the cities had so little to offer in terms of jobs, basic services, or even food for daily consumption.

The cities had little or no facilities such as paved roads, sewers, or urban services, and killing diseases were widespread. Inhabitants were routinely decimated by malaria, yellow fever, and other epidemics common in the tropics. Colon experienced a yellow fever epidemic in 1863, and in 1885 at least 5,000 people died from that disease out of a total of 15,000 dwellers.[10]

New arrivals in Panama found the place extremely taxing. David McCullough describes Colon, based on travel accounts of the times:

> Colon was the port of entry for all new recruits from France, for the thousands of workers from Jamaica, for all shipments of food from New York, and where everybody took the train to Panama City or to points along the way. . . . Colon had no services, no bathrooms. Garbage and dead cats and horses were dumped into the streets and the entire place was overrun with rats of phenomenal size.[11]

The modernization of the cities coincided with the first French effort to build a canal in 1880 and continued for the next two decades. In 1880, while the Compagnie Universelle began to move engineers and equipment into the country and to import large numbers of laborers to work on the canal project, improvements in the infrastructure of the cities were started. That year saw the setting up of public electric lighting on the main roads and avenues and the establishment of the *Cuerpo de Bomberos* (firefighters).[12] A year later the National Bank was inaugurated and telephone lines were laid linking Panama and Colon, as well as joining the two cities with towns in the interior of the country.[13]

In 1893 city dwellers were regaled with the appearance of trolley cars, and 1896 saw the start of the construction of an aqueduct to supply Panama City with potable water. Also in that year, work started on the installation of a sewer system. During that decade, coinciding with the second French effort at building the canal, parks were built, streets and avenues were paved, and the cities were beautified with promenades linking the main parts of town.[14]

The Panamanian upper classes made their living mostly as landlords or from financial ventures. They also took bureaucratic positions in local governmental agencies and sometimes took desk jobs provided by the foreign companies. They were hardly ever involved in ventures in which they actually had to perform any work. Thus the 1908 Commercial Census for the City of Panama shows that of the 653 commercial businesses 82 percent belonged to foreigners and that of the forty-five hotels and restaurants 98 percent belonged to foreigners, mostly of European extraction.[15]

The upper class was so small and so interrelated by marriage that Omar Jaén Suárez has called Panama "*la republica de los primos* [the republic of cousins]."[16] Panamanian landowners were notorious for making huge profits through the sale of property to foreigners. For instance, there are records of a piece of property bought for 90 pesos being sold a year later for 1,000 pesos and of another property purchased for 500 pesos and sold within a year for 10,000 pesos.[17]

The tertiary sector was so broadly developed, thanks to the services provided in the transit area, that according to some records of the time, they were "the sole reason for the cities' existence."[18] At the end of the nineteenth century there were fewer than twenty factories or industrial concerns in the city. Most produced goods for local consumption or processed agricultural products. The shops and factories included those that produced soap, beer, spirits, coffee, and chocolate. The most important of these was the ice factory.[19] Just about everything else was imported, including foodstuffs and everyday goods.

The Construction of the Panama Canal: The French Effort, 1889–1902

In 1880, fresh from the success of building the Suez Canal, Ferdinand de Lesseps began efforts to get the construction of the Panama Canal underway. However, Panama presented obstacles and challenges never imagined by the French. For the construction of the Suez Canal they had not had to cope with such high transportation costs, lack of available labor, nor devastating tropical diseases; this was also a more complicated engineering project because the canal had to accommodate the difference in tides between the sixteen-to-twenty-foot tides in the Pacific and the much smaller tides on the Atlantic or Caribbean side.

When de Lesseps embarked on the construction of the Panama Canal he was confident that it would be very similar to building the Suez Canal. By the time the French gave up in 1904 they had lost millions of dollars and thousands of lives and had jeopardized the futures of many middle- and working-class people in France who had invested their hard-earned savings on de Lesseps' dream. It was not the mismanagement of funds and other financial troubles that defeated the French. It was, instead, the enormity of the project and the incredible difficulties that they had to overcome: the climate, the diseases, and the lack of every conceivable necessity.

By 1882 there were about 2,000 laborers working for the Compagnie Universelle du Canal Interocéanique, and this number increased to more than 17,000 two years later. The level of workers was maintained at between 14,000 and 18,000 until 1888. (See Table 9.3.) To sustain that size workforce was a continual problem. For instance, McCullough estimates that in the first year of construction, of every 100 newly arrived workers only ten remained on the job after six months.[20] Workers were recruited from Colombia, Venezuela, Cuba, Barbados, Santa Lucia, and Martinica, as well as from some southern ports of the United States. Laborers also came from Senegal and from Europe, but the majority were recruited in Jamaica. Of 12,875 workers imported in 1885, 9,000 were from Jamaica. Omar Jaén Suárez estimates that about 43,000 workers in all were recruited from that island for the French project.[21]

During the French construction period, the percentage of unskilled laborers fluctuated between 82 and 97 percent of the total workforce. They were mostly pick and ax laborers, dirt movers, loaders, and common manual workers. The percentage of blacks among the laborers, in any given year, was between 89 and 92 percent.

The working and living conditions of these workers were abysmal. The men lived in barracks set on high concrete footings as a precaution against floods and rats.[22] "The men worked in constant fear of poisonous snakes (coral, bushmaster, fer-de-lance) and of the big cats such as puma and jaguar."[23] Not only did they have to contend with bugs and fierce animals, they also had to cope with the tropical climate:

> The effect of the climate on tools, clothing, everyday personal items, was devastating. Anything made of iron or steel turned bright orange with rust. Books, shoes, belts, knapsacks, . . . grew mold overnight. . . . Clothes seldom ever dried. Men in the field finished a day drenched to the skin from rain and sweat and had to start again the next morning wearing the same clothes, still wet as the night before.[24]

The workday lasted eleven to twelve hours, usually from 5:30 or 6:00 A.M. to dusk, around 6:00 P.M. Laborers worked under the blazing sun and in the torrential rains, in the brush, in the swamps, and in the inhospitable terrain. Nights were

TABLE 9.3 Workers on the French Efforts to Build a Canal: Panama

Year	Employees (annual average)	Laborers (%)
1881	967	85
1882	1,998	82
1883	6,941	89
1884	17,436	94
1885	15,784	91
1886	15,193	91
1887	16,873	92
1888	13,993	91
1889	1,938	88
1890	913	88
1891	870	91
1892	796	92
1893	717	93
1894	805	95
1896	2,715	95
1897	3,980	97
1898	3,396	96
1899	2,499	96
1900	2,000	94
1901	2,000	95
1902	1,449	95
1903	940	95

SOURCE: Omar Jaén Suárez, *La población del Istmo de Panamá del siglo XVI al siglo XX* (Panama: Impresora de la Nación, 1978), cuadro 74, 455.

taken over by mosquitoes and other insects to finish off the health of the workers, already debilitated and in a precarious condition from hunger and exhaustion.[25]

No one knows how many people died during the French construction period of the Panama Canal since the records are not good and many deaths were not recorded. U.S. doctors estimated that at any given time one-third of the workforce was sick.[26] It has been variously estimated that yellow fever accounted for anywhere from 15 percent to as much as 70 percent of all deaths.[27] According to French records, 21,000 French citizens died in the Panama effort, 16,000 of them from yellow fever.[28]

The salaries paid to the laborers were higher than those common in the Caribbean, but they were insufficient to cover basic needs since everything in Panama was expensive, and prices were constantly rising.[29] Having taken the jobs after being enticed by promises of being able to amass small fortunes, many of the laborers skimped on food, medicines, and clothing to try to return home with at least some small savings. In 1886 unskilled laborers earned $1.75 per day, experienced workers received between $2.50 and $2.75 per day, and white mechanics earned $5.00 a day.[30]

Apart from the laborers working directly for the Compagnie Universelle, there were also large numbers of laborers connected to the canal construction who worked for the railroad company, for the docks, and for independent contractors. Most of the laborers who worked for independent contractors, as well as the thousands who arrived looking for work, lived in the tenements in the city or built precarious shacks in the jungle near the two terminal cities. The railroad company had its own housing compound and also provided meals for the workers.[31] Fearful that the workers would run away, the company had its own private system of policing them, which included surveillance and corporal punishment (lashings) for those caught in an offense.[32]

The railroad was used to transport workers to and from the work sites and to move the excavated dirt to dumping grounds.[33] Railroad and dock workers were paid much lower salaries than the canal workers. In 1880 railroad workers earned $0.90 per day, a salary that had not changed for many years and that hardly covered their expenses. Meanwhile, the cost of necessities was higher than ever before, according to a local paper.[34]

The Caribbean workers considered employment in Panama somewhat like seasonal work, and there was a lot of movement to and from the islands. One author has noted that Jamaicans commonly tried to return to their homes for Easter.[35] According to the French Consul in Panama, Colon was almost a neighborhood of Jamaica, and in Panama City almost all the tailors, cobblers, cooks, and servants were Jamaicans.[36]

When the first French effort came to a halt, the number of railroad passengers plunged from 1.2 million in 1888, to 290,000 in 1889, and to 64,000 in 1890. The number of workers on the payroll decreased from 13,993 in 1888 to 913 two years later.[37] The bankruptcy of the French company and the halting of the construction project catapulted Panama into an economic depression that only ended in 1896 when the French reconstituted their assets into a new company and renewed construction of the Panama Canal. But the Compagnie Nouvelle du Canal de Panama (New Panama Canal Company) never really took off. The level of labor recruitment was much lower than in the previous decade, with the workforce hovering slightly over 2,000 men during all the years of operation. Salaries were also much lower, with common laborers receiving between $0.80 and $1.00 per day.[38]

Despite the dismal work situation, labor unrest was not very prevalent. Workers went on strike against the Trans-Isthmian Railroad Company but five times between 1868 and 1895, demanding better salaries. There are records of only two strikes against the Compagnie Universelle du Canal Interocéanique, in 1881 and in 1896.[39] Besides higher salaries, the strikers demanded better food and to be allowed to leave the housing camps on Sundays and go to the cities for drinking and relaxation.

U.S. Canal Construction Effort, 1904–1920

Shortly after the turn of the century it became apparent that the Compagnie Nouvelle was not making headway and that this second French attempt would also end in failure. The United States began negotiations with Colombia for the right to continue construction of the Panama Canal. To the frustration of the United States and of the Panamanian elite, the Herran-Hay Treaty that resulted from these negotiations was rejected by the Colombian Congress.[40]

The Panamanian elite, who had placed all their hopes on having Panama become a commercial emporium once the canal was in operation, let the United States know that they were willing to secede from Colombia and enter into direct negotiations with the United States. With support from a U.S. warship, the U.S.S. *Nashville*, off its shores, Panama declared independence from Colombia on November 3, 1903, and signed a treaty with the United States for the construction of the Panama Canal on November 18.[41]

The United States quickly resumed work on the Panama Canal. The U.S. phase of building the Panama Canal can be divided roughly into three periods: The first, between 1904 and 1908, was a period of taking stock and preparations. During this time great efforts and resources were poured into sanitizing and modernizing the facilities and services around the two terminal cities. New studies were also completed for the type of canal to be constructed, and the design was changed from a simple trench joining the two oceans to a lock canal. Special equipment was commissioned for the enormous job of dredging and earth removal that lay ahead.

The second period, from around 1908 to 1914, was the phase of heavy construction, which included moving the date of completion forward so the canal could be used by the U.S. military during World War I. Finally, the period between 1914 and 1921 involved putting the final touches on the already-functioning canal, as well as establishing the infrastructure and supports to sustain a community of civilian and armed forces that would run and protect the canal and the Canal Zone.

Because of the problems experienced by Jamaican nationals at the end of the French effort, when many were left stranded and had to be repatriated by British consular authorities, Jamaica was reluctant to engage in any arrangements for contract workers with the Panama Canal Company. In consequence, the bulk of contracted workers during U.S. construction were from Barbados. It is estimated that between 30 and 40 percent of all adult males, out of a total population of 200,000 in that island, went to work in the Panama.[42]

The United States undertook the construction of the Panama Canal much more intensively than the French had done, engaging a much larger number of laborers and investing considerably more resources than had their Gaelic counterparts. By 1906 the number of workers engaged on the works was 157 percent higher than during the peak year of the French effort. The number of workers would increase considerably more, reaching 56,600 in 1913, shortly before the canal was put into operation. In addition to the workers brought in by the company, many arrived on their own. Some were contracted because of their reputation as hard workers, especially those coming from Spain, Italy, and Greece. (See Table 9.4.)[43]

The problems encountered by the United States with regard to the workforce were similar to those the French had faced, and despite U.S. efforts and resources,

TABLE 9.4 Employees in the U.S. Panama Canal Construction

	Pan. Can. Co. Employees	*Laborer (%)*	*RR Workers*	*Contractor Workers*	*Total*
1906	19,485	80	4,416	2,646	26,547
1907	25,828	80	6,139	7,271	39,238
1908	23,964	82	5,863	14,063	43,890
1909	27,787	84	7,708	11,672	47,167
1910	29,098	84	6,044	15,660	50,802
1911	25,439	85	7,968	11,050	48,876
1912	28,982	85	5,855	16,056	50,893
1913	35,005	88	4,957	16,692	56,654
1914	25,289	85	4,343	14,697	44,329
1915	27,044	84	5,314	2,427	34,785
1916	21,190	84	5,349	8,637	35,176
1917	19,610	83	3,368	9,611	32,589
1918	15,561	82	3,067	6,892	25,520
1919	15,451	82	3,056	5,697	24,204
1920	17,777	79	2,598	298	20,673

SOURCE: Omar Jaén Suárez, *La población del Istmo de Panamá del siglo XVI al siglo XX* (Panama: Impresora de la Nación, 1978), cuadro 77, 460 and cuadro 78, 460.

many of these difficulties were hard to overcome. Until malaria and yellow fever were controlled, the death toll continued to be high, with about 90 percent of those that died being black laborers.

The workers contracted by the Panama Canal Company received a series of perks and benefits that the company allocated following a strict division by color line, which resulted in the establishment of a clear caste system. Known as the "gold" and "silver" roll based on the currency in which workers were paid, this highly discriminatory system spilled over to all other aspects of life. White managers or technically skilled workers, usually U.S. nationals, were paid in gold currency, while all others, mostly laborers, were paid in silver coins.

Within the silver roll there were different pay scales, with the smaller number of workers of European origin earning higher salaries than the main body of black workers from the Caribbean for the same task.[44] In 1910, for instance, the range of salaries for laborers of European origin was between $.16 cents and $.20 cents per hour, with about twice as many earning $.20 cents per hour, whereas the range for Caribbean blacks was between $.07 and $.20 cents per hour, with about 85 percent earning between $.13 and $.16 cents per hour.[45]

The silver and gold roll division affected every aspect of life, from having workers stand in different lines to get paid or at the post office to having different commissaries.[46] The contrast between the facilities and the provisions for white workers and workers of color was extreme. Whereas white workers had spacious living quarters surrounded by gardens, black workers lived in barracks on the outskirts of the U.S.-controlled area at both terminal points and slept on canvas cots packed as closely together as if they were in the steerage of a boat.[47] Many hundreds of laborers also lived in converted boxcars that were moved back and forth along the railroad line close to where they were working. Provisions were made for family living quarters for married white workers, but few were made for black workers. Wrote one visitor in 1913:

> The visitor who saw first the trim and really attractive houses and bachelor quarters assigned to the gold employees could hardly avoid a certain revulsion of opinion as to the sweetness and light of Isthmian life when he wandered into the Negro quarters across the railroad in front of the Tivoli Hotel [in Panama City] . . . or in some of the back streets of Empire or Gorgona.[48]

As a result of the conditions they encountered in the Canal Zone, "four out of five West Indians paid rent for wretched tenements in Panama and Colon, or they settled in the jungle."[49] The tenements that were hastily built in Panama City and Colon to house the laborers were two-story buildings made out of wood with zinc roofs and a communal bathroom in the courtyard on the ground floor.[50] These buildings had about thirty rooms per floor, which were rented to about that same number of families, and in Panama City they gave rise to the neighborhoods of El Chorrillo, Calidonia, Marañón, San Miguel, Granillo, and Malambo.[51]

The gold and silver division was maintained by the Panama Canal Company once the canal was completed and the communities to support its operation were established at either end of the canal. The new communities had separate housing and recreational facilities for each group, as well as separate schools for the children and separate bathroom and drinking fountains in the workplace.

After the United States took over the construction of the canal in 1904 there were a series of strikes and work stoppages, with demands for higher pay, better food, and better treatment. These actions were supported by the lodges, churches, and mutual aid societies that the Caribbean workers had established along similar lines to those prevalent in their own countries.[52] One group, the West Indian Protective League, even published a newspaper, *The Workman.*

Labor unrest in the transit area grew in size and frequency after the U.S. canal was completed. Between 1916 and 1920 there were six strikes. The most serious of these took place in February 1920 and involved over 17,000 laborers, almost the entire silver roll.[53] The workers' demands reflected concern not only with better salaries but also with the status of workers regarding housing privileges and other benefits. This strike was the first within the Canal Zone in which the government of Panama openly intervened, demanding that U.S. authorities keep the strikers within the Canal Zone. One outcome of the strike was the deportation of 2,000 blacks, including most of the movement's leaders.[54] Those who remained realized the precariousness of their situation since they had no legal status in Panama and all the privileges they received in the Canal Zone—housing, schools, medical attention, and far better pay than they would get if they worked in Panama—were contingent on the benevolence of their employers and on the workers acquiescence to their employers' authority.

The Labor Situation in Panama in the 1920s

Although the Canal Zone had bustled with energy during the construction of the canal, life proceeded at a much slower pace in the Republic of Panama. The Panamanian upper classes continued to make their living as landlords, service providers, and government officials in the recently independent republic. During the canal construction the productive capacity of the cities was not enhanced at all. Both the French and the Americans imported almost everything they needed. During the U.S. construction period, the Panama Canal Company spent $12 million annually on supplies, but only 17 percent of that amount benefited Panama through the local provisioning of charcoal, ice, hotel accommodations, and postage stamps.[55] Panama, on the other hand, paid the company for sanitation services, electricity, road construction, and even drinking water. There were so few basic supplies available in Panama that between 25 and 33 percent of what the country spent on imports was on foodstuffs and beverages.[56]

With the completion of the canal in 1914 Panama faced a period of deep depression. The Panama Canal Company began to let workers go, and these people could not find employment in Panama. By 1915 the company had reduced its labor force by 38 percent (to 34,785 laborers), and by 1921 the number of workers had decreased 75 percent (to 14,389 workers) from the peak year in 1913. The combined population of Panama City and Colon increased by 50 percent (from 66,500 to 99,800) during this period, when many of the unemployed workers decided to stay in the country rather than returning to their own countries.[57]

Prior to the 1920s the only labor organizations that could be found in the Republic of Panama were guilds and mutual aid societies of a highly incipient nature, such as the associations of butchers, bakers, typographers, barbers, carpenters, trolley car conductors, tailors, and blacksmiths.[58] The first workers' federation, the Federación Obrera de la República de Panama (Workers' Federation of the Republic of Panama), was founded in 1921. Several anarchosyndicalists who had arrived from Spain around that time helped organize this group. These included José María Blázquez de Pedro, who has been called the "father of Panama's labor movement" and was its most influential figure from about 1917 until he was deported in 1925.[59]

The more progressive members of the Federación Obrera (Workers Federation) formed a Grupo Comunista (Communist Group) in 1921, and shortly afterward conflict between the two groups developed. This was because the Federación Obrera prized the approval of the American Federation of Labor (AFL) and adhered to the tenets of that U.S. labor organization, whereas the Grupo Comunista wanted to promote more forcibly the ideas emanating from the Russian Revolution and the Third International. The Grupo Comunista broke off with the Federación Obrera in 1924 and formed the Sindicato General de Trabajadores (General Union of Workers).[60]

Although the Sindicato General de Trabajadores was short-lived, it was responsible for the first massive labor protest led by Panamanian workers. In 1925 the government announced an increase in property taxes to take effect in November of that year. By June the slum landlords had passed on the increase to their tenants, in many cases doubling their rent. The Sindicato General de Trabajadores organized a Liga de Inquilinos (Renters' League), promoted a boycott of rent payment, and called for a mass demonstration to be held in October. In mid-September the government jailed all foreign labor leaders, including José María Blázquez de Pedro, and deported them. They also denied a permit for the mass rally, which was held anyway, and the resulting clash with police left a toll of four dead and many injured.[61] Fearing popular reprisals, the government requested the United States to intervene. U.S. troops occupied the cities of Panama and Colon until the unrest had subsided. Mass arrests and many more deportations followed.[62]

By 1926 the government decided to curtail any activities in which labor groups were involved.[63] The problems between workers and their landlords did not subside. In the early 1930s a new period of turmoil erupted, which would be the last in which the working class would raise its voice until well after World War II. In 1932 labor and neighborhood groups made a new attempt at organizing a renters' strike, prompted by the same reasons as those that caused the 1925 strike. The precarious economic situation in Panama in the early 1930s was exacerbated by the effects of the market crash in the United States. Rents were exorbitant in both Panama City and Colon, and the level of unemployment was very high. Added to this, the government was paying part of its employees' salaries with IOUs, which were not accepted by landlords.

A new Liga de Inquilinos y Subsistencia (Renters' and Subsistence League) was formed. The Liga first demanded a 50 percent rent reduction, but when the landlords' association rejected this proposition, the Liga called a rent strike. In an effort to break the strike, the National Assembly, backed by the executive, suspended individual constitutional rights and signed the Law 8th of 1932, which, instead of lowering rents, allowed for a partial moratorium on rent payment and set up a tripartite Junta to deal with the matter.[64] These stalling tactics achieved their aim of defusing the situation, allowing the movement to lose momentum and die out.

Conclusion

The emergence of a working class in Panama at the turn of the twentieth century, its growth, and the resulting profile of this social sector are the outcome of unique features that single Panama out from the rest of the Central American countries. Even though Panama had the potential to develop a very strong working class thanks to the massive importation of laborers and even though many important labor leaders settled in Panama for a time and became instrumental in getting labor organizations started, a series of factors prevented the two segments of the labor sector from becoming integrated.

The opportunities that the canal construction brought to the two terminal cities allowed the Panamanian upper class to maintain a "parasitic existence" as landlords and bureaucrats[65] and to maintain strong economic ties with the U.S. But for the native working class the situation was different. These people, raised in the *arrabal* and dispossessed of power and material wealth, had sustained from the very start of the project extremely xenophobic feelings since they constantly competed with foreign adventurers and new arrivals for the meager opportunities to earn a livelihood.

The enormous waves of laborers arriving to work in the construction of the canal and the fact that thousands of mostly Caribbean workers remained in Panama did nothing to decrease the xenophobia of the Panamanian working class. The Caribbean blacks favored their situation in the U.S.-controlled Canal Zone because the pay and other benefits (housing, schools for their children, medical care) were far superior to what they could get elsewhere in Panama. Although there does not appear to have been much overt animosity between these two working-class segments, there were no compelling factors strong enough to bring them together.

Two key factors can be extrapolated from this analysis to give some perspective to Panama's development. First, there was no clear reason for the different segments of the laboring class to come together, which would have provided them a strong position from which to make demands and protect their interests. Second, the upper classes, who had the economic and political power, could always appeal to external forces, namely the United States, to restore order or to correct any unpleasant situation.

Although the barriers have been slowly eroding, the problems and cleavages that characterized Panama's union movement in its early years continue to prevent it from becoming a more effective advocate for the class it represents. The division between a group of foreign extraction and a native one, the ideological split in the orientation of the two large confederations, and the economic concentration on services and tertiary-sector activities in the urban area and on large plantation enclaves in remote rural areas are all factors that are present today as they were in the early 1900s.

Notes

1. The three main construction projects in the nineteenth and early twentieth centuries had to do with the development of the passageway (the trans-isthmian railroad 1852–1868, the French effort to build the Panama Canal between 1880 and 1889 and between 1894 and 1904, and the U.S. effort to build the Panama Canal between 1904 and 1914). The railroad and the French canal effort took place when Panama was a department of Colombia. The third enterprise, the building of the Panama Canal by the United States, provided Panama the opportunity to become independent from Colombia.

2. Omar Jaén Suárez, *La población del Istmo de Panamá del siglo XVI an siglo XX* (Panama: Impresora de la Nación, 1978), 32.

3. Estimates place the number of imported workers during construction of the railroad at about 7,000. Estimates for the numbers that actually arrived in Panama during the French and U.S. construction period are more difficult to determine, and none of the researchers that have studied these periods in detail will venture a guess at the actual numbers. We can imagine the magnitude and the impact on the terminal cities if we consider that at the highest point of the French period, in 1887, the labor force totaled almost 17,000 workers and that Panama City had a population of 30,000 and Colon had 15,000 inhabitants. During the U.S. period, the highest point in terms of the labor force was in 1913, when there were 56,654 people employed in that project, and the cities of Panama and Colon housed about 66,000 souls. (See Tables 9.2, 9.3, and 9.4.) See David McCullough, *The Path Between the Seas: The Creation of the Panama Canal, 1870–1914* (New York: Simon and Schuster, 1977); Suárez, *La población*; and Alfredo Figueroa Navarro, *Dominio y sociedad en el Panamá Colombiano (1821–1903)* (Bogotá: Ediciones Tercer Mundo, 1978).

4. Jaén Suárez, *La población*, 48.

5. During the California gold rush the fastest way of getting from the U.S. Atlantic coast to California was through Panama. Construction of the trans-isthmian railroad eased the crossing of the Panama land bridge, shortening the trip from four days to six hours; the train could carry 1,500 passengers and three steamship loads at once, thus putting out of business the lodges and rest places along the way. This boom period lasted for Panama until the construction of the intercontinental railroad was completed in the United States in 1869 linking the cities of the Atlantic coast and San Francisco; Jaén Suárez, *La población*, 318–322.

6. Ibid., 257.

7. Ibid., 256–257.

8. Panama City's climate is alleviated by ocean breezes, especially during the dry season, which lowers the humidity considerably.

9. Jaén Suárez, *La población*, 63.

10. Figueroa Navarro, *Dominio*, 33.

11. McCullough, *The Path*, 175.

12. Figueroa Navarro, *Dominio*, 263.

13. Jaén Suárez, *La población*, 330.

14. Figueroa Navarro, *Dominio*, 263.

15. Quoted in Jaén Suárez, *La población*, 536. Jaén Suárez points out that Panamanian businessmen had commercial interests in a few pharmacies and jewelry stores as well as owning one-third of the 192 local bars.

16. Jaén Suárez, *La población*, 534.

17. Figueroa Navarro, *Dominio*, 282–283.

18. Jaén Suárez, *La población*, 270.

19. Ibid., 271.

20. McCullough, *The Path*, 133.

21. Jaén Suárez, *La población*, 343.

22. McCullough, *The Path*, 133.

23. Ibid., 132.

24. Ibid., 135.

25. Luis Navas, *El movimiento obrero en Panamá (1880–1914)* (Panama: Editorial Universitaria, 1974), 70.

26. McCullough, *The Path,* 173. In 1884, for example, with a labor force of over 19,000 workers, probably 6,000 or more were sick.

27. Ibid., 171.

28. Figueroa Navarro, *Dominio,* 351.

29. *La Estrella de Panamá,* January 15, 1883 and October 25, 1883.

30. Navas, *El movimiento,* 82.

31. Ibid., 64.

32. Ibid., 65.

33. The number of passengers using the railroad increased by 490 percent between 1881 and 1883, and the tonnage of dirt moved increased from 168,000 tons in 1881 to 365,000 in 1888; Jaén Suárez, *La población,* 328.

34. *La Estrella de Panamá,* February 12, 1880.

35. Jaén Suárez, *La población,* 456.

36. Figueroa Navarro, *Dominio,* 349.

37. Jaén Suárez, *La población,* 331.

38. *La Estrella de Panamá,* August 8, 1895.

39. Marco A. Gandásegui et al., *Las luchas obreras en Panamá (1850–1978)* (Panama: CELA, 1980), 28–31.

40. Colombia was mired in one of its bloodiest civil wars, the War of the 1,000 Days, and could not give serious attention to an issue pertaining to one of its most remote provinces.

41. The Hay-Bunau Varilla Treaty, negotiated by a Frenchman trying to salvage some French assets, was much less favorable to Panama than the Herran-Hay Treaty had been.

42. The total population of 200,000 includes men and women; Robert E. Wood, "The Working Force of the Panama Canal," in *The Panama Canal: An Engineering Treatise,* ed. George W. Goethals (New York: McGraw-Hill, 1916), 195.

43. Between 1906 and 1908 about 8,000 workers were brought from Spain, 2,000 from Italy, and 1,000 from Greece. Most did not stay long because they found conditions in Panama very difficult; Navas, *El movimiento,* 120.

44. Hernando Franco Muñoz, *Movimiento obrero Panameño 1914–1921* (Panama: n.p., 1979), 15.

45. Navas, *El movimiento,* 130.

46. There were black wards at the hospitals, away from the best views and the breezes, and black schools where the ratio of pupils to teacher was more than double the pupil-to-teacher ratio in white schools; McCullough, *The Path,* 576.

47. Ibid., 502.

48. Willis John Abbot, *Panama and the Canal in Picture and Prose* (New York: Syndicate Publishing, 1913), 344–345, quoted in McCullough, *The Path,* 578.

49. McCullough, *The Path,* 577.

50. Samuel A. Gutiérrez, *Arquitectura Panameña* (Panama: Editorial Litográfica, 1967), 247.

51. Navas, *El movimiento,* 137.

52. Jorge Turner, *Raíz, historia, y destino de los obreros Panameños* (Mexico: UNAM, 1970), 22.

53. Franco Muñoz, *Movimiento obrero,* 20; Gandásegui et al., *Las luchas,* 40–43.

54. Gandásegui et al., *Las luchas,* 43.

55. Jaén Suárez, *La población,* 339.

56. Ibid., 340.

57. Life in the Canal Zone also became considerably more expensive at this time, and costs for the silver roll workers increased by 85 percent between 1914 and 1920; Jaén Suárez, *La población,* 336–343.

58. Franco Muñoz, *Movimiento obrero,* 31.

59. Ibid., 45.

60. Iván Quintero, *El sindicato general de trabajadores* (Panama: Centro de Estudios Latinoamericanos "Justo Arosemena," 1970), 14.

61. Alexander Cuevas, *El movimiento inquilinario de 1925* (Panama: Centro de Estudios Latinoamericanos "Justo Arosemena," 1980), 11–21.

62. Quintero, *El sindicato,* 17.

63. Ibid., 19.

64. Jorge Turner, *Sindicatos, nuevos movimientos sociales, y democracia* (Mexico: Universidad Obrera de Mexico, 1994), 52–61.

65. Jaén Suárez, *La población,* 535–536.

10
Urbanization, the Working Class, and Reform

Ronn Pineo and James A. Baer

Urbanization has long been viewed in two contradictory ways: as modern, exciting, and filled with the promise of tomorrow and as unsettling, troubling, and filled with danger. As the case studies here have shown, parts of both visions held true for the growing urban areas of Latin American in the late nineteenth and early twentieth centuries. The cities of Latin America overflowed with immigrants and migrants who had come in search of a better life. What these people found was often different: Employment could be very sporadic, housing expensive, and living conditions profoundly unhealthy. Yet people kept coming, drawn to these cities of hope.

In this concluding chapter we bring together some final reflections on urban conditions, reaching beyond the case studies to include available comparative information on other cities of this era. Building on the focus of several of the chapters here, we give special consideration to working-class housing and health conditions. Following this, we turn our attention to analyzing the process of urban reform. We have sought to identify the combinations of factors that could most advance or impede efforts to address various urban conditions and to trace some of the main pathways that led toward success in urban social reform.

In exploring the process of urban reform we see an identifiable array of key factors that interacted in complex combinations: the geographical setting, the racial composition and disease susceptibility of the urban population, the nature and performance of the economy, the extent of industrialization, the social structure and the distribution of political power, and the nature and strength of inherited political structures and institutions.[1] The chapters of this volume have highlighted the interactions among these components, focusing especially on the importance of workers' informal political actions in shaping the reform process.

Patterns in Urban Housing: Conditions and Cost

Housing issues became increasingly important throughout Latin America as the urban population increased. These issues centered on two related areas: conditions and cost. Overcrowded and unhealthy, working-class housing brought misery to those who had no other recourse and led to calls for reform by municipal authorities, who were appalled by the lack of privacy and modesty and who were fearful that contagious diseases might spread from these centers of infection to the rest of the city. However, these authorities had few means to address questions of overcrowding except to pass city ordinances that required no more than a certain number of tenants per room or per square foot. These ordinances, when enforced, led to evictions and increased concentrations of tenants in other buildings. By the end of the nineteenth century municipalities often turned to private enterprise to help provide worker housing or constructed subsidized housing that was available only to municipal employees.

Costs were an increasing problem in a market economy where the demand exceeded the supply of available housing. Taxes and import duties on construction materials were reduced in an attempt to encourage private firms to build more apartments and homes. Charities and cooperatives attempted to provide low-cost loans, but mortgage payments required deposits and a stable income for several years. Although many workers sought out vacant lots on the outskirts of the cities, those who needed to be near employment in the city center often continued to rent from month to month. These costs continued to escalate, especially during the first decades of the twentieth century.

David Parker's chapter on Lima describes some of the problems that occurred in that city as the government attempted to modernize the capital. With a municipal Institute of Hygiene and a national Public Health Department, officials began to inspect and fumigate worker housing and even to evict tenants from buildings that did not meet code. Their intent, however, was more to create the image of a healthy city than to improve the housing conditions of the poor. Parker reveals that Peruvian officials blamed the poor, whom they felt to be inherently inferior, for their conditions.

James Baer explains how poor conditions and high costs in Buenos Aires brought about the creation of tenant leagues that, in alliance with labor organizations, sought improvements. At first these movements focused on individual landlords and demanded reductions in rents. When these were not forthcoming, when rents increased instead, the tenants of Buenos Aires began a rent strike in 1907 that lasted more than five months. Although this rent strike was a dramatic event, it was only a harbinger of tenant reaction throughout Latin America during the next two decades. In São Paulo the 1917 labor rebellion was led by the Proletarian Defense Committee, which, in addition to demands for wage increases and an eight-hour day, called for an end to evictions and the reduction of urban rents.[2]

Both John Lear and Andrew Grant Wood analyze the rent strikes that erupted in Mexican cities in 1922. As in Buenos Aires, tenant leaders in Veracruz included women, both because they keenly felt the lack of water and facilities needed for a family to function well and because many worked out of their homes as laundresses or seamstresses. Prostitutes were among the first to join the strike in Veracruz in response to increasing rents charged for the apartments they used. The key to Wood's argument, as well as to Baer's, is the relationship of housing issues to political questions of reform. Pressure from the strike that united a broad segment of the working class in Veracruz with the anarchist labor movement brought a response from municipal authorities as well as the governor of Veracruz State. Like the rent law of 1921 in Argentina, that of 1923 in Veracruz brought government intervention through rent reductions and supervision of tenant-landlord relations.

The rent strike in Mexico City, also in 1922, suggests that housing issues were central to a working class whose labor unions had become the captive of the revolutionary government. Aware of the tenant movement earlier in Veracruz, working-class tenants in Mexico City formed a Renters Union in which women were also active. The Communist party of Mexico, sensing an opportunity in such a popular issue, supported the strike, and the widening political divisions among labor unions would weaken what had become a broad social movement. The Revolutionary government, still in formation during the presidency of Álvaro Obregón Salido (president 1920–1924), was reluctant to give in to the demands of a potentially powerful coalition of working-class groups, and the movement failed to achieve any significant gains in Mexico City.

Panama also had a rent strike, in 1925, as Sharon Phillipps Collazos's chapter notes. The construction of the canal had brought many Caribbean immigrants to Panama City, increasing its population and putting pressure on the housing supply. When a tenants' league demanded a reduction in rents, the government of Panama reacted as if this were a threat against its power and not just an economic confrontation between tenants and landlords. Government forces attacked tenants who were gathered in Santa Ana Park; several tenants were killed or wounded. This violence brought a reaction from the United States, which invoked its right to ensure stability and peace. The United States dispatched troops into the city to restore order. The offices of the tenant league were occupied by soldiers with drawn bayonets. Striking tenants were later deported, if foreign, or fired, if Panamanian nationals. Thus, once again, housing issues became part of the political arena, demonstrating the prime importance of consumer issues in the attitudes and actions of workers.

Patterns in Urban Health Conditions

Because the study of Latin American public health care is still in its infancy, comparison on all health care issues for all cities is not yet possible. Still, available evidence suggests that Latin America did develop some examples of at least partial success in addressing urban public health care concerns in these years.

Marked progress came to São Paulo, Brazil, as research by John Allen Blount has shown.[3] That any improvement came at all to public health conditions in São Paulo was fairly remarkable given the phenomenal population growth of the city: The population of São Paulo grew from about 31,000 in 1872 to nearly 600,000 by 1920.

São Paulo could not overcome all public health challenges. The city made little progress against measles, and the disease frequently killed over 100 children a year during this period. Smallpox also posed a serious threat, killing over 100 people in 1898, in 1908, and in 1912, although progress was gradually made, and by 1920 only fifteen died of that disease. Tuberculosis proved harder to defeat and remained the leading killer in São Paulo.

Nevertheless, São Paulo's progress was noteworthy. As Blount has summarized: "From 1897 to 1918 [São Paulo was] characterized by widespread application of sanitation measures and intensive combat against both epidemic and endemic diseases."[4] São Paulo, he adds, was "eminently successful in expanding health services, dramatically lowering mortality rates, and in placing the state of São Paulo on a level with many advanced nations [in the achievement of progress in public health]."[5] São Paulo was one of the first Latin American cities to eradicate yellow fever. The number of dead from yellow fever fell sharply: 732 died in the State of São Paulo in 1903, but only two died in 1904, two in 1905, and none in 1906.[6] By the 1920s São Paulo had nearly eliminated malaria, even though the disease remained a severe problem in much of the surrounding hinterlands. The number of annual deaths from malaria in the city of São Paulo fell below 100 in 1900 and never again reached that level. Bubonic plague was almost entirely defeated in the city and in the surrounding countryside. In addition, deaths due to dysentery and typhoid fever also fell considerably.[7] So despite the arrival of wave after wave of immigrants from Europe to São Paulo, city death rates fell dramatically.

Two key factors explain much of São Paulo's health care successes: the abundant richness of the coffee boom and the coffee barons' dire need to attract immigrant workers. The city and state political leadership launched sanitation reforms in São Paulo as part of a broader effort to induce European immigrants to come to Brazil. Without improvements in health conditions immigrants would not come, and without immigrants there would not be enough workers to harvest the coffee. The "members of the ruling elite . . . [realized] that a salubrious . . . image before the world was necessary" if workers were to be attracted.[8] The coffee elite realized that improving São Paulo's health reputation was critical to their own interests.

Fortunately, the spectacular performance of the coffee export economy made ample funds available for São Paulo's sanitation efforts, paying the cost of health care reform. There was, as Blount notes, "a considerable financial outlay on the part of the state government in São Paulo for the health of its citizens" from the 1890s to 1920.[9] Blount concludes: "[The] economic prosperity in São Paulo . . . [was] unquestionably an important precondition for the adoption of sweeping public health measures" in the city.[10]

Unfortunately, not all Latin American cities could match São Paulo's record of success. The extent of the health care challenge varied greatly from city to city. If some cities accomplished less in sanitation and health care reform, they often had the disadvantage of starting with more to do.

Port cities stood at constant risk of infection from exotic epidemics. For example, incoming vessels repeatedly transported yellow fever and other epidemic diseases to cities like Guayaquil, Ecuador; Veracruz, Mexico; or Panama City, Panama; among others.

Some cities had settings that were innately less healthy. Microorganisms and disease-bearing vectors flourished in marshy, tropical regions, and cities like Havana or Guayaquil, among others, suffered more because of their dank, tropical settings. Other cities had more favorable natural circumstances. For example, isolated mountain cities like La Paz, Bolivia, or Quito, Ecuador, were situated well above the level where the mosquitoes that spread diseases like yellow fever could live. Similarly, temperate-climate cities like Buenos Aires or Montevideo did not usually stand at risk from tropical illnesses such as malaria.

Crowded, densely packed housing conditions also facilitated the process of contagion, especially of tuberculosis, the leading urban killer of this era. Conditions were particularly acute in Valparaíso, Chile, where the situation was exacerbated by the lack of sufficient potable water supplies and proper sewage disposal. As a consequence, Valparaíso also ran a higher risk of the spread of cholera, typhoid fever, and dysentery, among other afflictions.

The racial composition of a population was also a key health variable because human populations differ so widely in their natural immunities to disease. Unacclimated groups moving into tropical cities were particularly vulnerable to novel illnesses. Hence the mestizo, Indian, or mulatto migrants to tropical cities confronted particularly high health risks. In Guayaquil, for example, death cut a wide swath through the ranks of Indian migrants who had previously lived in isolated hamlets high in the Andes.

The three Latin American cities that took in the bulk of international immigrants from Italy, Portugal, and Spain—Buenos Aires, Montevideo, and São Paulo—were also probably the three healthiest cities of Latin America in this era. Beyond the factors already mentioned, one additional reason was the age composition of their populations. Long-distance migration was highly selective of single young men; among all immigrants, single young men outnumbered all others by a ratio of at least 2 to 1. In these three cities, young men were greatly overrepresented.[11] Death preys most of all on infants and the elderly, not on young men in the prime of life. Under ordinary circumstances men this age do not die; if they do it is a mistake, an accident. The overrepresentation of this healthiest cohort helped further lower death rates in the three Atlantic cities of immigrants.

Comparison to Western European and United States cities of this era helps to place the overall situation of urban Latin America in context. Over the course of the nineteenth century the prosperous and advanced nations—the United States and the nations of Western Europe—led the world into the transition to modern demographic patterns by lowering birth and death rates. The fall in death rates stemmed from a combination of factors: improved urban sanitation, better urban potable water systems, wide advances in medical knowledge and medical care, and a generally higher standard of living for most workers, which meant better housing and, probably most important of all, an improved diet.[12]

The results of these advances were clearly reflected in the lower infant mortality rates (the number of deaths of infants aged 0–1 per 1,000 live births). Some comparative infant mortality figures from Great Britain help show the situation.[13] In Great Britain the infant mortality rate was about 155 to 160 from the 1860s to the 1890s; in 1905, it was 128; in 1910, 105; and in 1933, less than 60.

Similarly, the drop in death rates (the number of deaths per 1,000 in population per year) demonstrated the progress achieved in the leading cities of the world during this period. Urban death rates dropped from 22 in New York City in 1896 to 17 in 1908; and likewise in 1905 fell to 16 in London, to 17 in Paris, to 17 in Berlin, and to 21 in Rome; in 1908 to 19 in New Orleans, to 19 in Washington, D.C., to 14 in Chicago, and to 14 in Milwaukee.

Improvements in health conditions generally came more slowly to Latin America. As the chapters by Ronn Pineo and Sam Adamo show, available data suggest that the death rates in most Latin American cities typically remained in the 30s and infant mortality rates remained above 200, even in the 1920s. Overall, despite the advances in cities like São Paulo, Buenos Aires, and Montevideo, health care conditions in much of urban Latin America remained very poor in these years.

Patterns in Urban Reform

No single reason can explain why some Latin American cities of this era accomplished more in urban reform than others. The array of factors that might lead, for example, to a successful campaign to carry out a sanitation reform might not work to bring about a program to resolve workers' housing concerns. Reforms were not uniform. In nearly all cases the process of reform can only be understood if we recognize the changing and complex interaction among a variety of causal factors.

Most battles for reform were political struggles over scarce resources. Different groups focused on different concerns. Workers often fixed their greatest attention on issues involving inflation and were especially watchful over rising costs of food and rent. The middle class typically expressed its greatest concern over voting rights and public education. The urban elite generally showed the most enthusiasm for city beautification. Yet, as Baer and Wood have shown, there were areas of coincidence that could produce ad hoc coalitions and lead to reform.

Among the variables studied in the chapters of this book, the nature and performance of the export economy and the depth of resulting industrialization created large differences in available financial resources to pay for reform. But beyond this, the changing nature of the economy could create differing socioeconomic contexts. Of foremost importance was the size and political strength of both the middle class and the working class. There were different constellations of political forces in each city, and different outcomes of political contestation followed from this.

Two broad variables further conditioned this political contestation. The preexistence of stable, old political parties could channel reform impulses along traditional lines. As success in the export economy and industrialization created a wider middle class and stronger union movement, these groups' concerns could, under such circumstance, be gradually incorporated into the agenda of one or more of the existing parties. This proved especially important in softening the otherwise hard-line stances of workers.

The final broad factor is urban primacy. Primate cities controlled the national treasury. They were in a position to spend most of the national revenues on their own particular needs, ignoring the needs of other cities and rural districts, and many did exactly that.

The energy for reform, as shown by all the authors in this book (see especially the chapter by David Sowell), came from working-class initiatives. We have explored both formal and informal impulses, an approach to politics that we believe provides a broader understanding of urban contention and allows us to consider activities that otherwise might be overlooked or ignored.

Adam Smith, in noting the urban tendency for splintering work into less expensive but ever simpler and more mindless tasks, commented that the city worker would eventually become "as stupid and ignorant as it is possible for a human creature to become."[14] This uncharitable view of the modern urban worker was no doubt shared by many in positions of power in urban Latin America during the late nineteenth and early twentieth centuries. But even if Smith was correct in concluding that workers were finding less chance to express their human ingenuity at the workplace, what he did not see was that they nevertheless found ample opportunity to demonstrate great creativity in other forums. One such venue was in their public political response to urban conditions.

Workers had to be ingenious in crafting a response to the appalling urban conditions they confronted, for in most Latin American nations during the period from 1870 to 1930 the workers were disenfranchised. Only Argentina (in 1912) and Uruguay (in 1919) adopted universal male suffrage for citizens, but in these countries the near-majority of foreign-born, noncitizen residents among the working class considerably reduced the impact of this measure. Most worker politics in Latin America had to be informal, outside the institutions of political contestation. Moreover, even in Argentina and Uruguay the powerful influence of anarchist and anarchosyndicalist thought steered workers into direct action against employers and away from participation in formal politics, something they saw as sterile and controlled by the bourgeoisie.

To deal with their situation, the first response of working-class individuals was to strike out on their own, seeking to advance their own interests and those of their family rather than those of their community or class. In the case of urban tenants, this usually meant direct negotiations with their landlord. By acting as individuals, workers were seeking to go along with and succeed within the existing system, not to modify or overturn it. Only when they united with other workers could they provide the collective energy that might serve as the spark that could lead to reform.

As working-class conditions worsened, many workers began to feel more commonality of circumstances. In response to miserable conditions, urban workers in some places began to come together to build a collective, informal, political response. Some workers organized as producers. Workers built organizations arranged by trade, industry, sometimes by class, and, more rarely, in mass actions and insurgencies. Producer organizations of workers were generally the most militant form of worker organization. To the elite, they were also the most threatening.

However, Latin American cities did not typically have the conditions that would have fostered the development of a powerful working-class union movement. Industrialization, where workers labored in very close proximity under oppressive conditions, provided the best context for unionization. In Latin America, however, urbanization generally came without significant industrialization. Such industries as developed usually only appeared where the leading export required industrial processing prior to shipment. Significantly, where such processing was necessary, as for example in the meat-packing plants of Buenos Aires, stronger union organizing followed. Workers also came together most explosively in places like Orizaba, Mexico, where roughly a quarter of the labor force worked in the city's textile factories. Under such conditions, workers and their unions could and did play a key role in pressing for reform of their cities.

But because most Latin American exports of this age were shipped as unprocessed raw materials, little industry developed. For example, cacao (chocolate beans), an export important to Guayaquil, required no industrial processing prior to being bagged and shipped. Interestingly, one of the very few industries that Guayaquil developed in these years was a bag factory. This was not enough, however, to provide the foundation for a strong union movement. On the contrary, without significant industry Ecuador's labor movement remained one of Latin America's weakest.

Even though industrialization was key to successful worker organization, it also proved easier to organize workers in places where skilled workers occupied a strategic position commanding control over the flow of the critical export, a "choke point" for workers to grab. For example, in Buenos Aires dock workers certainly understood that they had their grip on an economic choke point, as they demonstrated in their November 1902 strike "timed . . . [to coincide with] the height of the harvest season."[15] Skilled railway workers also often enjoyed such an advantage, and they were usually among the first groups to unionize. In Montevideo and Buenos Aires, railway workers used this strategic position to launch large strikes after the turn of the century.

However, such strategic choke points were not common in the Latin American cities of this era. In Mexico, for example, exports were diversified. Closing off one export might hurt commerce, but it would not shut down the entire economy. To take another case: In Ecuador the entire export economy did depend upon just one product, cacao. However, here there was no clear bottleneck in the export flow. Even the railway could not be used as a choke point in Ecuador because all cacao was shipped downriver on rafts, not by rail.

Workers in high-profile foreign-owned firms also proved easier to organize into unions. In these cases, as for example with railway workers in Argentina and other countries, the employees could tap into explosive feelings of xenophobia, depicting themselves as patriotic workers being exploited by greedy, uncaring foreigners. Under such circumstances it was much more difficult for government to take management's side in any labor dispute lest they appear disloyal to their nation. Workers understood this well and used it to their advantage. However, in the period under study most urban workers in Latin America, even those in industry, were employed by domestically controlled firms whose owners were usually well connected with government.

Finally, workers located at critical spatial junctures enjoyed an advantaged position for labor organizing. For example, as the chapter by Anton Rosenthal shows, streetcars offered a moving stage for depicting urban life and provided a spatial focal point from which to organize protests or to broadcast workers' political views; alternatively, they could serve as a target for worker violence.

For all this, however, one overwhelming factor seriously undercut nearly all efforts at labor organizing in most Latin American cities of these years: the glut of labor. The urban economies in nearly all cases failed to create adequate employment opportunities for the waves of newcomers. In the surrounding urban hinterlands, large preexisting populations typically overwhelmed the demand for labor. Most of those who came to the cities could find but loosely arranged day-to-day jobs. Powerful worker organizations—aggressively defending the interests of their constituents—could scarcely develop in this unpromising socioeconomic context. Unemployed *jornaleros* (day workers) and women who take in laundry, cook, or serve as maids—that is, the bulk of the working class—made unlikely union members.[16]

Under such circumstances, workers in urban Latin America in these years found it difficult to overcome the many differences that divided them as a class: race, ethnicity, language, regionalism, religion, gender, skill level, or political ideology. The call for reform was generally faint because of the absence of effective worker organizations.

Nevertheless, under the right conditions—where there were industry, a growing demand for labor, a small preexisting local workforce (labor scarcity), an available economic bottleneck, and worker unity against foreign "exploiters"—labor could be stronger. The cities of Montevideo and Buenos Aires shared these conditions and thus they had the strongest and most militant labor movements in Latin America in these years.

However, even in these situations workers had to be careful not to become victims of their own success.[17] If workers' movements came to be viewed as too powerful, if they came to be too frightening to the elite, the movement would be repressed. In Argentina, for example, even the otherwise sympathetic government of Hipólito Yrigoyen (1916–1922, 1928–1930) lashed out at the labor movement with massive repression in the Semana Trágica during a wave of vast and menacing general strikes after World War I.

Workers were seen as less threatening and their voices were more likely to be heard when they organized as consumers and raised concerns about prices for food, housing, or transportation. Working-class families frequently organized as consumers, arranged by associations of neighborhood residents, and at other times in citywide mass actions. As Wood's chapter on the Veracruz rent strike shows, women could play leading roles in spearheading worker organizations when working-class families united to act on consumption issues. Women asserted their roles as homemakers and united to protest high prices at the marketplace or high rents. Whereas government found it easy to use repression against male workers who united as producers into menacing unions that directly challenged private property rights, governments were reluctant to use violent repression against women who united to protect their families. Consumer organizations were seen as less dangerous and were not usually repressed. As the studies by Baer, Lear, and Wood illustrate, consumer movements could win victories, at least short-term ones. Unfortunately for working families, it proved difficult to sustain a high level of mobilization in these wide organizations, and when energy flagged, rents rose.

Guiding the Reform Impulse: Patterns of Middle-Class Politics

Without active pressure from the working class the reform impulse lacked energy. On the other hand, where the working class showed too much strength and radicalism, the elite typically responded with repression. The urban working class had to strike a delicate balance. Yet it was often the case that even as radical movements were being repressed, the elite would offer some modest reforms to the moderate elements within the worker movement and to the middle class.

As John J. Johnson concluded in his classic 1958 study *Political Change in Latin America: The Emergence of the Middle Sectors:* "Since the middle sectors are predominantly urban, they favor . . . policies that assign a disproportionately large per capita share of public revenues to the urban centers."[18] Ruth and David Collier have likewise noted that "the middle sectors . . . play[ed] . . . [the] central role in initiating the change in government that brought the major challenge to oligarchic hegemony."[19] The case studies here have shown, however, that these middle sectors needed a push from the working class.

In Western Europe and the United States, triumphant economic success around the beginning of the twentieth century created a middle class powerful enough to push effectively for political inclusion and social reform. Historically, a large and politically powerful middle class was the group that played the critical role in reforming the cities, starting voluntary organizations, lobbying, voting, demanding that its needs be taken seriously, and defeating the entrenched interests that stood to lose financially from the passage of urban social reforms. However, the nature of economic development in Latin America did not produce such a mighty middle class.

For Latin America in the period under study, the middle class varied significantly in size and strength, from virtually nonexistent to a moderate presence. Only in the richer and most complex export economies, especially in Argentina and Uruguay, did the middle class show any significant development. In these years and in these places the composition of the middle class was changing from the old, static, intellectual, liberal professions, the essentially dependent groups, to more aggressive, independent groups of entrepreneurs in business and manufacturing.[20]

Certain middle-class occupations were more likely to lead to identification with the elite, such as jobs in the government bureaucracy; as lawyers, notaries, or tutors to the offspring of the elite; or in the arts that depended upon elite patronage. Other middle-class occupations, especially in small businesses, led to the development of a more independent identity. The more independent and progressive elements in the middle class at times joined in common cause with elements from organized labor, as Baer has indicated occurred in Buenos Aires. This was especially so when workers could vote and when middle-class politicians needed working-class votes. This interclass alliance was most likely to occur where workers were strong, and workers were strongest when they were industrial workers.

To this point we have sketched the general factors that shaped the process of urban reform. However, it will be easier to see and understand the interplay between these factors if we take a particular case in point. Montevideo, Uruguay, is a good example to consider, for in these years this city and nation led Latin America in progressive reform. "Between 1911 and 1915 . . . [Uruguay] enacted the eight-hour workday, one day off in five, unemployment coverage, minimum wage, free medical services, old age pensions, and other social legislation."[21] Montevideo illustrates how various forces interacted to produce successful reform.

Montevideo was a city of immigrants.[22] The lure was high pay scales, at least when compared against wages in Europe. In Montevideo, "almost one-third of the inhabitants in 1908 were foreigners."[23] Other than Argentina and southeastern Brazil, the remainder of Latin America was significantly less affected by immigration.

In Uruguay a combination of many factors led to the nation's leadership in urban social reform. Uruguay did not have a sizable preexisting indigenous population to exploit for its labor. When economic growth in the export of wool and grains came in the late nineteenth century, Uruguay experienced an acute scarcity of labor. This situation gave labor greater leverage in Uruguay.

Exports from Uruguay rose very rapidly, and significant industrialization also developed in Montevideo. "By the mid-1920's over 50 per cent of the gross national product was derived from the manufacturing and processing industries."[24] Uruguay had one of the highest proportions of the workforce in industry among Latin American nations in 1925, tied with Argentina at roughly 7 to 8 percent.[25] Most of Uruguay's industry was foreign owned. Reform-minded president José Batlle y Ordóñez (president 1903–1907, 1911–1915) openly sided with workers against the foreign-owned interests, as Rosenthal has demonstrated in the case of trolley companies. Batlle encouraged labor to organize, but he did not move to build government-controlled unions. Uruguay's labor unions became powerful and independent. In sum, in Montevideo three of the factors that we have identified as key to union formation were in place: a sizable industrial labor force, foreign ownership of industry, and, most important, labor scarcity.

In Uruguay the middle class enjoyed, in the words of John J. Johnson, the strongest situation of "leadership" in Latin America.[26] Nevertheless, middle-class control of national politics in Uruguay depended upon the support of organized labor and the votes of workers.

In moving from the old elite policies of repression of organized labor to new policies favoring labor's initial incorporation into the political process, some Latin American states moved faster than others.[27] Uruguay was first to accommodate labor in the political process. In 1903 Uruguay had adopted a restricted democracy (with literacy requirements and with no secret ballot) and by 1919 had expanded to a full democracy, one that lasted until 1933.

The early inclusion of the workers in the political process in Uruguay stemmed principally from two key factors. One was the large foreign component of the working class. In 1889, for example, there were 100,000 foreigners and 114,000 nationals in Montevideo.[28] Extending suffrage to workers still left about half of the working class, the foreign half, disenfranchised. The elite found some measure of reassurance in this. Moreover, Uruguayan workers were brought into the political process by a traditional and now dominant political party, Batlle's Colorado party. This party worked to channel working-class energy within the existing political structure and thereby served to modify, soften, and mainstream it.

By 1900 Montevideo's population of 300,000 totaled a third of all Uruguayans.[29] The government of the nation was highly centralized. Montevideo was the most primate of the many Latin American primate cities; as Martin Weinstein has noted, Montevideo was "almost a city-state."[30] The reforms that came to Uruguay—in sanitation, public works, education, and social security—almost exclusively benefited Montevideo. Batlle paid for his urban reforms by taxing the imports that came in return for the lucrative export trade in wool, meat, and hides and by ignoring rural poverty.[31] Montevideo was reformed; the rest of Uruguay was not. Taken together, this confluence of factors, especially the size and strength of working and middle classes, helps to explain why Uruguay was the "most progressive" nation in Latin America in these years.[32]

Conclusion

Ultimately, the possibilities for urban social reform in Latin America in these years were largely determined by the nature and performance of the economy. Economic prosperity, whether in industrializing cities or in those that exported highly successful primary products, meant more wealth, greater employment and investment opportunities, and, most important, more tax revenue. Economic success also brought foreign investment and loans, adding further resources to the local economy. Some cities were richer and had more to spend on reform. Stronger economies also tended to produce stable governments that had the power to carry out reforms.

But having the resources to pay for urban improvements did not mean that such reforms automatically followed. The appropriate political conditions had to be in place in order for reform to occur. The cities with more prosperous economies tended to develop more complex social structures, creating at once a broader middle class and a more powerful working class. This was especially so where workers were relatively scarce and in greater demand. As we have seen, a synergistic interaction between these two groups was critical in raising an effective call for urban social reform.

Working-class pressure was a critical factor; without it the elite felt no urgency in addressing urban conditions that did not directly affect their families or their pocketbooks. The case studies in this book have established the vital importance of worker pressure and the indirect achievements of their informal politics.

Yet by itself working-class pressure could not bring reform; the elite typically responded with fear and then repression to worker militancy. The key for workers was in raising enough pressure to increase the visibility of reform issues but not so much pressure as to frighten the elite into repression.

The presence of a strong and united middle class was equally important. The middle class could take the working-class energy and channel it, handling the task of assembling a moderate reform package acceptable to the elite. The pattern was one of repression of workers followed by partial acceptance of the reform agenda, especially if trustworthy and nonthreatening members of the middle class could be delegated the task of usurping some of the more modest planks from the workers' reform platform.

Some cities had more of the conditions that led to urban reform. The Atlantic cities of Montevideo, Buenos Aires, and São Paulo were in general the most advantaged. These cities were distinctive in that they were populated mostly by recent European immigrants and their children. These cities were also the fastest growing, the most involved with international trade, and the most economically successful in Latin America. They had more industry and stronger export economies, they generated more tax revenue, and they attracted more foreign capital.[33] Montevideo and Buenos Aires were also capital cities and as such had a special political advantage, for they controlled national revenues; their needs were addressed before those of lesser cities.

Most Latin American cities grew more slowly, chiefly from internal migrants (usually mestizos and mulattoes) rather than from European immigration. Moreover, large, preexisting populations of Indians, Africans, mestizos, and mulattoes typically overwhelmed the more modest increase in labor demand.

In most Latin American cities of this era, it fell to a small group of wealthy elite to oversee and direct urban progress. Although they cared about their cities, their notions of the correct order of priorities were not effectively challenged or tempered by large, organized, and powerful competing groups or classes.

In Rio de Janeiro in the 1920s, for example, the elite were largely left to guide urban progress without interference. Under these circumstances, the Rio "elite disavow[ed] . . . responsibility for the general welfare of the masses."[34] The wealthy concentrated instead on spending their money and "enjoyed their station more than at any other time in Brazilian history."[35] Elite-directed urban reform meant projects like cutting a wide boulevard through the center of Rio, a program explicitly meant to model Rio after Paris; the mayor even brought in French experts. Countless families were thrown out onto the streets as the path was cleared to build a Parisian boulevard in Rio. Elite-directed progress meant projects that enriched the elite, such as state-funded construction of transportation to the fashionable new beach communities or of exclusive beach parks.

Overall, the economic and political resources for confronting the dilemmas of urbanization varied considerably. Some cities did less well, notably those cities with comparatively less-successful economies and nonprimary cities that received less of the national budget. But ultimately the most disadvantaged cities of all were those that failed to develop a cohesive working class that would have fought for reform and a strong middle class to guide the political achievement of reform. For most ordinary men, women, and children, the cities of hope could not deliver on the promise of a better life.

Notes

1. To be sure, in some situations a single overriding factor might stand above all others in explaining why reform did or did not occur. Such situations were, however, rare.

2. See John D. French, *The Brazilian Workers' ABC: Class Conflict and Alliances in Modern São Paulo* (Chapel Hill: University of North Carolina Press, 1992), 31.

3. John Allen Blount, "The Public Health Movement in São Paulo, Brazil: A History of the Sanitary Service, 1892–1918" (Ph.D. diss., Tulane University, 1971).

4. Blount, "Public Health Movement in São Paulo," 98.

5. Ibid., 99.

6. Ibid., 117, 170–173, 203, 204, 206.

7. *New York Times,* 17 April 1893, cited in Blount, "Public Health Movement in São Paulo," 179.

8. Blount, "Public Health Movement in São Paulo," 17.

9. Ibid., 167.

10. Ibid., 185.

11. Herbert S. Klein, "The Social and Economic Integration of Portuguese Immigrants in Brazil in the Late Nineteenth and Twentieth Centuries," *Journal of Latin American Studies* 23, no. 2 (May 1991): 323.

12. For nearly all human history, cities had been correctly regarded as places that were considerably less healthy than the countryside. Though urban populations grew, that was only because of in-migration; deaths in the cities always exceeded births. But in the last part of the nineteenth century the prosperous cities of the West stood at variance from most other world cities; they were no longer population "sink holes."

13. Eric E. Lampard, "The Urbanizing World," in *The Victorian City: Images and Realities,* ed. H. J. Dyos and Michael Wolff, vol. 1 (London: Routledge and Kegan Paul, 1973), 10, 21, 24–25. In Vienna the infant mortality rate in the 1880s was 203; in urban Netherlands in the 1890s the rate was 195; in the United States in 1890 the combined figure for the twenty-eight largest cities was 237.

14. Quoted in Lampard, "The Urbanizing World," 28.

15. Carl Solberg, *Immigration and Nationalism: Argentina and Chile, 1890–1914* (Austin: University of Texas Press, 1970), 109.

16. For Buenos Aires, conversely, Robert Edward Shipley, in his excellent "On the Outside Looking In: A Social History of the 'Porteno' Worker During the 'Golden Age' of Argentine Development, 1914–1930" (Ph.D. diss., Rutgers, 1977) shows that labor unions and the Socialist party drove the movement for passage in 1905 of the mandatory Sunday rest law (83–84), the eight-hour workday (85), accident compensation for workers (87), legal aid for workers (89), child labor laws (91), the rights of women workers (92), and rent control (160) and that they led strikes to successful outcomes with government support (284). He also shows how the middle-class Radical party often supported reform and workers' causes in an effort to win the backing of working-class voters (passim).

17. These ideas are drawn from Dietrich Rueschemeyer, Evelyne Huber Stephens, and John D. Stephens, *Capitalist Development and Democracy* (Chicago: University of Chicago Press, 1992), passim.

18. John J. Johnson, *Political Change in Latin America: The Emergence of the Middle Sectors* (Stanford: Stanford University Press, 1958). By 1900, Johnson concludes, the new export economies helped to create new commercial and industrial middle-ranking groups of "managers, applied scientists, and highly trained technicians" that were added to the old middle-ranking groups: "members of the liberal professions, such as law and medicine; . . . writers, publishers, and artists; . . . professors in secondary schools and institutions of higher learning; . . . bureaucrats; . . . members of the secular clergy of the Catholic Church, and of the lower and middle echelons of the officer corps" (1–2). "But the differences . . . [did] not prevent large and ordinarily major segments of the middle sectors from finding common ground for joint political action" (4). James M. Malloy and Silvia Borzutzky, "Politics, Social Welfare Policy, and the Population Problem in Latin America," *International Journal of Health Services* 12, no. 1 (1982): 77–98, argue that elites allowed social reform to privileged worker groups, mostly skilled workers and the middle class, as part of the populist strategy of political co-optation of groups that were emerging with political power.

19. Ruth Berins Collier and David Collier, *Shaping the Political Arena: Critical Junctures, the Labor Movement, and Regime Dynamics in Latin America* (Princeton: Princeton University Press, 1991), 59.

20. Solberg, in his classic study *Immigration and Nationalism,* 59, describes the earlier formation as a "small middle class, which depended almost entirely on the patronage of the elites, and imitated their cultural values and followed their opinions on most questions."

The middle-class elements in colonial cities had been middle-ranking clergy, government bureaucrats, and middling military officers. See discussions in Franklin Knight and Peggy Liss, eds., *Atlantic Port Cities: Economy, Culture, and Society in the Atlantic World, 1650–1850,* passim. See also Johnson, *Political Change in Latin America,* passim.

21. Charles S. Sargent, "Uruguay," in *Latin America Urbanization: Historical Profiles of Major Cities,* ed. Gerald Michael Greenfield (Westport, Conn.: Greenwood Press, 1994), 483. See also Milton I. Vanger, *The Model Country: José Batlle y Ordóñez of Uruguay, 1907–1915* (Hanover, N.H.: Brandeis University Press, 1980).

22. In the nineteenth and early twentieth centuries people flooded out of Europe, especially Italy, Spain, and Portugal. This mass migration derived from broad demographic and economic forces. Europe's mortality rate was falling, and its population rose "from 187 million in 1800, to 266 million in 1850, to 401 million in 1900"; Magnus Mörner, with the collaboration of Harold Sims, *Adventurers and Proletarians: The Story of Migrants in Latin America* (Pittsburgh: University of Pittsburgh Press, 1985), 35, and see 36, 56, and passim. This created rural crowding and landlessness. During the same period inexpensive grain from the United States began to flow into Europe, bringing economic depression to European staple-producing regions. As a result of these and other forces, from 1830 to 1930 some 50 million Europeans left for overseas, 11 million of whom went to Latin America. Of this 11 million, 90 percent left for three Atlantic nations: Argentina, Brazil, and Uruguay. Cheaper and safer steamship passages to the New World by the late nineteenth century further facilitated this vast human migration, as did the travel subsidies offered by Argentina and Brazil.

23. Mörner with Sims, *Adventurers and Proletarians,* 77–78. Nearly half of the growth of Buenos Aires from 1895 to 1914 was due to European immigration; Mark D. Szuchman, *Mobility and Integration in Urban Argentina: Córdoba in the Liberal Era* (Austin: University of Texas Press, 1980). Population and immigration totals at the turn of the century were: Argentina, 4 million total population with 1 million immigrants (25 percent); Brazil, 14 million with 2.4 million immigrants (17 percent); the United States, 76 million with 10 million immigrants (14 percent); Uruguay, 978,000 with 90,000 immigrants (9 percent); Paraguay, 636,000 with 18,000 immigrants (3 percent); Venezuela, 2.6 million with 44,000 immigrants (2 percent); and Mexico, 14 million with 58,000 immigrants (0.4%); Pedro Lautaro Ferrer, *Higiene y asistencia pública en Chile: Quinta conferencia sanitaria internacional de las repúblicas Américas* (Santiago: Imprenta Barcelona, 1911), 118. Most of the immigrants to Atlantic Latin America ultimately settled in urban areas. As Magnus Mörner has noted: "In the city of São Paulo in 1900 there were two Italians for every native Brazilian. . . . In 1887, Italians alone made up 32 percent of the population of the Argentine capital," *Adventurers and Proletarians,* 77–78.

24. Johnson, *Political Change,* 54.

25. Collier and Collier, *Shaping the Political Arena,* 63; Sargent, "Uruguay," 481.

26. Johnson, *Political Change,* 45.

27. See Collier and Collier, *Shaping the Political Arena.*

28. Johnson, *Political Change,* 49.

29. Ibid.; Collier and Collier, *Shaping the Political Arena,* 63.

30. Martin Weinstein, *Uruguay: The Politics of Failure* (Westport, Conn.: Greenwood Press, 1975), xiii.

31. In a compromise with the landed elite, the vast holdings of the landed oligarchy were left "untouched . . . as long as they permitted and were willing to foot most of the bill for the programs of the urban-oriented *Colorados*"; Weinstein, *Uruguay,* 31.

32. Johnson, *Political Change,* 45.

33. Argentina and other nations took steps to attract foreign capital, including generous land concessions to the companies that built the railroads. Shipley, "On the Outside Looking In," 12, notes that "foreign capital poured into Argentina during these years. Foreign investment came in at such a rate that by 1913 almost one-half of the value of total fixed capital stock in the country was owned directly or indirectly by private foreign investors."

34. Michael L. Conniff, *Urban Politics in Brazil: The Rise of Populism, 1925–1945* (Pittsburgh: University of Pittsburgh Press, 1981), 7–9.

35. Conniff, *Urban Politics*, 7–9, 29.

About the Editors and Contributors

Sam Adamo received his Ph.D. from the University of New Mexico. He is currently employed as a researcher and planner by the Albuquerque Public School System. His publications include "Some Recent Works on Modern Brazilian History" in *Latin American Research Review* (1992) and *Disease, Death and Inequality: Rio de Janeiro and the 1918 Influenza Pandemic* (1992). He has received an ITT International Fellowship and a Mellon Travel Grant award.

James A. Baer received his Ph.D. from Rutgers University and is a professor of history at Northern Virginia Community College, Alexandria Campus. His publications include "Archivo Histórico de la Ciudad de Buenos Aires" in *Latin American Research Review* (1986) and "Tenant Contention and the 1907 Rent Strike in Buenos Aires" in *The Americas* (1993). He has received awards from the National Endowment for the Humanities and for a Fulbright-Hays travel seminar.

John Lear received his Ph.D. from the University of California, Berkeley, and teaches at the University of Puget Sound, Tacoma, Washington. He is currently working on a book on urban mobilization and organization in Mexico City during the revolution. Recent publications include "Mexico City: Space and Class in the Porfirian Capital (1884–1910)" in *Journal of Urban History* (1996), "Del mutualismo a la resistencia: Las organizaciones laborales en la Ciudad de Mexico desde fines del porfiriato a la Revolucion" in *Ciudad de Mexico* (1997), and *Chile's Free-Market Miracle: A Second Look* (1995).

David S. Parker received his Ph.D. in history from Stanford University. He is an assistant professor of history at Queens University, Kingston, Ontario. He is the author of *The Idea of the Middle Class: White Collar Workers and Peruvian Society, 1900–1950* (forthcoming) and winner of the Conference on Latin American History's James Alexander Robertson Prize in 1992.

Sharon Philipps Collazos received her Ph.D. from the University of New Mexico and is currently employed by the U.S. Department of Labor Women's Bureau in Washington, D.C., as a social science analyst. Her publications include *Labor and Politics in Panama: The Torrijos Years* (Westview Press, 1991) and "Panama" in *Latin American Labor Organizations* (1987).

Ronn Pineo received his Ph.D. from the University of California, Irvine. Currently, he is an associate professor of history at Towson State University, Towson, Maryland. His publications include *Social and Economic Reform in Ecuador: Life and Work in Guayaquil, 1870–1925* (1996). He has also published in *Latin American Perspectives* and in *Hispanic American Historical Review*. He has received numerous fellowships, including National Endowment for the Humanities Summer Stipend and Research grants and a Fulbright Fellowship to Ecuador. In 1992 he won the Sturgis Leavitt Prize for best article in Latin American Studies.

Anton Rosenthal received his Ph.D. from the University of Minnesota. He is currently an associate professor of history at the University of Kansas. He received a Fulbright Faculty Abroad Award and an Advanced Grant from the Social Science Research Council for research in Uruguay and Argentina in 1993. He has published articles on Montevideo in *The Americas, The Journal of Latin American Studies,* and *Studies in Latin American Popular Culture* (with Catherine Preston) and has work forthcoming in the *Journal of Urban History.*

David Sowell received his Ph.D. from the University of Florida and is currently associate professor of history and director of international programs at Juniata College in Huntingdon, Pennsylvania. His publications include *The Early Colombian Labor Movement: Artisans and Politics in Bogota, 1832–1919* (1992) and contributions to the *Encyclopedia of Latin American History.* He has received fellowships from the American Council of Learned Societies and the National Endowment for the Humanities. His current research is on the social history of medicine in the nineteenth-century Andes.

Andrew Grant Wood received his Ph.D. from the University of California, Davis. His dissertation is entitled "The Making of El Movimiento Inquilinario: Tenant Protest and the State in Postrevolutionary Mexico, 1870–1927." He is currently at work on a comparative study of working-class housing and popular culture in the Americas.

Index